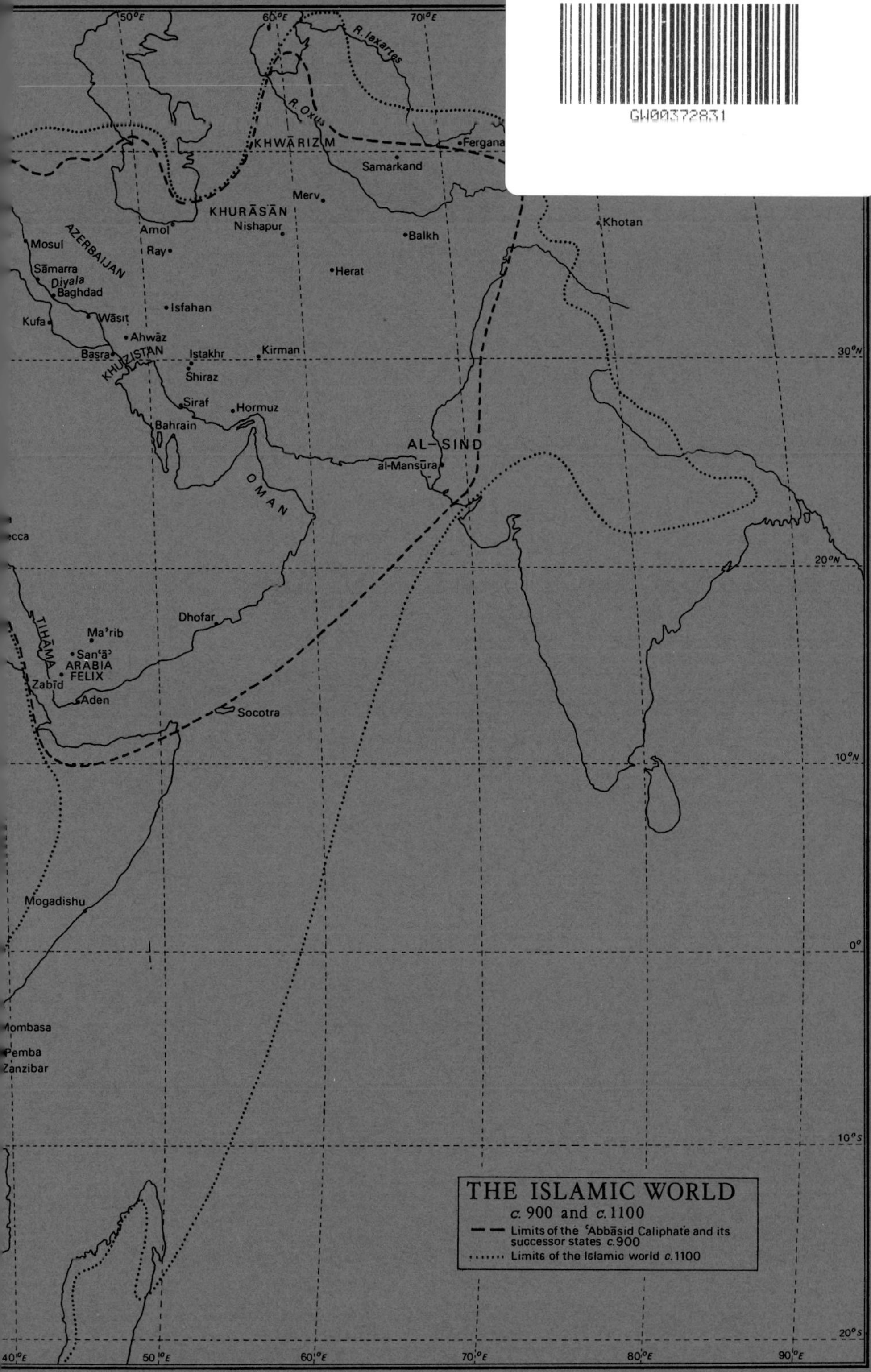
THE ISLAMIC WORLD
c. 900 and c. 1100
Limits of the ʿAbbāsid Caliphate and its successor states c. 900
Limits of the Islamic world c. 1100
R. Iaxartes
R. Oxus
KHWĀRIZM
Fergana
Samarkand
Merv
KHURĀSĀN
Nishapur
Amol
Ray
AZERBAIJAN
Mosul
Sāmarra
Diyala
Baghdad
Isfahan
Wāsit
Kufa
Ahwāz
Basra
KHUZISTAN
Istakhr
Shiraz
Kirman
Siraf
Hormuz
Bahrain
Balkh
Herat
Khotan
AL-SIND
al-Mansūra
OMAN
ecca
TIHĀMA
Ma'rib
Sanʿā'
ARABIA FELIX
Zabīd
Aden
Dhofar
Socotra
Mogadishu
ombasa
Pemba
Zanzibar
50°E
60°E
70°E
40°E
80°E
90°E
30°N
20°N
10°N
0°
10°S
20°S

Cambridge Studies in Islamic Civilization

Agricultural innovation in the early Islamic world

Cambridge Studies in Islamic Civilization

Other titles

BASIM MUSALLAM, *Sex and society in Islam*
ELIAS SAAD, *Social history of Timbuktu*
G. H. A. JUYNBOLL, *Muslim tradition*

Agricultural innovation in the early Islamic world

The diffusion of crops and farming techniques, 700–1100

ANDREW M. WATSON
Professor of Economic History
University of Toronto

Cambridge University Press
Cambridge
London New York New Rochelle
Melbourne Sydney

Published by the Press Syndicate of the University of Cambridge
The Pitt Building, Trumpington Street, Cambridge CB2 1RP
32 East 57th Street, New York, NY 10022, USA
296 Beaconsfield Parade, Middle Park, Melbourne 3206, Australia

First published 1983

Printed in Great Britain by the University Press, Cambridge

Library of Congress catalogue card number: 82-17773

British Library Cataloguing in Publication Data
Watson, Andrew M.
Agricultural innovation in the early
Islamic world. – (Cambridge studies
in Islamic civilization)
1. Agricultural innovations – History –
Islamic countries
I. Title
388.1'0917'671 HD146

ISBN 0 521 24711 X

UP

Contents

List of figures *page* vii
List of maps viii
Acknowledgments ix

1 Introduction 1

Part One: The chronology of diffusion

2 Sorghum 9
3 Asiatic rice 15
4 Hard wheat 20
5 Sugar cane 24
6 Old World cotton 31
7 Sour orange, lemon, lime, shaddock 42
8 Banana, plantain 51
9 Coconut palm 55
10 Watermelon 58
11 Spinach 62
12 Artichoke 64
13 Colocasia 66
14 Eggplant 70
15 Mango tree 72

Part Two: The pathways of diffusion

16 The routes 77

Part Three: The mechanics of diffusion

17 The agents 87
18 A medium for diffusion 91
19 The pull of demand 99
20 Facilitating supply: irrigation 103
21 Facilitating supply: land tenure 112
22 Facilitating supply: gardens 117

Part Four: The new plants in the economy

23 An agricultural revolution? 123
24 Agriculture in its context 129

Part Five: Later centuries

25 Agriculture in retreat 139

Notes 149
Works cited 215
Index 255

Figures

	page
Sorghum, designated as *Melita.* Manuscript, Österreichische Nationalbibliothek, Vienna	13
The sale of rice, probably from an apothecary's shop. Manuscript, Biblioteca Casanatense, Rome	18
The making of *trij*, or pasta. Manuscript, Österreichische Nationalbibliothek, Vienna	23
Sugar cane. Manuscript, Bibliothèque Nationale, Paris	25
An animal-powered mill for extracting juice from sugar cane. Engraving, *Description de l'Egypte... Etat moderne* II i, plates II	29
Gossypium herbaceum (cotton), as depicted in Dominique Chabré, *Stirpium icones et sciagraphia* (Geneva, 1677). Thomas Fisher Rare Book Library, University of Toronto	36–7
A member of the citrus family, possibly a sour-orange tree. Manuscript, Österreichische Nationalbibliothek, Vienna	43
A lemon tree. Manuscript, Bibliothèque Nationale, Paris	47
Two banana plants. Manuscript, Biblioteca Apostolica Vaticana, Vatican City	53
A coconut palm. Manuscript, Biblioteca Medicea Laurenziana, Florence	56
Watermelons. Manuscript, Österreichische Nationalbibliothek, Vienna	60
Spinach. Manuscript, Österreichische Nationalbibliothek, Vienna	63
Colocasia, as depicted in Prosper Alpino, *Historia Aegypti naturalis* (Leyden, 1735). Thomas Fisher Rare Book Library, University of Toronto	67
Eggplant, or *melongiana.* Manuscript, Österreichische Nationalbibliothek, Vienna	71
Carrying a frankincense tree: detail from carvings from the Temple of Deir al-Bahari dipicting the botanical expedition of Queen Hatshepsut to the Land of Punt. E. Naville, *The Temple of Deir el Bahari*, pt III (London, 1898)	88
A combination of *shādūfs* seen in Egypt by the Napoleonic scientific expedition. Engraving, *Description de l'Egypte... Etat moderne* I i, plates II	105
Cross-section of three *qanāts* in the environs of Kirman, Iran. After P. Beckett, "Qanats around Kirman", *Journal of the Royal Central Asian Society* XL (1953) 52	106
A water-driven noria. Manuscript, Biblioteca Apostolica Vaticana, Vatican City	109

Maps

The Islamic world *c.* 900 and *c.* 1100 — *Endpapers*

1 The diffusion of sorghum — *page* 10
2 The diffusion of Asiatic rice — 16
3 The diffusion of sugar cane — 27
4 The diffusion of cotton — 33
5 The diffusion of banana and plantain — 52
6 The names derived from "kolokasion" — 68
7 The routes of diffusion — 79
8 The diffusion of the *qanāt* — 110

Acknowledgments

This study has taken its author across the boundaries of many disciplines into realms that he could penetrate only with guidance. I owe a heavy debt of gratitude to a large number of scholars who, by generously giving of their time and wisdom, helped to initiate me into some of the mysteries of their disciplines. I am also much indebted to friends and colleagues in more familiar fields for advice on many points. To draw up a complete list of those who over the years have guided me now seems impossible. I should like, however, to thank the following scholars who have helped me along the way: the Rev. M. Anawati, Dr W. R. Anderson, Mrs Carlo Angelucci, the late Professor C. A. Ashley, Dr George Atiyeh, Dr Mohammed Aziman, Dr Miguel Barceló, Dr J. Vallvé Bernejo, Mr and Mrs Thierry Bianquis, Dr Lucie Bolens, Dr Henri Bresc, Mr Christian Bromberger, Mr Dominique Bromberger, Dr S. J. Brown, the late Harold Burnham, Professor Claude Cahen, Professor M. Gual Camarena, El-Emir Mustafa al-Chehabi, Miss Elizabeth Crowfoot, Mr Roger Dalton, Dr Jorge Dias, Professor G. S. Dikshit, Dr D. M. Dixon, Dr Claire Doyle, Dr Toufy Fahd, Dr Hasan Foda, Dr Gladys Frantz, the late Dr Veronika Gervers, Professor Thomas Glick, Dr Lisa Golombek, Professor A. K. Grayson, Professor J. Gulsoy, Dr Ahmad al-Harshni, the Rev. William Hayes, Dr Hans Helbaek, Professor Karl Helleiner, Dr J.-J. Hémardinquer, Professor Albert Hourani, Sir Joseph Hutchinson, Dr J. Eguaras Ibañez, Mr John Irwin, Mrs M. G. Johnson (Georgina Masson), Dr G. H. A. Juynboll, Professor Albertine Jwaideh, Dr ʻAbdullah Kanoun, Professor Nikki Keddie, Dr Hava Lazar, Dr L. Levine, Professor Seco de Lucena, Dr Louise Mackie, Professor Michael Marmura, the late Professor J. M. Millás Vallicrosa, Dr N. Millct, Profcssor A. Huici Miranda, Professor Pedro Martínez Montávez, Professor John Munro, Dr Roger Owen, Dr G.-B. Pellegrini, Professor Illuminato Peri, Dr Carlo Poni, Professor Evelyn Rawski, Dr Juan Reglà, Mr D. S. Richards, Professor J. Samsó Moya, Dr M. N. Sankary, Professor Roger Savory, Professor George Scanlon, Dr Hsio-yen Shih, Dr S. G. Stephens, Dr Frank Stewart, Dr Maḥmūd Ṣubḥ, Professor Ronald Sweet, the late Dr Vivi Täckholm, Miss Norah Titley, Dr Carmelo Trasselli, Professor Avrom Udovitch, Professor Juan Vernet, Mr C. Wakefield, Professor A. K. Warder, Miss Estelle Whelan, Professor K. D. White, Professor Lynn White, Dr R. O. Whyte, Professor

G. M. Wickens and Professor John Williams. I regret that momentary forgetfulness may have caused me to omit the names of others who offered valuable help.

Financial assistance for this study has come from the John Simon Guggenheim Foundation, the Canada Council and the University of Toronto, and material assistance from officials of the British Library, the Library of the Royal Botanic Gardens at Kew, The Bibliothèque Nationale in Paris, the Musée d'Histoire Naturelle, the Herbarium of Cairo University, the Library of Congress and the Institut Fondamental d'Afrique Noire. Permission to use portions of my earlier publications on this subject has been granted by the editors of the *Journal of Economic History*, by the Darwin Press and by the Royal Ontario Museum. To all of these I am grateful.

Finally, I wish to thank two former students who typed this book, Miss Mona Salloum and Mr Robert Cavanaugh. They attacked with intelligence and devotion a difficult manuscript. Many corrections and improvements are due to their care.

A.M.W.

International Centre for Agriculture Research in the Dry Areas
Aleppo, 1982

To KARL F. M. HELLEINER
Teacher and friend

Were the farmer not to plant, the builder would not build and the weaver would not weave.

Ibn Waḥshīya, *The Nabatean Book of Agriculture*

CHAPTER ONE

Introduction

Arab geographers, authors of farming manuals and other writers from the tenth century onwards tell of a countryside that had changed significantly from ancient times. In particular, they noticed many plants growing that had not been known – or had been little known – in pre-Islamic times. Some of these were of great economic importance for smaller or larger regions, often much more important than they were to be in modern times.

The new crops were mainly fruit trees, grains and vegetables; but the sources also mention new plants used as sources of fibres, condiments, beverages, medicines, narcotics, poisons, dyes, perfumes, cosmetics, nuts, wood and fodder. Many new flowers and ornamental plants had also appeared in the gardens these writers describe. So had some new weeds. It also seems certain that many new strains of old and of new plants were being grown in the early Islamic world, some pandering to different tastes and others having the merit of growing in different soils or climates.[1] If the writers are to be believed, these new cultivars abounded. To give only a few examples, al-Jāḥiẓ in the ninth century stated that 360 kinds of dates were to be found in the market of Basra, while in the following century Ibn Waḥshīya wrote that the varieties of dates in Iraq could not be counted; according to Ibn Rusta, who wrote in the early tenth century, there were 78 kinds of grapes in the vicinity of San'ā'; al-Anṣārī, writing of a small town on the North African coast about the year 1400, said that in the environs were produced 65 kinds of grapes, 36 kinds of pears, 28 kinds of figs, 16 kinds of apricots and so forth; in describing the different kinds of citrus fruits found in Egypt in the beginning of the thirteenth century 'Abd al-Laṭīf, a physician from Baghdad, stated that "these combine with one another to produce an infinity of varieties".[2] The exact figures, of course, should not be taken seriously, even when they do not approach infinity. What seems certain, however, is that the range of useful plants available to the cultivator – and to the consumer – was greatly increased in the early centuries of Islam by the diffusion of new plants and the development of new cultivars.

Although these introductions brought changes in patterns of consumption and land use, and were thus of economic as well as scientific importance, they have been little studied. The diffusion of sugar cane and citrus trees across the Islamic world has been treated in some detail in earlier works now in need of revision, but the other crops have been studied either only superficially or not at all.[3] What is more, the overall achievement of early Muslims in diffusing a wide range of useful plants over a large area has been the subject of only a few comments, some of them imaginative.[4] Virtually no attempt has been made to explore either the causes or the consequences of this phenomenon; perhaps understandably, scholars have shied away from the study of connections which, however important, are often complex, unobservable and uncertain. This book is an attempt to fill these gaps. It tries to follow as closely as possible the movement of eighteen of these new plants – seventeen food crops and one fibre crop – from their centres of origin through the early Islamic world and sometimes beyond. Although the crops were selected either for their economic importance or for the relative ease with which they could be studied, it is hoped they are representative of all the useful plants diffused in this period. This study then goes on to explore the interaction between these plants and the context through which they passed. It tries to identify the features of the early Islamic world which eased the new crops along their way and the ways in which this world was in turn affected by these introductions. Large questions these, to which certain answers cannot be found. But the attempt seemed worth making for the unusual way in which it might illuminate early Islamic society and economy and for the light it might shed on the broader, more general question of how in the past diffusion has taken place – or been blocked.

The picture which emerges from our enquiries is one of a large unified region which for three or four centuries – and in places still longer – was unusually receptive to all that was new. It was also unusually able to diffuse novelties: both to effect the initial transfer which introduced an element into a region and to carry out the secondary diffusion which changed rarities into commonplaces. Attitudes, social structure, institutions, infrastructure, scientific progress and economic development all played a part in the making of this medium of diffusion. And not only agriculture but also other spheres of the economy – and many areas of life that lay outside the economy – were touched by this capacity to absorb and to transmit. The end result of the prolonged operation of this medium was the emergence over a large part of the earth's face of a civilization that had a look of newness, fashioned out of elements that for the most part were old.

The crops diffused through this medium played a central role in the development of a more productive agriculture and were thus closely linked to important changes in the economy at large. The productivity of agricultural land and sometimes of agricultural labour rose through the introduction of higher-yielding new crops and better varieties of old crops, through more specialized land use which often centred on the new crops, through more intensive rotations which the new crops allowed, through the concomitant extension and improvement of irrigation, through the spread of cultivation into new or abandoned areas, and through the development of more labour-intensive techniques of farming. Agricultural changes were in turn bound up with changes in other sectors of the economy: with the growth of trade and the enlargement of the money economy, with the increasing specialization of factors of production in all sectors, and with the growth of population and its increasing urbanization. These factors bore on the agricultural sector and were in turn affected by it. Indeed, the interaction of the agricultural and non-agricultural sectors is so common and at times so intense that it seems impossible to unravel causes and effects. Population growth, for instance, must at times be viewed as a cause of rising agricultural productivity and at times a consequence. Sometimes they appear to act on one another simultaneously.

The greater part of the evidence on which this study is based is literary. For the Islamic period it consists mainly of manuals of farming, geographical works, travel accounts and botanical compendia; many of these have survived and more are continually being discovered.[5] Lesser – but sometimes crucial – help came from works of medicine, history and lexicography. These works are not easy to use in historical research. As their authors often plagiarized, sometimes from sources no longer available, the dating and reliability of their information are not always certain. For a study on cultivated plants these texts pose the additional problem of terminology: plant names varied over time and space so that one is sometimes not sure what plant a given name designated. Many times uncertainties were removed by consulting works of lexicography which give synonyms, works of botany which describe the plants and works of farming which recommend cultivation techniques. But sometimes doubt remained. Further difficulty arises from the relative lateness of most of the texts. With a few exceptions, the earliest are from the ninth century and the majority are from the tenth, eleventh and twelfth centuries. They are thus from a period when the diffusion of our plants was well under way and in some cases largely completed. All these difficulties notwithstanding, the early Islamic texts, by virtue of their abundance and the detailed information they contain, are by far the most valuable sources for a study of the cultivated plants of early Muslims. Carefully used, they throw much light on a process of diffusion that till now has remained obscure.

As this study is directed to readers not all of whom are Arabists, references are not always to the best Arabic edition of the texts. Where reliable translations are available, these have been cited. Special preference has been given to publications of the Arabic text together with an acceptable translation. When there was doubt about the translation of a critical passage, the translation was compared with the standard Arabic edition or occasionally with a manuscript. This procedure was intended to give readers access to many of the materials on which this study has been based without, it is hoped, any sacrifice of accuracy.

Whenever it was available, archeological material was also used. Paintings, bas-reliefs and other depictions – especially when they are unambiguous – have yielded valuable information which could not be obtained in any other way; such representations were particularly helpful when they could be precisely dated. Pollen and plant remains from excavations have also been used where these have been analysed and reported. But for the Islamic period the help from archeology is slight. Islamic archeology having for long been largely the preserve of historians of art, architecture and urban planning, there are few published reports of early Islamic plant materials or representations of plants. Moreover, recent research has shown that casual scrutiny of plant remains or depictions gave results that too often were unreliable, while the earlier techniques of dating led to other serious errors. Much of the early work in these areas can therefore not be used. Some research of the last two decades has yielded more trustworthy results, but it is only a beginning.[6]

Linguistic evidence has also at times been helpful in this study. The trail of words which a plant leaves behind tells something of its passage over the face of the earth, if only the signs can be correctly read. In the nineteenth century, the principles for such enquiries were laid down by the great French botanist Alphonse de Candolle in his pioneering study on plant origins.[7] His work has been carried further by another French botanist, Roland Portères, who has investigated the names for cereal plants.[8] To draw firm conclusions from this kind of evidence alone, however, would be dangerous indeed. In this study, linguistic evidence has been adduced for only two purposes: to support other evidence which in itself is not conclusive, and to frame tentative hypotheses when no other type of evidence is available.

The evidence of botany has been a valuable supplement to literary, archeological and linguistic evidence. By their present-day distributions, their variations of form and their genetic and biochemical characteristics, the plants themselves tell much about their history. Their evidence has been particularly useful in suggesting the genealogies of cultivated plants, their places of origin and their early diffusion from these centres.[9] To be sure, such inferences are perilous. For some plants – especially those which have been cultivated for millennia – no close relatives have yet been found growing wild; seemingly wild varieties often turn out to be escapes or imports. The wild ancestors of these plants may still be discovered, but they may have been the victims of ecological change or of continuous intercrossing with the cultivated forms and their escapes.[10] In the case of plants which developed in cultivation through crosses or mutations no genetically similar ancestor ever existed in a wild state and the genetic leap, if it cannot be repeated, can only be guessed at. Where a wild form can be identified, we cannot be certain that it is identical to the ancestor that was domesticated; nor can we be sure that the present-day distribution of the wild plant tells where it originated – let alone where it was first domesticated, where it was "ennobled" or where its annual varieties were produced.[11] The plant may no longer grow wild in the locus of its early development. But it may today be truly wild, and even show great diversity in its wild forms, in distant places which it reached through the agency of winds, rivers, tides, ocean currents, animals and men. Small wonder, then, that inferences based on the botanical evidence have generated much controversy or that botanists concerned with the early history of cultivated plants often resort to the help of textual, archaeological and even linguistic evidence.

But in spite of the great uncertainty prevailing in this area of enquiry, the botanical evidence points clearly to one conclusion which is important for this study. It shows that – with the exception of hard wheat and artichokes – the plants studied in this volume originated and were domesticated in parts of the world far removed and climatically distinct from the Mediterranean and the Middle East. To diffuse these exotic plants over a very large and, to varying degrees, hostile area was no mean feat.[12]

Indeed, the picture which this book gives of the cultivators of the early Islamic world may seem at variance with certain popularly held notions about the Arabs and their history, as well as with the opinions of some scholars. Ibn Khaldūn, writing in the fourteenth century, stated that "the places that succumb to the Arabs are quickly ruined. The reason for this is that the Arabs are a savage nation." The author continues with much more in the same vein.[13] This attitude has carried over into some scholarship of the nineteenth and twentieth centuries which has assumed on *a priori* grounds that the remains of Mediterranean irrigation works, castles, and villages all date from Roman times or earlier,[14] and that the Arabs when they appeared in the Mediterranean and the Middle East inevitably made agriculture less intensive (if they did not destroy it altogether), since they "had no agricultural traditions" and "knew only about the raising of stock".[15] Some of this scholarship is tendentious and may be dismissed. Some of it is the product of a habit, all too common amongst Islamic economic historians, of reading backwards from later centuries about which there is more information – sometimes even from the nineteenth century! – to the ill-documented centuries following the rise of Islam. The gross errors which this kind of scholarship has yielded have been uncovered in recent discussions of Islamic guilds, demography, "feudalism" and so forth. It is no different with agriculture. Here, too, the assumptions that the later centuries of Islam were similar to the early ones, and that at no point in Islamic history from the Arab conquests onwards were there significant discontinuities or even any reversals of previous long-term trends, have led to serious misreadings of the past. This study attempts to correct a few of these. At the same time it tries to make a modest contribution to the periodization of Islamic history.

The agricultural achievement of the early centuries of Islam was in fact the work of different peoples whose contributions combined in different ways. A part was played by the Arab conquerors and by later migrants from the Arabian peninsula, both of whom did have in their numbers many with a very long tradition of intensive, irrigated agriculture.[16] A part was played by the peasants and landowners whom they conquered, some of whom were left to farm their lands – albeit in an altered context – and some of whom in their migrations took their skills and their crops to distant regions.[17] A part was also played by the neighbours of the Islamic world, particularly the Indians, from whom early Muslims learned about new crops and new farming techniques. The economic and cultural environment of the early Islamic world encouraged the collaboration of peoples in this undertaking.

True, pastoral peoples living on the fringes of settled lands had long posed a threat to the agriculture of the regions the Arabs conquered, and they continued to be dangerous in Islamic times. As is shown in the conclusion to this book, Islamic farming suffered serious setbacks from nomadic incursions beginning in the eleventh century and lasting into modern times: not only from the Banū Hilāl, who caused so much destruction in North Africa and against whom Ibn Khaldūn inveighed so vehemently, but also from many other nomadic peoples – mostly non-Arab – who overran one part or another of the Islamic world, destroying much that lay in their path and bringing institutions and attitudes that were harmful to farming. But in the early centuries of Islam nomads were largely held in check. They did little to restrain the work in which peoples of diverse ranks and walks of life collaborated: rulers, who imported plants for their botanical gardens; their advisers, who urged the importance of a prosperous countryside;[18] jurists, who interpreted legal traditions so as to accommodate the needs of an expanding agricultural sector; botanists, who herborized the length and breadth of the Islamic world; agronomes, who produced a wealth of farming manuals; geographers, who wrote enthusiastically about the agriculture of the regions they visited; peasants and landowners who experimented with new crops; and many other urban and rural dwellers – mostly now lost from view – who showed on their tables their love of exotic foods and told of their love of greenery in their poems and in their gardens.

Part One
The chronology of diffusion

CHAPTER TWO

Sorghum, great millet *Sorghum bicolor* (L.) Moench.[1]

Arabic: *dhurra, durra, jāwars hindī, jawarsh*[2]

Uses

Sorghum is the world's fifth most important cereal crop. Its cultivation is still spreading rapidly today. Sorghum has tended to displace millets and other grains of antiquity because of its higher yields and the ability of some cultivars to withstand drought and to tolerate poor soils.[3]

The unground grain may be eaten raw or cooked to make cous-cous, porridges, soups and cakes. Thc flour is sometimes eaten uncooked and in Arab countries is widely used – usually mixed with other flours or starch – for making bread for the poorer classes. The seeds of red sorghum are the basis of a common beer, while the juice extracted from certain sweet-cane varieties is used to make both syrups and fermented drinks. The seeds and stalks are fed to cattle and poultry. Some varieties are used for thatch, fencing, baskets, brushes and brooms. The stalks are also used as fuel. Medieval texts mention several medical uses.[4]

Origins and pre-Islamic diffusion

The multitude of varieties of cultivated sorghum can all be traced back to the wild sorghums of Africa, which grow in the savanna lands lying to the north, the east and the south of the rain forest. Their cultivation began long before the Christian era and spread into several distinct zones; the different cultivated varieties so developed crossed freely with one another and with the wild sorghums of both Africa and Asia to produce a profusion of strains which confounds both the taxonomist and the historian. The scholar's difficulties are compounded by the very early appearance in India of new strains of sorghum, all developed from the African varieties, and by the crossing of these with African sorghums both in India and in Africa.[5]

Harlan has recently proposed a single wild progenitor – *Sorghum bicolor* var. *verticilliflorum* – which in the course of a number of domestications and diffusions may have given rise to all the cultivated sorghums of the world. The earliest domestication, he suggests, occurred in the region of Chad, Sudan and Uganda; and in the second millennium B.C., or perhaps even earlier, the

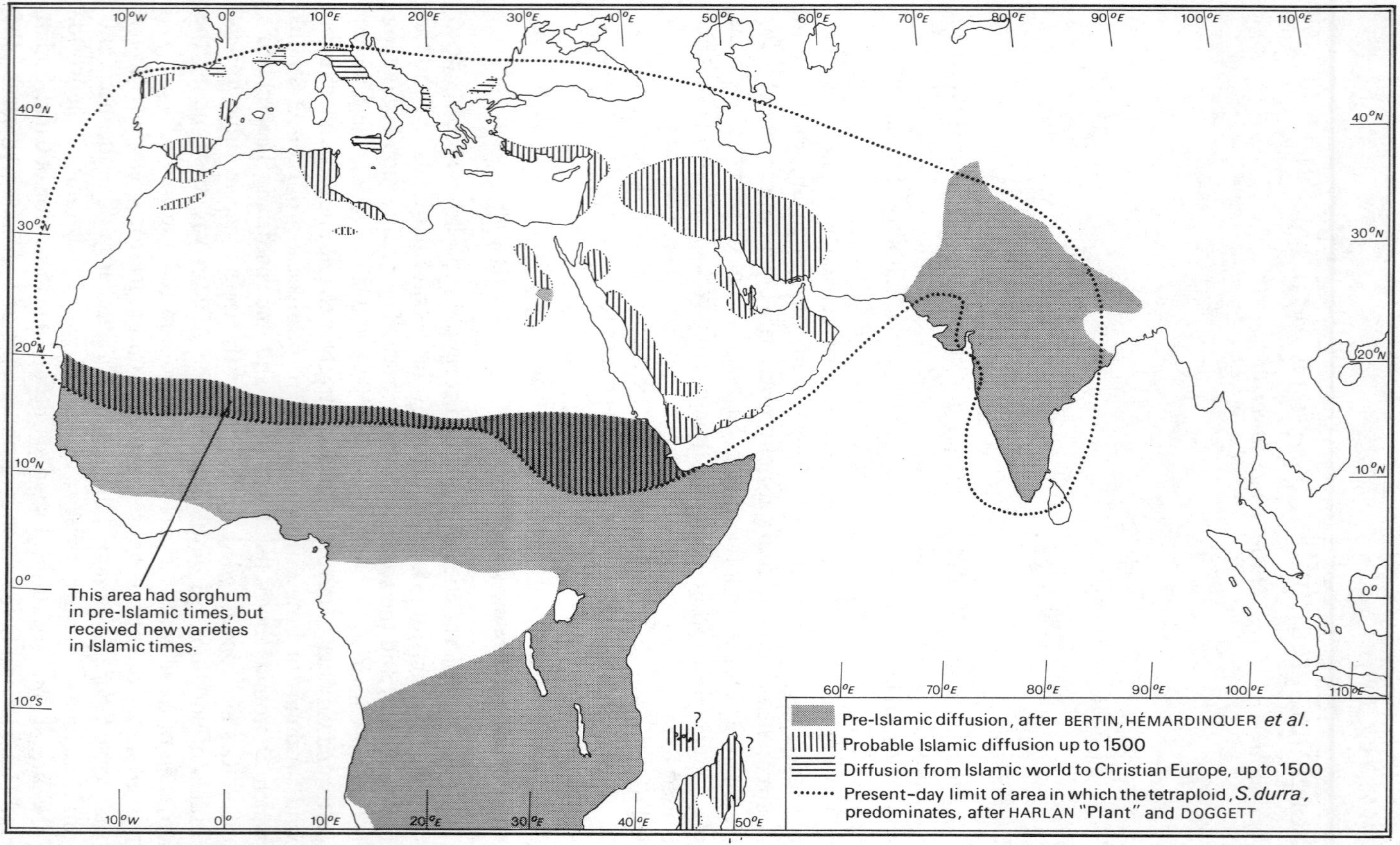
10°W
0°
10°E
20°E
30°E
40°E
50°E
60°E
70°E
80°E
90°E
100°E
110°E
40°N
30°N
20°N
10°N
0°
10°S
This area had sorghum in pre-Islamic times, but received new varieties in Islamic times.
Pre-Islamic diffusion, after BERTIN, HÉMARDINQUER *et al*.
Probable Islamic diffusion up to 1500
Diffusion from Islamic world to Christian Europe, up to 1500
Present-day limit of area in which the tetraploid, *S. durra*, predominates, after HARLAN "Plant" and DOGGETT
?
?

Map 1. The diffusion of sorghum

crop was diffused into western and south-eastern Africa and across the sea to India.[6] It may have reached India in the first half of the second millennium B.C., since a design on a pot found in Mohenjo-daro has been thought to represent the plant, and potsherds from Ahar in Rajastan have spikelets of sorghum mixed into the clay; the identification of the design as sorghum is, however, uncertain, and the material from Ahar – associated with artifacts dated 1725 B.C. ± 140 – was found at a disturbed site and thus may be more recent.[7] Firmer evidence dating from about 1400–1200 B.C. comes from Inamagon in Maharashtra.[8] A new variety was developed in India, *S. durra*, which was both high-yielding and drought-resistant.[9] Today *S. durra* accounts for about four-fifths of the sorghum grown in India; is virtually the only sorghum grown in the Middle East, North Africa, Arabia and along the southern fringes of the Sahara; and is the principal sorghum of Ethiopia.

From India sorghum may have fanned outwards to reach a number of widely separated regions in pre-Islamic times. The earliest transmission may have been to China. Several archeological finds, thought to date from about 1100 to 800 B.C., may contain sorghum seeds, stalks or leaves; but these have not yet been rigorously dated.[10] Other uncertain evidence has been dated between 400 B.C. and the time of Christ.[11] Contrary to what had previously been thought, there is no known literary evidence of sorghum in China before the thirteenth century.[12] Long before then, sorghum was probably taken to Southeast Asia and to Java;[13] there it may have crossed with the wild *S. propinquum* to produce the special characteristics of the Chinese *kaoliang*.

It is also possible that sorghum was diffused from India to Mesopotamia in the first millennium B.C. According to Piédallu, the plant is depicted in a bas-relief from the palace of Sennacherib (d. 691 B.C.) at Nineveh.[14] If this interpretation is correct, the "millet" of Mesopotamia, which in the fifth century B.C. Herodotus said was so tall that he would not be believed, could well have been sorghum.[15] However, Piédallu's identification has been challenged: the plant depicted may well be common millet, Japanese millet or one of several rushes.[16] Further doubt is cast on Piédallu's hypothesis by the lack of any clear description of sorghum in the reports of the Alexandrian expedition to Mesopotamia in the fourth century B.C. and in Dioscorides.[17] Sorghum is also not mentioned as one of the field crops of late Sasanian Persia by al-Ṭabarī or in the Babylonian Talmud.[18] It was also not known in ancient Egypt or in the pre-Islamic Levant.[19]

In pre-Islamic times African sorghum may have moved northward into lands that were later to be conquered by the Arabs – though this diffusion could have occurred entirely after the rise of Islam. Thus it was probably sorghum of African origin which was found in tombs of the sixth or seventh century at Thebes.[20] In North Africa the variety of names for sorghum in the Berber languages, most of which are unrelated to the Arabic names, is perhaps explained by an early appearance of sorghum from Africa in lands occupied by the Berbers.[21] However that may be, the entry of African sorghums into North Africa was not to be durable. As Doggett has convincingly shown, the sorghums of Africa – all diploids – are not grown today in the coastal regions of Egypt or the Maghrib. Their northerly limit is in hotter lands lying at a considerable distance from the sea. In fact they are hardly known north of the Sahara.[22]

A kind of sorghum may have been introduced into Italy in the first century of the Christian era, perhaps from Mesopotamia or perhaps from India, for Pliny describes a kind of black-grained "millet" that had come to Italy in his time.[23] This introduction, if it was one, does not seem to have been successful: sorghum is not mentioned again in Italy until the twelfth century, and the medieval varieties had red or white grains, not black.[24]

Islamic diffusion

The Middle East, North Africa and Europe received sorghum from India. On this point the botanical evidence is clear: the tetraploid *S. durra*, which today is almost the only variety grown in these regions, must have come from India where it was developed.[25] The linguistic evidence also helps us to glimpse a westward movement out of India. This evidence suggests that the movement of sorghum from India to the west did not begin in very ancient times; if it was pre-Islamic at all, it perhaps was initiated only a century or two before the rise of Islam. Thus from the Sanskrit *zoorna*, a word meaning "cereal" or, more particularly, "barley", came the complex of related words designating sorghum in the post-Sanskritic dialects of northern India; the Persian *gāvar hindī* or *gāvars hindī* and *gavarish*; the Arabic *jāwars hindī*; the *garawa* complex of words of Egypt; the *jahwarī* of Tunisia and the *junarī* of Morocco. The fact that the adjective *hindī*, or "Indian", was retained in early Arabic and probably in Persian of the early Islamic period suggests that the crop was not known from ancient times in Persia and Mesopotamia. Another linguistic chain starting with *zoorna* connects this word to the Persian *dura* and the Arabic words of the *dhurra* type, the terminology which was ultimately to predominate in the Arabic world. Whether originally the *jāwars* group of words designated a type of sorghum different from that referred to by words of the *dhurra* type – perhaps a lower-yielding variety diffused westward at an earlier date – is not certain, but the hypothesis seems likely.[26]

This westward transmission out of India cannot be easily followed in the texts. Part of the difficulty is that the earliest geographical and agricultural works which mention sorghum date from the tenth century, by which time sorghum was well known in the eastern parts of the Islamic world. In that century, al-Iṣṭakhrī and Ibn Ḥawqal spoke of it growing in the coastal regions of the Persian Gulf.[27] It was probably also sorghum which was intended by the term *jāwars* in the anonymous geographical work of the tenth century *Ḥudūd al-ʿālam*; according to this work *jāwars* had become the principal food in the region of Kirman in Persia.[28] In the same century it was seen by several

An illustration of sorghum, designated as *Melita*, from the *Tacuinum sanitatis*, which is the Latin translation of the medical work *Taqwīm al-siḥḥa*, by Ibn Buṭlān (d. 1066). The manuscript was probably made in Italy in the late fourteenth century. (Österreichische Nationalbibliothek, Ser. Nov. 2644, fol. 48v)

travellers in the southern Arabian peninsula, in parts of which, according to a later source, it was the staple.[29] Sorghum was also discussed at length in the tenth-century agricultural work of Ibn Waḥshīya, who said it was a very common crop in Iraq.[30] Early in the thirteenth century Yāqūt stated that it was grown in the region of Aleppo.[31]

By then it had already been observed in many parts of the Islamic west. Many writers saw it growing in Upper Egypt and along more southerly parts of the Nile valley, where it had clearly become the principal food.[32] It was also grown in certain inland and coastal regions in North Africa.[33] The appearance of sorghum in Spain seems to have been a little later than in the eastern reaches of the Islamic world. It was not mentioned in the tenth-century *Calendar of Cordova*, but was referred to by the eleventh-century agronome Abū al-Khair.[34] In the twelfth century, the growing of sorghum was discussed at length in the agricultural treatise of Ibn al-ʻAwwām.[35] By then sorghum seems to have passed over the frontier into Christian Spain and even into France: in the eleventh century al-Bakrī stated that, along with millet, it was the main crop in Galicia, and in the twelfth century, under the name *milhoca*, it was being sold in the market of Moissac.[36] Surprisingly, grains of sorghum dating from the ninth, tenth or eleventh centuries have been found in Poland.[37]

India, which had long before received sorghum from Africa, also sent back the new varieties which it had developed. These introductions probably occurred after the rise of Islam and through the agency of Arabs. The sweet-stemmed varieties probably came first, giving rise to the term "grain from the sea" in Abyssinia and possibly to the word *muhindi* on the east coast of Africa.[38] Later on, India sent various cereal sorghums to the east coast of Africa, where other sorghums may have long been known and where, by the early tenth century, the travellers Abū Zaid and al-Masʻūdī stated that black sorghum had become the principal food.[39] Linguistic evidence suggests that some of these later Indian introductions passed through the island of Pemba, where they were perhaps crossed with African varieties: the name for *S. conspicuum* in Tanganyika is *ma-pemba*, while the term *vary-apemby*, or "rice of Pemba", is one of several names for the genus *Sorghum* in Madagascar.[40] *S. durra* was also taken to the east coast of Africa, whence it penetrated into Ethiopia and across the southern fringes of the Sahara into West Africa.[41]

By the fourteenth century, if not earlier, sorghum had become of very great importance in many parts of India, Mesopotamia and Arabia. Perhaps by then – and if not, by a few centuries later – it had also become very important in Syria and Palestine, where the eighteenth-century traveller Niebuhr reported that it was the staple of the peasants.[42] In Upper Egypt, Ethiopia and Africa south of the Sahara it was the principal grain crop. But in the coastal parts of the Mediterranean it was less important. There wheat was the main cereal grown, except in certain irrigated or swamp regions where rice was the staple. In these lands sorghum was grown – and this was its real importance for the agriculture of these regions – mainly in areas unsuited to other grains: where the soil was too poor, the weather too hot or the moisture too little.

CHAPTER THREE

Asiatic rice[1] *Oryza sativa* L.

Arabic: *ruzz, aruzz, uruzz*[2]

Uses

In the cooking of medieval Arabs rice was prepared alone or with other ingredients. It was added to a number of soups. Many dishes combined it with fish, poultry or meat. It could also be used to stuff vegetables such as eggplants, or be wrapped in grape-leaves. Recipes abound for desserts – some famous in history – in which rice is cooked with milk and sugar or honey.[3] In certain regions, such as Tabaristan, the bread of the inhabitants was made from rice flour.[4] Medieval Arabs were aware that the Indians and Chinese made rice wine and vinegar, and in some places seem to have done so themselves.[5] The texts speak of several medical uses.[6]

Origin and pre-Islamic diffusion

Riziculture may have begun somewhere in India, Assam, Burma, Thailand, Cochinchina or China, or in several of these regions; and in remote times it spread outwards from its centre or centres of origin to the other regions, as well as into Southeast Asia, the Philippines and the Indonesian archipelago.[7] According to Strabo, who appears to cite Aristobolus, rice was grown in the second century B.C. in Babylonia, Bactria, Susia and "Lower Syria", this last term meaning perhaps the Jordan valley.[8] Chinese sources also tell of rice cultivation in a number of parts of Mesopotamia and Persia in the second century B.C. and again in the early Christian era.[9] Though the crop is not mentioned in the Bible, several references in the Jerusalem Talmud show that rice was grown in Palestine (probably in the Jordan valley) at some time between the third and eighth century.[10] Its cultivation in these regions, however, was probably limited: Chinese annals state – no doubt wrongly – that there was no rice in Sasanian Persia, while Jacob of Edessa speaks of rice as an Indian crop not grown in the Near East.[11] The plant does not seem to have been cultivated elsewhere in pre-Islamic times.[12] Though knowledge of rice gradually spread into the classical Mediterranean after the Alexandrian expedition to the east, and into pre-Islamic Arabia and East Africa as well, and small amounts of rice were imported into these regions for use as a

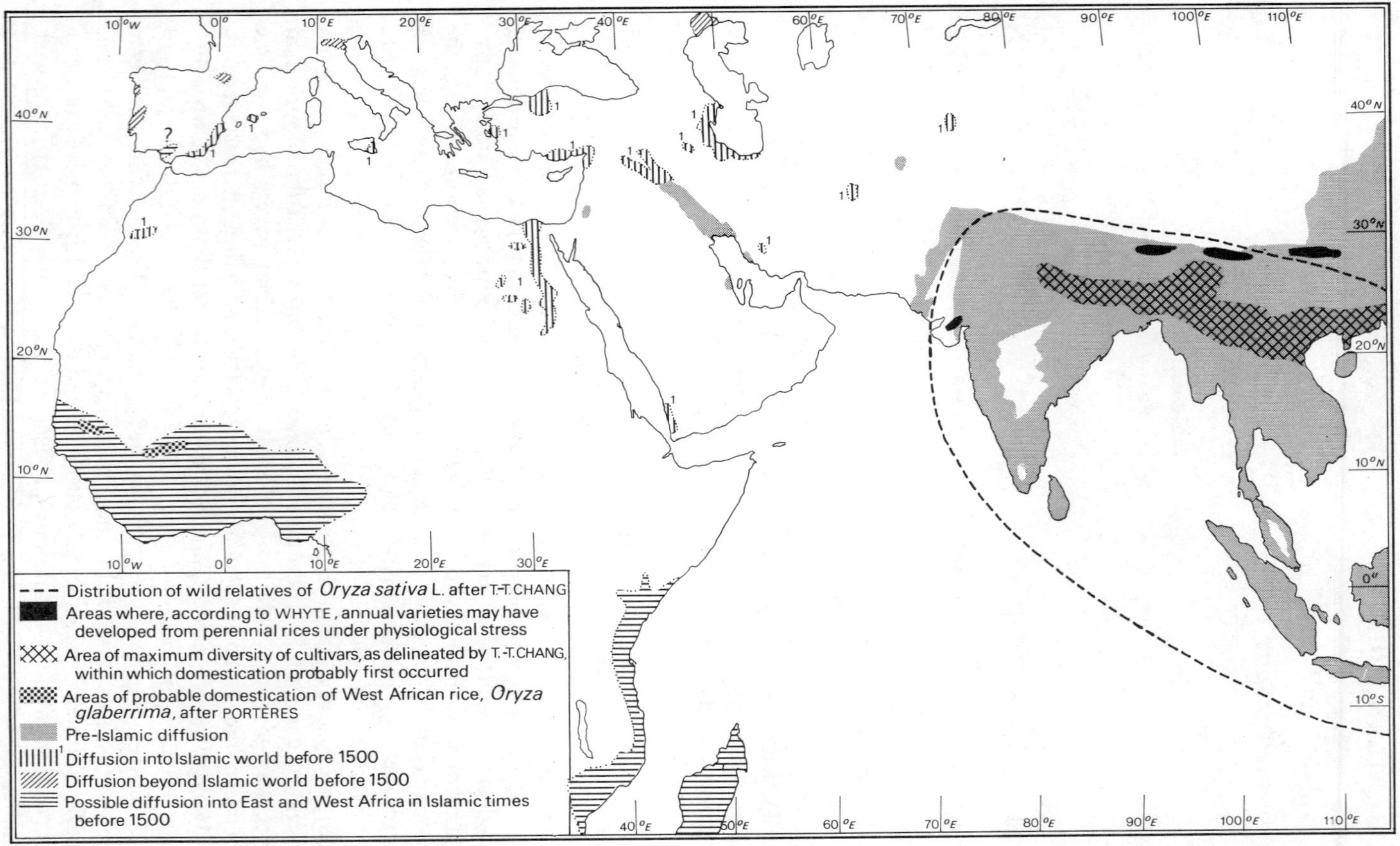

10°W
0°
10°E
20°E
30°E
40°E
60°E
70°E
80°E
90°E
100°E
110°E
40°N
30°N
20°N
10°N
0°
10°S
50°E
Distribution of wild relatives of *Oryza sativa* L. after T.-T. CHANG
Areas where, according to WHYTE, annual varieties may have developed from perennial rices under physiological stress
Area of maximum diversity of cultivars, as delineated by T.-T. CHANG, within which domestication probably first occurred
Areas of probable domestication of West African rice, *Oryza glaberrima*, after PORTÈRES
Pre-Islamic diffusion
Diffusion into Islamic world before 1500
Diffusion beyond Islamic world before 1500
Possible diffusion into East and West Africa in Islamic times before 1500

Map 2. The diffusion of Asiatic rice

medicine, the plant itself was not grown in any of these regions, it is believed, until after the rise of Islam.[13]

Islamic diffusion

Rice early came to be grown in the Islamic world almost wherever there was water enough to irrigate it. Although its overall importance never reached that of wheat or even of sorghum, it was very important in certain areas: in desert oases, in river valleys which were flooded naturally or artificially and in swamp lands. There rice was often the main crop and the staple food.

The sources allow us to delineate the regions where it was found. In the eastern part of the caliphate, where rice had been grown in ancient times, the early centuries of Islam saw an extension of its cultivation. It was grown in many parts of the lower Euphrates valley, along the canals which linked the Euphrates to the Tigris and on some of the tributaries of the Tigris in Khuzistan; it appeared in seemingly isolated pockets farther to the north, at Nisibin, for instance, around Divin, along the southern shores of the Caspian (where it was the staple food) and even beyond the frontiers of the caliphate in the valley of the Volga; it was also found in the Sind, where it was a very important crop, and in many other regions such as Siraf, Istakhr, Herat, Balkh and even as far to the north as Fergana.[14] In the Near East, according to al-Muqaddasī, it was grown along the Jordan River in the region of Baisan, which supplied the whole of Jordan and Palestine.[15] Several sources mention rice in the Yemen.[16] Although today rice is grown in Egypt only in the Nile Delta, it was found in early Islamic times in many other places: in the Fayyūm, where according to Ibn Ḥawqal it was the most important crop; in the southern oases; and along the valley of the upper Nile.[17] In the Maghrib, where perhaps most regions could not provide enough water for growing rice, it is mentioned only in the south of Morocco; and we have only one reference to it from Sicily, where, however, it may have been important.[18] From Spain there are many references to rice cultivation from the tenth century onwards. But as the regions in which rice is specifically mentioned as a crop are Valencia and – surprisingly – Majorca, we cannot be sure that rice was grown in the Muslim part of Spain after the Christian conquest of these areas in the early thirteenth century.[19]

Exactly what role the Arabs played in bringing Asiatic rice to sub-Saharan Africa is difficult to say. In the eastern part of the continent there is a *prima facie* case for Arab transmission on an important scale: in the twelfth century al-Zuhrī stated that in a part of Abyssinia the people lived on rice grown along the Nile; in the thirteenth century Marco Polo said that rice was the staple of the people in East Africa; and in the fourteenth century Ibn Baṭṭūṭa described a rice dish that was the main food in Mogadishu. In all probability rice began to be diffused through East Africa from the tenth century onwards.[20] The linguistic evidence does not support – but does not disprove –

The sale of rice, probably from an apothecary's shop, illustrated in a Latin translation of the *Taqwīm al-siḥḥa* of Ibn Buṭlān (d. 1066). The manuscript of this medical work is entitled *Liber magistri Ububechasym de Baldach.* It was probably made in Italy in the fourteenth century. (Biblioteca Casanatense, Rome, ms. 4182, fol. 26r)

this thesis: the terms of the *mpunga* and *panga* type found in Swahili and East African Bantu appear to be of Indian origin, suggesting that the grain, though not necessarily the cultivation of the plant, appeared in East Africa in pre-Islamic times.[21]

Whether Asiatic rice was also brought overland from the east coast into West Africa, or southwards across the Sahara, is still less certain. The linguistic evidence is confusing, since the names for the indigenous rice (*Oryza glaberrima*), which for millennia had been cultivated in West Africa, were sometimes transferred to Asiatic rice;[22] and in regions where words of the *aruzz* type are used, one cannot be sure that these words are of Arabic, and not Portuguese, introduction. But some inferences may be made. In the interior, along a band stretching from Lake Chad to the White Nile, words of the *aruzz* type prevail and strongly suggest an Arab introduction. In the west, where Asiatic rice is usually said to have been brought by the Portuguese, a case may still be made for an earlier diffusion by the Arabs: neither the medieval Arab travellers nor the early Portuguese explorers, who found some kind of rice growing in many parts of West Africa, mention that it was different from the rice they knew in their homelands.[23]

CHAPTER FOUR

Hard wheat *Triticum durum* Desf.

Arabic: *qamḥ, ḥinṭa, burr*[1]

Uses

Because of its high gluten content and the hardness of its grain, hard wheat has special uses. Husked but unground, or coarsely ground, it provides the most common *semoules* for the cous-cous of North Africa and some other parts of the Arab world,[2] as well as the *burghul* for pilafs and for Levantine dishes such as *tabbūla, kishk, kibba* and *bitfīn*. In Arab cooking, these *semoules* are also the basis of many soups, gruels, stuffings, puddings and pastries, and of preparations resembling the European *gnocchi* and *Knödel* (which are also often made from hard wheat).[3] A finer grinding gives the flour for macaroni, spaghetti and other dry pastas needing a large amount of gluten to bind the paste. This flour is also often used for making the flat round breads, pizzas, *galettes, torte* etc. of the Mediterranean and the Middle East. In many parts of the Arab countryside, hard wheat is picked green, roasted, hulled, sometimes (but not always) ground, and then eaten, either by itself as *farīk* or in soups, cous-cous or *manṣaf*.[4]

Hard wheat is a more versatile crop than bread wheat: it is sown in many parts of the world in dry, steppe regions where common bread wheats cannot be grown successfully. The low water content of the grain permits storage over exceptionally long periods.

Origin and pre-Islamic diffusion

Unlike the soft wheats, whose centre is Afghanistan, hard wheat originated either in Abyssinia or in the southern or eastern parts of the Mediterranean basin.[5] It probably developed from a mutation of emmer wheat (*Tr. dicoccum*) in not very remote times.[6] It seems to have been unknown in the Mediterranean of classical times. Two archeological finds from Byzantine Egypt show that in parts of that country its cultivation was spreading in the centuries just before the rise of Islam.[7] Elsewhere, however, there is not yet any evidence of this crop in pre-Islamic times. It goes unmentioned in the late classical works on farming, natural history, geography and medicine.[8]

Islamic diffusion

Whatever were the exact frontiers of the cultivation of hard wheat before the rise of Islam, it is certain that the Arabs diffused this crop widely in the Middle East and through the Muslim Mediterranean, from which it reached the Christian west. In much of this vast region hard wheat gradually displaced other forms of *Triticum* to become the principal – and often the only – wheat grown, giving rise to many typical dishes which are still part of the stable diet of this region today. The plant took so well to its new environment that many new varieties appeared: Spain, the Maghrib, the eastern Mediterranean, Central Asia, the Yemen and Abyssinia, if they were not the centre of origin, in effect became secondary centres for the plant's development.[9]

Unfortunately, however, its progress is difficult to trace, since there is no special word in classical Arabic to designate hard wheat. Only when an author elaborates on the special qualities of a kind of wheat do we catch glimpses of this revolutionary new plant. Thus Ibn Waḥshīya, in the early tenth century, was probably describing hard wheat, whose high content of gluten permits the making of pasta, when he wrote of a particularly "viscous" kind of wheat; his comment that it can grow in drier soils than other kinds of wheat makes this identification even more likely.[10] Similarly, in the same century, al-Hamdānī apparently described the hard wheat of the Yemen in this passage: "*burr* is not identical with *ḥinṭa*; for when the dough of *burr* has been kneaded and you then want to cut off a piece, the adjacent part is pulled out by the part you have cut off".[11] In the eleventh century al-Bakrī probably was writing of hard wheat when he mentioned a particularly dry kind of wheat seed sown in the region of Sijilmasa; this wheat seeded itself for three years running.[12] Either the black-grained or the so-called Alexandrian wheat mentioned in the Byzantine *Geoponika* as summer crops may also be hard wheat;[13] in any case there is clear archeological evidence of hard wheat from a tenth-century Byzantine site in Anatolia.[14] Several authors referred to the extraordinary durability of wheat in different regions:

In his book, *The Government of Kings*, Ibn Ẓāfir [1171–1216] reports that the wheat [of the Maghrib] could be stored for eighty years in silos, and then sown. The long period of storage increased its purity and quality.

(AL-'UMARĪ 88)

The air [of Toledo] is excellent and grain stays a long time without changing. One can store wheat for sixty-six years in silos without ill effect.

(AL-RĀZĪ "Description" 82)

One of the characteristics of Toledo is that its wheat never changes or goes bad over the years.

(AL-BAKRĪ *Jughrāfīya* 88)[15]

The wheat of Lorca lasts twenty years.

(AL-ḤIMYARĪ 207)

In Saragossa, you can find wheat which is a hundred years old.

(AL-MAQQARĪ *Nafḥ al-ṭīb* I 183)

These references can only be to hard wheat, which the citation from al-Rāzī shows had reached the interior of Spain by the tenth century.

New recipes in the cookbooks and references to the new dishes in other literature not only betray the diffusion of hard wheat but also show the ingenuity of the early Islamic world in finding ways to take advantage of this crop's special properties. Semolina and the most famous dish made from semolina, cous-cous, when they appear in our sources, do not prove the use of hard wheat, since today they are occasionally made with other grains.[16] But as no kind of semolina was known in the ancient world, and as the appearance of both semolina and cous-cous in the Islamic world is late, probably some centuries after the appearance of hard wheat itself, we may suppose that in medieval times these were both made almost exclusively from hard wheat: the new dishes using semolina were indeed probably invented especially for this new crop. In the twelfth century Maimonides wrote of semolina in his book of simples, and in the thirteenth century we learn of the making of cous-cous in Spain, Tunisia, Egypt and Iraq.[17] By the fourteenth and fifteenth centuries there are many other references to both semolina and cous-cous.[18]

The history of macaroni, spaghetti and other pastas made from hard wheat is more difficult to trace. A Genoese document of 1273 mentioned macaroni, which was again spoken of by Boccaccio in the middle of the fourteenth century.[19] By the fourteenth century an Italian treatise on foods mentioned many different kind of pasta, probably all made from hard wheat and all referred to by the generic name of *tria*, while two fourteenth-century Catalan works – a cookery book and a medical treatise – spoke of noodles known as *aletria*.[20] These words, which are found in many Italian and Iberian dialects in the fifteenth century,[21] are clearly borrowed from the Arabic *iṭrīya*, a word which has a long history in the languages of the Near East. In the fourteenth-century Arabic dictionary of al-Fīrūzābādī, *iṭrīya* is said to refer to a kind of noodle almost certainly made from hard wheat; and the word is also used to designate a kind of *pasta secca* in the thirteenth-century cookery book of Baghdad and in the medical treatise of Ibn Buṭlān (composed in the eleventh century but, unfortunately, frequently revised until the fourteenth century).[22] The word appears in earlier texts from the Middle East – in the ninth-century dictionaries of al-Jawharī and Isho Bar 'Alī – but although these works both make it clear that the word designates a kind of pasta, it is less certain that this was made from hard wheat.[23]

The transmission of another word from Muslim to Christian Spain and thence, apparently, to Italy also tells of the appearance of dry pasta in the late-medieval Islamic world, whence it may have been diffused to Christian Europe. In the anonymous Hispano-Muslim cookery book of the thirteenth century there are several entries concerning *al-fidawsh*, a kind of pasta.[24] This was said to be made in several forms: long strips, tiny spheres and thin paper-like sheets (possibly an early kind of *fīla* pastry); the spherical kind was

The making of *trij*, or pasta, depicted in the Vienna copy of *Tacuinum sanitatis*, a translation into Latin of the *Taqwīm al-siḥḥa* of Ibn Buṭlān (d. 1066). The manuscript was probably made in Italy in the late fourteenth century. (Österreichische Nationalbibliothek, Ser. Nov. 2644, fol. 45v)

said to be known also in Bougie, in North Africa. From the word *al-fidawsh* came the Spanish word for noodles, *fideos*, as well as similar words in other Iberian dialects; according to Corominas, this word passed from Spain into the dialects of northern Italy to give the Italian *fidelli*, *sfidelli* and *fidellini*.[25]

Whether the Italians are indebted to the Arabs for the invention and transmission of *pasta secca*, and (if they are) what is the extent of their debt, are still open questions. The probabilities are increasing, however, that the early forms of this high art, like the hard wheat from which it was made, did reach medieval Christendom from the Islamic Mediterranean.[26]

CHAPTER FIVE

Sugar cane *Saccharum officinarum* L.

Arabic: *qaṣab al-sukkar, qaṣab fārisī, qaṣab ḥulw, qaṣab hindī*[1]

Uses

"Capable of producing more human food per acre than any other crop",[2] sugar cane may be used in several ways. In early times, and long after the invention of ways of making sugar, the cane was sucked raw or cooked and eaten.[3] From the crushed cane came a juice which was drunk. The juice could be boiled to produce a syrup or further reduced to give a crystalline sugar which might be red, brown or yellow. Additional boilings of the syrup – in Morocco six boilings were common – allowed the removal of more impurities by skimming, filtering and decanting; amongst the clarifying agents used were first milk, and later on lime, ashes and certain herbs. The purified syrup could be turned into a "refined", white granulated sugar, loaves of crystalline sugar or hard rock-candy; loaf sugar could in turn be scraped, crushed or powdered.[4] The syrup and sugar in its many forms were used in the endless drinks, desserts, *confits* and confections for which Arab cooking is famous.[5] They also had a number of medical uses.[6]

Two by-products resulted from sugar manufacture: the discarded cane, which Ibn al-ʻAwwām says was an excellent cattle fodder,[7] and the part of the syrup which did not crystallize, known as molasses, which could also be given to animals, used in cooking, fermented to make various drinks or boiled again to extract the remaining sugar.

Origin and pre-Islamic diffusion

So long has sugar cane been grown by man, and in the course of this long period so much has the cultivated plant been transformed, that it has not been possible to identify its wild ancestor or to locate precisely its origin. Most botanists believe, however, that sugar cane derived from one or several of the *Saccharum* grasses which grow wild in India, Southeast Asia and Indonesia, or possibly from a now extinct or unknown relative of these. Early domestication and crossing may have occurred in the region of New Guinea, and the plants so developed may have been further hybridized with other wild relatives and "ennobled" both in the islands of the south-western Pacific and in India.[8]

Sugar-cane culture can be traced back to the time of the appearance of the

ومن خواصه انه اذا ضربت الحية بقصبة منه
ضربة واحدة لم تستطع ان تهرب وبقي في مكانها
وان ثني عليها الضرب هلكت وامكنها الذهاب
واذا دق القصب وهو رطب ووضع على العضو
الذي دخل فيه الحديد جذبه وقال ابن
البيطار منه الساحلي الى الرقة ما هو وجل الناس
يعرفونه اصله اذا تضمد به وحده او مع بصل النرجس
جذب من عمق اللحم ازجة النشاب وما اشبهها

Sugar cane, depicted in an anonymous work on natural history which is bound together with a fragment of Ibn al-Baiṭār's *Book of Simples*. The manuscript is probably fourteenth century. (Bibliothèque Nationale, Paris, ms. arabe 2771, fol. 184r)

Aryan peoples in India, though we cannot be certain that the plant was not cultivated in still earlier times either in India or elsewhere.[9] It probably appeared in southern China in the later part of the first millennium B.C. and spread northward in T'ang times (618–907).[10] From India the plant moved very slowly westwards. It may have been grown in Arabia Felix in the first century, as Pliny and Dioscorides suggest, but they may have been misinformed.[11] By the seventh century – but probably not earlier – sugar cane may have been grown, and sugar manufactured, in the Sasanian empire.[12] Though the ancients of the Near East and of the west had heard of sugar cane and of granulated sugar, and though small quantities of sugar had been imported into the Roman empire from the first century, the plant itself had apparently not been seen in the pre-Islamic west.[13]

Islamic diffusion

Legend has it that the Arab conquerors brought sugar cane with them, or had it brought after them, to the lands they overran in the seventh and eighth centuries, thus introducing the plant in the wake of conquest into Mesopotamia, the Levant, Egypt, North Africa, Spain and the islands of the Mediterranean. But though this legend may be true, no part of it seems to be based on established fact. Indeed, it is improbable on several grounds. In the first place, it assumes that the Arabs cultivated sugar cane in pre-Islamic Arabia and could therefore easily diffuse the complex techniques of its culture into other lands; but, as we have seen, apart from one or two statements of Latin authors of the classical period, who were not well informed, there is no evidence to suggest that the plant was grown in any part of the Arabian peninsula before the time of Muḥammad. With regard to Mesopotamia, the legend also assumes that the plant was not grown there in pre-Islamic times. But we we have suggested above, the plant may have been introduced to this region in Sasanian times, perhaps in the first part of the seventh century.[14]

Be that as it may, the early centuries of Islam saw a great expansion of sugar-cane culture in the lands of the former Sasanian empire. After mention of a tax levied in the time of the caliph ʻUmar (634–44) on lands planted with the crop in the valley of the Tigris and Euphrates, we learn nothing about the growing of sugar cane in this region until the tenth century, when sources become more abundant; but by then its cultivation is so widespread in both Mesopotamia and Persia that we may assume that its diffusion took place over much of the three preceding centuries. Sugar-cane cultivation appears to have been particularly concentrated in certain areas of the Islamic east: in the province of Sind, in north-western India; along the eastern shores of the Persian Gulf and inland in the province of Kirman, and especially in Siraf and Hormuz, the latter of which may, according to one scholar, have been the way station for the plant's diffusion from India to Mesopotamia; and all along the lower valleys of the Tigris and Euphrates, their connecting canals and their lower tributaries. In this last area Ibn Ḥawqal stated that there was no village which did not grow the cane. But it was also grown in many other parts of these eastern reaches of the Islamic world: in Jurjan, on the shores of the Caspian Sea; at Balkh, far to the east; and so forth.[15] Ibn Waḥshīya described in detail its cultivation in the valley of the Tigris in the tenth

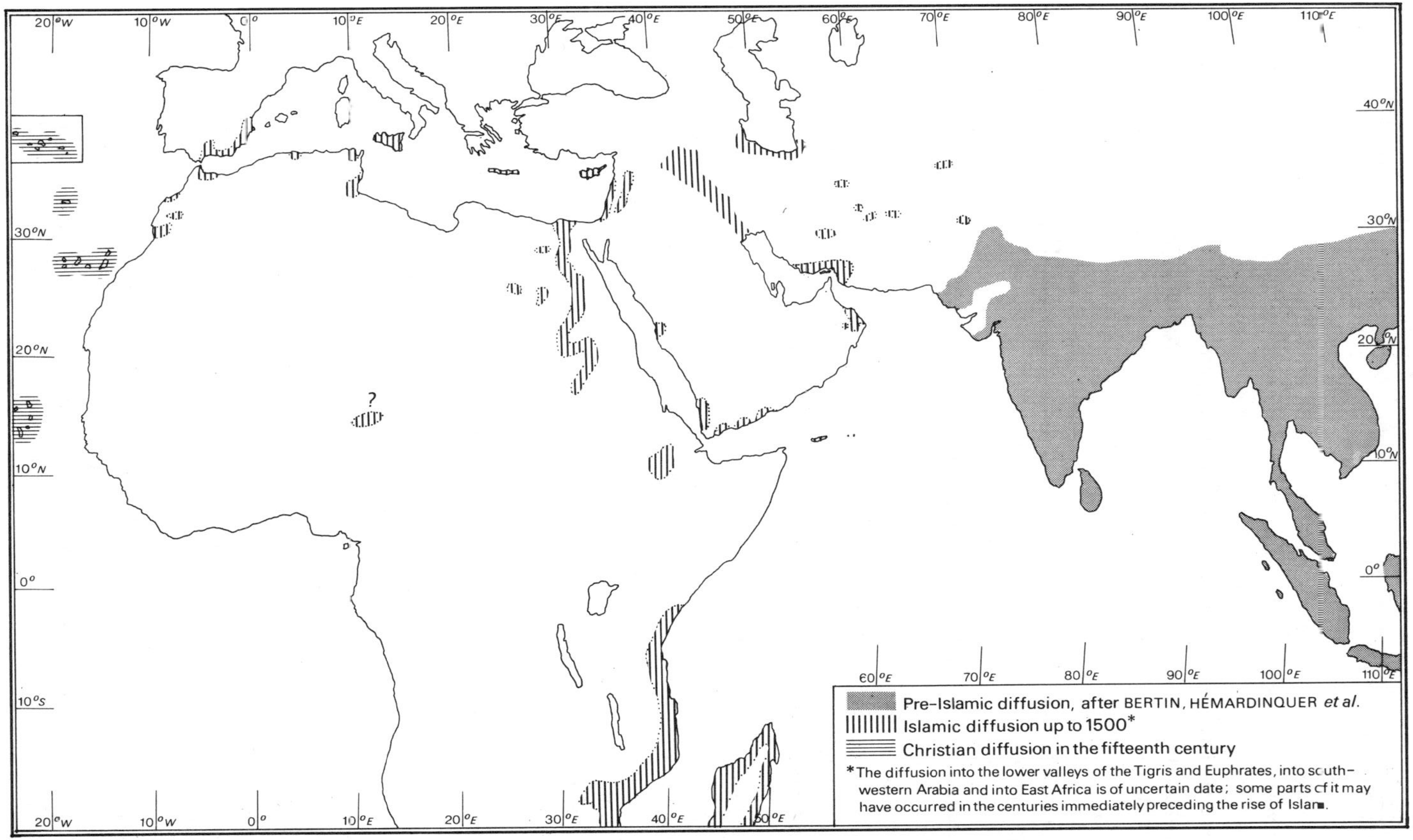
Pre-Islamic diffusion, after BERTIN, HÉMARDINQUER et al.
Islamic diffusion up to 1500*
Christian diffusion in the fifteenth century
*The diffusion into the lower valleys of the Tigris and Euphrates, into south-western Arabia and into East Africa is of uncertain date; some parts of it may have occurred in the centuries immediately preceding the rise of Islam.
20°W
10°W
0°
10°E
20°E
30°E
40°E
50°E
60°E
70°E
80°E
90°E
100°E
110°E
40°N
30°N
20°N
10°N
0°
10°S

Map 3. The diffusion of sugar cane

century,[16] and a treatise on sugar was written by a Baghadi doctor in the eleventh century.[17]

We do not learn of the cultivation of sugar cane in the Levant and the islands of the eastern Mediterranean until the tenth century,[18] by which time it was grown almost wherever land could be irrigated and weather permitted. In the interior of the Levant, cane was grown around the city of Damascus and on the shores of Lake Tiberias, and there were many plantations along the Jordan valley as far as Jericho. Another long band of cultivation – interrupted no doubt at many points – stretched along the coastal plains from Antioch southwards, with particularly important centres at Beirut, Tripoli, Sidon, Tyre and Acre. When the Levantine coast fell into the hands of the Crusaders, and even after the Crusaders left, this coastal band produced large quantities of sugar for export to Europe.[19] Though we have no record in any of the Arab sources of the cultivation of sugar cane in the islands they conquered in the eastern Mediterranean – indeed, the Arab sources say almost nothing whatever about these islands – we may suppose that the Arabs brought sugar cane there, perhaps from the Levantine coast, and that the Christians, at the time of their reconquest of the islands, found it growing and merely continued its cultivation. After the fall of the Crusader kingdoms in the Levant, Cyprus in particular became a very important source of supply for the Christian west.[20]

The first clear reference to the growing of sugar cane in Egypt comes from a papyrus of the mid eighth century, and the crop is mentioned in several papyri of the ninth century.[21] From the tenth century onwards many travellers, geographers and other writers spoke of its cultivation in Egypt. The plant was probably first grown in the Delta and along the lower Nile, the area around Cairo being described by al-Idrīsī as one well-watered field of sugar cane; but it was diffused early through Upper Egypt, where there were a number of important centres of cultivation and manufacture, and into the Fayyūm and some other oases of the desert.[22] A number of sources describe the technique of cultivation practised in Egypt.[23] So great was the total output that al-Mas'ūdī, in the tenth century, said that the Egyptians were the richest of all men in sugar, while in the following century the Persian traveller Nāṣir-i Khusraw also spoke of the abundance of sugar produced in the country.[24] Not all of it was consumed locally: Egyptian sugar of various qualities was exported all over the Mediterranean.[25]

The Maghrib, Sicily and Spain may well have received sugar cane in the century or so after the Arab conquest, but the first references to its cultivation are from the tenth century. Thereafter the crop was frequently mentioned in Sicily and Spain; wherever conditions permitted, it seems to have been grown on a wide scale.[26] By the twelfth century, sugar-cane cultivation seems to have spread across much of North Africa: important centres are described at Gabes, Sfax, Algiers, Ceuta, Saleh, Marrakesh and Sous; and a number of other centres, probably of less importance, are also mentioned.[27] The sugar

An animal-powered mill for extracting juice from sugar cane, as seen by the Napoleonic scientific expedition to Egypt at the beginning of the nineteenth century. The cane was fed into the mill by a man standing below two millstones which rotated at different speeds; the juice ran into a large earthenware jar beneath the stones. (*Description de l'Egypte... Etat moderne* II i, plates II)

of the region of Sous, in the south of Morocco, was said by several writers to be of very fine quality, to be produced in large quantities and to be exported all over the world. In Spain, where the manner of cultivating the plant is described in detail by Ibn al-'Awwām,[28] the plant seems to have been grown as far north as Castellón, which is probably the most northerly point in the world of its commercial cultivation. It was found in the irrigated plains lying all along the south-eastern coast of Spain, especially around Malaga; inland, it was mentioned along the shores of the Guadalquivir in the neighbourhood of Seville, in the Vega of Granada and on the coastal plain around Salobreña and Almuñécar.[29] There are not many references to the cultivation of sugar cane in Sicily, which was under Muslim rule for a relatively short period. By the tenth century the plant seems to have been grown around the city of Palermo and perhaps elsewhere in large enough quantity to be exported to North Africa.[30] When the island was captured by the Normans in the later part of the eleventh century, the industry still existed, but, as will be seen, its fortunes fluctuated.

Moving along a more southerly route, the "Sabean Lane", we can catch glimpses of the spread of sugar cane into Arabia Felix, Abyssinia and the islands and mainland of East Africa. In the south-eastern part of the Arabian peninsula, where, as we have seen, it is just possible that sugar cane was grown in pre-Islamic times, the earliest mention of the plant in Arab sources appears to be from the ninth century, and from texts of the tenth century and later we learn that it was grown in a number of areas of Arabia Felix.[31] Probably it was from here that the plant was diffused into Abyssinia at an unknown date; though it is mentioned in a number of sources from the twelfth century onwards, it was probably known earlier.[32] From Arabia Felix, too, or perhaps directly from Oman, the plant was brought to Zanzibar and the coast of East Africa, where it was seen in the tenth century and whence, according to Abū al-Ḥanīfa, the finest sugar came.[33] From Zanzibar the plant may have been taken to Madagascar.

A text of Ibn Sa'īd, who wrote in the thirteenth century, tells of a king of Kanem who introduced sugar cane into his fields. As other sources do not speak of the cultivation of sugar cane in West Africa, and as Ibn Sa'īd says the sugar obtained was of poor quality, this introduction may have been inconsequential.[34]

CHAPTER SIX

Old World cotton[1] *Gossypium arboreum* L. *Gossypium herbaceum* L.[2]

Arabic: *quṭn*, *'uṭub*, *kirbās*, *kursuf*[3]

Uses

The fibres of the cotton plant were used mainly to make thread, which alone, or combined with threads of silk, linen or wool, was woven into cloths of many qualities, and was widely used in sewing and embroidery. The fibres were also used for stuffing the quilts, pillows and mattresses which abounded in Arab houses, and sometimes in the making of paper, which was manufactured from the eighth century onwards and came to be the principal writing material in the Islamic world. The seeds of the cotton plant produce an oil used in cooking and in industry. There were also medical uses for the seed and its oil, the fibre, and the juice of the leaf.[4]

Origins and pre-Islamic diffusion

About the origin of the Old World cotton plants and their early development, botanical investigations have not yet yielded any certain answers. Until recently most botanists thought that the study of supposedly wild cottons in Asia and Africa would locate the primitive forms of *G. arboreum* and *G. herbaceum* and possibly throw light on the places and stages of their "ennoblement". Thus in the second half of the nineteenth century, Candolle, basing his conclusions on the work of a number of researchers, claimed that *G. herbaceum* was developed from certain wild cottons found in present-day Pakistan, notably *G. Stocksii*, and that the ancestors of the domesticated *G. arboreum* were to be found growing wild in Upper Guinea and along the valley of the upper Nile.[5] Following in his footsteps, other investigators have put forward other theories. A good many have maintained that both plants descend from the wild cottons of India, Pakistan and Baluchistan.[6] Some have suggested different origins: Arabia, the Sudan or other parts of the Sahara and the savanna lands surrounding this desert.[7] More recently, Hutchinson and others claimed that the primitive ancestor of the Old World cottons is *G. herbaceum* var. *africanum* Watt, which grows wild in South-West Africa and Angola.[8] As the seeds of this plant have no usable lint, and as the cultivation and use of cotton are not known to be ancient in this part of Africa, Hutchinson had further to postulate that this plant reached southern Arabia and the Persian Gulf in pre-historic times – perhaps as a weed or perhaps as a plant cultivated for the oil from its seed – and was developed there as a fibre plant.

Hutchinson and others, however, have recently modified their approach to the problem as it has become clear that many apparently wild cottons are in fact escapes descended from cultivars, or wild "associates" of the cultivated plants that have developed through intercrossing. Indeed, the ease with which intercrossing can occur in cotton suggests that in areas where cotton was domesticated the wild ancestor of the cultivated plant may have disappeared as it developed in association with cultivars. This hypothesis seems to explain the difficulty encountered in finding truly wild ancestors of either *G. arboreum* or *G. herbaceum.*[9]

Some clues about the origin of the Old World cottons and their early ennoblement are, however, offered by the archeological and literary evidence. This suggests that the north-western part of the Indian sub-continent was probably the cradle of cotton cultivation, from which an "ennobled" plant was diffused to other parts of Asia, the Middle East, Africa and Europe. Furthermore, the great antiquity of cotton culture in this region makes it unlikely that the plant originated or was improved in a very distant part of the world. The earliest clearly identified finds of cotton are from Mohenjo-daro in the Indus valley and may be dated between 2300 and 1760 B.C. ± 115. Microscopic examination suggests that the fibres came from a close relative of *G. arboreum.*[10] Archeological finds have also yielded bits of cotton fluff spun into silk and flax threads at Nevasa and Chandoli, which lie farther to the south; these may be dated between 1500 and 1000 B.C.[11] Although, rather surprisingly, no certain word for cotton can be found in the early Vedic literature, which probably dates from about the same period, there are many references to cotton garments – and a few references to the plant – from the fifth century B.C. onwards.[12] Thus Herodotus states that in India "wild trees bear wool more beautiful and excellent than the wool of sheep" and that the Indians made clothing from this "wool". Elsewhere he relates that the Indian contingent of the army of Xerxes wore clothes of cotton.[13] The *Kauṭilīya Arthaśāstra*, which perhaps dates from the late fourth century B.C., suggests that the cotton industry was already highly organized and an object of concern to governments: one learns in these texts of a Superintendent of Yarns who was to have thread spun by widows and crippled women, of "mills" for the weaving of cloth, and of a Director of Agriculture responsible for the collection and sowing of cotton seeds.[14] Other texts describe the different stages in the manufacture of yarn and cloth, and the ginning of cotton is depicted in a wall-painting at Ajanta which dates from about the sixth century.[15] By about that time the *Bṛhatsaṁhitā* implies that cotton was an important crop and the chief fibre for garments.[16]

Quite early, Indian cotton goods came to be traded over a wide area. In the fifth century B.C. Ctésias stated that the Indians traded cotton garments

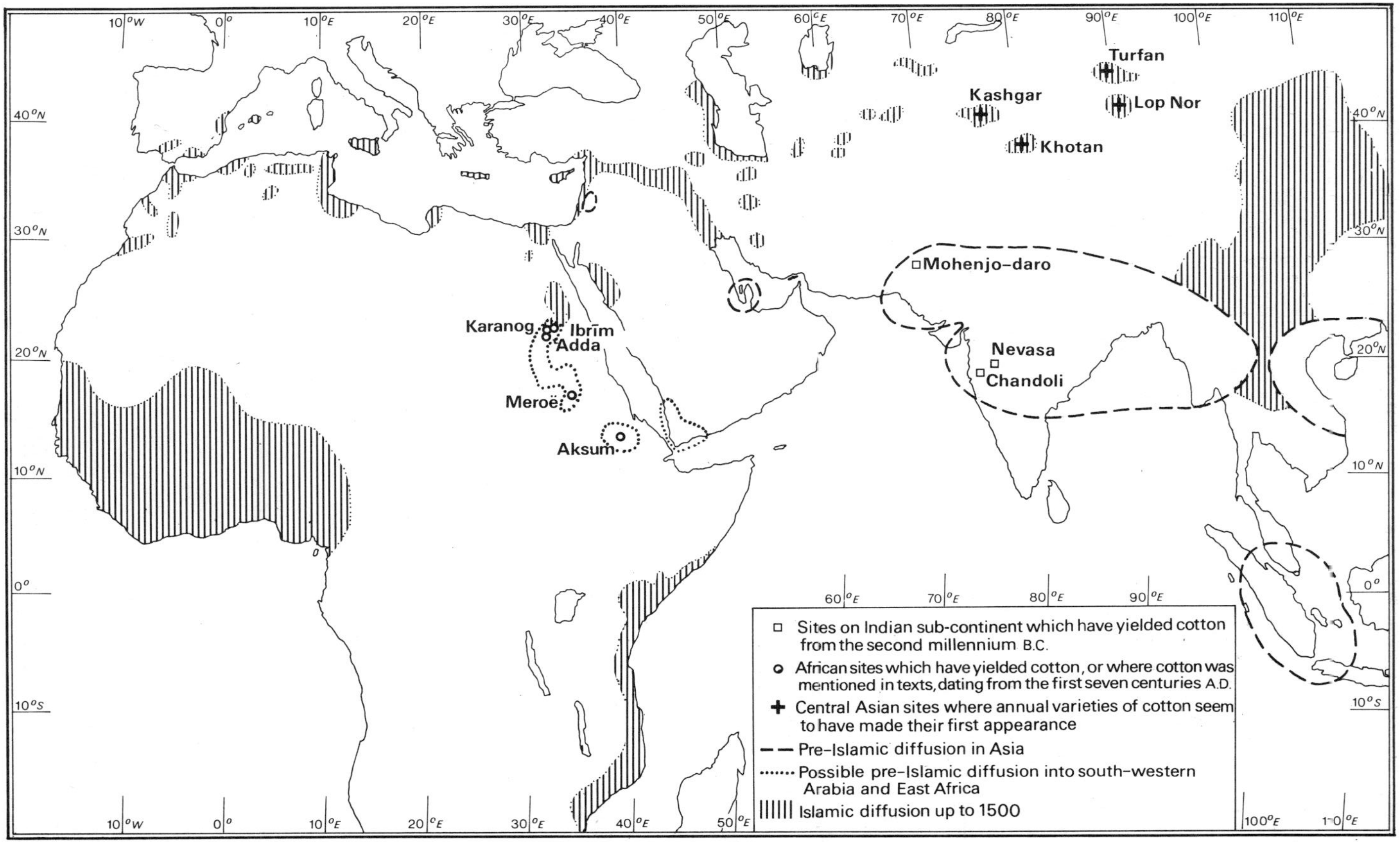
Turfan
Kashgar
Lop Nor
Khotan
Mohenjo-daro
Nevasa
Chandoli
Karanog
Ibrīm
Adda
Meroe
Aksum
Sites on Indian sub-continent which have yielded cotton from the second millennium B.C.
African sites which have yielded cotton, or where cotton was mentioned in texts, dating from the first seven centuries A.D.
Central Asian sites where annual varieties of cotton seem to have made their first appearance
Pre-Islamic diffusion in Asia
Possible pre-Islamic diffusion into south-western Arabia and East Africa
Islamic diffusion up to 1500

Map 4. The diffusion of cotton

with the "dog-headed" peoples who lived in the mountains to the north.[17] By the first century of the Christian era, Indian cottons were sent to Socotra, Eritrea and the Horn of Africa;[18] although the "Periplus" is not altogether explicit, it implies that Egyptian merchants obtained cotton goods both in the Horn of Africa and in India. In the early third century, Philostratus stated clearly that Indian cottons were imported into Egypt for sacred uses.[19] The appearance of Indian cotton goods in widely scattered places in Asia and the Middle East also seems to date from the early centuries of the Christian era. Thus in the first century they may have reached Mongolia,[20] and by the second or third century they probably appeared in Sinkiang, Turkestan and Palmyra.[21] In the early sixth century an Indian king is alleged to have sent cottons as a gift to the emperor of China, while from the seventh century onwards Chinese merchants could buy Indian cotton goods in Palembang.[22]

The cultivation of cotton also seems to have spread outwards from India at an early date, though about the extent of this diffusion there is much room for doubt. In ancient times it probably reached the island of Tylos, or Bahrain, and possibly other parts of the Persian Gulf, for accounts of the "wool-bearing tree" of the island were carried back by Alexander's naval expedition in the eastern seas in 325 B.C.[23] From the Persian Gulf, or perhaps directly from India, it may have spread to Arabia Felix: Theophrastus and Pliny, who are perhaps not reliable on this point, repeat reports that tree-cotton grew there, and the shrouds found in some Himyaritic graves were made of cotton which may have been locally grown.[24] The growing of cotton may also have spread into Ethiopia, Nubia and Upper Egypt: Julius Pollux and Pliny speak of the cotton "tree", "bushes" or "shrubs" which grew in Ethiopia and Upper Egypt, and an Aksumite inscription of the year 350 claims the destruction of Nubian cotton supplies.[25] Fragments of cotton cloth dating from the first seven centuries of the Christian era have been found at the Nubian sites of Karanog, Meroë, ʻAdda and Qaṣr Ibrīm, while other cloths dating from the fourth to seventh centuries have been found in the Upper Egyptian monastery of Phoebamon.[26] Whether the fibres from which these cloths were woven – or the stocks of cotton destroyed by the Aksumites – were locally grown is difficult to know; but microscopic examination of some of the cloths from Karanog suggests that the fibres may have come from a plant similar to a Sudanese variety of *G. arboreum*.[27] Cotton does not seem to have been grown in Lower Egypt or in the Mediterranean in pre-Islamic times.[28] Interestingly enough, however, it probably was cultivated by post-Biblical times in the area of Lake Tiberias and in the Jordan valley, for it is mentioned in both the Mishna and the Palestinian Talmud, and in the sixth century Gregory of Tours, writing of the area around Jericho, speaks of "arbores quae lanas gignunt" and of the whiteness and fineness of the cloths made from their fibres.[29]

While cotton cultivation was spreading westwards from India, it also seems to have been diffused to the east. From a work composed from Han materials between 318 and 445, we learn that the Ai-Lao "barbarians" grew cotton along the banks of the Irrawaddy River. Another Han work, written either in the first or second century, speaks of the cotton tree grown in Indo-China and in Kuangtung; and writings of the third to sixth centuries show that cotton – sometimes described as the cotton tree – was cultivated in the southerly provinces of Kuangtung and Yünnan.[30] Elsewhere in China cotton does not seem to have been grown before the seventh century, or even much later, and the Chinese seem to have been only slightly familiar with the exotic cloth woven from its fibres.[31] Although the diffusion of the plant into Southeast Asia is not well documented, it appears to have occurred there at about the same time as in China. In 430 a gift of cotton was sent from Java or Sumatra to the Chinese court, while in 523 a mission arrived in Nanking bearing cotton goods from either Sumatra or Malaya.[32] According to one legend, a Hindu from Indonesia or Malaya, shipwrecked in Japan, was responsible for introducing the cotton plant to that country in 799 or 800; but as there is no further mention of cotton growing in Japan for many centuries this introduction seems to have failed.[33]

Diffusion in Islamic times

One of the curious facts of the diffusion of cotton cultivation in pre-Islamic times is that it seems to have been strictly confined to regions with very warm climates where heavy watering was available from rainfall or artificial irrigation. In fact, the region of this early diffusion corresponds very closely to the present-day distribution of *G. arboreum*, which Harland gives as India, Malaya and South China, with some diffusion into Abyssinia and the Sudan.[34]

Was *G. arboreum* then the only cotton plant known in pre-Islamic times? This hypothesis receives some slight confirmation from the microscopic examination of archeological finds: the fibres of the very early pieces of cotton cloth from Mohenjo-daro and some early Christian fragments from Nubia appeared to those who examined them to be *G. arboreum*.[35] The literary evidence may also seem to confirm this suggestion, since all the descriptions of the plants speak of trees, shrubs or bushes. Even the ninth-century Persian scholar Abū Ḥanīfa al-Dīnawarī seems to have heard only of an arborescent cotton: "the cotton trees [in the lands of Kalb tribe] grow high until they look like apricot trees, and last twenty years".[36] But since there are perennial types of *G. herbaceum* which, after a number of years, take the form of a bush, we cannot be certain that *G. herbaceum* was unknown. Both species may have been cultivated over greater or smaller areas in their perennial forms.

What does seem clear, however, is that a fundamental obstacle to the northward diffusion of the cotton plant in pre-Islamic times was the absence of annual varieties which could mature in a shorter, colder season towards

XYLON SIVE GOSSIPIVM HERBACEVM: Germ. *B*
vvul: Belg. *Boomvvol*: Gall. *Cotton*: It. *Cotone*, *Bombac*

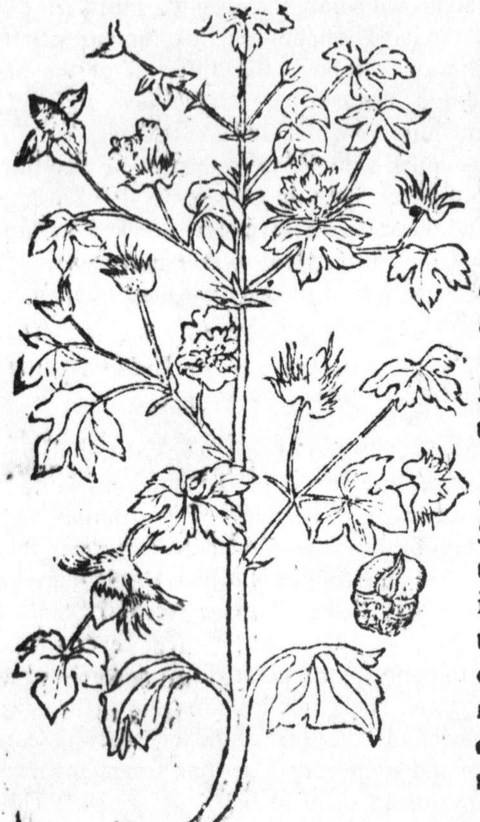

Xylon aliud *Arboreum*.
quo mox aliud *Herbaceum*
fert vtrumq; Nucem, quap
pter hunc locum ſibi v
dicant. Hocce veteribus p
riſque Græcis fuit incogni
vt illud Theophraſto. Dici
etiam Latinis *Bambax*, *Bo*
byx, *Bombax*, *Bombacium*, *B*
bacium, *Cotto*, *nis*: Cottonu
ni: Cottum, ti: & Cotum
Sed Lanugo ipſa propriè di
tur *Bombax*.

Calidis autem gaudet loc
& Martio atq; Aprili ſerit
Septembri & Octobri colli
tur. Olim plantabatur ſol
in Ægypto, nunc ferè per
tam Europam habetur. Vſu
quod attinet, nullum Lini g
nus eſt quod huic lanug
candore & mollitie præfe
tur.

Perhaps the first European writer to distinguish clearly between *Gossypium herbaceum* and *G. arboreum* was Dominique Chabré, in his augmented edition of Jean Bauhin's *Historia plantarum universalis* (Embrun, 1650–1). The page above is reproduced from Chabré's *Stirpium icones et*

XYLON, ſiue GOSSIPIVM ARBOREVM

Hujus arboris laniferæ, vt annotat Bellonius, primus mentionem fecit Herodotus, quem poſtea ſecuti sũt Theophraſtus & Plinius, ac plures alij, eſtque è numero ſemper virentium.

Diſſimile eſt ab Herbaceo proceritate caudicis, & glabritie foliorum, quæ in Herbaceo hirſuta ſunt: Eandem autem quam Herbaceum fere lanuginem.

Naſcitur in Ægypto & Arabia, authoribus Alpino & Bellonio: atque ex eo ſericeis ipſis tenuiores & ſubtiliores texunt Arabes telas.

Montbelgardi in S. Principis horto vtrumque Goſſypium coluimus. *Plura in Appendice.*

D

sciagraphia (Geneva, 1677). The picture of *G. herbaceum* was clearly copied from L. Fuchs, *De historia stirpium commentarii insignes* (Lyons, 1549). (Thomas Fisher Rare Book Library, University of Toronto) the end of which the days were markedly shorter. If *G. herbaceum* was known at all – and there is no clear evidence of it – it must have existed only in the perennial form. The annual varieties of both species, capable of a more northerly diffusion, had yet to be developed. This fact no doubt explains the apparent lack of success of an Assyrian king, Sennacherib, in introducing the cotton plant into Mesopotamia in the seventh century B.C.,[37] as well as the probable failure, already mentioned above, to establish it in Japan at the end of the eighth century.[38]

Where and when the new plant was developed is not certain, but there is now some evidence that it made an early appearance – if not its first – in the eastern part of Central Asia. A Chinese work of the late sixth and early seventh centuries stated that in the region of Turfan in Sinkiang "there grows in great abundance a plant, the fruit of which resembles a silk cocoon; the natives weave the fibre into a cloth which is soft and white, and send it to the markets of China".[39] By the eighth century other texts related that cotton was sent as tribute from the Turfan region to the Chinese court.[40] In the western part of Sinkiang, near Khotan, archeologists have discovered a small pile of cotton seeds dating from about the eighth century, which they take as clear evidence of cotton cultivation in the region.[41] Cotton seeds and fragments of cotton cloth have also been found at a ninth-century site near Kashgar in western Sinkiang; the seeds have been identified by the Chinese Academy of Sciences as *G. herbaceum*.[42] Archeologists have also discovered in the region of Lop Nor in Sinkiang a good many fragments of cotton cloth which appear to date from roughly the same period and which may have been made from locally grown fibre.[43] By T'ang times (618–907) cotton seems also to have been grown in the province of Lung-yu, corresponding approximately to the modern Kansu, from which cotton was exacted as official tribute.[44] Though the archeological reports of the finds of seeds and fragments of cloth do not specify the variety of cotton plant, it must in every case have been an annual variety of either *G. arboreum* or, more probably, *G. herbaceum* which could survive in the region's harsh, continental climate.

But the new plant seems to have encountered obstacles to its outward diffusion, for it did not make much progress for several centuries. Perhaps these difficulties were simply those which any new crop might meet where communications were poor and peasants conservative, compounded no doubt by the challenge of growing this particular crop in a hostile environment – especially in early times when the varieties available may not have been very resistant to drought or cold. But the operative factor slowing down the crop's diffusion may have had to do rather with industrial technology: workers may have learned only with difficulty the techniques of ginning, spinning or weaving this new fibre. Several modern writers have suggested that the widespread diffusion of cotton into China had to await improvements in the technology of ginning, while a Chinese source tells of a woman who, in the thirteenth century, brought to the lower Yangtze region superior spinning and weaving techniques which greatly improved the industry.[45] The evidence concerning the cotton or partly cotton cloths from the several regions of the early Islamic world, and even of this region in pre-Islamic times, may also be revealing. As early as the second century B.C., Julius Pollux wrote that cotton (perhaps grown in Upper Egypt or Nubia) was used only for the weft thread, linen being used for the warp.[46] Similarly, in the early Islamic world the earliest cloths in which cotton or partly cotton threads are found usually, though not always, had warps of linen, silk or wool.[47] The all-cotton cloths produced in the Yemen in the ninth and tenth centuries had warp threads which were very coarse and close together, while the weft threads were fine and widely spaced.[48] Very probably this evidence speaks of difficulties in using cotton for the warp, particularly in warp-weighted looms, which placed a special strain on the warp threads.

If any obstacles did slow the progress of *G. herbaceum* through more temperate climates, they were eventually overcome. For after a delay of several centuries following its apparent development the new plant was widely diffused through Asia, the Middle East and Africa; it also had a limited diffusion into parts of Mediterranean Europe.

Several scholars have suggested that cotton reached the central part of China by two routes: from Sinkiang in the west and from Indochina in the south. Since most of the cottons of central and southern China today are *G. arboreum*, the suggestion of two separate introductions along different routes is plausible. There is still no evidence, however, that *G. herbaceum* was known in Indochina before it appeared in China or even long afterwards. The western route therefore seems the more probable for the introduction of the annual varieties of this plant. From the sources we know only that by the thirteenth century cotton was sent as tribute by the eastern provinces of Hunan, Hupeh, Fukien, Chekiang and Kiangsu and the central provinces of Szechwan, Shansi and Shensi, where it was presumably grown.[49] A fifteenth-century source stated that "by our times [cotton] has spread throughout the Empire; it is used a hundred times more than silk or hemp".[50] Various texts on the cultivation of the plant describe what are clearly varieties of an annual, herbaceous cotton.[51] The stages in the processing of the fibre in China are outlined by several authors.[52]

To the west, the new cotton plant was diffused through the whole of the medieval Islamic world up to the frontiers of Christian Europe and pagan Black Africa. Although almost nothing is known of the process of diffusion, by the tenth century cotton was found growing in nearly every region of the Islamic world. Around centres of cultivation sprang up cotton industries, many producing specialty cloths or garments for export. A network of intermediaries arose to channel raw cotton to the workshop, the semi-finished product through the various stages of manufacture, and the finished good to its ultimate, often distant, destination.

In the eastern part of the Islamic world, cotton was grown on a very wide scale. A number of authors tell of its cultivation at many places in both Upper and Lower Mesopotamia; in the early tenth century, the technique of growing the plant there was described in detail by the agricultural writer Ibn Waḥshīya.[53] In Iran cotton is mentioned at scores of places and in almost every region.[54] Still farther to the east, it was found in various parts of Transoxania, and in the thirteenth century Marco Polo saw it growing abundantly in Kashgar.[55] The sources speak often of the great variety of cotton goods made in Iraq, Persia and Turkestan; they relate that Baghdad had a special wharf for the cotton merchants and a house for trading cotton.[56] In the Arabian peninsula, cotton was grown at Bahrain, in the Yemen and in the Hijaz; there were several famous centres of cotton manufacture in the Yemen and on the island of Socotra.[57] Many travellers saw cotton growing in different parts of Palestine, Syria and Asia Minor; probably from here the plant was taken to Greece, the Aegean islands and Cyprus.[58] By the twelfth century, cotton from the Levant and Cyprus was exported to Italy.[59]

Many places in the western part of Dār al-Islām – Egypt, the Maghrib, Spain and Sicily – also came to grow cotton and make cotton goods. There is much evidence that cotton was traded in Egypt in the early centuries of Islam;[60] one papyrus of the eighth or ninth century suggests that cotton was an article of common use in households.[61] By the end of the tenth century, the geographer Ibn Ḥawqal states that cotton was grown in Egypt.[62] But it may not have become an important crop until later: even in the eleventh century, al-Tha'ālibī remarked that "people know that cotton belongs to Khurāsān [in the region of Merv] and linen to Egypt".[63] On the other hand, the fact that a special section of the city of al-Fusṭāṭ was set aside for cotton merchants suggests that al-Tha'ālibī's information was out of date.[64] In any case, by the thirteenth century there is clear evidence that cotton had become a major crop in Egypt: the sources from this time onwards speak of it growing in Nubia, Upper Egypt, the Delta and the Fayyūm.[65] Although some cotton cloth was still imported into Egypt even in the fifteenth century, Egyptian cotton was also sent from Alexandria to Europe.[66] Farther to the west, Ibn Ḥawqal and later travellers noted cotton growing in Tripolitania, around Tunis and Carthage, on the island of Pantelleria and near several towns in present-day Algeria; cottons from Djerba, Tunis and other parts of Ifrīqiya were exported to Spain and Italy.[67] Cotton cultivation was probably taken from Tunis to Sicily, where it was noted in Islamic times or after the Norman conquest near Catania, Agrigento, Mazara and Giattini.[68] In Morocco, the sources speak of the growing of cotton in many places.[69] In Spain, cotton cultivation is first mentioned in sources of the ninth and tenth centuries.[70] Although the early references speak of its cultivation only in the south, notably in the Algarve and in the hinterlands of Seville and Elvira, later sources state that it was also grown at Guadix and – more surprisingly – in Valencia and Majorca.[71] The manner of growing cotton is described by the agronomes Abū al-Khair, Ibn Baṣṣāl and Ibn al-'Awwām.[72] Andalusian cottons were exported to other parts of Spain and to the cities of the North African coast.[73]

Cotton was diffused by Muslims not only to Mediterranean Europe but also to parts of Black Africa, both along the east coast and in the west. This diffusion was closely connected with the penetration of Islam into Africa, since Islam taught – in practice if not in doctrine – that the faithful should be clothed, preferably from the neck to the ankles, with only the face, neck, hands and feet showing. Wherever Muslims settled in Africa, or wherever converts were made, clothes appeared: the rich had expensive cotton garments made from imported cloth, while the poor, though they might have a fine robe for feast days, usually went about in simple cotton shirts or something which offered less cover. The greater part of the demand for cotton seems to have been supplied locally, for we learn of many places in which cotton was grown and many places where it was spun. Thus an entirely new demand came hand in hand with a radically new religion. And not long after – over the same routes – came an altogether new industry to satisfy that demand.[74]

By the end of the European Middle Ages, cotton cultivation had spread across nearly the whole of the Eurasian continent below the fortieth parallel, from the Atlantic to the Pacific, and in some places had reached still farther north. Cotton was also grown widely in Africa north of the Sahara and in many other parts of the continent. Over nearly all of this vast area – and beyond – cotton had become the chief fibre from which clothes were made and had revolutionized the textile industry. By 1500 the cotton plants of the Old World were at their zenith. In the centuries following the voyages of discovery they were in large measure eclipsed by new, long-fibred cotton plants from the New World. But the ease with which these new plants could displace the old may be explained by the tastes, agricultural skills and industrial techniques which had been acquired in the Old World with *G. arboreum* and *G. herbaceum* over a period of more than three millennia.

CHAPTER SEVEN

Sour orange, Seville orange *Citrus aurantium* L.[1]

Arabic: *nāranj*

Lemon *Citrus limon* L.[1]

Arabic: *līmūn, laimūn*

Lime *Citrus aurantifolia* Swing.[1]

Arabic: *līm, līma, līmū* (?)

Shaddock, pummelo *Citrus grandis* L.[1]

Arabic: *kubbād* (?)

Uses

Citrus trees were amongst the principal ornamental plants of the early Islamic world, figuring prominently in the gardens of the great and the modest alike. Their fruits were eaten raw, usually after sweetening; they were also preserved in syrup or brine and made into sugared *confits* and marmalades. The juices of the fruit were used for many kinds of drinks and to season meat, fish, poultry and sweets. The peels were soaked in brine or preserved in sugar. Essential oils, used for perfumes and soap, were obtained from the rinds, the flowers and the leaves. Some citrus trees were widely used as grafting stock. Medieval texts give several medical uses for the flowers, peels, seeds and juice.[2]

Origin and pre-Islamic diffusion

To confound both horticulturalist and historian, the cultivated members of the citrus family are unusually prone to variation. As ʿAbd al-Laṭīf remarked in describing the many kinds of citrus found in Egypt at the beginning of the thirteenth century, "these combine with one another to yield infinite variety".[3] Moreover, the new kinds of citrus so obtained seldom stay true to type unless propagated by grafting, budding or cutting. Otherwise they tend both to cross with other types or to revert to ancestral forms. These propensities have at once advantages and disadvantages. The hybridization of citrus plants has produced important new varieties, such as the grapefruit and the tangerine, which have no wild ancestors; in the second half of the twelfth century a Chinese treatise on oranges described as many as twenty-seven different kinds of oranges, many of which must have been hybrids.[4] On the other hand, the difficulty in keeping the plant true may have been a major obstacle to its diffusion. This problem was noted in the tenth century by al-Masʿūdī, who, in speaking of the transmission of the sour orange and a "round citron" from

A member of the citrus family, possibly a sour-orange tree, depicted in the Latin translation of the *Taqwīm al-siḥḥa* of Ibn Buṭlān (d. 1066). The manuscript was probably made in Italy in the late fourteenth century. (Österreichische Nationalbibliothek, Ser. Nov. 2644, fol. 20r)

India through the Arab world, lamented that these plants lost their fragrance when grown away from their Indian homeland.[5] Much earlier, in the first millennium B.C., a Chinese writer stated that "when sweet-orange trees are made to cross the river Hoaī and are planted to the North, they turn to sour-orange trees".[6] As late as the sixteenth century, García da Orta, comparing the citrus fruits of Portugal with those of India, found the latter much superior in size and flavour.[7] For the historian, too, these tendencies of citrus trees present problems: a proliferation of terms went hand in hand with the multiplication of kinds of fruits, making it not altogether certain today what were the citrus plants of yesterday.

The early history of citrus cultivation shows striking regional differences. Although the explorations of the Japanese botanist Tanaka have shown that most cultivated citrus originate from a relatively small area in Assam and northern Burma,[8] it was in the regions surrounding this centre – in China, India and Malaysia – that citrus cultivation began. Each region based its development on a different group of plants. Whereas in India the earliest citrus cultivated seem to have been the citron, the sour orange, and the lemon, in China citrus culture probably began with the kumquat (which is one of the few citrus native to China), the sour orange, various types of mandarines, the sweet orange and the poncirus; and in Malaysia the first citrus cultivated seem to have been the shaddock and the lime.[9] Exchanges among these three areas of early citrus culture occurred only sporadically, and sometimes relatively late. Even today, the kinds of citrus which predominate in China differ greatly from those common in India and the west.

Before the rise of Islam, some knowledge of the citrus family had reached the west, and one of its members, the citron (*C. medica* L.), had been diffused westward. Mentioned in ancient Sanskrit literature, and grown in Persia and Media by the fourth century B.C., the citron seems to have been known to the ancient Jews before the time of Christ.[10] Although it was mentioned by Roman authors of medical treatises in the first and second centuries, it was probably not grown in Italy or the western Mediterranean until later; Pliny relates that unsuccessful attempts were made to import citron trees in pots into western countries.[11] However, by the time of Palladius, who flourished at some time between the third and the sixth centuries, it seems to have been grown in Sardinia and around Naples, and in the early seventh century Isidore of Seville speaks as if it were known in Spain.[12] We may assume that before the Hegira the citron had been diffused through much of the Mediterranean, perhaps mainly by the Jews, for whom the fruit had become essential for celebration of the Feast of Tabernacles.[13]

Whether other citrus plants were grown in the pre-Islamic west is doubtful. One writer, on the basic of several mosaics and frescos from Carthage, Pompey and elsewhere, which seem to depict oranges and lemons, and in one case a lime, has concluded that these fruits were grown in Italy by the fourth century or earlier.[14] But while the resemblance is striking, the case for local cultivation of these citrus fruits, instead of importation, is shaky indeed; the artists may even have seen the fruits in the east. In any case, this iconographical evidence is not borne out by any literary or paleobotanical evidence. Nor is there any other evidence whatever to suggest that citrus fruits excepting the citron were grown in other places lying to the west of India.[15] If these plants were in fact grown in the Mediterranean, they can have been only rarities which soon disappeared from view and had, much later, to be reintroduced.

Islamic diffusion

The Islamic writers from the seventh, eighth and ninth centuries are mute on the subject of citrus fruits other than the citron, but by the tenth century there are many sources which tell of the cultivation of sour oranges, lemons and limes. Most, but not all, of the references are from the eastern part of the Islamic world, where these fruit trees must first have appeared and had perhaps been known for a century or more. Their introduction into the western reaches of the Islamic world must still, in the tenth century, have been very recent.

Exactly how and when the sour orange came to the Islamic world is not known. Quite probably it was seen in the second decade of the eighth century by the Arab conquerors of the Sind in north-western India, and was then gradually diffused westward. According to a fifteenth-century Yemeni treatise on farming, which may not be reliable on this point, the caliph Ma'mūn (813–33) brought sour-orange trees from north-eastern Persia to Rayy.[16] A more nearly contemporary report, and one which is more trustworthy, comes from al-Mas'ūdī, who relates that after the year 912 the sour orange and the "round citron", which might be the lemon, were brought from India to Oman and thence via Basra through Iraq and into Syria, Palestine and Egypt, where they were previously unknown; by his time, towards the middle of the tenth century, these trees had already become common in Syrian and Levantine houses.[17] But al-Mas'ūdī's date for the introduction of these plants is too late. Not only does it not seem to allow enough time for transmission over such long distances, and for the plant to become a commonplace in the eastern Mediterranean, but it also cannot be tallied with certain other texts. As early as the first decade of the tenth century, Ibn Waḥshīya devoted a whole chapter in his treatise on agriculture to the sour-orange tree, which he said came from India but was suited to other countries; and only a few years later, in his book on farming, Qusṭūs also discussed its cultivation, saying that it might be grown in both tropical and temperate climates.[18] A number of Arab poets of the early tenth century also wrote rapturously of the fruit, which seems to have come in many colours, and later in the century geographers spoke of it growing in Amol, Balkh and Palestine.[19] Around 976, the chamberlain al-Manṣūr planted the Patio de los Naranjos in Cordova, an example which was to be followed in the courtyards of many Spanish mosques, palaces and houses.[20]

If many of the early references to sour oranges tell of royal plantations, in which the tree was perhaps mainly ornamental, and if the sources suggest that rulers were often responsible for the first introductions of the sour orange, the tree soon became popular throughout the length and breadth of the Arab world, where it was grown by rich and poor alike and its fruits used in a number of ways. Though today the sour orange is little valued except as an ingredient in marmalade and as a source of candied peel, its fruits were precious indeed in an age when few other citrus fruits were known and most of these were bitter and not juicy. Later sources testify to widespread culture of the sour orange – sometimes on a commercial scale – in the eastern provinces, Mesopotamia, the Levant, Egypt, the Yemen, the Maghrib, Spain and probably Sicily.[21] At an unknown date the sour orange was introduced into parts of Africa lying south of the Sahara: it was noted by travellers to West Africa in the fourteenth and sixteenth centuries, and was found growing along the coast of East Africa by the Portuguese voyagers of the sixteenth century.[22]

Although the early history of the lemon tree is obscure and does not go back so far as that of the sour orange, this plant was introduced into the Islamic world and diffused across it at roughly the same time as the sour orange or only slightly later. In India, where the plant was probably first brought into cultivation, there were several Sanskrit names for it, but these are all of uncertain antiquity. According to one guess, the lemon tree was not cultivated in India until some time between the fourth and the ninth centuries.[23] The first clear literary reference to the lemon in any language dates from the beginning of the tenth century and is from an Arabic source: Qusṭūs, in his book on farming, noted that the *laimūn* tree is very sensitive to cold, a factor which may have delayed its diffusion until hardier varieties were found.[24] Slightly later in the century, the geographer al-Iṣṭakhrī related that at al-Manṣūra, the most southerly Muslim outpost in India, there was a fruit called *līmūna* which was the size of an apple and very sour. This account of the fruit is repeated by Ibn Ḥawqal, who wrote around 988, and by several later geographers.[25] Although Ibn Ḥawqal and his contemporaries speak at length of the crops grown in every part of the Muslim world, none of them mentions the lemon tree except in the region of al-Manṣūra. Nevertheless, its westward diffusion had probably already begun. Perhaps it was the lemon that al-Mas'ūdī refers to as the "round citron", which, he says, was brought with the sour orange from India to Oman some time after 912 and then diffused through Iraq, the Levant and Egypt.[26] In any case, the plant seems to have spread through the Islamic world during the tenth, eleventh and twelfth centuries. Towards the end of the twelfth century, Ibn Jāmi', the personal physician to Saladin, wrote a treatise on the lemon, and the fruit had by then been the subject of several poems.[27] From the twelfth century onwards, geographers and agronomes mention the lemon tree in almost every part of the Islamic world, even in distant Balkh where, one might have supposed, the winters were too severe. The later authors speak of several kinds of lemons – sweet and sour, yellow and green, and so forth – which we cannot with certainty identify.[28]

The progress of the lime through the early-Islamic world is more difficult to detect, partly perhaps because we cannot be sure that the word *līmū* and similar words were always used to designate it, and partly because its most important diffusion was through Saharan and sub-Saharan Africa, about which the sources tell us little. The lime tree is probably the tree referred to

A lemon tree, depicted in an anonymous work on natural history which is bound together with a fragment of Ibn al-Baiṭār's *Book of Simples*. The manuscript probably dates from the fourteenth century. (Bibliothèque Nationale, Paris, ms. arabe 2771, fol. 202v)

in the tenth century by Ibn Waḥshīya as *al-khashīshā*, which he said was known in Persian as *al-līmū*. He stated that it grew in Ibla, which lies to the west of Babylon, but apparently it had not yet reached Ibn Waḥshīya's homeland in Mesopotamia. He went on to say that the fruits were small, round and yellow; they later turned green, though there was one variety which tended to become reddish. The juice had only a little acidity.[29] In the literature of later centuries there appear sporadic references to *līmū*, *līma* and *līm*. In *The Thousand Nights and a Night*, for instance, we are told of a "lime of sweet scent, which resembles a hen's egg, whose ripe fruit is ornamented by its yellowness".[30] Geographers, travellers and chroniclers mention the tree growing in a number of parts of the Islamic world: in the Sind, around Basra, in Egypt, in the Yemen and in the Maghrib.[31] Under the names *lumi*, *lumía* and *limó* it also appeared in documents from Christian Sicily and Spain, where it had probably been introduced in Islamic times.[32] But as the lime is the most sensitive to cold of all citrus trees, it seems likely that its advance through Mediterranean lands had to wait the development of hardier strains. On the other hand, it has become the most widely grown citrus tree in the warmer parts of Africa – both in the Sahara and in tropical and semi-tropical regions – and its names in a multitude of African languages betray the role of the Arabs in its diffusion.[33]

Whether the Arabs diffused any other citrus trees during the Middle Ages is uncertain. New types of citrus may have appeared under old names: as *utrujj*, a term which specifically designated the citron, the first citrus plant known west of India, but which may sometimes have meant citrus fruits in general and could also have been used for new kinds of citrus which had no name; or as the "round citrons", "sweet citrons", "hairy citrus" and so forth which from time to time crop up in the texts, though these may equally well have been only new varieties of familiar types of citrus. A few new names also appear – *kubbād*, *zanbū'* and *bustanbūn* – which may designate new types of citrus or may be simply local names for types already known.[34] The term *turunj* and its derivatives also sow confusion; originally another name for the citron, the word came to designate other types of citrus in languages other than Arabic, and may have been used in the same way in parts of the Arab world.[35] There is thus much room for speculation. Amongst the candidates which have been proposed as other Arab introductions in medieval times are the shaddock or pummelo (*C. grandis* L.), the sweet orange (*C. sinensis* L.), the bergamot (*C. bergamia* L.), the mandarine (*C. reticulata*) and the poncirus (*Poncirus trifoliata* L.). But most of these claims seem doubtful indeed. Only for the shaddock can a reasonable case be made. Probably of Malaysian origin, and perhaps brought to India by the Arabs, the shaddock may be the round citron which al-Mas'ūdī says was brought with the sour orange from India into the Arab world some time after 912, though, as we have suggested, this could easily be the lemon.[36] It could be the "round lemon" which Ibn al-'Awwām says is the size of a colocynth and yellow.[37] It is probably the fruit called *kubbād* which was said by al-'Umarī to grow in Syria and which was mentioned a number of times in *The Thousand Nights and a Night*;[38] in the sixteenth century, Ibn Iyās mentioned the *kubbād* as one of the fruits of Egypt.[39] But if the shaddock was introduced to the Islamic world in medieval times it cannot have been common; the references to it are too few and, as will be seen, it did not appear in the lists of citrus fruits of different regions with which the Arab sources abound.

In spite of many claims to the contrary, there is no clear evidence to support a medieval introduction of the sweet orange. Several authors have cited a statute of the year 1379 from the Italian town of Fermo which they say mentioned sweet oranges; but in fact the statute itself says nothing about sweet oranges, which were the invention of a commentator.[40] In Islamic texts there are misleading passages which have tripped up translators: when, for instance, al-Bakrī says that "there are no oranges as sweet as those of Touzer", he is probably speaking of a relatively sweet kind of sour orange, not of the sweet orange.[41] Thus although translations of Arab and Persian texts often mention sweet oranges, reference to the original invariably shows that the author mentioned only the citron, the sour orange, the lemon or the lime.[42] The only unambiguous reference to the sweet orange comes from the fourteenth-century traveller Ibn Baṭṭūṭa, who says that in India there are many sweet oranges and few sour ones.[43] As Ibn Baṭṭūṭa goes on to list the fruits known in his homeland and in other parts of the Arab world, and does not mention the sweet orange, this kind of citrus seems not to have been known in the Arab world in his time. The claim for a diffusion by the medieval Arabs is therefore doubtful. Certainly the linguistic evidence points to a different agent and route of diffusion: in nearly all of the Mediterranean and Middle Eastern languages – including even the Pashto of Afghanistan and some dialects of the Yemen – the word for the sweet orange is of the *portugallo* type, suggesting that it was the Portuguese who brought the plant westwards; while in Berber dialects words such as *shīna* and *lah-shīn*, like the Portuguese *laranja da China* and the German *Apfelsine*, suggest that the plant reached the west directly from China.[44] Very probably the Portuguese did bring the sweet orange to the west; but as the sweet orange was well known in southern Italy and Sicily by 1525, only a few years after the Portuguese had reached China, the first trees must have been brought from India, not China, soon after the circumnavigation of Africa. The oft-repeated legend that the tree was brought to Portugal from China by a Jesuit priest in the year 1548, if it contains any truth at all, refers to a later introduction – possibly of another cultivar.[45]

Perhaps excepting the shaddock, then, the only citrus fruits widely known in the Islamic world – and in Europe – up till the end of the fifteenth century seem to have been the citron, the sour orange, the lemon and the lime. The others were either entirely unknown or were only oddities. Although this thesis runs counter to many statements in the literature, it is abundantly supported by the texts. Time and again the Arabic authors – geographers, travellers, lexicographers, agronomes, botanists and pharmacists – list the citrus fruits known in a certain region or all over the Islamic world, and almost invariably the only fruits they mention are these four;[46] the occasional reference to what might be another type of citrus could equally well be to one of these, to a special strain of one of these or to the shaddock. The European writers confirm the impression left by the Arabs: Jacques de Vitry, speaking of the citrus of the Holy Land, mentions only *citrones*, *orenges* and *limones*; the *Tacuinum sanitatis* gives only *citra*, *limoni* and *citroni*, the last of which the editor takes for sour oranges; a fourteenth-century Catalan cookery book mentions *limons*, *taronjes* and *neronges*; in his description of the fruits of Valencia in the fourteenth century, Francesc Eiximenis lists *teronjes*, *aranges*, *llimons*, *llimes* and *adzabrones*, the last of which is probably a variant of the mysterious *zanbūʿ*; a fourteenth-century document from Tuscany speaks of *cedri*, *aranci*, *lumie* and *limoni*; and a Catalan text of 1469 speaks of *toronjes*, *oranges*, *limon* and *limes*.[47] Even García da Orta, writing of the citrus of India in the sixteenth century, mentions only *çidroés*, *laranjas*, *limoées* and *limas*; he does, however, find that the oranges (*laranjas*) of India are greatly superior to those of Portugal, and we may suppose that some of these oranges were sweet oranges which were still unknown, or just becoming known, in the Arab world and in the Christian Mediterranean.[48] Thus if any citrus other than the citron, the sour orange, the lemon and the lime was known anywhere west of India before the voyages of discovery, it must have been very rare. In the literature it went unnamed and indeed unmentioned.[49]

CHAPTER EIGHT

Banana *Musa sapientium* L.[1]

Plantain *Musa paradisiaca* L.[1]

Arabic: *mawz, ṭalḥ*[2]

Uses

The ripened fruits of the banana plant may be eaten raw, and the unripe fruit may be steamed, boiled, baked, roasted or sun-dried. The fruits of plantains are normally, but not always, cooked. In many parts of East Africa a beer is made from the fruit; in some places the fruit is made into a flour. Less commonly, the leaves, inner stems and rhizomes are cooked and eaten in much the same manner as *Ensete*, a distant relative of *Musa*. The leaves may also be fashioned into containers and mats, and in the Far East fibres from the leaves are made into cloth and cord. Medieval texts mentioned several medical uses.[3]

Origins and pre-Islamic diffusion

Cultivated from a remote antiquity – for so long indeed that through improvement, hybridization and probably mutation they have become sterile and can reproduce only from corms – the banana and plantain are descended from certain *Musaceae* which grow wild in Assam, Burma, Southeast Asia, Indonesia, the Philippines and probably India.[4] As cultivated plants, denoted by the Sanskrit words *mochaka* and *kadali*, they were mentioned in Indian literature from perhaps as early as the fifth or sixth century B.C.[5] By at least the fourth century the banana was known in China.[6] The botanists of the Alexandrian expedition to India saw the plant in the Indus valley in 325 B.C. and brought knowledge of it to the Hellenistic Mediterranean.[7] How far the banana and plantain had spread westwards by the time of the Islamic conquests of the seventh century is not certain; just possibly they had already reached Mesopotamia and the Arabian peninsula.[8]

Islamic diffusion

The Islamic conquests were followed by a far-reaching diffusion of banana culture. As early as the ninth century, the plant was referred to by a number

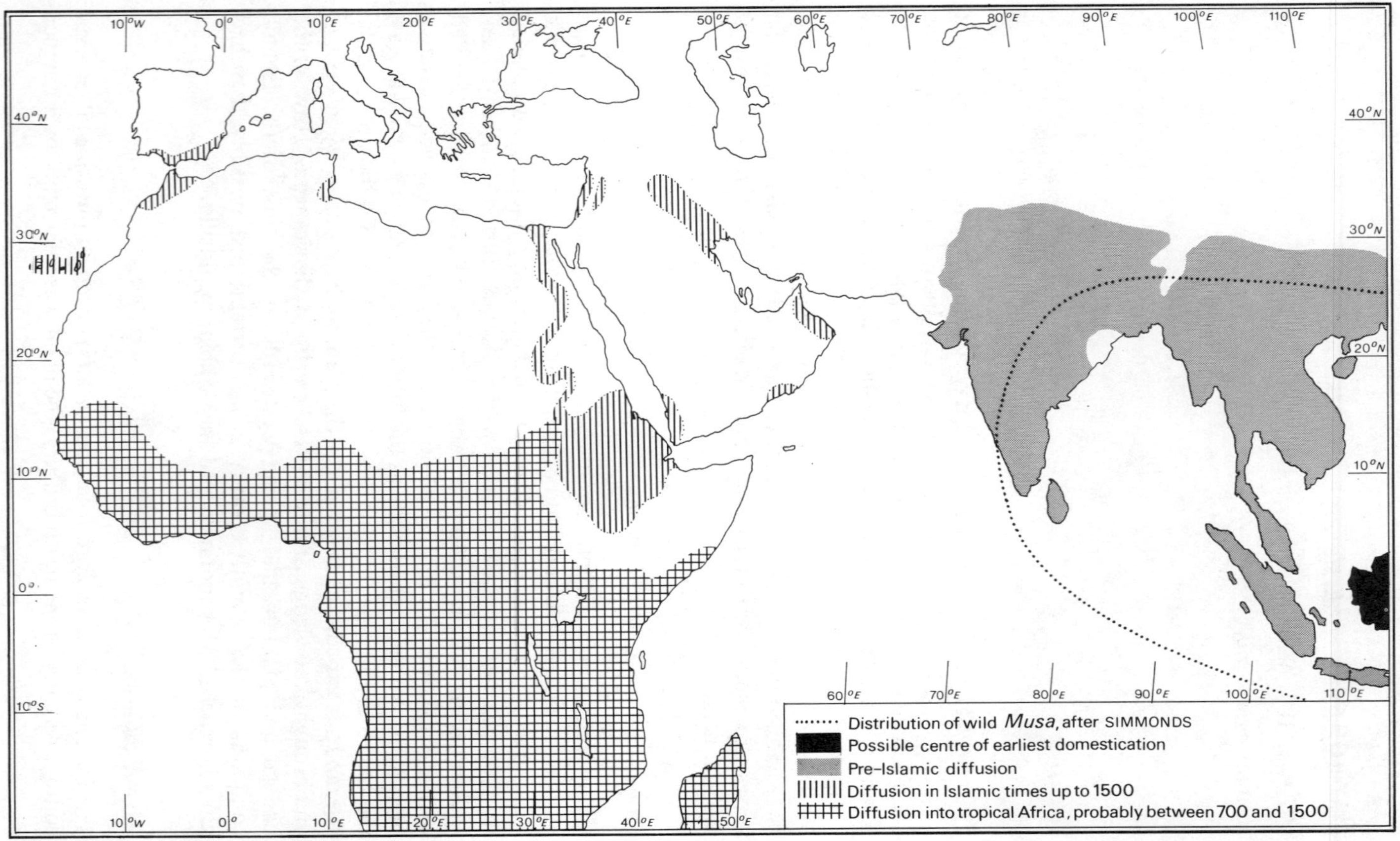

Map 5. The diffusion of banana and plantain

A drawing of two banana plants from the sixth-century *Christian Topography* of Cosmas Indicopleustis. The manuscript was made in Constantinople in the ninth century. The caption reads: "These are the so-called moza, the Indian fig [or palm?] tree." A similar illustration, showing two stems of fruit on each plant, is found on fol. 146r of the manuscript of this work in St Catherine's Monastery in Sinai. The original drawing was probably made by Cosmas himself. (Biblioteca Apostolica Vaticana, Greek ms. 688, fol. 15r)

of writers from the eastern part of the Arab world: it was the subject of an ecstatic poem by Ibn al-Rūmī (d. 896),[9] was mentioned in a number of Sunnī *ḥadīths* collected in Kufa and was described by Abū Ḥanīfa.[10] In the tenth century it was treated by Qusṭūs, Ibn Waḥshīya, Ibn Māsawaih and al-Mas'ūdī.[11] By the tenth century, too, it was found by al-Muqaddasī near Jerusalem and Jericho; later descriptions of the Levant, both Christian and Muslim, also mentioned banana production in this area.[12] A ninth-century papyrus tells of banana cultivation in Egypt, and in the tenth century it is mentioned by Ibn Rusta, al-Mas'ūdī and Ibn Ḥawqal, the last of whom related that the town of Maḥallat Masrūq produced excellent bananas which were exported to al-Fusṭāṭ.[13] For later centuries there are many references suggesting that the banana was grown on a wide scale in Egypt; al-Maqrīzī stated that it was one of the most abundant fruits in Cairo.[14] Probably from Egypt the banana was taken westwards across North Africa and into Spain. The earliest mention of it in North Africa is late: in the eleventh century al-Bakrī stated that it was grown at Gabes.[15] But by then it had already appeared in Spain, for it was mentioned by al-Rāzī in the ninth century and in the *Cordovan Calendar* of the tenth century.[16] Later sources told of banana cultivation in the Vega of Granada, at al-Shamajla and on the coastal plains around Salobreña and Almuñécar; from this coastal region, it was said, came some of the best bananas of the Arab world.[17]

Glimpses may also be caught of the westward progress of the banana along another route, farther to the south. Probably from Oman, where Abū Ḥanīfa thought the plant originated, and which Ibn Ḥawqal found "rich in bananas" in the tenth century,[18] the banana was taken around the Arabian peninsula to the coast of the Red Sea, where Muḥammad may have been familiar with it in the seventh century and where it was found in many places by later writers.[19] Certain modern writers claim that it had appeared in Abyssinia at some time between the sixth and the ninth century, and from there it has been suggested on the basis of an oral tradition that it arrived in Uganda perhaps as early as the year 1000.[20] Be that as it may, we have more certain knowledge that it was known in Zanzibar in the tenth century: al-Mas'ūdī stated that the banana was as abundant on the island as in India.[21] Al-Qazwīnī, in the thirteenth century, and al-'Umarī, in the fourteenth century, stated that it grew in Abyssinia.[22] Ibn Baṭṭūṭa saw it in the fourteenth century at Mogadishu and Mombasa, where he related that one of the main staples of the people was a dish made of boiled green bananas seasoned with fresh ginger and mangos.[23] Probably the Arabs of the east coast of Africa took the banana across the continent to the Atlantic coast, where it was found in the fifteenth century by the Portuguese.[24] It is also possible that the Arabs were responsible for its introduction farther south along the east coast of Africa and into Madagascar.[25]

CHAPTER NINE

Coconut palm *Cocos nucifera* L.

Arabic: *jawz hindī, nārajīl*[1]

Uses

"Perhaps from a world point of view our most important cultivated plant",[2] the coconut palm has many uses. In addition to their milk, the nuts yield an edible white meat which in dried form is known as copra; from the milk and meat may be extracted an oil used in food preparations and in the making of soap. The fibrous husk which surrounds the fruit is combed into coir for matting and ropes. From the sap are made sugar and wine. The trunk is used in building, while the leaves and leaf stalks are used in thatching, basket-making and wicker work. Several medical uses are mentioned in medieval texts.[3]

Origin and pre-Islamic diffusion

The coconut palm probably originated in the Malayan archipelago or in Oceania.[4] In ancient India, where it was known by the Sanskrit name *nārikeli*, the tree was grown from at least the fifth century B.C., for it was mentioned in early Buddhist texts; its cultivation in Ceylon was recorded in the first century B.C.[5] In the sixth century the tree was seen in India by Cosmas Indicopleustis, who described the "great Indian nuts".[6] The fruit of the tree seems to have been imported into China from Indochina from the second century B.C. onwards, but except in the extreme south the tree was seemingly not grown in China.[7] The fruit was also known, but probably not produced, in Sasanian Persia, where it was prized as a delicacy in the royal palace.[8]

Islamic diffusion

As the plant will not grow well in most of the regions conquered by the early Muslims, the Arabs learned of it mainly from geographers describing India, the islands of the Indian Ocean, and the East Indies.[9] They also gained firsthand knowledge of it in the Arab province of the Sind in north-west India, which was brought into the Islamic world early by conquest in the eighth century. The fruit appears to have been imported into Iraq in the early tenth century,[10] and as it is mentioned in nearly all the collections of *materia medica*

A drawing of a coconut palm from the sixth-century *Christian Topography* of Cosmas Indicopleustis. The manuscript was probably made in the Iviron Monastery on Mount Athos in the eleventh century. The label reads: "The Indian nut tree". A similar illustration, with the same label, may be found on fol. 203r of the manuscript of this work in St Catherine's Monastery in Sinai. The original drawing was probably made by Cosmas himself. (Biblioteca Medicea Laurenziana, Florence, ms. Plut. IX, Cod. 28, fol. 270r)

it must have been known, at least as a medicine, in much of the Arab world.[11] In an account of the traveller Abū Zaid we learn of Omani sailors who were in the habit of visiting certain Indian islands, where they cut down the coconut trees, used the wood and fibre to make ships, and set sail for Oman bearing cargoes of coconuts.[12]

Perhaps it was also the Omani, with their close ties to India, who were responsible for introducing, at an uncertain date, the coconut palm into Dhofar on the southern shore of the Arabian peninsula; in the fourteenth century – probably long after its first appearance – Ibn Baṭṭūṭa saw it there.[13] From here, or perhaps directly from India, it was probably brought by Arabs to East Africa, where al-Mas'ūdī in the tenth century stated that the coconut was one of the main foods of the people of Zanj, and where it was seen by the Portuguese explorers at the end of the fifteenth century.[14] It may have been taken from East Africa across the continent to the west coast or perhaps southwards to Madagascar, but we have no evidence for such diffusions and think them improbable.[15] Even the diffusion of the plant to East Africa cannot yet be proved to have been the work of the Arabs: a transmission from Malaysia via Madagascar in pre-Islamic times is another possibility. But as the banana, eggplant, colocasia, the improved watermelon, certain strains of sorghum, and the mango appear to have come to East Africa, and in some cases to Madagascar, over this northern route, we may tentatively conclude that the coconut palm also travelled along the "Sabean Lane", at least as far as the island of Zanzibar.

Attempts to introduce the plant into cooler climates met with failure. Ibn Waḥshīya tells of an unsuccessful effort to bring it from India into "Babylon",[16] while other sources describe similar undertakings – which also failed – in Egypt in the sixteenth and nineteenth centuries.[17] Though the Arabs were successful in acclimatizing many tropical plants in the Middle East and Mediterranean basin, neither they nor others were to succeed with the coconut palm.

CHAPTER TEN

Watermelon *Citrullus lanatus* (Thumb.) Mansf.

Arabic: *baṭṭīkh, baṭṭīkh hindī, baṭṭīkh al-sind, baṭṭīkh akhḍar, baṭṭīkh aḥmar,* (*baṭṭīkh*) *al-khirbiz, dullāʿ* (*al-sind*), *jabas*[1]

Uses

The flesh is normally eaten raw. In the wild or semi-wild varieties, however, the sometimes bitter flesh is cooked into soups, jams and conserves; the rinds of all varieties are used in similar ways. Both flesh and rinds are sometimes dried in the sun to allow storage. Edible oil is extracted from raw seeds. The roasted seeds may be eaten whole, pounded into a paste or crushed into cakes. Medieval texts speak of several medical uses.[2]

Origin and pre-Islamic diffusion

The wild ancestor of the cultivated watermelon is native to the steppes and savannas of Africa which encircle the tropical rain forest and verge on the desert. The centre of origin – from which the wild plant may have diffused outwards by natural means – lies perhaps in the eastern equatorial part of the continent.[3] The fruit of the wild plant is about the size of a grapefruit or even smaller, and most often is bitter.

Like many other plants which grow wild in the Nile valley, the primitive watermelon may have had a more northerly limit in ancient times than nowadays, and it is probable that the ancient Egyptians knew it as a wild plant. Wall-paintings in Egyptian tombs perhaps depict it, but may in fact represent the colocynth (*Citrullus colocynthus* Schrad.), which closely resembles the watermelon. Contrary to what has previously been supposed, it may now be stated that there is no evidence whatever of watermelon seeds or leaves from pre-Islamic tombs or other sites in Egypt.[4] Nor does the linguistic evidence support the thesis that watermelons were cultivated, or even used, in pre-Islamic Egypt: a hieroglyphic word *betton-ka*, whence derive the Coptic *betuke* and perhaps the Arabic *baṭṭīkh*, may denote melons in general, and more particularly *Cucumis melo* L. That the unimproved plant was taken from ancient Egypt to Palestine seems even more unlikely; the Hebrew and Aramaic words *avatiach* and *abattichim*, and other related words, probably denote the colocynth or the common melon.[5] An early diffusion into North Africa is more probable, since the Berber word for watermelon, *te-dalāt*, seems to have given rise to the medieval Arabic word *dullāʿ*.[6] In pre-Islamic times the watermelon may also have spread into West Africa, where today a semi-wild variety known by many unrelated names is widely used.[7] But whatever the exact limits of its pre-Islamic diffusion, the watermelon of early times was an inferior plant, very different from the cultivated varieties of today. It was appreciated mainly for its seeds, and perhaps also for its cooked rind. Its flesh was usually – perhaps always – bitter. That it was cultivated, and not merely gathered, is not known.

The "ennobled" cultivated plant, much larger in size and with sweet flesh, was almost certainly developed in India rather than Africa. How this process occurred is not known. Like sorghum and certain other plants, the watermelon probably moved eastwards along the "Sabean Lane" – up the east coast of Africa, along the south coast of Arabia, and into north-west India. As there was a Sanskrit word for the plant, *chaya-pala*, but no known Vedic word, it probably arrived in India between the fifth century B.C. and the eighth century A.D. The development of improved forms may have been rather late, since the plant was not taken to China till the late eleventh century, and its arrival in Malaya also seems to have been relatively recent.[8]

Islamic diffusion

Owing to the multitude of varieties of melons known in the Arabic world – so many, as Ibn Waḥshīya remarked, that they could not be counted – and to the profusion of names for these, the spread of the improved, or Indian, watermelon through the Islamic world is not easily traced.[9] But the main direction of movement seems clear from the linguistic evidence. The Afghan word *hindvana* and the New Persian word *hindawānah*, or Indian fruit, both betray the Indian origin of the fruit. Several of the classical Arabic terms are still more explicit. *Baṭṭīkh hindī* or *dullāʿ al-hind*, for instance, mean simply the melon of India. A similar term, *al-baṭṭīkha al-sindīya*, or the melon of the Sind (in north-west India) was carried right across the Islamic world to give the Castilian *sandía* and the Sardinian *sandria*.[10] Certain of the words for watermelon in dialects give us glimpses of successive stages in the plant's westward transmission: a term used in Egypt was the "Palestinian melon", while in Valencia it was called the "melon of Algiers".[11]

In Islamic literature, the watermelon first appears in works of authors from the eastern part of the Muslim world, and first of all in works of pharmacology and philology. Thus it is mentioned from the ninth to eleventh centuries by al-Rāzī, Ibn Sīna and Abū Ḥanīfa, and in the tenth century was the subject of a poem.[12] Although there are many references to melons of one kind or another in Ibn Waḥshīya, and a very long section on their cultivation and us, the watermelon is mentioned only once in passing.[13] It is not mentioned clearly by Qusṭūs. Nor is it unambiguously reported by any of the early geographers. This evidence suggests that even in the eastern parts of the

Watermelons, shown in the *Tacuinum sanitatis*, a Latin translation of the *Taqwīm al-siḥḥa* of Ibn Buṭlān (d. 1066). The manuscript was probably made in Italy in the late fourteenth century. (Österreichische Nationalbibliothek, Ser. Nov. 2644, fol. 214)

Islamic world it did not early become a common crop; it was perhaps used first mainly as a medicine, possibly even imported as seeds or in dried form. But by the twelfth or thirteenth century the watermelon had become common in Egypt, where many authors mention it, and in other parts of the eastern Islamic world.[14] In the thirteenth century, al-Qazwīnī stated that the watermelons of Aswan were so large that a strong camel could carry only two of them.[15] In the west, the plant appeared early: it was clearly mentioned in the *Cordovan Calendar* of 961, and by the eleventh and twelfth centuries it was discussed in some detail in several Hispano-Arabic farming manuals.[16] By then we may suppose that it was also grown in North Africa, though the first clear indication of its arrival in the Maghrib is from the fourteenth-century writer al-'Umarī, who saw it in Ifrīqiya – modern Tunisia – where he says it was rare, and in Morocco. The same writer also noted the watermelon in Abyssinia, while a contemporary wrote of it in the Yemen.[17]

CHAPTER ELEVEN

Spinach[1] *Spinacia oleracea* L.

Arabic: *isfānākh, isbānakh, isfānāj* etc.[2]

Uses

As a food, spinach was cooked in various ways, either alone or with meat. It also had several medical uses.[3]

Origin

Primitive forms of *S. oleracea* are found in north-west India and Nepal, and the plant was probably domesticated in these regions.[4]

Diffusion

This "queen of the vegetables", as it was called by Ibn al-'Awwām,[5] was unknown to the ancient world;[6] the first references to it are from Sasanian Persia,[7] and in 647 it was taken from Nepal to China, where it is still known as the "Persian green".[8]

Its westward diffusion was almost certainly the work of the Arabs. The earlist references to it in Arabic literature are from the beginning of the tenth century: it is mentioned in the medical work of al-Rāzī[9] and in the agricultural treatise of Ibn Waḥshīya,[10] and is discussed in some detail by Qusṭūs al-Rūmī, who describes its cultivation and medical uses.[11] Although it became a popular food in the Arab world, grown in some places throughout the year[12] and prepared in a variety of ways,[13] the plant was little mentioned in the literature of geography and travel, and hence its progress towards the west is difficult to trace. By the later part of the eleventh century, however, it had appeared in Spain, where it was mentioned by Ibn Wāfid, Abū al-Khair and Ibn Baṣṣāl, and where it was the subject of a special treatise by Ibn Ḥajjāj.[14] In the works of later writers from various parts of the Arab world, it was mentioned as a common plant.[15]

An illustration of spinach from the *Tacuinum sanitatis*, a Latin translation of the *Taqwīm al-siḥḥa* of Ibn Buṭlān (d. 1066). The manuscript was probably made in Italy in the late fourteenth century. (Österreichische Nationalbibliothek, Ser. Nov. 2644, fol. 27r)

CHAPTER TWELVE

Artichoke *Cynara cardunculus* L. var. *scolymus*

Arabic: *kharshuf*, *ḥarshuf*, *kharshūf*, *qinārīya*, *kankar*(?)[1]

Uses

The receptacle and the fleshy base of the calyx bracts are edible after boiling. The stems of the young plants are also sometimes boiled and eaten. The receptacle, or "heart", may be pickled in a brine and vinegar solution in the manner of other *mukhallalāt* of the Arab world. There were probably also medical uses.[2]

Origin and pre-Islamic distribution

The artichoke does not grow wild. It seems to have been developed from the cardoon (*Cynara cardunculus* L.), a native of the Mediterranean which does grow wild and is also cultivated. The cardoon is prized mainly for its stalks and leaves, but its receptacle and roots are sometimes eaten; the calyx of the cardoon is not edible. Contrary to what is sometimes stated, only the cardoon was known to the Greco-Roman world, designated by such names as *kaktos*, *cynara*, *carduus*, *scolymus* and *spondylium*. There is no reference in Classical literature to a plant of this family with edible flesh on the bracts.[3]

Islamic diffusion

In all probability, the artichoke was developed in the Islamic world and diffused through it before 1500. Unfortunately, it does not seem possible to identify its point of origin, which is just possibly the Maghrib, where there are several Berber words for the plant – *taga*, *tifrhūt* and *fegane*[4] – which are all different from the Arabic. Nor is it possible to chart the artichoke's advance through the Islamic world, since the Arabic terminology for the cardoon and the artichoke is utterly confused. Indeed, the term *ḥarshuf* and its variants, used most often for these two plants, seem at times to be used to designate still other unidentified plants. Very probably, however, these terms as used in the agricultural and pharmaceutical literature of the Arabs sometimes in fact refer to artichokes,[5] and almost certainly the plant called *qinārīya* in thirteenth-century Spanish sources is the artichoke.[6] But we can have no idea of the plant's progress until it begins to move into Europe in the late Middle Ages, bringing into all the European languages names derived from the Arabic.[7]

CHAPTER THIRTEEN

Colocasia, taro, coco-yam, eddo, dasheen *Colocasia antiquorum* Schott.

Arabic: *qulqās*, *qulqāṣ*[1]

Uses

The tubers or corms are eaten, sometimes raw but most often cooked; medieval texts proposed a number of recipes, of which parboiling followed by frying was a favourite.[2] The young greens are also sometimes eaten. Several medical uses were recommended in medieval Arabic works.[3]

Though it may be grown in all parts of the Mediterranean basin, colocasia has become a particularly important crop in tropical and semi-tropical regions because of various advantages: its exceptionally high per-acre yield of starch, which it produces in an unusually digestible form; its ability to withstand slightly colder weather than, for instance, the greater yam; its short growing season, which allows two or three crops of it to be grown on the same land in a single year; and the easy preservation over many months of the fresh or dried tubers, which made it useful for tiding people over barren seasons or for taking on sea voyages.

Origin and pre-Islamic diffusion

Various origins have been proposed for colocasia: Assam and Upper Burma, Thailand, Malaya and Indonesia.[4] By the second century B.C. it had reached China, where it has become the most important tuber crop grown.[5] The ancients of the west had heard of this plant but probably not seen it: they appear to have confused it with the lotus, the water lily, the arum lily, the beet, the turnip and the Egyptian bean.[6]

Islamic diffusion

By the tenth century, colocasia seems to have been known in Mesopotamia, the Levant and Egypt. Ibn Waḥshīya mentions it twice, though strangely he does not discuss its cultivation or uses in detail; from the way he speaks, however, we may infer that the plant was familiar to the author and his readers in the valley of the Tigris and Euphrates.[7] A thirteenth-century Baghdadi cookbook gives five ways of preparing it.[8] In the Levant, it is mentioned by two writers in the tenth century and two others in the thirteenth

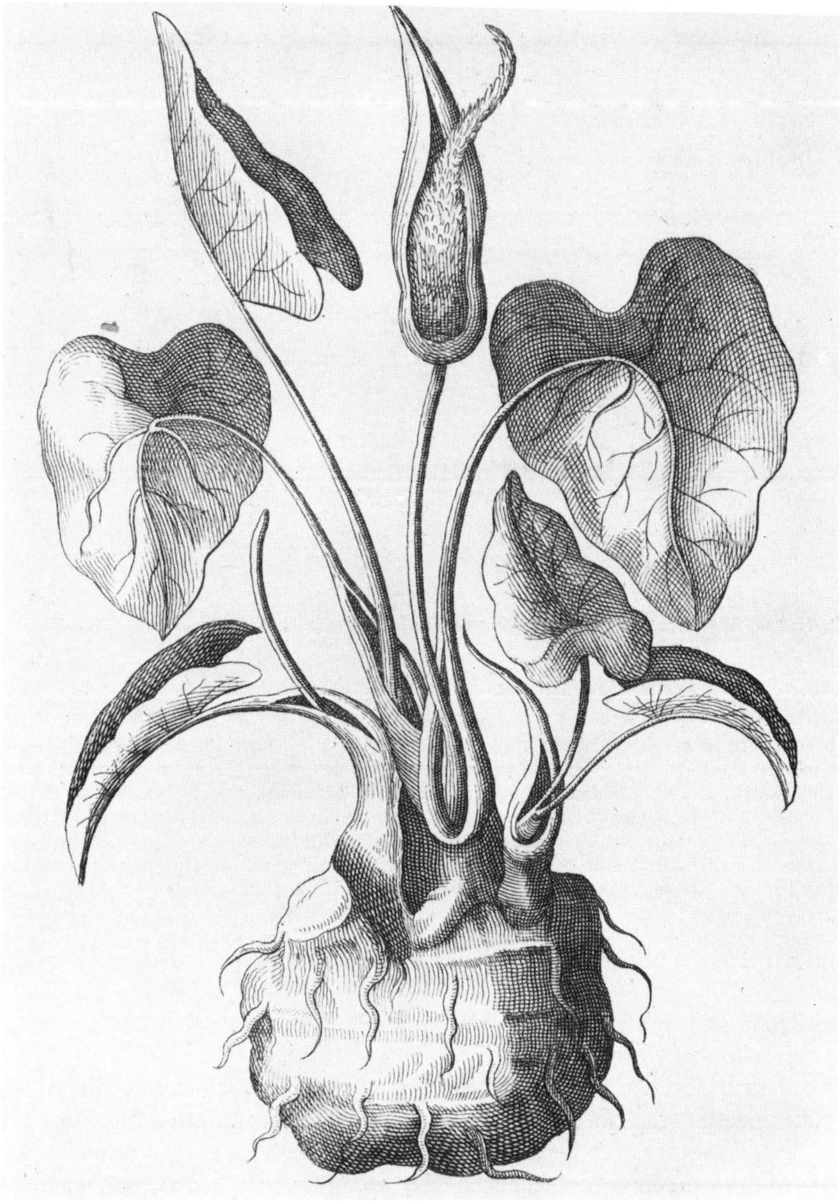

Colocasia, as depicted in Prosper Alpino's *Historia Aegypti naturalis* (Leyden, 1735). (Thomas Fisher Rare Book Library, University of Toronto)

century; though 'Abd al-Laṭīf says that it was not common in Syria, al-Dimashqī states that large quantities of it were grown in the environs of Tripoli.[9] In Egypt, where it seems to have been an important crop, it is frequently discussed in the texts.[10] It does not seem to be mentioned in Morocco until the fourteenth century, when al-'Umarī stated that it was

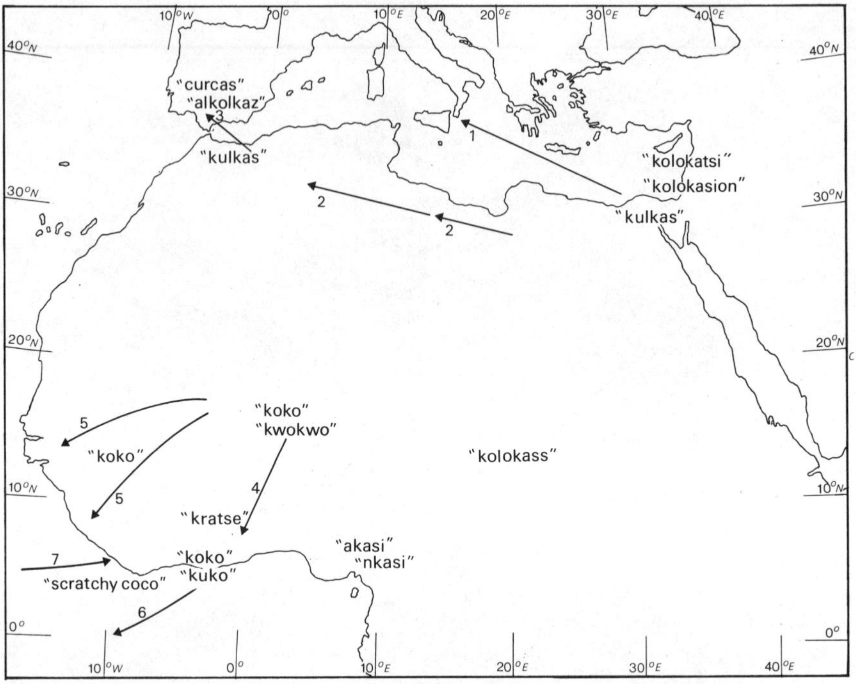

Map 6. The names derived from "kolokasion". Arrow no. 1 shows the carrying of *Colocasia esculentum* to Italy; no. 2, the advance of the Arabs which carried the name and probably the plant westwards; no. 3, the extension of Berber agriculture into Spain, by which the crop was brought to Spain and Portugal; no. 4, the possible Fante migration which carried the name "koko" to the coast; no. 5, lines of tribal movement of the Mandinka; no. 6, "koko", or "coco", carried to the West Indies; no. 7, the name brought back to Liberia etc. "Scratchy coco" is bazaar English from "kratse" plus "koko". (After BURKILL "The contacts" 86–7)

grown there only as an ornamental plant.[11] In Spain Ibn al-'Awwām discussed its cultivation, citing Ibn Waḥshīya and the Moorish author Abū al-Khair, and in the sixteenth century L'Ecluse stated that it grew along the river valleys of Portugal.[12]

Linguistic evidence strongly suggests the diffusion of colocasia by the Arabs at an uncertain date into tropical and semi-tropical regions of Africa, in some parts of which the crop became a staple. From southern Arabia, where it was known as *zanj*, colocasia seems to have been taken to East Africa, where in Usambara it is called *m'sanga*. It may have been diffused from there to Madagascar: one of the Malagasy names for the plant is *saunjo*, though other names seem to be of Indian or Malayan origin.[13] Whether West Africa received the plant from the East African coast or from North Africa is not certain, but the existence all over West Africa of names of the *kolkos* or *koko* group suggests that the plant came either down the Nile valley and then westward or from the Maghrib directly across the Sahara.[14] A plant resembling colocasia – doubtless one of the many varieties of it – was observed in the fourteenth century by both Ibn Baṭṭūṭa and al-ʿUmarī in the kingdom of Mali, where it was said to be the favourite food. In spite of the apparent popularity of the dish amongst the Malians, it was not well received by Ibn Baṭṭūṭa: he himself was sick for two months after eating it, and one of his fellow diners died the next day.[15]

CHAPTER FOURTEEN

Eggplant, aubergine, brinjal *Solanum melongena* L.

Arabic: *bādhinjān*[1]

Uses

Said by Ibn Waḥshīya to be a cause of death when eaten raw, and mentioned by him in his book of poisons,[2] eggplant was cooked in a great many ways in the medieval Islamic world. One cookbook alone gives eighteen recipes for preparing the fruit.[3] The texts also mention various medical uses.[4]

Origins and pre-Islamic diffusion

Botanists generally agree that the eggplant originated in India as an improved form of the wild *Solanum insanum* Roxb.; one variety, however, may have been developed in China.[5] The existence of several Sanskrit names for the plant (including *vangana*, from which has descended a long line of names for the plant) suggests some antiquity for its use. The plant had apparently been taken from India to China by the early sixth century,[6] but was not known in the ancient west.[7]

Islamic diffusion

The Arabs probably found the eggplant already established in Persia at the time of its conquest, for Ibn Waḥshīya says that "it is a plant from Persia which has spread over all the regions of the world"[8] and Abū Ḥanīfa states that the Arabic name was taken from the Persian.[9] But the existence of several other ancient Arabic names for the plant, two of which seem to have come directly from other Indian names, suggests that the plant may also have reached the Arabian peninsula direct from India in pre-Islamic times or shortly after the Hegira.[10] However that may be, in the ninth century the eggplant was the subject of a number of Sunnī *ḥadīths* compiled in Kufa, and in the following century, when the sources for the eastern reaches of the Arabic world become more abundant, the plant was known to all the main writers; it was mentioned many times and dealt with at length in the *Nabatean Book of Agriculture*, and was treated by Qusṭūs, Ibn Sīna, al-Rāzī and Ibn Māsawaih.[11] Several poems sang its praises.[12] From the east it was taken to Egypt,[13] across North Africa[14] and into Spain, where it was mentioned several

Eggplant, or *melongiana*, depicted in the *Tacuinum sanitatis*, a Latin translation of the medical work *Taqwīm al-siḥḥa* of Ibn Buṭlān (d. 1066). The manuscript was probably made in Italy in the late fourteenth century. (Österreichische Nationalbibliothek, Ser. Nov. 2644, fol. 31v)

times in the *Cordovan Calendar* of the tenth century and treated in later centuries by Abū al-Khair, Ibn Baṣṣāl and Ibn al-'Awwām.[15] By the fourteenth century it had appeared in Abyssinia and at Kanem.[16]

From the accounts of our authors, we learn that the Arabs were at an early date familiar with several varieties of eggplant. Ibn Waḥshīya spoke of six kinds, each different from the others in colour, shape and origin.[17] Ibn al-'Awwām, quoting Abū al-Khair, described four varieties known in Spain: the "local", the Cordovan, the Egyptian and the Syrian.[18] A Chinese visitor to Samarkand in 1221 was surprised to find eggplants with elongated fruit, the original wild plant and the cultivated eggplant of China both having round fruit.[19] In the fourteenth century, a variety with a pure white fruit, believed to have come from China, was grown in the gardens of a Yemeni king.[20]

CHAPTER FIFTEEN

Mango tree *Mangifera indica* L.

Arabic: *ānbaj*, ʻ*anbā* etc.[1]

Uses

The ripe fruit was eaten raw. Ripe or unripe fruits were cooked into "chutneys", preserved in vinegar or made into sugared *confits*. There were also medical uses.[2]

Origin and pre-Islamic diffusion

The mango tree was developed from a plant that grows wild in India, Malaya or Indonesia.[3] It has been cultivated since very ancient times in India, where it was later noted by several Arab authors.[4] Though it was probably grown widely through much of Southeast Asia in pre-Islamic times, from the sources we learn of it only in Cambodia, and not until just before the rise of Islam.[5]

Islamic diffusion

Abū Ḥanīfa stated that by the end of the ninth century the mango tree was common in the region of Oman.[6] From there it must have been taken to the more southerly parts of Iraq, for mangos were listed amongst the contents of the treasury of the caliph Hārūn al-Rashīd (786–809).[7] By then, or slightly later, it is said – improbably – to have reached Central Asia: a Chinese source of the T'ang period is alleged to mention the mango tree at Fergana.[8]

How and when the mango tree reached East Africa is not clear. None of the Arab travellers who visited the "Land of the Zanj" in the tenth century wrote of it. In the fourteenth century, however, Ibn Baṭṭūṭa saw it in Mogadishu, where he stated that one of the staple dishes of the inhabitants was made from boiled green plantains (or possibly *ensete*?) seasoned with lemon, fresh ginger, pepper and mangos.[9]

But in spite of the obvious appeal of the mango fruit, the tree seems to have enjoyed only a limited diffusion before the European voyages of discovery. It may have been taken to parts of the interior of West Africa before then, but this diffusion is not certain.[10] Even in East Africa its existence may have been precarious, for in some parts it seems to have been introduced only in the last century. The use in many parts of Africa and of the Arab world of names of the *manku* type, which derive from Indo-Malay or Tamil words, suggests a relatively late introduction over a different route. Very probably, the northerly diffusion of the mango tree, into Egypt and southern China, for instance, where it is now widely grown, had to await the development of new, hardier varieties in the past century and a half. In warmer areas, the difficulty of propagating the tree may have slowed its progress: it should be grafted by in-arching since, if grown from seed, it will yield fruit that is stringy and ill-tasting.[11]

Part Two
The pathways of diffusion

CHAPTER SIXTEEN

The routes

The dates of the earliest known appearances of these crops in each region often reveal, or at least suggest, the routes over which the new crops travelled. There is also the odd contemporary account telling of the pathways of diffusion. These appear to have been relatively few. They are worth studying not only because of their importance for the spread of the crops studied in this volume but also because they were the arteries of diffusion along which travelled many other new crops and much else that was to shapc thc carly Islamic world.

Although the new crops were of diverse origins, most of them passed through India on their way to the Islamic world and were often "ennobled" there. One group came from the great centres of origin of cultivated plants lying farther to the east: Assam, Burma, Southeast Asia and the Malaysian archipelago. It included rice, colocasia, the sour orange, lemon and lime, and very probably also the coconut palm, sugar cane, bananas, plantains and mango trees (though there is some possibility that these last four plants were first brought into cultivation and improved in India). Their entry into India cannot be precisely dated, partly because some arrived in pre-historic times and partly because the Sanskrit and Vedic texts, which may testify to an introduction in historical times, cannot be narrowly dated. It seems likely, however, that the movement began early in the second millennium B.C., gained momentum during the first millennium B.C. and continued into the early centuries of the Christian era. During part of this same period, another group of crops reached India from Africa. In addition to several crops which do not concern us here (including finger millet, pearl or bulrush millet and the cowpea) this group included sorghum and possibly cotton and watermelons (though it may be that cotton was developed from a plant once native to India but now extinct). Travelling along the "Sabean Lane", these plants probably moved up the east coast of Africa, across the southern shores of Arabia and into north-western India.[1] In India itself another of our plants – the eggplant – was first brought into cultivation and a number of varieties were developed, probably during the first millennium B.C. In thus domesticating, improving and diffusing these and many other useful plants, as well as in other ways which will become apparent later on, ancient India played a crucial role in the development of Eurasian and African agriculture in general and in the agricultural revolution of the Islamic world in particular.[2]

From India these plants were diffused eastwards and westwards during the first millennium of the Christian era, leaving behind as evidence of their westward passage many chains of plant names. For the westward movement these linguistic chains start with the Sanskrit or Vedic words, pass through Persian and Arabic and reach into many of the languages of Europe and Africa. This movement began, but did not progress very far, in pre-Islamic times. Probably some of the crops moved into the Sasanian empire in the fifth, sixth and seventh centuries. These may include sugar cane, sorghum, eggplants, spinach, bananas, plantains and rice, the last of which (along with cotton, which was not grown in the Sasanian empire) was also grown by the sixth century in the Jordan valley, where the extremely warm climate and the availability of irrigation favoured its introduction. Since the sources which throw light on late Sasanian agriculture are few, uninformative and difficult of interpretation, we cannot be sure that even this limited diffusion from India into the Sasanian empire occurred in pre-Islamic times. About nearly all of these possible introductions there is good reason for doubt. But as much else was transmitted from India into the syncretic civilization of the Sasanians, it does not seem improbable that at least a few of our crops were also diffused. From India, too, and also in pre-Islamic times, another route for westward diffusion may have been operating. Moving along the Sabean Lane, but in the opposite direction to that of the earlier diffusion along this path, several of our crops may have spread to Arabia Felix before the time of Muḥammad, and one or two may even have penetrated as far as Abyssinia and Nubia. These may include bananas, plantains, cotton and sugar cane, though so little do we know about the crops of pre-Islamic Arabia and Abyssinia that we cannot be sure that any of these crops were introduced there. Once again, however, the case for an introduction at least into Arabia Felix seems plausible not only because of documentary and archeological evidence but also because the climate of South Arabia favoured such crops, because intensive irrigated agriculture was widely practised in this region in pre-Islamic times, and because many trading voyages linked India and the Persian Gulf to South Arabia and Abyssinia.

After the rise and spread of Islam, this movement from east to west gained momentum. As we have suggested, some of the crops may have been obtained by early Muslims in the lands of the fallen Sasanian empire and diffused westwards from there. More, however, were probably found on the Indian sub-continent, where the new province of the Sind, conquered in 711, gave early Muslims a foothold in a part of India where most of the new crops were already known. In the transmission of these crops from India into Persia and Mesopotamia, an important role was probably played by the sailors and merchants of Oman and Siraf who plied between India and the headlands

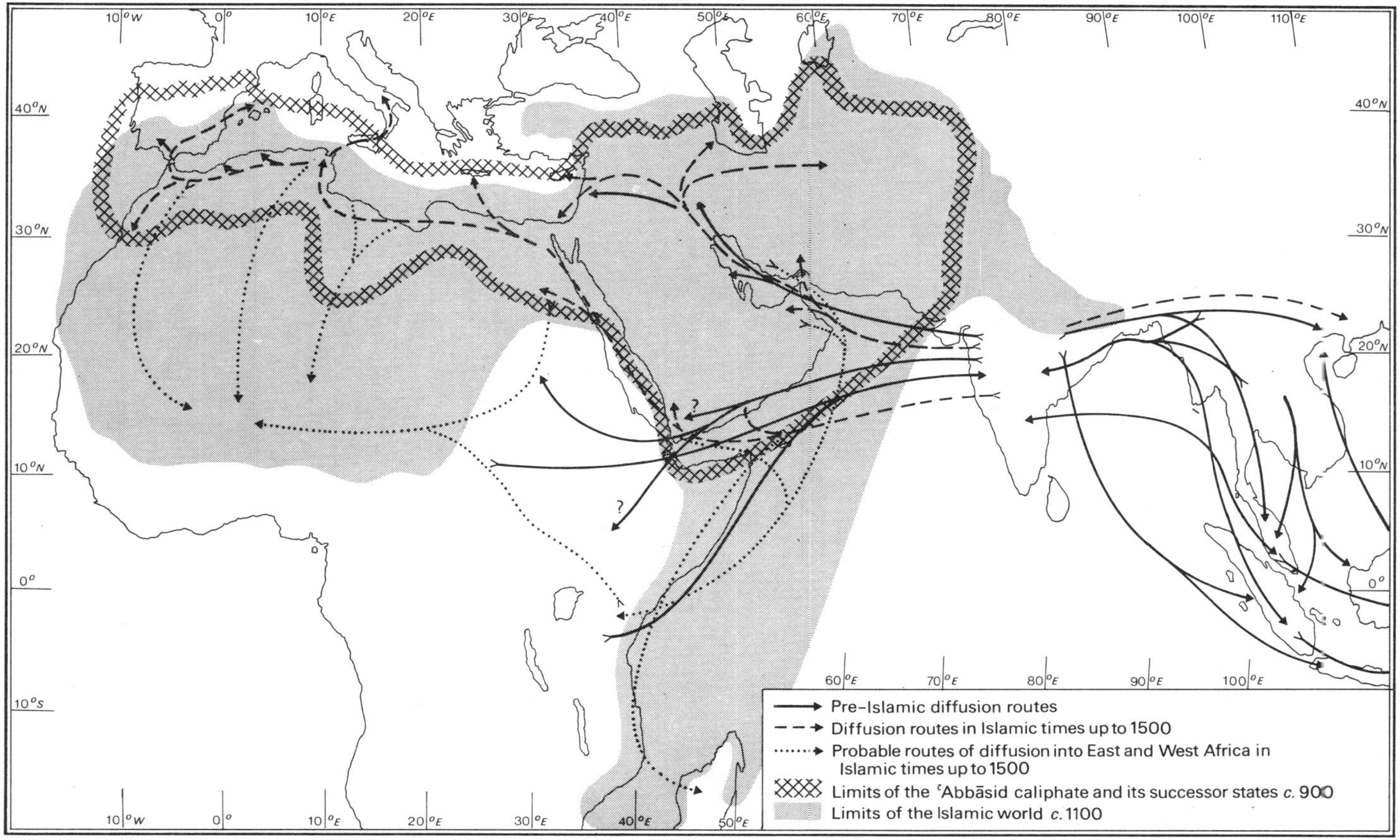

Map 7. The routes of diffusion for crops studied in this volume

of the Persian Gulf.[3] Oman itself may have been a halfway-house in which these plants from India were acclimatized before being passed farther to the north and, as we shall see, in other directions as well. This hypothesis receives some confirmation from al-Masʿūdī, who tells that after the year 912/13 the sour-orange tree and the "round citron" tree (which may be the lemon tree) were brought first to Oman, where they were planted, and then to Basra and other parts of Iraq; from there, he relates, they passed into Syria, Palestine and Egypt, where they were previously unknown. In another passage, al-Masʿūdī states that the caliph al-Qāhir (932–4) imported sour-orange trees from India via Oman and Basra.[4] Though these introductions of the sour-orange tree were probably not the first (since Ibn Waḥshīya, writing *c.* 904, stated that the plant was already known in Mesopotamia),[5] al-Masʿūdī's accounts may well give a true picture of the path followed by many plants in their westward progress. Again, the statement by Abū Ḥanīfa al-Dīnawarī (d. *c.* 895) that the banana tree was native to Oman, though it is incorrect, may indicate the source from which the Persians and Iraqis received this plant.[6]

From Persia and Iraq all the crops received from India were diffused westwards and arrived in the most westerly parts of Dār al-Islām by the tenth or eleventh centuries, if not earlier. The eastern part of the Islamic world was thus the gateway through which passed on their westward journey all the crops of the agricultural revolution except mango trees and coconut palms (which could be grown only in tropical climates). There were a number of stages along the route to the western reaches of the Islamic world. The crops probably first arrived in al-Jazīra, where some of them may have been acclimatized only with difficulty; they then, as al-Masʿūdī suggests, were probably carried to the Jordan valley, the Levantine coast and Egypt. From their footholds on the south-eastern shores of the Mediterranean, the crops were transmitted still farther to the west: across the Maghrib, into Spain and Sicily, and from one Mediterranean island to another. Feeding into the westward movement from Egypt across North Africa and into Spain and Sicily may have been another stream. This also can be traced back to India, but it passed through Arabia Felix and thence up the Red Sea or down the valley of the Nile. Nothing is known about the movement of our crops over this route. But many of the new crops may have been introduced into southern Arabia and thence into the upper Nile region in the centuries immediately before and after the rise of Islam, and many of the new farming techniques may also have appeared there very early; it seems likely, for instance, that the Yemeni who came to settle in Egypt, the Maghrib and Spain, bringing with them into Spain their irrigation laws and administration, were also the carriers of new crops, irrigation technology and systems of more intensive land use.[7]

Arabia Felix played a role – along with other parts of the Islamic world – in the diffusion of some of the new crops over another route: south-westwards into Ethiopia, along the east coast of Africa, into the islands of Zanzibar and Pemba, and quite possibly into Madagascar. The exact importance of Arabia Felix in this transmission into Africa is not certain, but it seems likely that many of the crops which were acclimatized in south-western Arabia were then passed further to the west and south by the sailors of the Hadramaut and the Yemen who sailed along the East African shores.[8] However, some of the plants may easily have been carried into these new regions by other agents travelling the same or different routes: by Omanis and Sirafis who, from perhaps as early as 700, traded over this coast, founding colonies in Somaliland in the ninth and tenth centuries and at Kilwa in the eleventh century; by Persian merchants and settlers who in the course of various migrations from the time of Hārūn al-Rashīd (786–809) onwards established colonies in Zanzibar, Pemba and Kilwa; and by Indian sailors from Dabhol, the "Wadebuli", who arrived on the coast of East Africa at an uncertain date, brought by boats whose sails were said to be fashioned from palm leaves.[9] Here, as elsewhere, there may have been many successive "introductions" of the crops which were noted in different parts of East Africa from the tenth century onwards, first by the Arab geographers and travellers and later by the Portuguese explorers. Among the crops they mentioned are sorghum (some of the varieties improved in India), sugar cane, sour oranges, lemons, limes, mango trees, coconut palms, cotton, bananas, plantains, colocasia, eggplants and rice.

From the east coast of Africa some of these plants may have been taken to Madagascar, which Arab and Shirazi traders frequented (and the historian al-Mas'ūdī visited more than once) and where, from the eleventh century onwards, Muslims from East Africa settled. Linguistic evidence points to this direction of flow in a number of cases: the various names of sorghum in Madagascar, for example *hova ampemby*, suggest an introduction via Pemba,[10] while the Arabic origin of the names of certain of the plants in some of the Malagasy languages speaks for a transmission from peoples who spoke Arabic or Swahili.[11] That some of these crops also reached Madagascar direct from Malaya or Indonesia is not impossible; they may have come in the course of undatable but probably pre-Islamic migrations which led to the original settlement of the island, or through later direct contacts with Indonesia which continued at least until the thirteenth century.[12] But contrary to what is often maintained, it seems probable to us that many of the crops reached the island first in Islamic times and by travelling along the northern and eastern shores of the Indian Ocean, brought by carriers who may have been Indian, Persian or Arab.

Some of the crops also moved into West Africa in medieval times. The evidence of this diffusion is partly documentary, since certain of the crops were seen by Arab travellers who visited West Africa from the eleventh century onwards and some were noted by the Portuguese in the fifteenth century. For a number of the crops there is also linguistic evidence pointing to an Arab introduction: the names of several of the new crops in the languages of the interior of West Africa seem to be derived from the Arabic names.[13] On these grounds, therefore, it is almost certain that in medieval times West Africa received cotton, colocasia, bananas, plantains, sour oranges and limes. It may also have obtained sugar cane, Asiatic rice and varieties of sorghum improved in India, though the existence of indigenous rice and sorghum makes it difficult to date the arrival of new species and varieties of these from the east. The introductions were all the more precious since the range of crops previously available was extremely limited, especially in the tropical rain forest area,[14] and many of the indigenous crops gave little nutrition in relation to the amount of land or labour required.

For this diffusion several routes were possible. Some of the crops may have come across Central Africa from the east coast; we think it unlikely, however, that many crops moved over this route, which was not an important avenue of either trade or migration. Possibly some of the crops did travel over the Nilo-Chadian route which stretches from the White Nile across the savanna lands into West Africa – a route along which there was considerable movement of men and goods from about 1000 onwards.[15] But most of the crops were probably brought from the Maghrib over the caravan routes which crossed the Sahara. A few appeared relatively early: thus in areas where Islam spread, the converted almost immediately began to wear clothes – as their religion enjoined – and soon cotton came to be grown in many places to cater for a growing demand.[16] But for many crops the diffusion seems to have been difficult and slow. The Sahara, that barrier which prevented the transmission of the plough (known in Egypt in the third millennium B.C.) to any part of sub-Saharan Africa except Ethiopia, must have been one obstacle. Others were probably the still heavy dependence of the area on hunting and gathering and its relatively primitive agricultural practices; the tribal and village land tenure systems; the multiplicity of tribal and linguistic groups; and the slow and limited penetration of those unifying factors which helped to create an efficient medium of diffusion in other parts of the Islamic world – the Islamic religion, the Arabic language and trade.[17]

In time the new crops also moved northwards into Christian Europe. They reached Christendom through Spain, Sicily and Cyprus. Some may also have passed from the Muslim to the Christian world via Byzantium or the Crusader kingdoms; but, contrary to commonly held views, there is no evidence to support such a thesis, and a number of factors make the latter regions unlikely intermediaries for the transmission of our crops.[18] Whatever its routes, the diffusion into Europe contrasts strikingly with the earlier rapid movement across the Islamic world. It began late – many centuries after the crops had reached the frontiers of Christian Europe – and it proceeded slowly. Spinach was one of the earliest crops to be received into Europe, but it did not appear until the thirteenth century, when it seems to have made rapid progress.[19] Sorghum, too, is mentioned in Italy by the late twelfth and thirteenth centuries, by which time it had arrived in the south of France.[20] Sour oranges and lemons appear to have spread slowly through parts of Italy and Spain in the thirteenth and fourteenth centuries, but their use seems very limited.[21] Hard wheat probably appeared in the thirteenth century.[22] Rice was not grown on the plains of Pisa until 1468 or in the Po valley till 1475.[23] Only by the later part of the fifteenth century and throughout the sixteenth century did Christian Europe show itself more receptive to these and other exotic plants, many of which were introduced as oddities but soon came to be used on a wider scale.[24]

To account for the slowness of this diffusion into the Christian world several factors may be suggested: the lack of skills of the European peasantry, which may have been a serious barrier since some of the crops were very difficult to grow in the new environment; the inability of feudal landholding arrangements to receive certain of the new crops, particularly specialty crops; the limited use of irrigation in European agriculture and in particular the near absence of very heavy irrigation; and the lower population density of medieval Europe, which made it unnecessary, and perhaps uneconomic, to find ways of getting very high returns from the soil. The unfavourable climate of Europe also placed a northward limit on the diffusion of some of the new crops, and may have delayed diffusion into certain regions until hardier varieties were developed. But the importance of climate seems in many areas to be secondary. In Sicily, Spain and the Crusader kingdoms, the Christians conquered lands in which the new agriculture had already been practised for some centuries and where probably all the new crops (except coconut palms and mango trees) were grown. Yet, with the exception of a part of the coastal plain in the Holy Land and some of the lower Jordan valley, these crops – often previously grown on a wide scale – tended to disappear from the conquered regions as a type of land use was introduced that was centred much more heavily on grazing and the cultivation of wheat, barley and the traditional crops of European agriculture. Thus we find in the first half of the thirteenth century Frederic II of Sicily sending to Tyre for experts in sugar production, the sugar industry having apparently died out in Sicily.[25] In the following century, Jaime II of Aragon sent to Sicily in an effort to reintroduce sugar and cotton cultivation into the lands he had conquered; but it seems unlikely that his mission was altogether successful, since sugar growing did not revive (on any scale at least) in Sicily till the fifteenth century.[26] In the same way, many of the other crops – especially those which were difficult to grow – seem to have disappeared from the lands which the Christians recaptured from the Muslims. Lacking skills, incentives, favourable attitudes and receptive institutions, Christian agriculturalists seemed unable or unwilling to accept the new crops even when they got them on a platter.[27]

The contrasting performances of Europe and Black Africa on the one hand, and the Islamic world on the other hand, suggests that the unusual receptivity and powers of conduction of the latter deserve more study. In particular, more attention should be given to the main corridor of Islamic diffusion – agricultural and other – with its openings on India, Persia and Iraq in the east and its termini in the western Maghrib, Spain and West Africa. Over it were to travel not only the new crops, irrigation technology and farming techniques of the agricultural revolution but much else that was to contribute to the "orientalization" of the western parts of Dār al-Islām, serving at once to unify the Islamic world and to set it apart.

Part Three
The mechanics of diffusion

CHAPTER SEVENTEEN

The agents

Who introduced the new crops into the Islamic world, and who transmitted them from one part of that world to another? Did rulers play a leading role by bringing exotic plants from afar to ornament their gardens or to grace their tables? Or did great landowners and other wealthy people import these plants, either to add to their collections or for commercial production? Or were the vectors of the new crops simple peasants who in the course of their migrations westwards brought with them the plants they had been used to growing – and eating – farther to the east? We cannot be sure, since with a few exceptions the sources are mute about how our plants were moved from place to place. We may suspect, however, that all three groups were variously involved in the work of diffusion. Before it came to be a common crop in a region, a plant may have been brought there on a number of different occasions by agents who belonged to different social classes, were actuated by different motives and operated independently of one another. And after an initial introduction, other carriers may have been responsible for the secondary diffusion which could make the plant a commonplace.

The near but not complete silence of our sources about the agents who transmitted the crops studied in this volume suggests that the unsung heroes of this story were often common people who in their travels – or more probably their migrations – carried over shorter or longer distances the crucial seeds, roots, cuttings or live plants. For a few of the crops, such an agency seems almost certain. Thus sorghum, for instance, appears to have been considered an inferior grain by the wealthy and is not even mentioned in the aristocratic cookbooks of the thirteenth century, though it was by then a very common crop in many parts of the Islamic world. If rulers and other wealthy people grew the plant at all, they wanted it to look at and not to eat. It was rather peasants who were interested in sorghum as a food plant: they began growing it, we may suppose, for their own consumption and that of their animals, though later, as new tastes spread, possibilities of producing for the market may have opened up.[1] Quite possibly, peasants were also responsible for the introduction of those exotic plants which could be grown only with difficulty in the hostile environment of the early Islamic world. The Indians,

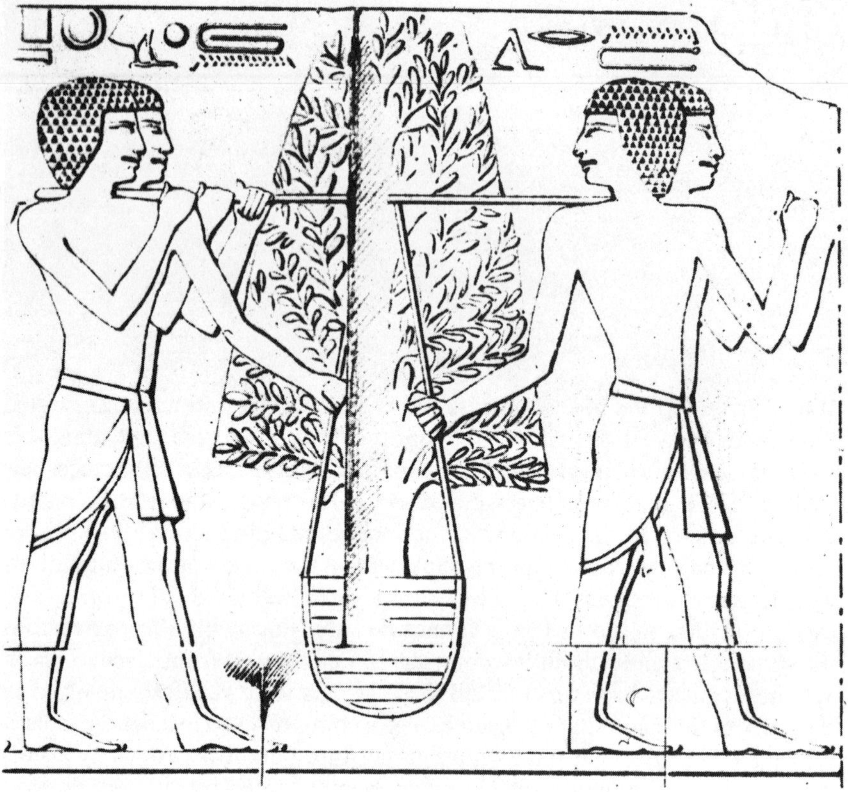

Carvings from the Temple of Deir al-Bahari depict the botanical expedition of Queen Hatshepsut to the Land of Punt, *c.* 1495 B.C. This detail shows the carrying of a frankincense tree. (E. Naville, *The Temple of Deir el Bahari*, pt III (London, 1898))

Persians, Yemeni, Hijazi and Syrians who migrated westward may have carried not only these new plants but also the crucial techniques of growing them. As we know from the study of industrial technologies, difficult skills are most readily diffused by the migration of those who possess them. Only with great difficulty are they learned afresh by other people in other places.[2]

On the other hand, the surviving documents that tell of early plant introductions stress – and perhaps exaggerate – the role played by rulers and their entourage of courtiers, administrators, soldiers and scientists. Kings might receive exotic plants as gifts from other rulers or as tribute from conquered provinces; or they might send out expeditions, botanical or other, that brought back new plants. The earliest recorded plant introduction was the result of a royal expedition: Queen Hatshepsut of Egypt, probably in 1495 B.C., sent ships to the land of Punt, which may have been the Somali coast, and these brought back *inter alia* thirty-one incense trees.[3] Similarly, the Assyrian king Tiglath-pileser I (1115?–1102 B.C.?), claimed that "I took cedar, box-tree and Kanish oak from the lands over which I had gained dominion – such trees as no previous king among my forefathers had ever planted – and I planted them in the gardens of my land. I took rare orchard fruits not found in my land and filled the orchards of Assyria with them."[4] A later Assyrian king, Sennacherib, told in a text of 691 B.C. that he "made a large park wherein are planted all worth-while plants, fruit trees such as grow in the mountains and in Chaldea...as well as cotton" – the last of which introductions appears to have failed.[5] In the fourth century B.C. Alexander's expedition to the Persian Gulf and India brought back knowledge of many exotic plants, though perhaps not the living plants,[6] while in the second century B.C. a Chinese emperor sent to western Asia a military expedition which introduced to China the grape vine and alfalfa.[7] Similarly, plants and agricultural produce could be sent as gifts or tribute to a ruler: in 430 the Chinese court received cotton as a gift from Java or Sumatra,[8] and in 647 it was sent spinach plants of Nepal.[9]

The literature of classical Islam offers many similar examples of rulers who were given or who sent for plants from afar. Having exotic plants, whether useful or merely ornamental, may have appealed variously to rulers' collecting instincts, their scientific interests, their love of gardens, their *gourmandise*, their desire for new cures or their eagerness to make money. Many of these alleged introductions occurred in the eighth and ninth centuries. A vizier of the caliph al-Mahdī (775–85), for instance, sent envoys to India to study the medicinal and other plants of that country, specimens of which were almost certainly brought back to Baghdad.[10] The '*Abdallāwī* melon of Egypt (= *Cucumis melo* L. var. *Chate* Naud.) is said to have been brought there from Khurāsān in the year 825 by the governor, 'Abd Allāh ibn Ṭāhir.[11] Slightly later, the Ṭūlūnid ruler of Egypt, Khumārawaih (884–95), made an outlandish garden beside his palace where he grew many kinds of rare plants.[12] In Spain, 'Abd al-Raḥmān I (756–88) is said to have filled the park which surrounded his palace, al-Ruṣāfa, with trees from all over the world; this ruler sent an agent to Syria who returned with many seeds and plants which were grown in this garden.[13] According to one source, a particularly fine kind of pomegranate, the *safarī*, was brought by his agent from Syria to al-Ruṣāfa, whence it was diffused through all of Muslim Spain;[14] another source states, perhaps incorrectly, that the first date palm in Spain grew in this garden.[15] The *boñigar* fig is said to have been brought to Spain from Constantinople by an emissary sent to that city by 'Abd al-Raḥmān II (822–52).[16] Even in much later times the interest of Islamic rulers in exotic plants had not completely disappeared: one Yemeni sultan, whose grandfather had introduced a new kind of tree from India, is said to have received in the year 1369 an embassy from Calicut bearing large numbers of rare plants and birds, while another ruler sent an envoy to Abyssinia for cuttings of the *qāt* bush, which prospered thereafter in the Yemen.[17]

A few such legends speak specifically of crops studied in this volume. Thus, as has already been mentioned, a fifteenth-century Yemeni treatise on farming relates that the caliph al-Ma'mūn (813–33) brought sour-orange trees from north-eastern Persia to Rayy,[18] while the tenth-century writer al-Mas'ūdī tells that the caliph al-Qāhir (932–4) planted in Baghdad a courtyard with sour-orange trees brought from India via Oman and Basra.[19] Although this second account can hardly refer to the first appearance of the sour orange in Iraq, it may tell of a reintroduction of this plant or of the introduction of a special variety; as we have already suggested, successive reintroductions of a plant to a region may have been common, and could have permitted selection of the most suitable varieties as well as secondary diffusion within the region. An episode similar to the one just mentioned may account for the introduction of the sour orange to Spain: in about the year 976 the Chamberlain, al-Manṣūr, allegedly planted the Patio do los Naranjos in Cordova, an example which was followed in the gardens of many mosques and palaces in other parts of Spain.[20] With the coming of the Spanish *taifas*, or petty kingdoms, in the eleventh century, much more secondary diffusion within Spain may have occurred as courts were established in many cities and rulers competed with one another in patronizing learning, building palaces and planting gardens.[21] The geographer al-'Udhrī relates that one such king, al-Mu'taṣim ibn Ṣumādiḥ of Almería (1051–91), introduced into his palace gardens many rare plants including the banana and sugar cane – which, as we have seen, had already made their first appearance elsewhere in Spain.[22] In the Yemen, towards the end of the thirteenth century, the sultan al-Mālik al-Ashraf introduced the growing of rice into the valley of Zabīd; this same sultan also made a royal garden in Zabīd where many unusual trees were planted.[23] From West Africa comes one final example illustrating the role that monarchs can play in crop diffusion: a text tells of a sultan of Kanem who attempted to grow sugar cane; the experiment, however, appears to have been unsuccessful, for later sources say nothing of the growing of sugar cane in Kanem, or indeed anywhere in West Africa.[24]

Thus the little the sources tell about the vectors of the crops studied in this volume, and of useful plants in general, affords some glimpses of rulers who played a role in the diffusion process. Since our information on this subject is so fragmentary, we may suppose that the sources tell only a part of this story of royal activity: there must be many other instances – condemned to oblivion – of kings and their officials who introduced or reintroduced plants that came from afar and provided the impetus that sent these plants still farther along their paths of diffusion. But what the sources say, and do not say, about the doings of rulers in the kingdom of vegetables can only give a distorted view of the agencies by which new crops were transmitted across the early Islamic world. In fact, the diffusion of the new crops must have been the achievement of thousands of mostly unknown individuals from many levels of society who moved plants over shorter or longer distances for many different reasons. Great or humble, they unwittingly collaborated in a vast undertaking that was to enlarge considerably the range of useful plants available over a large part of the known world. They also prepared the stage for still further migrations of these same plants in the early modern era.

CHAPTER EIGHTEEN

A medium for diffusion

The context in which the agents of diffusion operated seems to have favoured their activities. Indeed we shall argue that the early centuries of Islam saw the creation of a medium for diffusion of great efficiency: it was peculiarly receptive to novelties and favoured their transmission. Many areas of life were touched by its powers of conduction, of which agriculture was only one.

The creation of this medium began with the Muslim conquests of the seventh and eighth centuries which united – or began to unite – a large part of the known world, bringing the conquered territories for a time under one rule, and more durably under one language, one religion and one legal system. Although Muḥammad's State was a very loose alliance depending on allegiance to the Prophet, and although centrifugal forces at all times worked against centralizing tendencies, the relatively strong State which emerged under the Umayyads and the early 'Abbāsids was an umbrella under which other kinds of unification took place.[1] Gradually, Arabic displaced indigenous tongues as the language of administration, of higher culture and – to varying degrees – of common speech.[2] In time, more and more of the conquered peoples were converted to the religion of the Prophet, so that although non-believers were at first very numerous and religious minorities remained important throughout the period of classical Islam, the State came to be an Islamic state and the people it governed came to be predominantly Muslim. The apparatus of the State was the means for other kinds of unification: of law, of coinage and of weights and measures.[3] It also forged, when it did not inherit them, links of communication – roads, caravan routes, ports, postal and courier services, and a far-reaching network of smoke and flame signals – which drew still more closely together the far-flung territories of the caliphates.[4]

The area thus united was not only large but highly diversified. Its heartland lay in the semi-arid and arid lands of the southern and eastern Mediterranean, the Middle East and the Arabian peninsula; but it included tropical and semi-tropical regions in sub-Saharan Africa, monsoon-drenched lands in the Yemen and north-west India, near-temperate lands in the interior of Spain, and regions with a severe continental climate in Central Asia. The variety of plant life was very great.[5] So was the variety of human achievement: as the regions of this empire had developed in varying degrees of isolation from each other, they had produced a wealth of different traditions in every sphere of life from scholarship to agriculture. They thus had much to teach each other and much to learn. What is more, the empire was strategically located, with footholds on all three continents of the Old World. By reaching beyond the frontiers of Islam still further into these continents, the Arabs and the peoples they conquered came in contact with the still greater diversity of this wider world, where, *inter alia*, other useful plants and agricultural practices were to be found.[6] In fact, from the period of classical Islam until the European voyages of discovery, Muslim scholars were unique in their extensive knowledge of the different parts of the known world.[7]

Within the area of Arab dominion, and to some extent beyond, there was much movement of men, of goods, of technology, of information and of ideas. Ibn Khaldūn wrote of the Arabs that "all their customary activities lead to travel and movement",[8] and so it was to become not only for those of Arabic stock but also for the conquered peoples. The very conquest and settlement of new areas often led to important displacements of peoples. When an area was overrun by Arabs and their allies, the conquering soldiers – mostly from distant places – were often encouraged to settle in the conquered lands.[9] Another wave of migrations occurred when the Jews of formerly Byzantine, Sasanian and Visigothic territories, many of whom had collaborated with the invading armies, began to spread out through the early Islamic world. Further movements followed the conquests with the flight of some conquered peoples, their forcible displacement and the long-distance trade in captured slaves. After a very short time, most regions of the Islamic world showed an astonishing mixture of peoples. Early Basra, for instance, had important groups of Indians, Persians, Yemeni and other Arabs.[10] The region of Baalbek was settled by Persians and Yemeni.[11] Muslim Spain was settled by Berbers from North Africa, as well as by Yemeni, other Arabs and other easterners.[12] Visitors to Palermo in Sicily found in the city a population which included Greeks, Lombards, Jews, Slavs, Berbers, Persians, Tartars and Negroes.[13] These cases were not exceptional. In almost every part of the early Islamic world an amalgam was forming of indigenous and foreign elements, the latter coming from diverse, often distant, places and bringing to their new homes much that was exotic.

To the movement of peoples initiated by the conquests and their aftermath were soon added other kinds of displacement. The pilgrimages that Muslims made in great numbers, and especially the pilgrimage to Mecca, brought together people from the far corners of the earth and thus were a vehicle of prime importance for cultural transmission. In Mecca itself, according to Ibn Jubair, was to be found every kind of fruit, merchandise and *agrément*, coming from India, Abyssinia, Iraq, the Yemen, Khurāsān, the Maghrib and elsewhere. "These things", he states, "can neither be counted nor named...

There is no merchandise or precious object on earth which is not to be found in this town at the time of the pilgrimage."[14] Many pilgrims took advantage of their displacement to indulge in further travel: to carry out business, to visit relatives, to study in foreign centres of learning and just to see sights.[15] Trade by professional merchants also led to much movement. Very soon after the rise of Islam, Muslim and Jewish merchants were penetrating to the outer limits of the caliphate. By the middle of the eighth century they had reached far beyond these bounds and established counters in India, China and East Africa.[16] Hand in hand with trade went missionary activity, as holy men followed in the footsteps of merchants to preach to isolated Muslim communities abroad and to convert the heathen.[17] Thus both trade and religion linked distant outposts into a network which spanned the continents. Like men of religion, scholars also travelled widely to study and to teach; the authors of the Arabic manuals on farming, botany and pharmacy which have been used as primary sources for this book nearly all travelled far and wide, some the whole length and breadth of the Islamic world.[18] Finally refugees, of whom the political fragmentation and instability of the Islamic world brought forth an increasing number, account for still more movement. Many scientists were forced by changes of rulers to move to new patrons or new centres of learning – and in some cases to move several times. For similar reasons humbler people, too, sometimes had to resettle.[19]

But perhaps any attempt to explain, or even to describe, the widespread movement of people across the early Islamic world is doomed to fail. All through the literary sources from the medieval Islamic world are found accounts that suggest an almost incomprehensible amount of coming and going across huge stretches of land and water. Every class of people, it seems, was prone to this restlessness; all travelled: the rich and the poor, the scholar and the illiterate, the holy and the not so holy. Poverty was no obstacle, as one could move by foot, begging along the way; relatives could be imposed upon endlessly; patrons were readily found for scholars or holy men, or those who posed as such; a place to bunk, and perhaps to eat, was available outside the main mosque in most cities.[20] Lured on in search of money, adventure or truth, Muslims from every region and of every station left home and roamed to and fro over the continents, taking with them knowledge of the farming techniques, plant life and cookery of their homelands and seeing on their way the agricultural practices, plants and foods of new lands.

In their travels the early Muslims were on the lookout for whatever could be learned or bought. This was an attitude which went back to the earliest days of Islam. Perhaps because the Arabs came out of a cultural (and sometimes an actual) desert, and overran centres of high and ancient civilization, they were from the beginning aware of their intellectual and material deficiencies, very receptive to the new, eager to learn from those who could teach, avid to ape the fashions of the great centres.[21] Particularly keen to assimilate the ways of their imagined betters was a class of people that was to become a permanent feature in medieval Islamic society, though its membership was constantly changing: the wealthy, privileged groups of rulers, their families, their favourites, their ministers and others who rose to positions of power around the rulers and their courts. They were at once most sensitive to their shortcomings and best able to remedy these. The uncertain duration of their fortunes only encouraged them to enjoy immediately and to the full whatever benefits wealth and power could bring. But they were not alone. On the contrary, they were followed to varying degrees by other people of means, particularly the great merchants and landowners who formed an important element in the cities of classical Islam. Together, these wealthy classes set about acquiring the trappings of wealth and culture with all the enthusiasm of the *nouveau riche*.[22]

To overcome their sense of inferiority, many began collecting in the grand manner, building up collection of whatever took their fancy or whatever they thought might impress: rare birds, wild animals, exotic plants, beautiful slaves, jewels, porcelain, and books – all from all over the world.[23] An unkind soul might go on to remark that the books themselves were often little more than collections of long lists of foreign or archaic words and their meanings; of odd facts; of names and descriptions of plants, medicines or places; or of sayings, doings and judgments; and so on. They offered little in the way of theory or interpretation. The modern reader may find such books indigestible, but they delighted the mind that sought to possess, enjoy and doubtless to show off all the good things the world had to offer.

Nowhere indeed is the collecting instinct of the early Islamic world more clearly seen than in its scholarship, which, often with royal support, set out systematically to collect the knowledge of all ages and of all peoples. In Umayyad times (661–750) we catch a glimpse of an activity which shortly afterwards was to become of the greatest importance. The *bait al-ḥikma*, or library, of the first Umayyad caliph, Mu'āwiya I, passed into the hands of his heir, Khālid ibn Yazīd ibn Mu'āwiya, who avidly collected manuscripts and surrounded himself with copypists, translators and scholars. Of himself, Khālid is reported to have said, "I am not a scholar...I am only a collector of books."[24] With the establishment of the 'Abbāsid caliphate in 750, the task of assimilating the knowledge of the ages was pursued still more vigorously. The early caliphs in Baghdad were nearly all bibliophiles; some were also scholars. They collected books on a grand scale, sending out expeditions to procure rare works and sponsoring an ambitious programme of translation: works of all kinds were translated into Arabic from Greek, Syriac, Pahlavi, Persian, Sanskrit and Hindi.[25] Private families in Baghdad built up smaller collections of books and also patronized scholars to make translations.[26] Amongst the books translated were a good number on agriculture, botany and pharmacology, all of which helped to make early Muslims familiar with plants they had not seen. Several early lexicographical works, such as those by al-Aṣma'ī (d. 828?) and Abū Ḥanīfa al-Dīnawarī (d. 895), were largely devoted to the identification of plants.

The fashion in Baghdad was soon copied by Islamic rulers elsewhere, and by the end of the tenth century there were bibliophile rulers in Cairo and Cordova who had amassed great collections of books. According to al-Maqrīzī, the Fāṭimid caliph of Egypt al-ʻAzīz (d. 996) had a library which numbered between 120,000 and 160,000 volumes.[27] The library of his successor, al-Ḥākim, was supposed to contain the greatest collection of books any prince had ever assembled.[28] By Ayyūbid times we learn of an Egyptian book collection which was said, doubtless with exaggeration, to contain as many as a million volumes.[29] Similarly, in Muslim Spain the buying of culture was pursued with a vengeance. Almost all of the Umayyad rulers of Spain went to great lengths to attract scholars from eastern centres of learning and to build libraries; expeditions were sent out to buy eastern books, which, it was said, became available in Spain before anyone had read them in the east. By the time of al-Ḥakam II (961–76), the royal library contained, according to al-Maqqarī, some 400,000 volumes, the listing of which filled forty-four index catalogues of twenty folios each. Translators, copyists and bookbinders were legion.[30] But although royal libraries were naturally the largest, they were by no means the only big collections of books in the early Islamic world. Almost all important mosques had libraries and there were also many large private collections of books.[31] Great or small, royal or private, religious or lay, these collections of books were at once a sign of the great amount of diffusion which had taken place in the early Islamic world and a vehicle for still more diffusion.

In the medium for diffusion which was being created in the early centuries of Islam there were many directions of flow, as an essentially syncretic society snapped up whatever seemed useful or amusing in all of the areas that had been brought under common rule. Thus Greek, Roman, Byzantine, Egyptian, Persian and Indian and Chinese elements were all taken up where they were found and diffused outwards. But there was one main artery of diffusion. It traversed the whole of the Islamic world from its eastern to its western extremities, beginning in north-western India and Persia and ending in Spain, Morocco and West Africa. The eastern aperture of this channel was opened with the conquest of Persia in the seventh century and the conquest of the province of Sind, in the north-west of the Indian sub-continent, early in the eighth century. It became operative almost immediately, as merchants, peasants, scholars and soldiers began moving into and out of Persia and Sind. Of the early diffusion of eastern culture, technology and learning towards the western parts of the Islamic world, there are many signs. In the Umayyad desert palaces on the fringes of the Transjordanian desert, for instance, are found many Persian influences.[32] In the seventh century a monk at a monastery on the upper Euphrates wrote a treatise on astronomy and geography in which for the first time outside of India there is mention of Indian numerals.[33] In the eighth century, Persian scientists used the tables of the Indian treatise on astronomy *Siddhanta*, and later translated this work from Sanskrit into Arabic.[34] In this same period Arabs and others in the early

Islamic world must have been exposed to many new crops which they saw growing in the fields and gardens of Persia and India.

With the rise of the 'Abbāsid caliphate in 750 this opening on Persia and India became of very great importance. The 'Abbāsid capitals at Baghdad and Sāmarra were the gateways through which eastern influences of all kinds entered the Islamic world and began their passage westwards. In particular, Persian traditions to varying degrees displaced those of Arabia and the Mediterranean. The 'Abbāsid court was modelled on the Sasanian court, and courtiers and wealthy people set out to ape the customs of that brilliant pre-Islamic society, whose rulers "remained in popular memory as the most powerful princes in the world".[35] Sasanian society, having itself been syncretic, had already absorbed many Indian and some Chinese influences which thus indirectly reached the 'Abbāsids.[36] But the 'Abbāsids also had direct contacts with India which were to be of great importance. In the time of the caliph al-Mahdī (775–85) a mission was sent to India to study Indian medicine; by the time of Hārūn al-Rashīd (786–809) a number of Indian physicians of repute were established in Baghdad, one of whom – a court physician – wrote a book of Indian remedies. Because many of the plants used in Indian medicine were still unknown or little known in the Arab world, these contacts were important not only for medicine but also for botany and agriculture.[37] By the tenth and eleventh centuries, although the province of Sind had been lost to the 'Abbāsids, knowledge of India had increased greatly: there was a whole chapter on India in al-Mas'ūdī's *Golden Meadows*, and al-Bīrūnī (d. after 1050), "the most original and profound of medieval Islamic scholars", wrote an impressive book on India and translated several works from Sanskrit to Arabic.[38]

The fragmentation of the 'Abbāsid empire by no means ended the flow across the Islamic world. Long after the end of political unity, a sense of nationhood, of belonging to a community or *umma*, prevailed amongst the inhabitants of Dār al-Islām, favouring the same kinds of contact among different regions that had occurred in high 'Abbāsid times.[39] Political disintegration may even for a time have accelerated the flow. For in the eastern part of the Islamic world there appeared kingdoms with new capitals where scholarship flourished and further discoveries of Persian and Indian learning were made;[40] the penetration of the Ghaznavids into northern India in the early eleventh century reopened for a time the door – by then almost closed – on Indian learning. And farther to the west, there sprang up a whole series of kingdoms whose rulers and courts consciously set about to import the learning and the fashions of the east. Thus in Ṭūlūnid Egypt (868–905), the founder of the dynasty, Ibn Ṭūlūn, and his successor, Khumārawaih, who had both lived in the 'Abbāsid capital at Sāmarra, followed 'Abbāsid models. Mosques, palaces, gardens, court etiquette, textiles, pottery and cookery were all copied from the east, making the Ṭūlūnid capital "un bloc asiatique transporté dans la Vallée du Nil".[41] As one writer points out, "fashions which had seemed strange and exotic in the 'Abbāsid capital had become commonplace in Egypt a century later".[42] A new wave of migration from the east into Egypt helped this process of assimilation: scholars, functionaries, craftsmen, merchants and others from Persia and Iraq migrated to Egypt from the ninth to the eleventh centuries, allowing eastern influences to penetrate into Egypt long after the fall of the Ṭūlūnids.[43] By the eleventh century, too, Muslim merchants were trading on a large scale directly between Egypt and India.[44]

Similarly, the Maghrib was ruled from the eighth to the tenth century by a number of dynasties which drew heavily on oriental inspiration: the Fāṭimids, the Aghlabids, the Rustamids and the Idrīsids. The last three of these were founded by immigrants from the east and attracted still other oriental immigrants who were responsible for the importation of traditions from Egypt, Syria, Mesopotamia and Persia. The theology, learning, secular and religious architecture, ceramics and cookery of this region all bear the imprint of the east.[45]

Lying at the end – or one of the ends – of this corridor of diffusion was Muslim Spain, the Far West of the Islamic world and for some centuries a backwater. At the time of the conquest of Spain, many Syrians, Yemeni and other easterners had settled in al-Andalus, bringing eastern ways to a region that in Roman times had been relatively isolated. The *orientalización* of Spain was hastened by the Spanish Umayyad emirs and caliphs, themselves of Syrian origin, who set about importing on a grand scale eastern administrative practices, law, architecture, plants, fashions, *objets d'art* and, as we have seen, learning. They took as their model first Umayyad Damascus, then 'Abbāsid Baghdad; Egyptian influences were also seen in their courts.[46] They were followed by their richer subjects, some of whom showed an almost indecent haste to ape the fashions of the east: Ziryāb, a musician who came to Spain from Baghdad in 821–2, was said to have "taught the people of al-Andalus to use vessels of crystal instead of gold and silver; to sleep on a soft couch of leather instead of on cotton blankets...Change of clothing according to the seasons was another of the improvements introduced."[47] The collapse of the Spanish Umayyad dynasty from 1008 onwards and its replacement by a host of petty kingdoms, or *taifas*, only speeded up the process of diffusion from the east into Spain and within Spain itself. For the rulers of the new kingdoms competed to establish courts and capital cities modelled on the capitals of the east, on Umayyad Cordova, and on those of neighbouring rivals. When some of the northern kingdoms, such as Toledo, fell to the Christians in the eleventh century, further diffusion occurred as courtiers and scholars from the conquered regions found new patrons in the south.[48]

By the twelfth century, however, this great corridor of diffusion which spanned the Islamic world had largely ceased to be operative. At its western end much diffusion was still occurring within Spain itself, between Spain and North Africa, and from North Africa into West Africa; there was even a reverse flow from Spain back to Egypt and the Near East.[49] But the flow from the eastern extremities of the Islamic world towards the west had dwindled – though not stopped – as the eastern doorway to China and India was gradually closed and the Islamic world – once so open to the outside – turned in upon itself. In time, the east was drained of its novelties and, as the western regions developed, its cultural ascendancy was no longer recognized. The unity of the world of classical Islam began to fragment, as that world entered upon a period of long, though often interrupted, decay.

But for a period of four centuries or more that world was a medium of diffusion of unusual efficiency through which were transmitted new demands and the means to satisfy these demands. Across it travelled not only the new crops and agricultural practices studied in this volume but all the other elements from which classical Islamic culture was to be fashioned. And as strong new links were forged across space, the links with the past were nearly everywhere weakened and to a surprising degree severed. A civilization was appearing that looked outwards rather than backwards.

CHAPTER NINETEEN

The pull of demand

But a medium of diffusion, however great its receptivity and its powers of conduction, was not enough. For the new crops, and with them changes in agricultural practice, to be disseminated on a wide scale much more was needed. On the one hand there had to be a substantial demand for the new crops as foodstuffs or, in the case of cotton, as a textile fibre – a demand which had to be created, since the crops were new. And on the other hand producers had to be able and willing to supply the crops at prices which would permit supply and demand curves to intersect at significant levels of production. These conditions were satisfied, it seems, by the action of a number of factors, some of which served to create a growing demand while others helped to facilitate supply. They were at work in every part of the Islamic world. Together, they constituted the economic framework in which the carriers of the new crops could successfully operate.

One could of course argue that demand is not a problem: supply will create its own demand. Once a plant had been introduced as an oddity, perhaps in a royal garden or in a peasant's plot, its possibilities would be seen by a few who would start to use it, and as a matter of course demand would grow. This explanation is perhaps correct for a few of the new plants. But in the main we do not believe that the process was so simple. What was in fact a radical change in diet and in habits of dress was not likely to occur so easily. The evidence suggests that the process of enlarging demand was more complex, more deserving of study.

In fact, many of the new crops first came to be known in the Mediterranean and Middle East as medicines used in India.[1] Some of these had been described in the *Enquiry into Plants* of Theophrastus (d. *c.* 285 B.C.), who had learned of them through Alexander's expedition to the Persian Gulf and India.[2] They had then passed into the *Materia medica* of Dioscorides (fl. first century) and into other classical books of simples. As a result, small quantities of sugar and rice, for instance, were imported into the classical Mediterranean as medicines, though they were not grown there. In the Sasanian empire of Persia (226–651), which extended to the Indus valley, further knowledge of Indian medicinal plants was obtained as Indian scientific books were studied and Indian cures imported.[3] After the rise of Islam this knowledge of Indian plants gradually passed into the Islamic world. Greek, Roman, Syriac, Persian and Indian works of medicine were studied and often translated.[4] In the time of the caliph al-Mahdī (775–85) a mission was sent to India to study the drugs and other natural products of that country; this mission was headed by Yaḥya ibn Khālid, the vizier of the caliph and tutor to Hārūn al-Rashīd.[5] By such means the inhabitants of the early Islamic world become aware of the alleged medicinal properties of many exotic plants. We may assume that some of these were imported and sold at high prices as medicines, though nothing is known about this trade until a later period. It is also possible that this market for foreign medicines favoured import substitution and that some of the plants studied in this volume thus came to be grown locally instead of being imported. However, we think this unlikely. The market for exotic cures must at all times have been small, composed largely of wealthy faddists willing to pay high prices to treat real and imagined ailments. By itself, it probably would not have stimulated any significant amount of import substitution, particularly as most of these plants were difficult to grow in the climate of the Islamic world.

The next step was therefore the enlargement of demand – and its transformation. Instead of being used mainly or exclusively as medicines, the new plants came to be demanded as foodstuffs or, in the case of cotton, as a textile fibre. As early as the first century, India exported to the east coast of Africa rice, sugar, cotton goods and indigo, all of which were later, probably in Islamic times, introduced into East Africa as crops.[6] It seems unlikely that this was a commerce in medicines: rice and sugar were almost certainly imported into East Africa as foodstuffs, cotton in the form of cloth and clothing, and indigo as dye. The quantity demanded would almost certainly be larger than when these products were used merely as medicines. The way was thus being prepared for the later introduction of new plants into the agriculture of East Africa. A similar growth of demand may be seen in the Sasanian empire. Trade with India probably familiarized Persians and others in the empire with the plants described in the Indian works on medicine and pharmacy, which undoubtedly mentioned nearly all the plants studied here. In time, many of these came to be used as foods as well as medicines, and as demand for them grew a few of these Indian plants were introduced into the agriculture of the Sasanian empire. The extent of this Sasanian import substitution, however, was very limited: it occurred in the case of a very few crops and it affected only restricted areas.[7] For most of our crops and for most of the areas conquered by the Arabs, the crucial enlargement of demand did not occur until the centuries following the rise of Islam.

The broadening of demand in the early Islamic world was effected through the activities of many people in many walks of life. Migrants must have played a part: after the conquests a crucial role may have been played by Indian settlers who moved into Persia and by Indians and Persians who moved into

Iraq, while the later movement of easterners into the western parts of the caliphate must have carried new tastes farther to the west. Travel by westerners to the east must also have enlarged demand as westerners saw, tried, adopted, brought home and popularized the fashions of the great eastern centres. But we believe that rulers and their courts were also very important. The Arabic historians tell of great feasts offered by the caliphs, who spared no expense to regale guests with exotic dishes whose ingredients sometimes came from afar. Thus at a banquet offered by the Umayyad caliph Muʿāwiya (661–80), for instance, courtiers were given pies of sugar and milk; at a feast held in the ʿAbbāsid court in Sāmarra towards the middle of the ninth century guests were served sour oranges, a fruit which was said to be extremely rare.[8] In fact we cannot be sure that sugar was produced in Syria or sour oranges in Iraq at the time of these feasts; both may easily have been imported. Similarly, we learn of many new dishes served at these feasts, some of which were of Indian or Persian origin and not a few of which used our new plants. As the caliphate fragmented and new kingdoms appeared in both east and west, their rulers consciously set about recreating in their new capitals the life-styles of the eastern courts; they, too, sought to amaze guests with rare foods and exotic recipes of eastern origin.[9]

Rulers, moreover, helped to spread new demands not only horizontally but also vertically – down the social ladder as well as across space. For with an eagerness which is perhaps characteristic of societies which look abroad for their models, rulers were imitated to varying degrees by their courts, by the wealthy landowners, merchants and administrators who lived in early Islamic cities, and even by those of more modest station.[10] What was served on the tables of the very rich was soon being eaten by the slightly less rich. All the while demand for exotic foodstuffs grew.[11]

Eventually a critical point was reached in a particular region when demand was seen to be great enough to justify import substitution. Probably with great difficulty at first, perhaps even after many a setback, local sources of supply developed. Though these may in the beginning have been expensive, they probably cheapened as skills were acquired and the scale of production grew. With lower prices the market no doubt widened still further.

Occasionally the texts afford us glimpses of stages in this process. In the treatise of the tenth-century geographer Ibn Ḥawqal, we learn of a landowner, an emir of Mosul, who seized the right moment, after demand had become great enough, to start growing new crops: he planted some of his lands with cotton and rice, and as a result of these and other changes doubled his revenues.[12] This landowner was certainly not the first to grow these crops in this region; but he was able to take advantage of what seems to have been a continuous growth in demand for these crops, and his success in turn no doubt had a "demonstration effect" on other landowners and perhaps on peasants. The process must have worked in much the same way elsewhere, being repeated time and again in one part of the Islamic world after another, making available what had been costly imported foods and medicines to a wider market. By the thirteenth century, from which a few cookbooks have survived, the new foods seem to be commonplace, at least in the kitchens of those for whom the books were written – often, admittedly, well-to-do people.[13] Virtually all the crops are mentioned in these books. For most there are many recipes: there were dozens of different ways of preparing eggplants; sugar had become the main sweetening; the juice and flesh of sour oranges and lemons were widely used in preparing meats, fish, poultry and desserts; the uses of rice were legion; so were those of hard wheat. The enlargement of demand thus seems to have been carried to its conclusion by the time these books were written; indeed, since some of the dishes described in the recipe books were mentioned in much earlier texts, and were probably made in the same way in earlier times, the books may reflect a state in the culinary arts – and hence a broadening of demand – that had been reached some centuries before.

Something of the same process may be seen in the movement of cotton across the Islamic world. The first cotton or partially cotton cloths found in Egypt appar to be of Persian manufacture, doubtless imported by the rich who were adopting foreign fashions, perhaps not only in dress but in interior decoration.[14] Partially cotton cloths of slightly later manufacture, dating from the eighth and ninth centuries, were probably actually made in Egypt, but still imitated Persian designs and may still have used raw cotton imported from the east.[15] By the tenth century some cotton was grown in Egypt to cope with the increasing demand, though even then eastern designs were still being used; later centuries saw cotton become a much more important crop. In West Africa, in the following century, we catch another glimpse of a stage in the changing of taste: al-Idrīsī, writing of Silla and Takrūr, relates that "the rich wear clothes of cotton; the common people dress in wool".[16] This single sentence, seemingly trivial, speaks worlds to those who have ears to hear its message. It shows wealthy West Africans copying what had become the manner of dress of many Egyptians, who in turn had copied the easterners. We do not know when cotton growing was introduced into this region where today cotton is an important crop and the principal fibre from which clothes are made, but we may suppose that it was some time after the fashion set by the rich was sufficiently widespread, and hence the demand for cotton great enough, to induce some landowners and peasants to experiment with its cultivation. In much the same way, cotton must have moved from Egypt farther west, across the north of Africa into Spain and from one Mediterranean island to another.

CHAPTER TWENTY

Facilitating supply: irrigation

By itself an increase in demand could not bring about diffusion if there were obstacles which made the introduction of new crops too costly, thus preventing supply and demand curves from intersecting. We shall argue that the four centuries following the Arab conquests saw many changes in the countryside of the Islamic world which on balance facilitated supply or – to put it another way – moved supply curves downwards. One such change was in irrigation.

To grow many of the new crops on a large scale in the lands of the early Islamic world important advances were required in irrigation. Because they mostly originated in tropical or semi-tropical areas where there was a season of heavy rains, the new crops could be grown only with difficulty in the Middle East and the Mediterranean, where rainfall was not only low but also undependable. Even the light rain which did fall in the area into which they were introduced came largely at the wrong time of the year: in the winter instead of in the summer. Thus for most of the new crops artificial irrigation was required in the summer months and often over a longer period. Some were particularly demanding of water. Sugar cane, for instance, when grown along the Nile, required not only the river's annual flooding – or the equivalent amount of water artificially brought to the land – but twenty-eight subsequent waterings by noria; in Spain sugar cane was watered every four to eight days.[1] Though rice was grown as a non-irrigated crop in parts of China from the tenth century onwards, and could, according to Ibn al-ʻAwwām, be grown without irrigation in parts of Spain where rains were heavy, it was almost always grown in the Islamic world in swamps or on irrigated lands. Ibn Waḥshīya taught that it was to be sown on level land that was continuously covered with water from planting till harvest, and according to Ibn Luyūn it needed to be watered twice before the seed germinated and twice weekly thereafter.[2] Similarly, many of the other crops required heavy waterings through much of their growing season, especially in the summer months: bananas, mango trees, colocasia and cotton, for instance, were typically irrigated through long periods.[3] Most of the other crops, depending on where they were grown, either required shorter periods of irrigation or at least gave much greater yields if watered at the right time.[4]

Additional water was required on account of the novel rotations in which the new crops were used. As will be shown below, the new crops, being nearly all summer crops, were often combined with winter crops so that the land was under continuous, or nearly continuous, cultivation. The long periods of fallow of earlier agricultural traditions, during which the land regained its moisture, were to varying degrees done away with. Extra moisture had therefore to be supplied artificially.[5]

To be sure, the lands which the Arabs overran – and parts of the Arabian peninsula itself – had known irrigated agriculture for a long time: the Yemen, the Hadramaut, Egypt, the Levant, Mesopotamia, Persia and limited areas in Transoxania, North Africa and Spain had elaborate irrigation works, nearly all of which can be traced back to a remote antiquity. Most of these flourished as never before in the early centuries of the Christian era. But in the centuries leading up to the rise of Islam the irrigation systems of antiquity nearly all declined markedly. Governmental neglect, over-taxation and insecurity no doubt all played their part in the decay of irrigated agriculture.[6] So, too, did population decline, which seems to have afflicted the western Roman empire from the third century onwards, culminating in the disastrous plague of the sixth century.[7] Nearly everywhere canals, tunnels and aqueducts were allowed to silt up and were not cleaned out. Dams and weirs collapsed and were not rebuilt. Irrigated land was abandoned. Finally, a number of great disasters overtook these ancient irrigation systems: in the late sixth century the great Yemeni dam of Ma'rib broke, after which time there is no evidence that any Himyaritic irrigation works were in operation;[8] in the sixth century, too, floods submerged the whole of the Nile Delta, wreaking great damage;[9] and in the year 627 a huge flood on the Tigris and Euphrates destroyed many embankments and dams, including the great dam of Nimrud, leaving the lower reaches of the river a marshy quagmire.[10] In short, by their conquests the Arabs fell heir to systems of irrigation which nearly everywhere were in an advanced state of decay, if not in ruins.

Another problem with the Arab heritage of irrigation works was that, by and large, it did not provide the kind of irrigation the new crops required, namely watering through the summer months. Pre-Islamic irrigation had consisted mainly in the temporary trapping of rain water or river floods and the spreading of them by gravity flow over the land. It therefore brought water mainly in one season, the time of the rains or floods, and it irrigated mainly those lands which could be reached by gravity flow. Little or no irrigation water was provided in summer, when indeed it had not been wanted. To these general limitations there were certain exceptions. Some devices for lifting water out of wells and rivers were known either in pre-Islamic Arabia or in some of the lands the Arabs were to overrun: the *dalw*, or pail pulled by a rope passing through a pulley;[11] the *baddāla*, or pivoted trough;[12] the *shādūf*, or pole with a pail on one end and a counterweight on the other;[13] the *ṭanbūr*, or Archimedes' screw;[14] and certain but perhaps not all kinds of *nā'ūra*, or

A combination of *shādūfs* seen in Egypt at the beginning of the nineteenth century by the Napoleonic scientific expedition. The system was installed on the edge of the Nile as the river's flood subsided and was extended as the water level dropped. At the lowest level four men are shown lifting water into four channels, from which it flows into a reservoir; the next level is manned by three workers, and the higher levels by only two. As depicted, the system raised water a distance of 6 metres. (*Description de l'Egypte... Etat moderne* I i, plates II)

noria, a device for lifting water in a succession of revolving pots or boxes. However, all but the last of these devices used large amounts of human labour to lift relatively small amounts of water only a very short distance; by themselves they could not provide the kind of irrigation needed to make the new crops economic. The most efficient of these devices, the noria, was not used widely in pre-Islamic times, and the kind that was powered by animals – which was later to be the most common – may have been known in only one form or not at all.[15] Similarly, short-term storage was provided by some water-spreading dams, allowing the irrigation season to be prolonged for a month of more, and perennial storage could be had from basins, cisterns

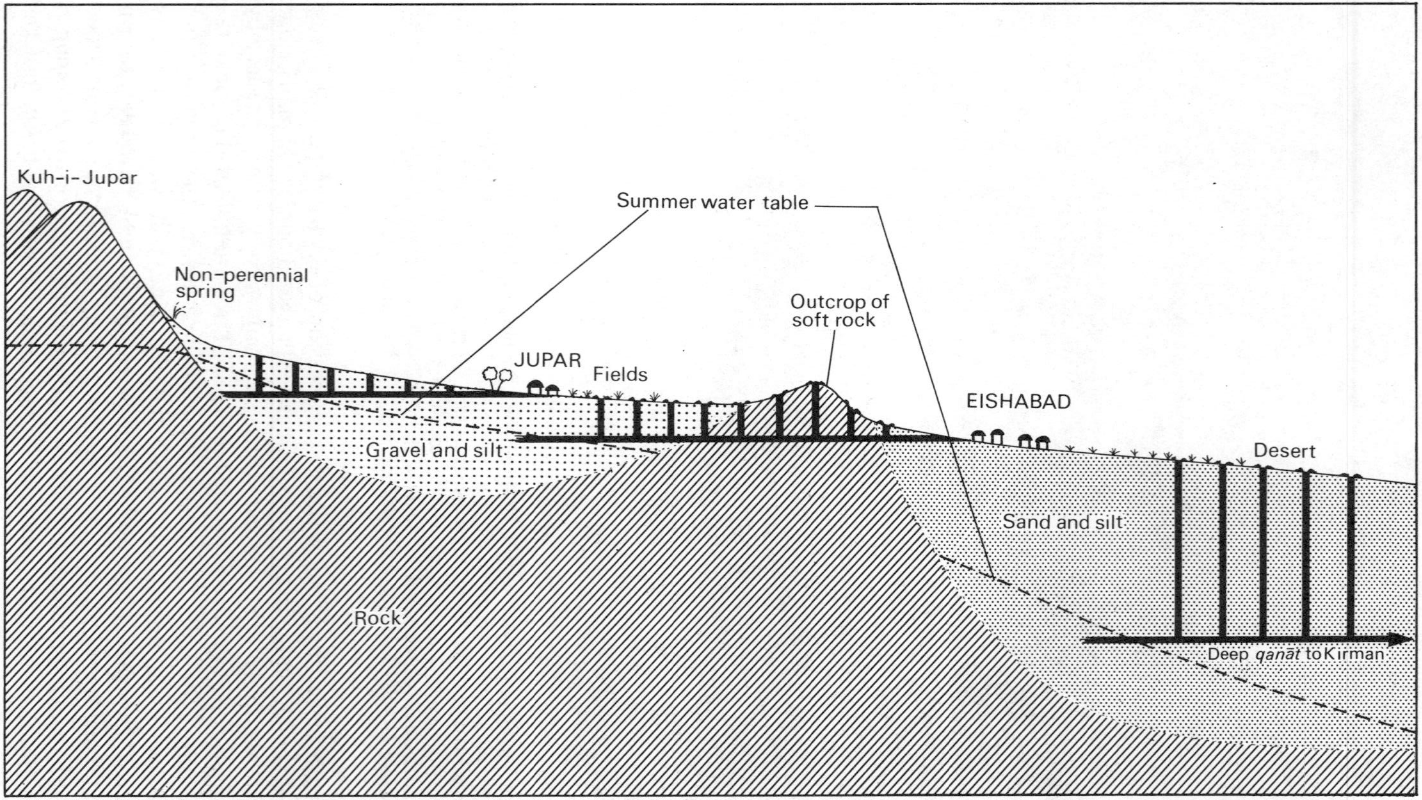

Cross-section of three *qanāts* in the environs of Kirman, Iran. The heavy lines show the slightly sloping underground canals, which tap ground water at three different levels, and the vertical access shafts. (After P. Beckett, "Qanats around Kirman", *Journal of the Royal Central Asian Society* XL (1953) 52)

or other kinds of reservoirs; but these latter techniques were used mainly for domestic water supplies and relatively little in agriculture.[16] Again, a flow of water over a longer period, or sometimes through the whole year, could be obtained from wells or from an underground canal – the *qanāt* or *kārīz* – which tapped an aquifer, sometimes at a great distance. But wells could usually provide only small amounts of water and required efficient lifting devices to be effective in agriculture; and the *qanāt*, a much more useful technique in the right environment, was used mainly in the agriculture of Persia, Mesopotamia and eastern Arabia, though it was known (but little used for agriculture) in the Levant and a few parts of Egypt.[17]

Thus on the eve of Islam the irrigation systems of the ancient world were in the main not ready to receive the new crops, at least not on a large scale. They brought too little water to too little land – and over too short a season. Before the new crops could move into most areas and certainly before they could have an important impact, the ancient system needed radical changes: extensions in the area of land irrigated, increases in the amount of water reaching the land in a given period of the year, and a lengthening of the season of irrigation to cover, if possible, the whole year.

These changes, it seems, soon came. Although the small amount of evidence available suggests that in the decades immediately following the Arab conquests the decay of irrigated farming may have continued, and perhaps even accelerated,[18] the process was soon reversed. With the consolidation of the Islamic state and the return of a greater measure of security, the attention of government, landowners and peasants soon turned to ways of increasing the productivity of the land. Rulers, their families and their officials were interested in increasing private and state revenues from the land; they also seem to have perceived, at least dimly, that the growth of old and new towns alike depended on a parallel growth of food and water supplies.[19] Indeed, the construction of hydraulic works to supply water to towns was often still more closely linked to agriculture, since the facilities that brought water to the towns were often also used to irrigate the countryside: the canal of Ḥailān, for instance, which brought water to Aleppo, also watered the fields of villages along its route, while the river which supplied the town of Aghmāt Warīka in southern Morocco was diverted onto fields, according to al-Idrīsī, on Mondays, Tuesdays and Wednesdays.[20]

But irrigated agriculture was promoted not only by the repair of old irrigation works and the construction of new ones: it was also advanced by the use of a wide range of techniques to catch, channel, store and lift the water that ultimately – when it was needed – was put on the land. Rainwater was captured in trenches on the sides of hills or as it ran down mountain gorges and into valleys; other surface water was taken from springs, brooks, rivers and oases; and underground water – the supply of which varied least through the seasons and over the years – was tapped by creating new springs, by cutting channels down to aquifers and by digging various kinds of wells.

Water thus obtained could be moved along underground tunnels carved through bedrock, many of which were miles long;[21] in surface ditches dug through the earth or cut through rock; in canals made from stone or brick or in pipes of tile or lead; or above the ground, in various kinds of aqueduct.[22] At different points in its flow, water could be diverted, held and raised by weirs, diversion dams and – to an extent – storage dams; additional storage could be had from artificial lakes, basins, pools, reservoirs and cisterns.[23] To raise water to lands not reached by gravity flow there were the various lifting devices described above, powered by men, animals or moving water: the *dalw*, the *baddāla*, the *shādūf*, Archimedes' screw and the noria. The last of these, the noria or water wheel, could take many forms. It could be turned by men, animals or water, and could raise water in pots, buckets or boxes attached either to a chain turned by the wheel or to the wheel itself. By using very long chains or very large wheels, the noria could raise water to considerable heights.[24]

In all this profusion of irrigation technology there was much that was old and only a little that was, strictly speaking, new. One striking innovation is the type of cistern, dating from Umayyad and Aghlabid times, that was used around Qairawān and in much of the rest of Ifrīqiya.[25] Another innovation, it has been suggested, may have been made in the technique of digging wells;[26] and quite possibly certain types of noria – particularly those driven by animals – did not appear until after the Arab conquests.[27] It is also possible that progress was made during early Islamic times in the technique of building storage dams.[28] But for the most part the technology used by the Arabs and those they conquered was old: it formed part of the legacy of irrigation devices which passed from the ancient to the early Islamic world. The Islamic contribution was less in the invention of new devices than in the application on a much wider scale of devices which in pre-Islamic times had been used only over limited areas and to a limited extent. For instance, the *qanāt*, or underground canal tapping a source of ground water, had been little known in pre-Islamic Egypt and was probably entirely unknown farther to the west; in early Islamic times it was diffused across the whole of North Africa and into Spain, becoming of great importance in much of the interior of the Maghrib.[29] Similarly, the noria, known but little used in ancient times, proliferated all over the early Islamic world in a multitude of forms.[30] For some regions the effect of the diffusion of so much irrigation technology may have been revolutionary. A further contribution of Islamic agriculture to the development of irrigation may have been in the devising and wider use of ingenious combinations of the available devices. Instead of using the techniques in isolation or in relatively simple combinations, irrigators seem to have found ways of integrating different techniques into complex systems. Water that was captured in a variety of ways could then be successively channelled, stored and lifted by a wide variety of techniques; with a number of devices to choose from for each operation, the possible combinations were

A water-driven noria from an illustration of an episode in the tale of Bayāḍ and Riyāḍ. The manuscript, which dates from the thirteenth century, was probably made in Spain or Morocco. (Biblioteca Apostolica Vaticana, ms. arabo 368, fol. 19r)

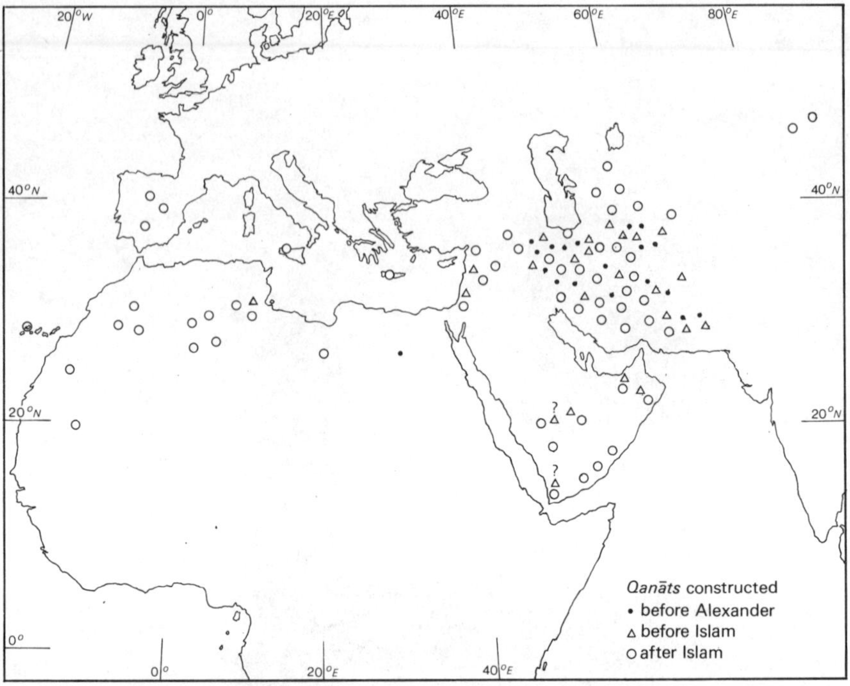

Map 8. The diffusion of the *qanāt*. From its apparent place of invention, Iran, the *qanāt* was diffused slowly outward in the pre-Islamic period. After the rise of Islam diffusion was much more rapid and extensive in all directions, but particularly in the western part of the Islamic world. (After GOBLOT "Dans l'ancien Iran" 504–5)

almost infinite. Opportunities thus opened up to irrigate land more cheaply and more extensively than in the past, and to bring water to land which, in times gone by, it had been impossible or uneconomic to irrigate.

The end result was to endow the early Islamic world with an extensive patchwork of irrigated lands. These varied widely in the degree of watering: at one end of the spectrum were many areas which were heavily watered through the entire year and which could support intensive, nearly continuous cultivation; in the middle range were lands irrigated less heavily through the year or for only parts of the year; and at the other end were lands watered only once or twice in a season through the capture, for instance, of a flash flood or by sparing use of small amounts of water stored in a cistern. The available water resources were generally used to the full extent allowed by known technology. In many regions it would be only a slight exaggeration to say that there was hardly a river, stream, oasis, spring, known aquifer or predictable flood that was not fully exploited – though not always by irrigators, who had to compete with urban and domestic users. In the Huerta of Valencia, for example, the experience after the Reconquista showed that the area of irrigated lands could not be increased without provoking serious water shortages in years of low rainfall.[31] Similarly, Professor Susa has calculated that the area in the Sawād of Iraq which was subject to the land tax, and presumably irrigated, amounted to nearly 50,000 square kilometres, which was "almost certainly the total cultivable area".[32] In a section below we shall show how the development of heavily irrigated agriculture in the early centuries of Islam allowed many regions to support a density of settlement which has not been equalled since – and sometimes had not been previously reached.[33] Of course in this period there were also regions where irrigated farming declined or was abandoned, as patterns of settlement and land use changed, rivers altered their course and some irrigated lands became too saline; and for some areas it will be debated whether irrigation advanced or declined in the early centuries of Islam.[34] Elsewhere, the fortunes of irrigated lands fluctuated with changes in rulers: with almost monotonous regularity, periods of large-scale investment and careful control were followed by periods of neglect and maladministration. But what matters here is that in many, perhaps most, areas indisputable progress was made in both the quantity and quality of irrigation, so that by the ninth or tenth century virtually every part of the Islamic world had countless areas, great and small, which were heavily irrigated and into which the new crops could easily move – or had already moved. An environment fundamentally hostile to tropical and semi-tropical crops had been transformed into one in which, for a time at least, they were grown with astonishing success.

CHAPTER TWENTY-ONE

Facilitating supply: land tenure

Supply was also facilitated during the early centuries of Islam by important changes in the ways in which land was held, exploited and taxed. Unfortunately, for lack of records of landed estates, our knowledge of these changes comes mainly from legal sources which present the historian with a number of problems – most notably, the obvious disagreements among different schools of law and the less obvious (but no doubt common) discrepancies that must have existed between legal theory and actual practice.[1] Yet there does emerge from legal texts and from other sources which corroborate them a picture of a legal and administrative framework for agricultural activities which is markedly different from that of earlier times. Though some historians have stressed the continuity of local practices and institutions in certain regions, it seems to us that in essential matters – that is, those which affect most directly the productivity of agricultural land and labour – the two centuries following the Arab conquests saw a sharp break with the past.

One change of paramount importance was that in practice, if not in legal theory, the early Islamic world recognized that virtually all cultivated land was owned by an individual who had the right to sell, mortgage or will it, and could farm it or have it farmed as he liked. To be sure, legal and religious authorities sometimes paid lip service to fictions according to which the ultimate ownership of all land resided in God, his Prophet or his temporal–spiritual ruler, or that some or all conquered land belonged to the State or the Muslim community.[2] But such doctrines had almost no practical application; they seldom clouded the title of the individual who exercised the rights of ownership as these are normally conceived and paid the usual taxes to the State. The law, in fact, accorded full individual ownership over several categories of land: lands owned by Muslims who had acquired them by concession, purchase or inheritance, or by reclaiming dead lands; and lands owned by non-Muslims, whose ownership had been confirmed by the State at the time of the conquest or later on. Jurists distinguished several other categories of agricultural land over which, in principle, individuals did not have rights of ownership: State lands acquired through conquest, confiscation, purchase, gift or commendation, which were administered by the ruler; and conquered lands belonging to the Muslim community, some of which were administered by the ruler and on some of which the previous tenants or owners enjoyed usufruct (which they could alienate) in return for the payment of *kharāj* or land tax.[3] But in actual practice both these categories of land appear quickly to have reverted to what was in effect private ownership – if indeed they were in reality ever publicly owned. State lands and some lands belonging to the Muslim community were usurped as private property of the ruler or were granted by him as ownerships to individuals, while the effective ownership of other lands in theory belonging to the Muslim community seems to have fallen to those who enjoyed the usufruct and paid only the appropriate land tax.[4]

The prevalence of property rights over agricultural land was of great economic importance. Privately owned land became a fully marketable commodity.[5] Through the action of the market it tended to fall into the hands of those who could use it most productively, since they could pay the highest rents or purchase price; the least productive users could find themselves forced to put their land on the market as the pressure of competition made their undertakings unviable. Slowly or quickly, therefore, land tended to gravitate away from non-innovating users towards the practitioners of the new agriculture.

What is more, the early Islamic owner of farm land appears to have exercised not only the full right of alienation but also the full right to determine land use. His ability to decide how, or whether, land was to be cultivated in a given year does not appear to have been curtailed by any rights of other parties over the same land. Cultivated land in the early Islamic world was nowhere, so far as one can tell, subject to communal rights to graze on stubble, and the owner was therefore not obliged to grow a crop which could be harvested at a particular time and thereafter leave his land idle. Nowhere do we find village-wide systems of rotation which dictated what must be grown on a particular plot of land and when.[6] Nor were the rights of the owner compromised by the claims of a peasantry with lifetime or perpetual tenancies: tenants appear to have had leases for clearly defined periods of time, most often for only one year.[7] In short, the progressive landowner or his tenant could easily effect changes in land use which made land or labour more productive. They were not constrained by the multitude of claims over their land which in the pre-Islamic world and in medieval Europe could hamstring innovation or even obscure the locus of ownership.

Although we have little information about the size of the units of agricultural exploitation, there is good reason to think that in this regard, too, the coming of Islam brought changes favouring innovation. The large estates, which everywhere had come to dominate – and usually to monopolize – agriculture,[8] were often broken down into smaller ownerships. This division of large properties might occur when effective ownership was given the former tenants after landowners had fled, been killed or been expropriated, as seems to have happened in parts of the Sawād, Sicily and elsewhere.[9] In other regions, such as parts of Spain and North Africa, it resulted from the distribution of captured lands to soldiers in the conquering armies.[10] Laws giving the ownership of dead or abandoned lands to those who reclaimed them may also have favoured the creation of smaller proprietorships, some of them gained from large estates.[11] The continuous breakdown of large accumulations of property must have been effected also by partible inheritance, which was enjoined by Islam, and possibly also by the frequent confiscation and regranting (perhaps in smaller units) of property belonging to those seen to have become excessively rich or dangerously powerful. Of course, many large estates survived the conquest, and others were built up afterwards; indeed, the process of creating large estates must have gone on continuously. But for some centuries the large estates had to compete with alternative forms of exploitation which must often have been more efficient: medium-sized and smaller estates, as well as even smaller proprietorships which could be operated by a peasant, his family, and perhaps a hired worker or two. Small undertakings, often irrigated by a noria or some other means, dominated the lands around cities, which were almost everywhere given over to market gardens and orchards.[12]

Such a panoply of forms of exploitation no doubt favoured innovation. The very existence of alternatives which competed with the large estates must have encouraged the introduction of more profitable crops and techniques of production in undertakings of various sizes; and the gradation of the size of units of production allowed the easy upward mobility of successful peasants and landowners, of whatever grade. For some kinds of production – perhaps particularly crops demanding much labour and great care – the smaller unit was probably more efficient than the large estate; its example, and competition from it in the marketplace, may at times have stimulated more productive land use on the large estates.[13] Where the owner was also the operator, moreover, some kinds of innovation were more likely to occur: in many cases there was a greater probability that a need or opportunity would be perceived by an owner in close touch with the work on the land, and that the appropriate change would be introduced when the innovator stood to capture the greater part of the gains. Furthermore, even the large estates were free of many of the retrograde features which held back agricultural progress in many parts of the pre-Islamic world and on the European manor. They had no demesne, in the sense of an important part of the estate which the owner operated with involuntary tenant labour. Holdings of both owners and their tenants seem to have consisted most often of consolidated blocks or a small number of fragments; there was nothing to correspond to the scattered strips in the open-field system of northern Europe. Nor do we learn of any cultivated land over which the tenants exercised any kind of collective rights, or any operations (except the construction and upkeep of irrigation works) which required co-operation.

Relatively low rates of taxation on the land and its produce also seem to have encouraged agricultural progress. These were in marked contrast to the oppressive rural taxation that prevailed in the late Roman, the late Sasanian and much of the late Byzantine empires, and that were to prevail afterwards in the decaying Islamic world.[14] The Prophet himself had been concerned that levels of taxation be kept reasonable, and later rulers and legal writers echoed this concern.[15] True, in the first decades following the conquests, the pre-Islamic system and rates of taxation may in some parts have continued; and these rates may have been heavy for some conquered peoples.[16] But the information on tax receipts after the conquest of the Sawād, seemingly showing a marked decline in state revenues, suggests that there taxes were lighter.[17] In any case, the system of rural taxation was reformed in the reign of the caliphs al-Manṣūr (754–75) and al-Mahdī (775–85), and in the next century or so the reforms were introduced through most parts of the Muslim world with the exception of Egypt.[18] Under the new system, known as *muqāsama*, producers paid a proportion of their output as taxes to the State: usually a tenth or a fifth, depending on the status of the land or its owner, but – as will be seen below – sometimes still less or even nothing.[19] Moreover, as these rates of taxation were argued to have been enshrined by tradition, they were in principle inviolable. Special levies were imposed in times of crisis, but normal taxes could not legally be raised by rulers. They might, on the other hand, be lowered: indeed, the State frequently forgave the taxes of those unable to pay.[20]

Light rates of taxation were one factor helping to keep alive a class of smaller, independent landowners and a relatively prosperous peasantry. They slowed down, or even reversed, the tendency, so common in the ancient world, for large estates to dominate the countryside and for the peasantry to be exploited and finally enserfed. What is more, the fact that these rates of taxation were in theory immutable encouraged innovation. Landowners and tenants alike were reasonably assured that a substantial part of the gains of agricultural improvements would be theirs. At least in the early centuries of Islam increased profits could not easily be scooped off by capricious tax collectors or a greedy State.

Other provisions of the tax laws also worked to promote the new agriculture. Although traditions differed on many of these points, there was widespread agreement among authorities that fruits and vegetables should either not be taxed at all or that only one-twentieth of their output should be paid.[21] According to some writers, sorghum and cotton were also not to be taxed.[22] Some even maintained that no summer crops were taxable – though in point of fact it seems clear that rice and sugar cane were always taxed.[23] Fruit trees were also not to be taxed until they had begun to yield, and several authorities held that even mature trees should not be taxed unless they were planted so close that nothing else could be grown on the ground.[24] As many of the new crops fell into one or more of these categories, it seems clear that these favourable rates of taxation, where they were applied, gave a strong incentive to switch from traditional to new crops. Similarly, the introduction of waterlifting devices and hence the expansion of irrigated agriculture were promoted by laws which taxed at only one-twentieth of output any land watered by bucket (i.e. the *shādūf*) or, in an extension of this principle, land watered by noria.[25]

Still other laws favoured agricultural progress in other ways. The whole corpus of irrigation law, which attempted to give explicit answers to any possible dispute over water, and wherever possible assigned property rights over water, must on balance have encouraged investment in irrigation both by creating a climate of confidence and by making some water rights, like rights over land, a marketable commodity.[26] Other laws encouraged the reclamation of dead lands and swamps by giving the rights of ownership to Muslims (and perhaps others) who put such lands under the plow and by taxing these lands at only one-tenth of produce instead of at any higher rate that might have applied. On the other hand, the abandonment of cultivable land was strongly discouraged by laws transferring the ownership of abandoned land to the State, which could then reassign it; and by taxes on any uncultivated land which had access to water.[27]

The legal and institutional framework for the use of another factor of agricultural production – labour – also seems to have encouraged agriculture in general and the diffusion of new crops in particular. With rare exceptions, slaves do not appear to have been used in agricultural undertakings during the early centuries of Islam.[28] Nor, it seems, was the peasantry anywhere reduced to a state of serfdom or even effectively tied to the land.[29] It performed no corvée for the landowner – though it was perhaps at times conscripted, as was the case later on, for labour on irrigation works.[30] Instead, the legal and actual condition of the overwhelming majority of those who worked on the land was one of freedom. Labour was supplied for the most part by the self-employed and by sharecropping and other tenants.[31] It was also sometimes supplied by an essentially new form of labour, which perhaps appeared to help fill the void left by the near disappearance of slaves from the agricultural labour force: the hired worker who sold his labour for a wage.[32] Owner-operators, sharecropping tenants and even hired labourers – all working of their own volition – were more likely than slaves or serfs to work hard, to be responsible and to innovate. Tenants and hired labourers were also more mobile.[33] They tended to move from less to more profitable undertakings: presumably from the old agriculture to the new, and from long-settled, overpopulated areas – where intensive agriculture might have reached its limits – into new lands offering new opportunities.

The Arab conquests thus appear to have freed the countryside from many arrangements which were economically retrograde. New modes of production brought more agricultural land and labour, as well as their product, into the market place, and the forces of competition thus released were intensified by laws rewarding innovators. Although laws and institutions later became less flexible, less responsive to the claims of the agents of change, they were for some centuries remarkably favourable to agricultural innovation in general and to the introduction of our new crops in particular.

CHAPTER TWENTY-TWO

Facilitating supply: gardens

To be disseminated new plants had to be available. Although we have earlier suggested that the agents of diffusion were in many cases peasants and landowners who brought exotic plants from afar and introduced them into the agriculture of their region, we shall argue here that gardens, royal and private, often served as halfway-houses in the diffusion of plants between one region's agriculture and that of another.

Indeed, many of our plants may first have been brought to an area as ornamental plants or botanical oddities, and were only later prized as useful plants and grown on a commercial scale. We have already spoken of the collecting instincts of the upper classes in the early Islamic world. For collecting plants, however, they had a special penchant. Possibly because some of their ancestors had come from the desert, and in most places where they lived the desert was still near at hand, sometimes within eyesight, ever ready to encroach on the land that had been claimed from it, the inhabitants of the early Islamic world were, to a degree that is difficult for us to comprehend, enchanted by greenery.[1] This love of plants is clearly shown in a genre of poetry, the *rawḍīya* or garden poem, probably of Persian origin, which came to be one of the main poetic forms in the ʻAbbāsid orient from the eighth to the tenth century.[2] In the garden poem, the author exclaimed at the coolness of the shade, the heaviness of the perfume, the music of the running water, the lushness of the foliage and so forth – in short at all the features of the artificially contrived environment which contrasted so strongly with the arid natural world. By the ninth century the genre had arrived in Spain where it was to reach its greatest heights in the eleventh century; gardens became, according to Henri Pérès, probably the most common of all Arábigo-Ándaluz poetic themes.[3]

These were not mere words; they corresponded to a reality. Early Muslims everywhere made earthly gardens that gave glimpses of the heavenly garden to come. Long indeed would be the list of early Islamic cities which could boast huge expanses of gardens. To give only a few examples, Basra is described by the early geographers as a veritable Venice, with mile after mile of canals criss-crossing the gardens and orchards;[4] Nisibin, a city in

Mesopotamia, was said to have 40,000 gardens of fruit trees, and Damascus 110,000;[5] al-Fusṭāṭ, with its multiple-storey dwellings, had thousands of private gardens, some of great splendour;[6] in North Africa, one learns of a multitude of gardens, surrounding and even inside cities such as Tunis, Algiers, Tlemcen, and Marrakesh, places which today are not conspicuous for their greenery;[7] in Spain, writers speak endlessly of the gardens and *lieux de plaisance* of Seville, Cordova and Valencia, the last of which was called by one of them "the scent-bottle of al-Andalus".[8] The most spectacular gardens of all were those of rulers, many of which are described in the sources: the garden of al-Mu'taṣim at Sāmarra;[9] the great royal parks of the Aghlabid *amīrs* of Tunisia, situated near Qairawān, and later the famous garden of the Ḥafṣid rulers of Tunisia;[10] those of the Fāṭimid caliphs of Egypt, and of the vizier al-Afḍal;[11] the gardens surrounding the royal palaces at Fez and Marrakesh;[12] the great botanical gardens of 'Abd al-Raḥmān, the first Umayyad *amīr* of Spain;[13] the Huerta del Rey in Toledo; the gardens of many of the other Taifa kings of Spain;[14] those of the Īl-Khāns and Tīmūrids at Tabriz and elsewhere;[15] and that of Maḥmūd of Ghazna at Balkh.[16] One of the more elaborate gardens was that of Khumārawaih, a Ṭūlūnid ruler of Egypt in the later ninth century, who made a royal garden said to be in the Persian manner. According to al-Maqrīzī, the glory of this garden was its palm trees, whose trunks were covered with gold; behind this covering were pipes which brought water up the side of the trees and sprayed it out from various openings into pools.[17]

"A garden in the Persian manner..." In fact, we believe that Arab gardens were usually constructed on the Persian models; and one wonders if rulers imitating Persian layouts might not also have tried to introduce Persian or other exotic plants.[18] In this way royal gardens might have been focal points in the process of plant diffusion. The evidence we have suggests that this was actually the case. It was in stocking their gardens with rare and exotic plants that many rulers gave full reign to their collecting instincts. We are told, for instance, that the first Umayyad *amīr* of Spain, 'Abd al-Raḥmān, was passionately fond of flowers and plants, and collected in his garden rare plants from every part of the world. He sent agents to Syria and other parts of the east to procure new plants and seeds. A new kind of pomegranate was introduced into Spain through his garden. The date palm, too, was probably introduced, or reintroduced, by him. By the tenth century, the royal gardens at Cordova seem to have become botanical gardens, with fields for experimentation with seeds, cuttings and roots brought in from the outermost reaches of the world.[19] Other royal gardens, in Spain and elsewhere, also became the sites of serious scientific activity as well as places of amusement. A very important recently discovered geographical manuscript, that of al-'Udhrī, relates that al-Mu'taṣim, a Taifa king, brought many rare plants to his garden in Almería; these, we are told, included bananas and sugar cane (both of which, however, were already known in other parts of Spain).[20] At the other end of the Islamic world, in Tabriz, the garden of the Īl-Khāns was used to acclimatize rare fruit trees from India, China, Malaysia and Central Asia.[21]

In many parts of the Islamic world this royal interest in botanical research and agricultural innovation outlasted the agricultural revolution by several centuries: the sources tell of Syrian plants introduced into his garden in Cairo by the Mamlūk sultan Qalāwūn;[22] of a thirteenth-century king of Kanem who experimented with the growing of sugar cane in his garden;[23] and of a number of fourteenth-century Yemeni sultans who were seriously interested in botanical and agricultural research, one of whom wrote an agricultural treatise while another imported exotic trees and was the first to plant rice in the Valley of Zabīd.[23]

Another sign of the serious nature of these undertakings is the fact that such gardens were often in the charge of leading scientists: that of the Īl-Khāns was directed by a Persian botanist who wrote a book on the grafting of fruit trees;[25] al-Tignarī, the author of an important Andalusian farming manual, made botanical gardens for a Spanish Taifa king and then for the Almoravid prince Tamīm;[26] in the garden of a sultan of Seville, the author of an anonymous botanical treatise domesticated rare Iberian plants and acclimatized exotic ones;[27] in the twelfth century the famous botanist and physician al-Shafrān collected plants from many outlying regions of Spain for the garden of an Almohad sultan at Guadix;[28] the Huerta del Rey in Toledo was directed by two of Spain's leading agronomes, Ibn Baṣṣāl and Ibn Wāfid, both of whom carried out agricultural experiments and wrote important manuals of farming, the texts of which have recently been discovered. Ibn Wāfid was also the author of a book of simples, which gives, *inter alia*, the names and uses of many of the new plants being introduced into Spain. After the fall of Toledo in 1085, both scientists moved to the south of Spain and continued their work there; Ibn Baṣṣāl planted another botanical garden in Seville for his new patron, al-Mu'tamid, the Taifa king.[29]

Thus the gardens of the medieval Islamic world, and particularly the royal gardens, were places where business was mixed with pleasure, science with art. By being part of a network which linked together the agricultural and botanical activities of distant regions, they played a role – perhaps one of great importance – in the diffusion of useful plants. Only many centuries later did Europe possess similar botanical gardens which helped to make it the same kind of medium for plant diffusion that the Islamic world had been in the Middle Ages.[30]

Part Four
The new plants in the economy

CHAPTER TWENTY-THREE

An agricultural rcvolution?

Hand in hand with the new crops came changes in agricultural practice, some of which were to affect the growing of traditional as well as new crops. So many were these changes, and so far-reaching were their effects, that one is perhaps justified in using the term – alas, so hackneyed – agricultural revolution.[1]

One important change was the opening of a virtually new agricultural season. In the lands of the Middle East and Mediterranean the traditional growing season had always been winter, the crops being sown around the time of the autumn rains and harvested in spring; in the long hot, dry summer the land almost always lay fallow, usually even in irrigated regions where at least some of the crops available to the ancients could, with special care, have given satisfactory yields.[2] Those crops mentioned as summer crops in the classical Roman manuals – *trimestre* wheat, millets, sesame and various legumes, as well as a few garden crops – played a minor role in some parts of the northern Mediterranean, where the summer was relatively cool, though even there they seem to have been little used and were not integrated into any systematic rotation.[3] But in the southern and eastern parts of the Mediterranean they were practically never grown, at least not as summer crops. There the summer season was to all intents and purposes dead. Since, however, many of the new crops originated in the tropical regions of India, Southeast Asia and Central Africa, they could be grown only in conditions of great heat. In particular, rice, cotton, sugar cane, colocasia, eggplants, watermelons and sorghum were all summer crops in the Islamic world, though rice could also be a winter crop in certain very warm areas.[4] Several other important new crops which we have not been able to study in detail were also grown in summer, such as indigo, henna, safflower and the green gram.[5] The introduction of such summer crops on a wide scale radically altered the rhythm of the agricultural year as land and labour which had previously lain idle were made productive.

More than this, the opening of a significant summer season was one of several factors – perhaps the principal one – permitting systems of rotation which made much more intensive use of the land. In Roman, Byzantine and

Judaic agricultural traditions, the universal practice was to crop the ground only once every two years or in exceptional circumstances once every year.[6] Long periods of fallowing were deemed necessary to allow the land to regain its fertility, heat and moisture. Even in Byzantine Egypt, where the flooding of the Nile would seem to make prolonged resting of the land unnecessary, fields were often sown only once in every two years; they sometimes bore a legume crop in intervening years but never grain crops in successive years.[7] In the Islamic world, however, these periods of rest for the land were often done away with. Fallowing was not recommended – or even discussed – in most of the agricultural manuals. It has even been suggested by one writer that there was no specific word in classical Arabic meaning "to fallow".[8] Instead most land, and certainly all irrigated land, seems to have been cropped at least once a year and given no regular period of rest. Fallowing *is* discussed in the farming manual of Ibn al-ʻAwwām, but he recommends it only for the preparation of newly cleared or long-abandoned land of middling or inferior quality. Elsewhere, he seems to imply, it was unnecessary and for some soils undesirable.[9]

Still more intensive cropping of the land became common in places that were fertile and well watered, for in these areas a summer crop could be planted immediately after the spring harvest. Ibn al-ʻAwwām even seems to suggest that summer cropping was preferable to summer fallowing: some soils left bare in the summer, he states, were liable to scorching.[10] In certain areas three or more harvests per year could be had from the same plot of land. This heavy cropping, moreover, could continue year after year without letup.[11] Although the new crops were of fundamental importance in opening up the summer season, the summer crops which were known, but little used, in antiquity also played a role: in particular, *trimestre* wheat,[12] barley and catch crops[13] were used much more by Muslims than by the ancients. The Islamic manuals were also much less rigid on the subject of what was a winter and what was a summer crop. Many crops, thought by the ancients to be suitable for one season only, were given in the manuals as both summer and winter crops: wheat, broad beans, flax and sesame are but a few examples.[14]

The possible combinations were thus countless. New crops could be combined in rotations with old ones. An irrigated season could follow a dry one. We are told that in the High Yemen the land around Ma'rib was cropped three times yearly, while that near Sanʻā' yielded two harvests of wheat per year or three to four harvests of barley.[15] In early Islamic Egypt, according to several modern scholars, artificial irrigation seems to have allowed many lands to produce crops two or three times every year.[16] In many parts of the early Islamic world a winter crop of wheat could be followed by a summer crop of sorghum; this rotation was even recommended for improving hard soils.[17] In Cyprus, where the practice had no doubt been introduced during the Arab occupation, a traveller noted that a summer crop of cotton could just be fitted in between two crops of winter wheat in successive years.[18] In

Iraq winter rice could be followed by summer rice.[19] Where plants with a shorter growing season were used, such as spinach, colocasia and eggplants, three or more harvests per year were common.[20] The many areas of market gardens, especially around the great cities, showed no sharp breaks in the agricultural year: Nāṣir-i Khusraw remarked that the fruits and vegetables of Egypt could be produced in any season,[21] while al-Ḥimyarī, writing of the Vega of Granada, stated that the land was artificially irrigated (and hence under crops) through the entire year.[22]

Like most of the new crops, the system of multiple cropping seems to have reached the Islamic world from India.[22] Before the rise of Islam it may have moved from India into Arabia Felix and even Abyssinia,[24] where climate favoured its introduction. It was the achievement of Islamic times, however, to bring this system into colder and drier regions where its practice was much more difficult – and more dangerous.

Naturally, such heavy cropping depleted the soil of its fertility and, in the case of unirrigated land, of its moisture; it could give satisfactory results over the years only if strenuous efforts were made to maintain the productivity of the soil. Of the ways to keep the land in heart the manuals of farming had much to say. They spoke of using dung of sheep, goats, pigs, cows, horses, mules, buffaloes, gazelles, wild and domesticated donkeys, pigeons, doves and wild birds, as well as night soil, each with its peculiar virtues and uses. Other animal products recommended for certain soils included blood, urine, and powdered bones, horns and ivory. Vegetable matter of many types was also to be used where indicated – for instance, sediment from olive oil, lees, seeds, straw, husks, leaves, rags, shavings, different kinds of ashes and unused parts of the plant which was to be grown. Mineral matter, too, had its role: the manuals told when it was appropriate to add different kinds of soil, sand, gravel, "dust", chalk, marl, lime, crushed bricks or broken tiles.[25] Again, the manuals urged much ploughing (normal and deep ploughing), hoeing, digging and harrowing, both at the time of planting and during the shorter periods when the land was at rest; turning and breaking the soil were seen as partial substitutes for both fallowing and fertilizing the soil, and on occasion preferable.[26] Finally, the choice of the right sequence of crops was important since it was understood that crops depleted the soil to different degrees, at different levels and of different nutrients; it was also known that some crops restored nutrients to the soil or improved its structure.[27] The ways of caring for the soil were thus many. Used alone or in an almost infinite number of combinations they could serve not only to maintain fertility of heavily cropped areas but also to improve – or even change – the soil. As Ibn Waḥshīya remarked, "the earth does not keep one form but changes over time"; changes in the quality of the soil, he urged, should be effected by the cultivator where desirable.[28] While some of the techniques described in the manuals clearly required a considerable investment and must therefore have been uneconomic where extensive dry farming was practised, others were simpler. They may have contributed materially to increases in the productivity of agricultural land in the early Islamic world.[29]

But the agricultural revolution was by no means confined to heavily irrigated and fertile areas where multiple cropping on the Indian model could be introduced. On the contrary, though the impact of the revolution was greatest in such areas and though they may perhaps be regarded as the spearheads of agricultural advance, the new agriculture overflowed their bounds to affect the whole spectrum of land types – from best to worst – that the early Islamic peasant tilled. Virtually all categories of land came to be farmed more intensively. In part this spillover was made possible by the fact that there was no sharp break between irrigated and unirrigated lands. Rather investment in irrigation works and the spread of irrigation technology had endowed the early Islamic world with a gradation of artificially watered lands, ranging from those receiving heavy, perennial irrigation through those which were watered less heavily or for shorter periods down to lands on which rainfall was supplemented only by one or two artificial waterings. On partially irrigated lands, too, more intensive cropping appeared: winter fallowing was often reduced and some summer cropping could be practised. Even the capture of a flash flood or the sparing use of water stored in a cistern could make lands bear in a season when previously they had lain barren.

The possibilities of intensifying land use were compounded by the widening of the range of crops available and by the growing knowledge of their special requirements and potentialities. There were all the crops of traditional agriculture; there was seemingly an explosion of new cultivars of these, some more productive or more versatile than the older strains;[30] and there were the new crops. All these, moreover, could be more closely matched than before to the available soil, climate and water, for the authors of the Islamic manuals of agriculture understood more than their predecessors about the choosing of crops to suit local conditions. They identified more kinds of soil, each suited to particular plants, and differentiated them further by taking into account a soil's moisture and temperature through the growing season. They also considered the effect of different types of water on each phase of a plant's growth cycle.[31] The enlightened landowner or cultivator thus had before him an almost infinite variety of flexible cropping patterns, each suited to special conditions – in contrast to the small number of rigid rotations of antiquity and medieval Europe. The proper choice of cropping pattern could increase the productivity of nearly any kind of land.[32] Particularly spectacular results were achieved when advantage was taken of local soil variations and microclimates.

Even on lands which in earlier times had been thought too dry, too hot or too infertile to use, and which no artificial watering could reach, the new agriculture made important advances. Here again certain of the new crops were crucial. Though it required some moisture in the early part of its growing season, sorghum, for instance, could mature in a summer that was very hot and dry; it could also, as the Arab manuals pointed out, be grown on hard and sandy soils which other crops would find inhospitable, and it even helped to reconstitute these lands.[33] Hard wheat could also endure much heat and drought, and could also be grown on poor soils. Though of less importance, watermelons and eggplants also yielded satisfactory returns on lands once thought too dry or too sandy to use. These crops thus allowed the frontier of cultivation to be pushed back into large areas of steppe and savanna – lands which previously had been used only for sporadic grazing or occasional cultivation, or had gone unused. Similarly, sugar cane, rice, colocasia, coconut palms and eggplants could be grown on salty soils, where cereals could not be grown, and helped to improve these. They therefore encouraged an extension of cultivation into swamp lands lying along seacoasts and at the mouths of rivers, into lands watered by brackish springs, and into lands which after centuries of irrigation had become too saline for other crops.[34] Again, we learn from Ibn al-ʿAwwām that cotton was grown on the worst lands of Spain and Sicily, and we may assume that this crop also helped to enlarge the frontiers of sedentary agriculture.[35] More generally, the manuals have much to say about the steps to be taken to bring into cultivation land which has been newly cleared or long abandoned. They give the impression of a society pressing hard on the margins of cultivation, seeking to put under the plough lands which in earlier times had gone unused. They assume that all categories of land will be used to their full potential – even inferior and downright bad lands, which the ancient writers did not deign to consider.[36]

One of the direct consequences of the new agriculture was higher and more stable agricultural earnings. The total income generated by the agricultural sector was higher because more land was farmed, because more cultivated land was irrigated, because land was cropped more intensively, and because there was a wider variety of crops to choose from – some much more profitable than anything available in earlier times.[37] But the new agriculture also helped to stabilize agricultural incomes. No longer was the rural community so dependent on a single harvest, the size of which was at the mercy of an undependable climate. Instead an increasing number of producers could rely on two or more crops which matured at different times of the year and whose exact time of maturation, in the case of irrigated crops, could to some extent be controlled by regulating the flow of water.[38] Moreover, with more land under irrigation, the damage inflicted by climatic fluctuations was greatly reduced, since the flow of irrigation water, coming from rivers, aquifers and wells, varied much less than rainfall; on this account, too, the level of output – and hence earnings – varied less. The fact that hard wheat and sorghum could be stored over very long periods allowed speculators and governments to build up surpluses in years of high production and low prices which could be released onto the market in years when production was low and prices high.[39] Because such activities tended to keep supplies of grain on the market more stable, they also helped to stabilize prices and incomes – though the tactics of unscrupulous speculators and governments sometimes had the opposite effect. More stable incomes were important not only in alleviating the periodic misery which punctuated the lives of rural dwellers in earlier agricultural systems; they also made it easier for peasants to meet their obligations to landowners and to the State, and thus were one factor helping to keep intact for a time a relatively prosperous and free peasantry and to prevent the excessive buildup of large estates.

Higher and more stable agricultural earnings were achieved, however, by applying more capital and labour to the land unit. In this sense the new agriculture was both highly capital-intensive and highly labour-intensive. More capital was required per land unit for the construction of irrigation works and for the levelling or terracing of land to be irrigated. The reclamation of land could also require a heavy investment. In a less obvious but perhaps important way the new agriculture also demanded a higher investment in tools, draft animals and outbuildings. Operating capital was greater on account of the larger amounts of seed, fertilizer and labour used on a given land area in the course of a year. At the same time, much more labour was required per land unit: to construct, operate and repair the irrigation works; to plant, tend and harvest crops on land that was more frequently cropped, some of the new crops – such as sugar cane – making very high demands on labour;[40] and to carry out the large amount of ploughing, digging, hoeing and harrowing, as well as the extensive fertilizing, which were needed to maintain the fertility and moisture of heavily cropped land. Though some of the tasks came in what had been dead or slack seasons in earlier agricultural systems, and could therefore be performed by labour that otherwise would have remained idle, more hands were undoubtedly needed per land unit. Thus the new agriculture was based on a shift in the relative proportions of the factors of production – land, labour and capital – that were used in the production of food. Land was economized as more labour and capital were applied to it. This shift was an economically rational response to changing conditions: to a growing scarcity of land and to increasing supplies of labour and probably capital. It suggests a responsiveness in the agricultural sector which is typical of an economy experiencing rapid growth, if not transformation.

CHAPTER TWENTY-FOUR

Agriculture in its context

Agricultural revolutions do not occur in a vacuum. On the contrary, they are part and parcel of larger, more general changes in economy and society extending far beyond the bounds of the agricultural sector. In the case of the Arab agricultural revolution, there were many crucial linkages between what happened in the fields and what happened elsewhere, and only by exploring some of the more important of these can we begin to understand the causes of this revolution and its consequences.

For one thing, the agricultural revolution was bound up with an ill-documented but none the less real demographic revolution which seems to have touched most parts of the Islamic world from roughly the beginning of the eighth till the end of the tenth century. Rising population levels and increasing levels of output of foodstuffs must continuously have interacted: though both were affected by other factors, at times demographic growth must have been the result of agricultural progress, at times its efficient cause.

Much of the increase in population was rural and one of the signs of this growth was the expansion of settlement into new areas – onto lands which had never before known sedentary agriculture and onto once-cultivated lands which had long been abandoned. To this general pattern there were of course exceptions: in the first century and a half of Islam the frontier of settlement retreated in parts of the Negev and possibly in some regions of western Syria and Palestine.[1] In ʿAbbāsid times we learn of the contraction of settlement in other regions.[2] These countertendencies are not surprising when it is remembered that in many parts of the early Islamic world the occupation of the countryside had always been precarious, depending for its continuation on a delicate balance of military, political, demographic, ecological and other factors. As circumstances changed, the limits of cultivation continually ebbed and flowed, and there was much relocation within occupied areas. But in the early centuries of Islam areas of contracting or disappearing settlement seem to have been unusual. In most parts of the early Islamic world there was a strong tendency for settlement to move outward. The Prophet himself seems to have looked down on nomadic peoples and strongly favoured sedentary life,[3] and he was followed in this by Umayyad and ʿAbbāsid rulers, who settled nomads and encouraged new settlements by giving protection against bandits and nomadic raiders.[4] A number of other factors, some of which have already been mentioned, also contributed to this outward thrust: new crops which could be grown on lands previously thought unusable, new techniques of improving soils that were poor, the bringing of irrigation water to new lands, new laws which gave ownership to the person who had reclaimed land which had been "dead" for three years and taxed this land at a low rate,[5] other laws which took away grants of land that went uncultivated for a period of years,[6] the pressure of large and growing cities on food supplies, and finally the growth of rural population itself, which must have forced many sons of peasants to seek holdings on land not yet under the plough – sometimes in places lying far afield.

The evidence, though it is of varying reliability, comes from nearly every corner of the early Islamic world. In Turkestan, for example, the construction of new irrigation works drew settlers into lands lying along the tributaries and lower reaches of the Oxus and along the tributaries of the Iaxartes, as well as into the hinterlands of the great oases.[7] In Persia, new lands were opened up not only through the construction of irrigation works but also, as in Khwārizm, by the clearing of forests.[8] In Iraq and al-Jazīra we learn of particularly important extensions of irrigated agriculture in the hinterlands of Basra, Wāsiṭ, al-Nīl, Baghdad and Sāmarra; but on a smaller scale, often through private rather than public initiatives, the areas of irrigated and non-irrigated land must have grown in other areas too.[9] In eastern Arabia, the Hijaz, Transjordania and eastern Syria the margin of settlement seems in many places to have been pushed eastward into the desert, where the so-called "desert palaces", once surrounded by extensive irrigated areas, are only a few signs of a more general advance into the desert of sedentary agriculture.[10] In the Maghrib, where the early centuries of Islam saw new roads reaching farther and farther into the interior, sedentary agriculture seems to have moved into many new areas as the water in rivers, streams, wells and aquifers came increasingly to be used for irrigated crops, and as rainfed farming – aided no doubt by the low water requirements of sorghum and hard wheat – pushed farther and farther south.[11] This extension of cultivation in North Africa continued in most regions until the early or mid eleventh century and somewhat longer in the southern part of Morocco.[12] In Spain the expansion of settlement in early Islamic times cannot yet be well documented; but the heavy distribution of Arabic place-names and the multitude of Islamic archeological remains in nearly every part of the peninsula show clearly that the Islamic penetration of Iberia was much deeper than the Roman.[13]

At the same time as the total inhabited area was being enlarged, the density of rural settlement seems to have been rising. Again, there were no doubt exceptions – possibly the Diyala plains are an example;[14] but although the evidence is often not very exact or reliable, and sometimes contains an obvious element of exaggeration, the overwhelming weight of it suggests that in most regions villages were becoming larger, more numerous and more nearly contiguous, especially along the great river valleys and around the big oases. Chroniclers, geographers and travellers tell that there were 360 villages in the Fayyūm, each of which could provision the whole of Egypt for a day;[15] that there were 12,000 villages along the Guadalquivir, which, if this were true, must have reduced greatly the amount of cultivable land;[16] that the coastland between Tangier and Melilla, which today is almost entirely abandoned, was densely settled and prosperous;[17] more generally, that between Ifrīqiya and Tangier there was a wide band of settlements whose agricultural hinterlands touched one another;[18] that on the road between Gafsa and Feriana, a part of Tunisia which today is desert, there were 200 villages;[19] and that along the Tigris settlement was continuous, so that before dawn crowing cocks answered one another from housetop to housetop all the way from Basra to Baghdad.[20] The 1975 archeological survey of the east Jordan valley showed that the densest settlement in the area occurred in Ayyūbid and Mamlūk times, and was closely linked to the cultivation of sugar cane; similar surveys in the eastern part of Saudi Arabia have shown that the highest density of population was reached in the early centuries of Islam.[21] Even in the savanna and forest lands of West Africa, villages became larger and more numerous as new crops introduced in Islamic times made the soil much more productive.[22] Other kinds of evidence support the thesis of denser rural settlement with perhaps slightly greater precision: an eighth-century census of 10,000 villages in Egypt was said to show that no village had fewer than 500 male Copts, while data from the seigneurie of Monreale in Sicily suggest that some hundred years after the Norman conquest of the island – by which time depopulation may already have set in – the rural areas of the seigneurie, amounting to some 1,000 square kilometres, had about 20,000 inhabitants.[23] Occasionally there are signs that the density of settlement was the maximum that could be supported by available resources and techniques: seventh-century taxation data from the Sawād indicate that the area subject to the land tax was 125,000 square kilometres, which one scholar has calculated to be virtually all the cultivable area,[24] and in the Huerta, or irrigated hinterland, of Valencia the experience after the reconquest suggests that no more land could be irrigated without endangering city water supplies in years of drought.[25] That the early Islamic countryside should have had many rural areas that were densely populated is not surprising. They are the concomitants – causes and effects – of a system of agriculture in which the average unit of cultivated land both required and fed more people.

The consequences were far-reaching. The filling up of many empty spaces, the appearance of denser and more nearly continuous settlement had important, if elusive, effects on the growth of communications, on the speed at which agricultural and other innovations were diffused, on the spread of trade through the countryside and the consequent specialization of agricultural land and labour, and on the role played by the State in rural life. In turn, changes in these areas influenced the course of agricultural development.

So considerable were the increases in food production generated by the agricultural revolution that the countryside seems to have been able to feed not only much heavier rural populations but also large urban populations. For during the early centuries of Islam new cities were founded in nearly every part of Dār al-Islām,[26] and the new and many old cities grew – sometimes spectacularly. Indeed, it is likely that in the early Islamic world the proportion of the total population living in the cities rose. This increasing urbanization of the population, if it occurred, implies a rising productivity of the agricultural labour force: those who tilled the soil could produce not only enough to feed themselves and other rural dwellers but also a surplus big enough to provision cities whose populations grew more rapidly than total population.[27] As they expanded, urban markets offered greater incentives to the surrounding countryside to increase the productivity of land and labour, and at the same time they drew larger and larger hinterlands into their gravitational field. The areas of land that were thus pulled into the sphere of urban economies must in many cases have been very large, since the cities were themselves, at least by contemporary European standards, very large. The agricultural surplus needed to feed the cities was even a little greater than the size of a city's population might suggest, since, as we have seen, in most early Islamic cities there was a substantial element of wealthy people who lived – and ate – very well, and whose eating habits, we have suggested, played an important role in the introduction and diffusion of new crops.[28] Indeed, the cities seem to have contained large numbers of rich and not so rich people who depended on the countryside not only for their food supply but also for much or all of their incomes. Rulers and their courts, bureaucrats and soldiers, and the not insignificant class of rentier landlords lived to varying degrees – but often mainly – on revenues generated by rural producers but diverted to urban dwellers in the form of profits, rents, taxes and bribes.

About the absolute size of early Islamic cities there has been, and will be, much debate. In the absence of census data, the geographers and other contemporaries who give population statistics (or figures from which these might be estimated) had to rely on hearsay or personal impressions. No doubt they were often prone to exaggerate. On the other hand, many modern scholars have gone to the opposite extreme: they have made obviously low guesses, apparently on the grounds that it is more respectable to underestimate than to overestimate.[29] Some seem to suppose (almost equally irrationally) that early Islamic cities could not have been bigger than the cities of medieval Europe, notwithstanding the glaring examples of very large cities in the classical Mediterranean and in medieval China.[30] They ignore the fact that the growth of Islamic cities was not constrained – at least not to the same degree – by many of the factors that held back the growth of cities in early medieval Europe: the extreme decentralization of power and the concomitant insecurity; the inadequate network of communications; the shortage of precious metals and the limited scope of the money economy; the low density of rural populations and the availability for many centuries of new agricultural lands; the comparative immobility of agricultural labour; political and economic institutions in the cities that became increasingly exclusive; and, last but by no means least, agricultural institutions and techniques that did not favour – indeed often prevented – intensive farming of the land. In all these respects the early Islamic world offers a marked contrast. Furthermore, one factor positively encouraged the growth of Muslim cities: town dwellers, unlike rural folk, were often not taxed.[31]

But in spite of all the difficulties in making accurate estimates, an idea of the magnitude of early Islamic cities and hence of their importance for the growth of agriculture may be had from the calculation of city populations that various scholars have made, even though all of the estimates are very rough and some seem intentionally on the low side. The population of Baghdad, perhaps the largest of all Islamic cities in the ninth and tenth centuries, has been variously estimated: at 2,000,000 in the 1911 edition of the Arabic *Twentieth-Century Encyclopedia*, at 1,500,000 by Levi della Vida and by Aḥmad ʻAzīz al-Dūrī, at more than 1,000,000 by Herzfeld and at between 200,000 and 600,000 by Lassner.[32] A figure between 500,000 and 1,000,000 does no seem unreasonable. Sāmarra is estimated by Herzfeld, who excavated it, also to have had nearly a million inhabitants;[33] the figure seems high for a city which was the capital for only fifty-six years, but the inhabited area of the city was immense. Fusṭāṭ–Cairo, another large city whose size is difficult to gauge, has been given various population levels on the eve of the Black Death: 600,000 by Clerget, 500,000 by Abu-Lughod and between 450,000 and 600,000 by Dols.[34] Tinnis, claimed by Ibn Iyās to have been one of the greatest cities of Egypt until it was flooded by sea water, was said by Nāṣir-i Khusraw to have had 50,000 male adults in the eleventh century, a figure which would imply a total population of about 200,000; al-Suyūṭī states that the 83,000 adults in the city were subject to poll tax, a figure which would suggest a still higher population.[35] On the eve of the Black Death, by which time it was well past its peak, the population of Damascus is estimated by Ziadeh at 100,000 and by Dols at 80,000. The Ottoman census of 1520–30 counted 57,000 people.[36] Ziadeh estimates the population of Aleppo before the Black Death to have been about 100,000.[37] Poll-tax information published by Dennett allows Russell to calculate a population of 340,000 for Hims and district and of 440,000 for Marv and district.[38] The population of Kufa is estimated by Massignon at a maximum of 400,000,[39] while the estimates for Basra in the eighth and ninth centuries range between 200,000 and 600,000.[40] Isfahan, described by Nāṣir-i Khusraw as the most populous city he had seen, is conservatively estimated by Lambton to have had 100,000 inhabitants in the tenth century.[41] Bulliet estimates the population of ninth-century Nishapur to have been between 100,000 and 500,000 people.[42]

In the western part of Dār al-Islām there were also large cities, for some of which estimates are available. Doubtless Cordova was the greatest of these, estimated to have a population between 500,000 and 1,000,000.[43] In the twelfth and thirteenth centuries, Fez is estimated by Fitzgerald to have had a population of 400,000.[44] Talbi suggests that in the ninth century Qairawān had a population of "several hundred thousand".[45]

To be sure, these estimates, conservative though some of them may be, and very incomplete in coverage though they are, may nevertheless give an exaggerated picture of the rate of urbanization. For the growth of new cities was in part at the expense of some of the conquered cities. Carthage, Alexandria and Antioch – great coastal cities of antiquity – all declined as inland cities burgeoned; and the Sasanian capital, Ctesiphon, was eventually abandoned altogether. Nor did all the early Islamic cities reach their apogee at the same time. There was much shifting of populations between neighbouring cities as trade routes changed or as rulers moved capitals, administrative centres and military posts. On occasion, one city might rise almost out of the ruins of another. Still, the decline of the cities of late antiquity in early Islamic times was often – even in some of the most spectacular cases – not very significant in absolute terms;[46] and the fact of migrations between towns can only qualify, and not invalidate, the thesis that this world was becoming more citified. What is perhaps more important to remember is that the figures cited are for only a few of the great cities of the early Islamic world, and that in addition to the great cities there was a host of lesser towns. Al-Maqqarī wrote that in Muslim Spain there were 80 cities of the first rank, 200 of the second rank and countless small towns and villages.[47] Other parts of the early Islamic world must also have had their greater and their (more numerous) lesser cities. Great and small, they stood as witness to the progress of the agricultural sector from which their populations were fed.

The new crops were also bound up with the rise of linked industries which in their turn stimulated still other economic activities – some of which were in the agricultural sector. One backward linkage has already been noted: the growth of the irrigation industry, which absorbed much capital and employed great numbers of functionaries and labourers.[48] As we have seen, progress in irrigation was a prerequisite for the spread of the new crops. However, the forward linkages should perhaps be stressed here. Since many of the new crops had to be processed before they could be used, their introduction gave rise to employment and sometimes investment outside the agricultural sector. Some of the processing could be performed as usufacture: the drying, cooking, pickling and milling of some of the crops, for instance, could be done in the home of the user. Often enough, however, the workers who carried out even these simple tasks sold their products or their labour on the market. Other tasks required such a degree of skill or such expensive equipment that they were more often carried out by a specialized labour force. In this way the new crops brought new industries into being. The milling of rice was such an industry. Rice could be milled by hand-operated querns in the home; but the work was often – probably most often – done by mills driven by animals, water or wind.[49] Two such forward-linked industries became very large: the refining of sugar and the processing of cotton. They appeared in many parts of the Islamic world, employing large numbers of people and, in the case of sugar refining, tying up large investments in plant and machinery.[50] Their finished products in turn gave rise to other industries: sugar to the making of the sweets, pastries and confectionery which, for better or worse, are so loved in the Islamic world, and cotton to the manufacture of clothing, paper and household articles made of cotton cloth or cotton wool.[51] Cotton manufacture also acted in turn on the agricultural sector by creating a demand for dyestuffs, such as indigo (another new crop), and other fibres, such as linen and silk, which were often mixed with cotton. Still other industries depending on the new crops were the manufacture of medicines, cosmetics, perfumes and oils; and these, too, because they sometimes combined the new crops with other produce of the land, often linked back to the agricultural sector.

Finally, the rise of the new agriculture was bound up with a growing trade in agricultural produce and to a deeper penetration of the money economy into the countryside. City markets, as we have seen, attracted surpluses from hinterlands that grew as the cities themselves grew.[52] In the rural areas thus pulled into the urban economy production became increasingly specialized as it came to be governed less by the needs of the tenant or the landowner and more by the requirements of the market. Growing specialization of rural land and labour raised still more the productivity of agriculture in several ways: by reducing the loss of time involved in changing from one task to another, by giving workers a better chance to acquire special skills (and several of the new crops required very skilled labour), and by using land for more productive crops. The growth of long-distance trade in some of the crops carried the specialization of the countryside – and the spread of the money economy – still further. Cotton (and cotton thread and cloth), rice, sugar, coconuts (as well as the fronds, branches and trunks of the coconut palm) and doubtless some other new crops, not to mention many of the traditional crops, were traded over long distances in the Islamic world. Some were exported on an important scale beyond the limits of Dār al-Islām: sugar and cotton, for instance, were sent from many parts of the Muslim Mediterranean to Christian Europe.[53] Besides affecting the economy of both the producing and consuming region, all this trade, both local and long-distance, generated an important class of intermediaries trading in foodstuffs; and these merchants in turn were serviced by transporters, financiers and the owners of warehouses.[54] To the extent – still unclear – that rural producers were able to buy from the cities as well as sell to them – to the extent, that is, that their cash incomes were not removed from them as rents and taxes or in some other way – rural dependence on the cities carried still further the specialization of rural labour, stimulated the growth of urban industries, and enlarged still more the class of intermediaries.[55]

What one glimpses, even from such a superficial survey, is an agricultural sector developing within an economy which was also developing, each acting upon the other to determine the overall pattern of growth. The ways in which this interaction took place are numberless and sometimes they are obscure; to trace in a serious fashion all the strands in this economic skein would take many years or lifetimes, if indeed it were possible. But from the brief sketch of some of the interconnections presented above we may conclude that the interacting parts of the early Islamic economy were on the whole responsive to the needs of each other: one part seems generally able to supply what was demanded by another. Blockages there must have been, to be sure, and inadequate responses, and these biased the course of development in ways that are worth identifying and explaining. But the overall responsiveness of the different parts of the economy is impressive. This in turn implies an elasticity in many other areas which impinge on economic life: in attitudes, tastes, skills, labour supplies, resources, institutions, laws, technology and money supplies. All these connections would be still more difficult to illuminate, though they are worth pondering. But the point remains that it is in the context of the performance of the whole economy, and indeed of the operation of many factors usually deemed to lie outside the economic sphere, that we should study the flowering of Islamic agriculture – and its later decline.

Part Five
Later centuries

CHAPTER TWENTY-FIVE

Agriculture in retreat

The end of the tale is the story of the decay of Islamic agriculture in general and the waning importance of many new crops in particular. Decline set in at different times in different places and once initiated it proceeded at different speeds. On occasion it was accelerated by seemingly exogenous factors that impinged on the Islamic world from without: the Black Death and the almost unrelenting rise of the European economies are examples, even though their consequences cannot be understood except against a background of ongoing rural decadence.[1] At other times the process was momentarily arrested, or even reversed, as smaller or larger regions experienced periods of revival: Egypt in the thirteenth and early fourteenth centuries, Tunisia in the thirteenth and fifteenth centuries, and parts of the Ottoman empire in the sixteenth century.[2] But the general trend was clearly downward. As decay proceeded, much of what had been achieved was undone. Agricultural land and labour gradually – or on occasion quickly – became less productive, and some land was abandoned. The decline affected the new crops studied in this volume, many of which could be accommodated only with increasing difficulty. Some disappeared altogether.

At the pinnacle of its development, early Islamic agriculture had probably accomplished all or nearly all that was possible with the known resources and technology. Virtually all exploitable land and water were used to their potential, except where these were claimed by cities. Rural settlement had become very dense in many regions of ancient agriculture and the frontiers of cultivation had been pushed back into new areas supporting settlements that, in keeping with the possibilities, were sometimes dense and sometimes sparse. As the upper limits to growth were approached, the forward momentum of agriculture – and whatever else in the economy had depended on it – was lost. Growth could have been sustained only by eliminating constraints, for example through the introduction of new or improved crops and technology, or by the discovery or conquest of new lands. But for various reasons, some of which will be discussed below, the Islamic world failed to remove the barriers to further expansion.

It may even be argued that the growth of the agricultural sector in the early centuries of Islam was excessive: it was carried beyond the point that was safe. Lands may have been irrigated or cropped so intensively that they finally became too saline or too infertile for intensive – or perhaps any – cultivation; and the pushing of the frontier of cultivation into marginal lands and forested regions may have led to the erosion of soil and the lowering of water tables. Thus the initial decline of Islamic agriculture may have been triggered by the excesses of its period of expansion – by its at first unnoticed but later more apparent overextension.[3] As settlement retreated from certain areas and as the productivity of some occupied regions declined, a process of economic contraction was unleashed which – fed perhaps from other sources as well – gained its own momentum.

Regardless of whether this argument is correct, – and doubt is permitted – it seems clear that at its peak the new agriculture was exceedingly fragile. Overextended or not, it could sustain production at high levels only if a great many conditions were satisfied. The fertility and moisture of the soil had to be protected by techniques that were often very labour-consuming and which might not be effective in the face of climate changes; water tables, on which some irrigation works depended, had to be maintained by preventing excessive runoff of rainwater and by husbanding groundwater. The irrigation works themselves had to be kept in repair, often at great cost. There had to be ways of settling water disputes fairly. At the margin of settlement and sometimes elsewhere cultivators had to be protected from attack. What is more, the high degree of specialization of land and labour in many agricultural regions depended on a high degree of specialization in other agricultural regions and in other sectors of the economy, and this specialization in turn depended on much else: on an adequate money supply, on the maintenance of land and water transport, on the security of trade routes and cities, on the sustained demand for agricultural products in their markets, and so forth. Failure in any of these areas could undo some of what had been achieved. Sometimes even temporary failure could have long-lasting or permanent results, as orchards and vineyards which had take years to mature were destroyed in a moment, or as trees and soil cover were irrecoverably lost. When it was at its peak, then, Islamic agriculture was also at its most vulnerable. It had none of the resilience of the agriculture of early medieval Europe, where largely self-sufficient communities of peasants lived by the extensive cultivation of a small part of the land area. Instead it could survive only in a complex environment protected by a government that was centralized, powerful and sympathetic.

Still other weaknesses were inherent in the pattern of settlement of the early Islamic world. Although the early centuries of Islam had seen a rising density of population in the countryside and a gradual filling up of many empty spaces, the end result was still an occupation of the land that was highly discontinuous. The bands of settlement along the great river valleys, the enclaves around the lower reaches of wadis, the pockets surrounding oases were separated from one another by greater or smaller – but usually greater – stretches of land that were in some places suitable for non-intensive, dry farming but for the most part could be used, if at all, only for nomadic grazing. Whereas the growth of population in Europe in the Middle Ages led to the clearing of new lands and gradually to a continuum of settlements which stretched virtually across the whole continent and were interrupted only occasionally by a mountain range or other unusable land, in the early Islamic world, even when population had expanded to its limit, the settled areas were still very scattered. The disadvantages to patchwork settlement were serious. The great empty spaces added to the cost of – and hence inhibited – trade, communications, centralized administration and defence. For isolated communities of peasants virtually no protection whatever could be provided by central governments, and even larger settled areas were usually easy prey for invading armies or nomadic raiders. When conditions of life became difficult for frontier communities, either because of pressure from foreign powers seeking to enlarge their territories or through harassment by the bedouin, the only solution must often have been withdrawal. For lack of defence the frontier of settlement must often have retreated and cultivated areas reverted to desert.

Although the agricultural history of the Islamic world in its period of decadence is still largely unwritten, we can sometimes catch glimpses of the process of decay. As early as the ninth century settlement retreated from the eastern frontier bordering the desert in the Hijaz, in Transjordania and in much of Syria.[4] The reasons for this precocious abandonment of land are still obscure, and it may have nothing to do with what was to follow; indeed, it ran counter to the general expansion of agriculture in almost all other parts of the early Islamic world at that time. Possibly this region is an example of the overextension of sedentary agriculture into the desert; possibly the cause was a change in the weather which progressively desiccated areas on the fringe of the desert; possibly governments were no longer able, or willing, to protect this frontier of settlement against nomads. Whatever the explanation, this area was in its time exceptional. Elsewhere agriculture prospered and even expanded, it seems, until well into the tenth century and in many places through much of the eleventh century; as we have mentioned, there were sporadic, localized examples of rural prosperity even in later centuries. Thus the early abandonment of settlement along the north-western fringes of the Arabian desert is perhaps best seen as a sign: it showed the precarious hold of cultivation in much of the early Islamic world where sedentary agriculture – often very intensive in its use of the land – had been imposed on regions that in their natural state were desert or near-desert.[5]

By the tenth century – or even slightly earlier – the administrative environment in which the agricultural sector had flourished seems to have begun its slow deterioration. Tax farming, unknown in the first decades of Islam, appeared in Khurāsān in 715, and had become more widespread by the tenth century.[6] The authors of taxation manuals inveighed against the practice, claiming that the collectors used force to take more than was due and thereby discouraged both investment and production.[7] To defend themselves against tax collectors, as well as from other lawbreakers and invaders, small landowners commended their lands, and perhaps their persons, to the protection of more powerful landowners or to the ruler. The *talji'a*, as this commendation was called, allowed the former landowner the right to alienate his holding, as his land had now become, but the locus of ownership was clouded as some property rights were assumed by the new protector. In particular, the protector collected payments from the former landowner which were considerably higher than mere land taxes and might be changed arbitrarily: they presumably included payment for protection and probably also a component that was akin to rent. With the State becoming less able to protect the weak, protectors could intimidate reluctant landowners into commending their lands. Small and even medium-sized ownerships were thus caught in the growing web of the large estates. Their formerly free owners found themselves reduced to a state of dependence.[8]

By this time, too, there had appeared a landholding institution, the *waqf* or *mawqūf*, which, as it spread over the whole of the Islamic world, was to have devastating effects on agricultural productivity. Known in the eighth century and perhaps even earlier, the *waqf* was at first relatively harmless: early examples seem to involve the transfer of income but not ownership of small properties to relatives, often for limited periods of time.[9] In such cases both the owners of the property and the beneficiaries of the *waqf* might be expected to take an interest in the efficient management of the land. By the tenth century, however, there had appeared *waqf* endowments which were larger in scale and for the benefit of institutions rather than individuals: for instance of mosques, schools and caravanserais. What is more, the ownership of the property as well as its income seems to have been lost forever by the donor, while the beneficiary held the land in mortmain and was thus unable to alienate it. As a general rule, those in charge of the institutions that received such endowments had not the time, inclination or expertise to see that their property was efficiently managed. This task was made still more difficult by the fact that the lands from which their income derived were often not only distant but also scattered.[10] Frequently their revenues declined and, as al-Maqrīzī complained, were inadequate to support the institution. The farming out of their income to managers in return for fixed sums and for limited periods only made matters worse as the holders of the farm attempted to maximize short-term revenues at the expense of both land and labour. As time wore on, more land was immobilized in *waqf* endowments. A study of sixteenth-century Syria shows that in nearly every district very high proportions of total agricultural income were committed in *waqf*; in many places all rents were so claimed.[11] By later Ottoman times the "dead hand" of the *waqf* had touched three-quarters of all agricultural land in the empire. In places the proportion was still higher.[12]

From the eleventh century onwards, however, agricultural decline becomes more evident, and more general, as one region after another fell prey to successive waves of invaders: the Saljūqs, Crusaders, Ayyūbids, Mamlūks, Mongols, Tīmūrids and Ottomans in the east, and the Banū Hilāl, Almoravids, Almohads, Normans and Spain's *conquistadores* in the west. With the changes in rulers decline early became apparent. It was particularly visible during and after invasions, which often ruined irrigation works, destroyed permanent crops, closed down trade routes, and caused peasants to take flight. But the aftermath of the invasions sometimes had more long-lasting, if less obvious, effects. Because the conquerors had come from regions where less intensive use was made of the soil, they were on the whole unsympathetic to the kind of agriculture which the early Islamic world had so brilliantly created. They understood and supported systems of farming and land tenure which favoured cereal crops and grazing. The entrepreneurial and administrative environment thus became less and less favourable to specialty crops. Matters were made worse in many areas by failure to maintain irrigation works, by excessive taxation and the corruption of tax collectors, and probably by breakdowns in the rule of law. In many areas the balance of sedentary agriculture and nomadic life once again tipped towards the latter form of land use. Settlements were abandoned. The desert encroached on land that for some centuries – or millennia – had been tilled.[13]

Where the new rulers were Muslim – and hence the conquered lands remained within the Islamic world – the decay of agriculture was probably hastened by new ways of governing regions and collecting taxes. From the tenth century onwards, some regions escaped from central tax collection, and to a large extent from central administration, as a result of two nearly identical types of concession, the *muqāṭaʿa* and the *īghār*, granted to notables and to tribal groups such as Kurds, Turkomans and some bedouin. In return for various immunities, the recipients agreed to pay a fixed sum to the central government.[14] The inhabitants of such concessions, however, were subject to high and arbitrary rates of taxation, without recourse to centrally administered justice. Where these concessions were granted to tribal groups without long traditions of sedentary agriculture, the grazing of flocks might be expected to gain over cultivation.

Another type of concession, which appeared in the tenth century and gradually became very widespread, was also to have discernible and adverse effects on land us over nearly all of the Islamic world. This was the *iqṭāʿ*, a military benefice whose grantee was given the right to collect – and often kept – all taxes from the area conceded.[15] Land so alienated by the State could cover vast spaces: in Mamlūk Egypt probably at least half of the land was granted in *iqṭāʿāt*, while in many other parts of the Islamic world the proportion was much higher.[16] Although the effects of these concessions on agricultural output have yet to be studied in detail, some generalizations may be hazarded. With the exception of Egypt, where the worst evils of the system seem to have been avoided,[17] the *iqṭāʿ* appears to have everywhere discouraged intensive use of the land. In early times, grants were for limited and often unpredictable periods, and even in later times they were not always hereditary; recipients thus tended to maximize revenues over the short run by oppressive rates of taxation, doing little to maintain – let alone develop – either land or irrigation works. Heavy and arbitrary taxation also discouraged landowners and peasants from initiatives which would increase the output of the land. To make matters worse, the holders of *iqṭāʿāt* sometimes were granted or usurped other functions of the State, such as protection and justice, and thereby managed to gain control over the land and people in their concessions – and beyond. Some of the rights of ownership of land tended to be assumed by the holder of the *iqṭāʿ*, while the peasantry by virtue of its debts, its contracts and its weakness tended to become tied both to him and to the land.[18] With revenues thus reduced, central governments played roles of diminishing importance. Increasingly, their functions were assumed by local potentates whose control over land and men thus grew. By Ottoman times the area of *milk*, or privately owned land, had been greatly reduced and the proportion of the agricultural labour force that was free had also fallen considerably. The factors of agricultural production were thus locked into a system that was much less responsive than in the past to economic opportunities. Growth of the agricultural sector became increasingly difficult. Further decline was easy.

Parallel developments may be seen in the lands overrun by the Christians – Spain, Sicily and the Latin kingdoms in the east.[19] Although the experience of each of these regions under its European conquerors was not identical, a general pattern may be glimpsed; only the coastal strip of the Holy Land and the island of Cyprus stand out as exceptions.[20] Almost everywhere the appearance of Christian soldiers and overlords caused many Muslim peasants and landowners to flee, leaving large tracts of *agri deserti* and much other land which, though not completely abandoned, came to be farmed less intensively. The flight of peasants continued intermittently for some centuries after the conquests, as a result of local persecutions by the Christians and unsuccessful uprisings by the Muslims.[21] The departing peasants were to some extent replaced by immigrants from the heartland of feudal Europe; but the newcomers seem to have been less numerous than those who left, and they were familiar with crops and agricultural techniques different from, and inferior to, those of the Muslims. It is not clear whether some of the most retrograde features of the European manor appeared in the conquered lands – the cultivation of a demesne by servile labour, the communal grazing of flocks on stubble, and the concomitant village-wide rotation of crops on the great fields. Quite possibly they did not. Here as in other newly colonized areas settlers may normally have been granted consolidated holdings free of labour services and communal grazing rights.[22] What is clear is that other, less intensive, features of European agriculture were introduced. More land was given over to grazing, as the European system of mixed farming on large estates came to predominate.[23] On cultivated lands less intensive rotations were used, the soil usually being cropped once every two years.[24] And the crops which had been introduced in early Islamic times tended to disappear They were replaced – even on irrigated land – by the traditional crops of European agriculture: wheat, barley and legumes.[25]

A final blow was dealt to the new crops in the Islamic world by the circumnavigation of Africa and the discovery of the New World. A sign of things to come appeared in the fifteenth century when the Spanish and Portuguese introduced sugar cane into the islands of Madeira, the Canaries, Santiago and São Tomé.[26] By the later part of the fifteenth century and the early sixteenth century sugar from these islands was flooding onto European markets, with ruinous effects on the sugar industry of both the Christian and Muslim Mediterranean.[27] But still greater opportunities were presented by the opening of sea routes to continents with vast tropical and semi-tropical regions where the new crops could be grown more easily – and more cheaply – than in the inhospitable climate and with the costly labour of the Middle East and the Mediterranean basin. Rice, sugar cane, cotton, indigo and some of the other crops brought to the Arab world in the early centuries of Islam began to be grown for export in India, East Asia and the New World and were sent in ever larger quantities to the Islamic world and its former European export markets.[28] New, superior varieties of crops such as cotton, sugar cane and bananas also seem to have given overseas producers an advantage.[29] By the end of the seventeenth century rice, bananas, sugar cane and cotton had largely disappeared from the Mediterranean basin, where they had once been so important, and from some parts of the Middle East.[30] Long ago inroduced into the Islamic world as import substitutes, these crops were in turn replaced by imports; their disappearance contributed to the general decline of the Mediterranean in the seventeenth and eighteenth centuries.

Had it been different, Islamic science might have shown Muslims the way to further agricultural progress. But the advance and decline of Islamic agriculture went hand in hand with the progress and decay of Islamic science. The centuries of agricultural expansion had seen progress in the science of agronomy, as agronomists became familiar with more useful plants and identified more types of soils, winds and waters. Comparable advances were made by this civilization of collectors in other realms of science: in areas related to agriculture, such as botany and pharmacology (where the main achievement seems also to have been the addition of new plants to the lists of those known and used), as well as in such distant branches of science as geography and philology (where progress was made principally in collecting information about more places and more words). In these and many other areas the scientists of the early Islamic world attained knowledge of great breadth – for the time, of almost universal breadth. But in the end there was a limit to what could be achieved by continuing in this direction. When all that was accessible had been collected, identified and catalogued, this kind of science could go no further. Its contribution had been made. Ultimately it was to fall to other peoples – not such avid collectors as the early Muslims, but driven by a strange urge to peer beneath the surface of things and see how they worked – to carry science not only further, but along another road. Islamic science, like Islamic agriculture, was increasingly removed from the mainstream of world development. It became part of a world that had largely closed in upon itself.

True, the expanding geographic horizons of early modern times had familiarized men in many parts of the world with a widening range of useful plants. Some of these were to become of great economic importance in new places far from their old homes. In Islamic agriculture the modern era saw the introduction of maize, tomatoes, tobacco, sweet oranges and other plants from the New World and the Far East.[31] But these new plants, though they may have slowed the downward slide of Islamic agriculture, could not arrest – let alone reverse – the decay of a world in which too many factors conspired against agricultural progress. Inept governments, changing patterns of world trade, a deteriorating physical environment and perhaps changes in the climate all worked not only to limit the effects of these new introductions but to erode still further the achievements of the early centuries of Islam. The kind of development which new plants had initiated long before could not be repeated in a context that had radically altered.

Notes
Works cited
Index

Notes

1. Introduction

1 In the chapters on individual crops, we show that there were developed in Islamic times new botanical varieties of sorghum, cotton and citrus fruits, many of which were better suited to the environment of the Middle East and the Mediterranean. Many new cultivars also appeared.

2 Al-Jāḥiẓ, cited in PELLAT *Le milieu* 236; IBN WAḤSHĪYA "Filāḥa" III 545–6 and AL-DŪRĪ *Ta'rīkh* 60; IBN RUSTA 125; text of al-Anṣārī in TORRES BALBÁS "Las ruinas" 290–4; 'ABD AL-LAṬĪF *Kitāb al-ifādah* 66. AL-BADRĪ *passim* states that in the region of Damascus were to be found 21 cultivars of apricots, 50 cultivars of raisins, 6 cultivars of roses etc. See also 'ĪSÀ 100–1. There are, of course, many other accounts of the great varieties of agricultural produce in different regions. BOSWELL 177 states that three new cultivars of cauliflower were introduced into Spain in the twelfth century, but gives no source.

3 For the diffusion of citrus trees, see TOLKOWSKY, and for sugar cane, see DEERR and LIPPMANN.

4 Some general discussion of the diffusion of new plants through the early Islamic world is to be found in SCHWEINFURTH "Aegyptens"; RENAUD; MEYERHOF "Esquisse" and "Essai"; CHEVALIER "Le rôle joué"; ABŪ AL-NAṢR; and 'ĪSÀ.

5 The Arabic manuals of farming are surveyed in SHIHĀBĪ "Al-filāḥa" and "Kutub"; SHIHĀBĪ *et al.* "Filāḥa"; MILLÁS VALLICROSA *La ciencia*; CAHEN "Notes pour une histoire"; and the introduction to IBN AL-'AWWĀM tr. Clément-Mullet. The geographical and travel literature up to the middle of the eleventh century is reviewed in MIQUEL, and EBEID lists the relevant works of medicine, pharmacy and botany.

6 Pioneering work in the identification of ancient plant materials has been done by Dr Hans Helbaek of Copenhagen, many of whose publications are listed in the bibliography of this book. For further discussion of recent advances in methodology, see RENFREW 1ff.

7 CANDOLLE 20–8.

8 PORTÈRES *Appellations.*

9 The pioneering work in determining the origins of cultivated plants was carried out by the great French botanist Alphonse de Candolle, who used all the kinds of evidence that were available in the middle of the nineteenth century. For a description of his methodology see CANDOLLE 8–28. In spite of the variety of evidence which he brought to bear on his enquiries, Candolle placed great emphasis on the locus where plants grew truly wild as an indicator of their origin. This approach was refined by Russian botanists N. Vavilov and P. M. Zhukovskij, who argued that plants have developed where they show the greatest variety in the wild forms, and by the German botanist Elizabeth Schiemann, who put forward the idea that there are secondary centres of plant development in places removed from the centres of origin. See VAVILOV *Tsentry*, *The Origin* and "Geographische Genzentren"; ZHUKOVSKIJ *passim*; and SCHIEMANN *Die*

Entstehung and "Gedanken zur Genzentrentheorie". More recently, however, this heavy reliance on the distribution of the wild plant has been overtly criticized by HARLAN "Agricultural", and an implicit criticism may be found in the whole thrust of the work of RENFREW. For a discussion of further difficulties in this kind of enquiry, see HELBAEK "The Fyrkat".

10 As will be seen in the chapter on cotton below, intercrossing amongst the wild, cultivated and escaped forms of Old World cotton may be what confounds attempts to locate the wild ancestor.

11 The appearance of annual varieties, which were developed from perennial varieties, has been little studied. See, however, the pioneering works of WHYTE "Cytogenetical", "The botanical" and "An environmental", where it is argued that annual varieties were developed when the perennial varieties were subjected to environmental stress, e.g. where the climate was too cold or the days too short. The development of annual varieties of Old World cotton, discussed in the chapter on cotton below, may be a case in point.

12 As will be seen below, this difficult diffusion was made possible partly by altering the environment of the Middle East and the Mediterranean through irrigation and partly by the development of new varieties.

13 IBN KHALDŪN *Muqaddimah* I 302–5.

14 SOLIGNAC *Recherches* 7 *et passim* points out that French archeologists and others working in Tunisia had consistently assigned to the Romans many irrigation works which he shows clearly to be Arab; see, for instance, GAUCKLER. A similar mistake may be seen in BEADNELL 167ff where all the *qanawāt* of the Libyan desert are attributed to the Romans. SAUVAGET "Remarques" shows that many of the palaces of the Transjordanian and Syrian desert, once thought to have been Roman or Byzantine, are in reality Arab. See also the introductory remarks in CHERBONNEAU, and GLICK *Irrigation* 168ff. See also p. 191 n. 34.

15 REIFENBERG 99 *et passim*.

16 As is now well known, there were cities of some importance in parts of the pre-Islamic Arabian peninsula; these were fed mainly with the surplus produced in settled regions lying nearby. In the Yemen and in Oman intensive, irrigated agriculture was highly developed before the rise of Islam. The Arab armies which took part in the later conquests contained many Yemeni who settled in the conquered lands. For the Yemeni settlers in Spain, see AL-MAQQARĪ tr. Gayangos II 20ff; GLICK *Irrigation* 230; RIBERA Y TARRAGÓ II 212ff; GUICHARD "Le peuplement" 105, 111; and LÉVI-PROVENÇAL *Histoire* I 44ff, 81ff. Information on Yemeni settlement in Syria, Iraq, Egypt and Azerbaijan is to be found in AL-BALĀDHURĪ I 435–6; AL-YA'QŪBĪ 173, 174, 176, 177 *et passim*; AL-MAQRĪZĪ *Description* I 298; SPULER *Iran* 249; DJAÏT; and VADET.

17 It is clear that in many regions the Arabs either settled in lands not previously occupied (see AL-BALĀDHURĪ I 278) or appeared in previously settled lands as landowners who left farming to the indigenous peoples. On the other hand, many non-Arabs migrated during the early centuries of Islam, bringing with them the agricultural tradition of their homelands. On the Persian influences on North African agriculture, see SOLIGNAC "Travaux" 563. LÉVI-PROVENÇAL *L'Espagne* 159 argues that the majority of settlers coming to Spain were Maghribi and that these had a long tradition of settled agriculture.

18 For example, IBN 'ABDŪN 9 urged that "the Prince should insist that greater encouragement be given to the cultivation of the land. The soil should be preserved; the peasants should be treated well... The Prince should order his ministers and the powerful people in the capital city to have their own landed estates... For agriculture is at the base of civilization: all life flows from it." LAMBTON *Landlord* xxvii ff cites Najm al-Dīn Rāzī's exposition of the duties of a *vazīr*: "let the *vazīr* be continually solicitous concerning the condition of the *amīrs*, prominent persons, the peasants and the military, so that he will provide the peasants with equipment... and will not lay heavy burdens upon them. This will be achieved when the *vazīr* strives to develop material prosperity and agriculture." LAMBTON *Landlord* xix also cites the instructions given to Mālik al-Ashtar in 658/9: "give greater

attention to the development of the land than to the collection of the *kharāj* because the *kharāj* can be obtained only by the development of the land". According to AL-MASʻŪDĪ ed. Barbier de Meynard VII 104, the caliph Muʻtaṣim said that "agriculture has many advantages. It feeds domestic animals, lowers the price of foodstuffs, increases the sources of commerce and contributes to well-being." See also GRABAR *et al.* I 163 and LAMBTON "Reflections on the role" 294ff. Much more in the same vein can be found in the literature.

2. *Sorghum*

1 We intend to treat mainly those sorghums which are grown as cereals, leaving aside broomcorn (*S. bicolor* var. *technicum*) and sweet-cane sorghum (*S. saccharatum*). As has been pointed out by DOGGETT 57, 65ff and GARBER 319ff, the available taxonomy for the cultivated sorghums – mostly developed in SNOWDEN – is no longer satisfactory. For some purposes the simplified classification proposed by HARLAN AND STEMLER and HARLAN AND DE WET is useful; this divides the cultivated sorghums of Africa into five main races: bicolor (the first to be domesticated), guinea (grown in West Africa), kafir (grown in south-east Africa), caudatum (grown in Sudan, Chad and Urganda) and durra (which is virtually the only sorghum grown in the Islamic countries, and which is very important in India and Ethiopia). But in certain parts of our treatment it has been necessary to retain the taxonomy of SNOWDEN.

2 Various problems connected with the Arabic words for sorghum are discussed in the text and notes below. The main sources of information are ABŪ ḤANĪFA ed. Lewin 183; PORTÈRES *Appellations* 109ff; ADRIAN AND GAST 14; CLÉMENT-MULLET 219–24; SCHWEINFURTH *Arabische* 121, 160; and TRABUT *Répertoire* 246. Here it should be noted that ABŪ ḤANĪFA ed. Lewin *loc. cit.* states that *dhurra* is *jāwars hindī*, and in this he is followed by *Glosario* 211. Whether the unmodified *jāwars* usually designates sorghum is unclear. *Tuḥfat* 44–5 states that in parts of Morocco *jāwars* is the term for sorghum. But IBN WAḤSHĪYA "Filāḥa" II 201ff treats *jāwars* as distinct from both *dhurra* and *dukhn* (which is described in IBN WAḤSHĪYA "Filāḥa" II 202; IBN AL-ʻAWWĀM ed. Banqueri II 81; and which designates common millet, the word may have been used in the eastern reaches of the early Islamic world to designate another kind of millet – or just possibly a variety of sorghum introduced before *S. durra.* In Arabic ms. 4947 of the Bibliothèque Nationale in Paris, which is the Arabic translation of Dioscorides' *Materia medica*, there is an illustration of *jāwars*, which is unfortunately not clear enough to permit identification. The fact that this manuscript makes no mention of *dhurra*, though it does speak of *dukhn*, suggests that *jāwars* was probably another kind of millet known in the eastern Mediterranean long before *dhurra* was introduced.

3 In the eighteenth century NIEBUHR I 289–90 noted a yield/seed ratio of 400:1 in the coastal part of the Yemen.

4 MONTAGNÉ 974; ADRIAN AND GAST 25ff; DOGGETT 50. The making of bread from sorghum is described in IBN WAḤSHĪYA "Filāḥa" II 202; IBN AL-ʻAWWĀM ed. Banqueri II 81; and IBN AL-BAIṬĀR II 418. EL-SAMARRAIE 89–90 notes that in the tenth-century Iraq bread made from sorghum was preferred to rice bread. GOBERT 539 describes its use in soups and pastries in medieval Tunisia. Medical uses are given in IBN AL-BAIṬĀR II 147 and IBN BUṬLĀN ed. Ricci II 42.

5 SNOWDEN 240 *et passim*, which is the fundamental (but now outdated) work on the subject; WET AND HUCKABY; PORTÈRES "Vieilles" 494–7 and "Berceaux" 201ff; DOGGETT 59; BURKILL "Habits"; GARBER 333; BOIS IV 180.

6 HARLAN "Plant", "The origins" and *Crops* 153ff.

7 The supposed depiction of sorghum is reproduced in MARSHALL, photograph 5 of pl. LXXXVII. The material from Ahar is reported in VISHNU-MITTRE "Protohistoric" 96; *Evolutionary Studies* 21; and in the discussion by Allchin which follows JOSEPH B. HUTCHINSON "India".

8 VISHNU-MITTRE *loc. cit.*; HUTCHINSON *loc. cit.* This find revises the views of ALLCHIN 325 and ALLCHIN AND ALLCHIN 266 that sorghum was not grown in India until the early part of the first millennium. At Nevasa the earliest evidence of sorghum comes from the level of Period V, which is dated between 200 and 50 B.C.; see SANKALIA *et al.* 67, 530. There is no certain name for sorghum in Sanskrit: words of the *zoorna* and *juwar* groups seem to have referred to the principal cereal of a region or sometimes more specifically to barley, while the meaning of the other words adduced is uncertain. See WATT *Commercial* 1032–3, whose thesis that there are "wild sorghums native to India" has been disproved by Snowden; PORTÈRES *Appellations* 114ff; BURKILL *Dictionary* II 2057. On the other hand, the possibility that sorghum may at a very early date have spread from India to China, and perhaps even to Java, Mesopotamia and Italy, speaks for the antiquity of its cultivation in India; see the discussion which follows in the text of this chapter.

9 See n. 6 above and STEMLER, HARLAN AND DE WET. This work seems to have refuted the thesis of Doggett that *S. durra* was developed in Ethiopia.

10 HO *The Cradle* 380–4; YIN AND LI. I am indebted to Professor Evelyn Rawski for translating the latter article for me. W. WATSON 398–9 doubts this evidence, stating that the cereals of Neolithic China were millet and possibly wheat and rice.

11 HO *loc. cit.*

12 BRETSCHNEIDER *Botanicon* II 147 and *On the Study* 9 maintained that there was literary evidence for sorghum in China from the fourth century. This claim has been refuted by HAGERTY. In any case sorghum cannot have been common in China until later times: see *Food in Chinese* 27, 147.

13 BARTLETT 13 shows that Javanese tradition gives the year 371 as the date of the introduction of "maize" into Java. As such an early introduction of maize seems impossible, he suggests that the word now used to designate maize may earlier have referred to sorghum.

14 This relief, now in the British Museum, is reproduced in PIÉDALLU pl. I facing p. 32. DOGGETT 61 wrongly states that the relief is from Timgad. A similar, probably identical, plant is depicted in a relief of the fifth century from Taq-i-bostan; this is reproduced in GHIRSHMAN *Parthes* 194–6.

15 HERODOTUS I 242–3 (bk I 193): "As for millet and sesame, I will not say, though it is known to me, to what height they grow, for I am well aware that what I have said regarding corn is wholly disbelieved by those who have never visited Babylonia".

16 WET AND HARLAN 133 state that the plant represented is almost certainly a common reed, *Phragmites communis*.

17 BRETZL *passim*. The various grains mentioned in DIOSCORIDES ed. Wellmann I 173–4 (bk II 96–8) appear to be barley, common millet and foxtail millet.

18 AL-ṬABARĪ 242ff; NEWMAN *passim*.

19 DIXON "A note" 135. LÖW *Aramäische* has no Aramaic word for sorghum. LÖW *Flora* 1740–6 seems to be wrong in suggesting that various words of the *dukhn* and *arzan* groups may refer to sorghum; almost certainly they refer to millet. RENFREW gives no evidence of sorghum in the pre-Islamic Near East or Egypt. See also PIÉDALLU 21ff; TÄCKHOLM, TÄCKHOLM AND DRAR I 520–41; MOLDENKE AND MOLDENKE 222–3; and HARTMANN 53. Certain words in GALEN fasc. I 14–15 and the Bible (Matt. XXVII 48, Mark XV 36 and John XIX 29) have sometimes been thought to refer to sorghum, but all these attributions are extremely doubtful.

20 WINLOCK AND CRUMM 61. Schweinfurth identified the specimen as *S. durra*.

21 TRABUT *Répertoire* 246; PORTÈRES *Appellations* 135–8, 153–4. One of the terms mentioned by Trabut is *ṭamm*, which is also the word for sorghum in the Yemen (see SCHWEINFURTH *Arabische* 121, 160). A separate diffusion of sorghum – or simply the name – may have occurred from the Yemen to North Africa.

22 Map in DOGGETT 51–2 and *passim*.

23 PLINY V 224 (bk XVIII 10): "A millet has been introduced into Italy within the last ten

years that is of black colour and has a large grain and a stalk like that of a reed; it grows seven feet in height, with very large hairs... It is the most prolific of all cereals, one grain producing 3/16 of a peck. It should be sown in damp ground."

24 NICCOLI 189. CRESCENTIIS (d. 1321) 76ff (bk III 7) mentions sorghums with red and white seeds; the black-seeded variety seems to have been unknown to him. See also SACCARDO *Cronologia* 9.

25 See n. 22 above.

26 The hypotheses advanced in this paragraph are based on the evidence presented in PORTÈRES *Appellations* 109ff. See also the references cited in n. 5 above. The identification by certain lexicographers of the Sanskrit *zoorna* with sorghum (PORTÈRES *op. cit.* 114) is almost certainly an anachronism. *Jāwars hindī* is given by ABŪ ḤANĪFA ed. Lewin 183 as meaning *dhurra*, and was thus probably also the term used in Persian at the time.

27 AL-IṢṬAKHRĪ 79; IBN ḤAWQAL I 53.

28 *Ḥudūd* 124, 147 *et passim.*

29 AL-HAMDĀNĪ *Südarabien* 94, 95, 130, 179, 267–9. It is probably also sorghum (designated as *jāwars*) that is mentioned in the South Yemen by *Ḥudūd* 147. In the fourteenth century, IBN BAṬṬŪṬA II 197 stated that sorghum was the principal crop around Dhofar.

30 IBN WAḤSHĪYA "Filāḥa" II 201ff; see also I 27, 134, 170, 171, 176, 186, 188 and II 228, 345. See also AL-DŪRĪ *Ta'rīkh* 30 and ABŪ ḤANĪFA ed. Lewin 183, who mentions white and black varieties.

31 YĀQŪT II 308.

32 AL-IDRĪSĪ *Description* 6, 24; IBN ḤAWQAL I 53; AL-ZUHRĪ 184; AL-MAS'ŪDĪ ed. Barbier de Meynard II 383; YĀQŪT IV 820; 'ABD AL-LAṬĪF *Relation* 32. All of these writers find sorghum growing only in the upper Nile region. The cultivation of sorghum, however, is discussed by the Egyptian agricultural writers AL-WAṬWĀṬ ch. 3 and AL-GHAZZĪ *passim.*

33 AL-YA'QŪBĪ 205 and 225 noted it at Zawīla in Tripolitania and at Sijilmasa in Morocco; YĀQŪT I 400 spoke of it at Ozghart; and AL-'UMARĪ 101 mentioned it in Ifrīqiya.

34 See *Calendrier* IBN AL-'AWWĀM ed. Banqueri II 78–82 stated that it was discussed by Abū al-Khair.

35 *Loc. cit.*

36 AL-BAKRĪ *Jughrāfīya* 80; HÉMARDINQUER 450–1. DOÑATE SEBASTIA 10–12 publishes fourteenth- and fifteenth-century documents from the Archivio Municipal of Villarreal which speak of *paniç* and *dacsa.* These he suggests are forms of maize. The more plausible interpretation is that they are forms of *panicum* or millet, but since one document mentions both of these along with *mill* they may refer to types of sorghum. The suggestion seems all the more likely since the documents speak of red and white kinds.

37 LANGE 65.

38 PORTÈRES *Appellations* 143–4. Some sorghums may also have come to East Africa from the Yemen, for the Yemeni name, *ṭamm*, seems to have given the Swahili *ma-tama.* It is possible, however, that only the name was transmitted. The Yemeni names are given in SCHWEINFURTH *Arabische* 121, 160, and the Swahili name in PORTÈRES *op. cit.* 109.

39 ABŪ ZAID 127; AL-MAS'ŪDĪ ed. Barbier de Meynard III 30.

40 PORTÈRES *loc. cit.*

41 HARLAN "Plant" and *Crops* 153ff; HARLAN AND STEMLER 477. Many medieval geographers and travellers mentioned sorghum – though not necessarily *S. durra* – in West Africa and the Sudan: YĀQŪT II 822 and 933, who spoke of it at Tibir and Zaghawa in the kingdom of the Sudan; AL-'UMARĪ 9, 44, 50, 61, who found it in Kanem and Mali as well as in Abyssinia and Nubia; IBN BAṬṬŪṬA IV 394, 433–4, 437, 438–9, who mentioned it in Mali, in the regions of the Bardama tribe (whose principal food it was), in Timbuktu, in Takadda and elsewhere; AL-BAKRĪ *Description* 300, who saw it at Awdaghast; and IBN AL-FAQĪH 51, who stated that it was the staple in Ghana. (In a number of these references the word *dhurra* has been mistranslated as "millet".) It was possibly sorghum, referred to as *milho zaburro*, that the Portuguese explorers of the late fifteenth and early sixteenth

centuries found growing in various parts of the West African coast. See, for example, FERNANDES 15, who saw this grain in the Senegambia region, where the inhabitants made a kind of cous-cous from it. TEIXEIRA DA MOTA AND CARREIRA *passim* suggest that this grain may be *Pennisetum*, but the sixteenth-century herbal of DODOENS 538 clearly states that the term "milium saburrum" designates sorghum.

42 NIEBUHR I 289–90.

3. Rice

1 The term "Asiatic rice" is used here to distinguish *O. sativa* L. from a rice native to Africa, *O. glaberrima* Steud., which has been cultivated in certain parts of West Africa for perhaps over three millennia. See PORTÈRES "Vieilles", "Géographie" and *Appellations* 176ff. There are, of course, many varieties of Asiatic rice, and the Chinese local gazetteers of the Ming period distinguished among these; see RAWSKI 39–44. In the Arabic agricultural manuals, however, different varieties of rice were not identified. But as rice was put to various uses in the early Islamic world, and was clearly grown in different ways, quite different varieties must have been known. A glutinous kind of rice was probably used for wine and vinegar, another kind for bread and so forth.

2 ABŪ ḤANĪFA ed. Lewin 45 also gives *runz*, apparently derived from the Persian or Sanskrit, as an "incorrect" Arabic term.

3 MUḤAMMAD IBN AL-ḤASAN 44–7 (where *inter alia* the recipe for *muḥallabīya* is given), 195, 199, 200; "Kitāb al-ṭabīkh" 184–5, 187, 190, 192, 199; RODINSON "Recherches" 135–7; AL-MAS'ŪDĪ ed. Barbier de Meynard VIII 401, 404–5, where descriptions are given of the famous dishes *aruzza* and *judāba*; IBN WAḤSHĪYA "Filāḥa" II 299, 321, 324, 328, 332, 341; CANARD 120ff, who makes the interesting point that in many coastal and swampy areas dishes which combined rice and fish (possibly the origin of paella) were very common; LIPPMANN 110. Other recipes are given in IBN AL-'AWWĀM ed. Banqueri II 62. See also CANARD 120ff.

4 *Ḥudūd al-'ālam* 134. IBN BAṬṬŪṬA II 5 wrote of the rice bread eaten by some Ṣūfīs in Wāsiṭ. IBN AL-BAIṬĀR I 43–4, quoting Dioscorides, also spoke of rice bread, and the making of bread from rice flour was discussed by IBN WAḤSHĪYA "Filāḥa" I 186 and II 200–1, 228, 243, 345 and by IBN AL-'AWWĀM ed. Banqueri II 63.

5 The Chinese and Indian practice of making rice wine and vinegar is mentioned in IBN RUSTA 149; *Akhbār* 11; and POLO 161. IBN AL-'AWWĀM ed. Banqueri II 63, IBN WAḤSHĪYA "Filāḥa" II 201, 301 and POLO 276 wrote of rice wine and vinegar as products of the Islamic world.

6 AL-RĀZĪ *Kitāb* V 225, 251, VI 190–1, 251 and VIII 25, 28, 40, 48; IBN AL-BAIṬĀR I 43; IBN WĀFID *Libre* 35; SCHMUCKER 58; *Syrian Anatomy* 164, 363, 549; IBN BUṬLĀN ed. Unterkircher *et al.* I 74.

7 For the views of botanists on the origin of the rice grasses, see VAVILOV *The Origin* 24; SCHIEMANN *Die Entstehung* 304; GRIST 3–6; COYAUD *passim*; CHATTERJEE 18ff; ANGLADETTE 11ff; ZHUKOVSKIJ 9; *Evolutionary Studies* 56–7; and other recent literature referred to below. T.-T. CHANG "Origin and evolution" 425ff and "Origin and early" 9ff has argued convincingly that the progenitors of the cultivated species of Asiatic rice originated on the Gondwanaland continents. They are now represented by perennials which grow wild in the swamplands of a large area stretching from Bengal to South China and Southeast Asia; BARRAU 71 would have this area extended to include "Indo-Oceania". The large area over which the progenitor grows wild has given rise to a number of contenders for the locus of domestication of rice: India (T.-T. CHANG "Origin and early" 12 and "The rice cultures"; VISHNU-MITTRE "Changing economy" 574–5), China (HO "The indigenous" 440ff and *The Cradle* 61ff; K.-C. CHANG *Early* 14–15) and Thailand (GORMAN "Modèles" 54ff and "*A priori* models". Gorman claims much earlier beginnings in Thailand on the basis of evidence that is still circumstantial. But WHYTE "Cytogenetical", "An environmental" and "The botanical" has pointed out that, although rice does grow wild

over a large part of Asia, the annual varieties, which were almost certainly the ones domesticated, could have developed only in limited areas where the perennial varieties suffered physiological stress: where climate became drier or colder, where there were wide fluctuations in temperatures, or where soils were desiccated through overgrazing. He suggests that the annual varieties must have appeared "in a belt from north-east India (Bengal) to south-eastern China (Kwangsi, Kwangtung and Fukien)". Domestication could have begun at various points in or near this belt, and the domesticated plant could have been carried southwards and northwards. Recent attempts to infer a chronology of rice cultivation from the archeological material seem premature, since the amount of evidence is small and its dating sometimes uncertain; in the near future other finds will probably overturn most or all of the proposed theories. Various finds of rice grains in Indian, dating to the early fourth millennium B.C. K.-C. CHANG goes on to postulate that material may date from as early as 3500 B.C. See *Evolutionary Studies* 12–13, 15, 29, 59; ALLCHIN AND ALLCHIN 259, 264 *et passim* (and for the dating of these finds, 336, 337); CLUTTON-BROCK *et al.* 30; VISHNU-MITTRE "Changing economy" 574–5. It is not certain, however, whether the earliest finds were of cultivated or wild rice. Carbonized remains from China have been dated about 3215 B.C. ±115; see HO "The indigenous" 440. For evidence of the spread of rice cultivation in pre-historic and early historic India, see the above *passim* and ALLCHIN 325, 327; *A Concise History* 372–3; and CHAUDHURY 23–5. Recently HO *The Cradle* 61ff and K.-C. CHANG *Early* 14–15 and *The Archaeology* 34, 136, 140, 142, 167, 169, 181 have suggested that certain Chinese finds are earlier than the Indian, dating to the early fourth millennium B.C. K.-C. CHANG goes on the postulate that in China rice may have been domesticated by northern farmers of the Lungshanoid culture, who were used to the cultivation of other cereals and who encountered wild rice in the course of their southward expansion. It should be pointed out, however, that the dating of the Chinese material seems to be a little less certain than that of the Indian material.

8 STRABO VII 27–9 (bk XV i 18). Rice cultivation in Mesopotamia is also mentioned in the first century B.C. by DIODORUS IX 265 (bk XIX 13). The existence of a word for rice in Assyrian shows that the grain was known in Mesopotamia as early as the seventh century B.C., but there is no proof that the plant was cultivated there until later. See THOMPSON 106–7. In fact, HERODOTUS I 243 (bk I 193), writing in the fifth century B.C., mentions wheat, barley and millet as the cereal crops of Babylonia, and in the fourth century B.C. THEOPHRASTUS I 319 (bk IV 4) knew of rice cultivation in India only.

9 LAUFER *Sino-Iranica* 372–3; the author of an account from the second century B.C. speaks of rice in Fergana, Parthia and Chaldea, the last two of which, however, he did not visit.

10 *Le Talmud de Jérusalem* II 138, 144–5, 339. See also LÖW *Aramäische* 358–9 and JEHUDA 151, 165.

11 LAUFER *loc. cit.*; HJELT 572. Some evidence for the cultivation of rice in late Sasanian Persia is given by AL-ṬABARĪ 244, who mentions a tax on rice plantations. *The Pahlavi Text* 43 (in the Arabic text but not in the Pahlavi) and CHRISTENSEN 471 also give evidence for the use of rice, but not its cultivation, in late Sasanian Persia. Passages in the *Gemara* suggest that rice was cultivated in Babylonia in the fifth century; see NEWMAN 79.

12 CANARD 113ff argues that rice was not known in pre-Islamic Arabia. A Yemeni treatise on agriculture of the fourteenth century states the contrary without, however, giving any proof; see MEYERHOF "Sur un traité" (1943–4) 53. Rice was clearly not grown in pre-Islamic Egypt: see DIXON "A note" 136–7; SCHNEBEL 100; DARESSY; and TÄCKHOLM, TÄCKHOLM AND DRAR I 412. In the "Periplus of the Erythraean Sea", which dates from the first century, it was stated that rice was sent every year from India to Socotra and to the Horn of Africa, and in the latter region it was obtained by Egyptian merchants. See "Periplus" 64, 94.

13 BRETZL 201–3 discusses the Greek discovery of rice in India at the time of the Alexandrian expedition. See also THEOPHRASTUS I 319 (bk IV 4). Rice is mentioned in many classical works on medicine, e.g. CELSUS I 197, 201, 331, 411, 490; DIOSCORIDES ed. Wellmann I

173 (bk II 95); and PLINY VII 77 (bk XVIII 28), who in V 235–7, 249 (bk XVIII 13, 20) says that rice is imported from India or "the east". The rice mentioned in *Diokletians Preisedikt* 100, which dates from the year 301, may be assumed to have been imported from India, as were several other commodities mentioned in the same section. The term *alica* used in the fourth-century *Expositio* 182–3 to denote a grain grown around Smyrna was translated by Rougé as "rice". As ANDRÉ 23 points out, however, the meaning of the term is obscure; it probably refers to a kind of wheat, but almost certainly not to rice. LANGE 65 reports a find of rice grains at the first-century Roman site of Neuss, near Cologne. These were certainly imported, probably as a medicine. The rice mentioned in a diploma of the abbey of Corbie, dated 716, was clearly imported, as were many other exotic products listed; see LEVILLAIN 235–7.

14 IBN ḤAWQAL I 207 and II 251, 330, 371, 382, 425, 459; AL-MUQADDASĪ *Aḥsan* 76; *Ḥudūd* 137; IBN KHURDĀDHBIH 239, 284; ABŪ ḤAMĪD 203, who saw rice in the region of the Volga; AL-QAZWĪNĪ II 102; IBN WAḤSHĪYA "Filāḥa" I 198ff *et passim*; YĀQŪT I 668, 669, II 492, 496–7 and IV 23, 773; SPULER *Iran* 387, 406, 508, 510; AL-DŪRĪ *Ta'rīkh* 27, 30; EL-SAMARRAIE 87–9.

15 *Aḥsan* 180, 219.

16 IBN RUSTA 122; AL-HAMDĀNĪ *Südarabien* 173; POLO 182; MEYERHOF "Sur un traité"; and AL-BALĀDHURĪ, citing Yaḥyā ibn Ādam (b. 757), wrote of rice growing at al-Ṭā'if. ABŪ ḤANĪFA ed. Lewin 45 stated simply that rice was grown in the land of the Arabs.

17 The earliest references to rice cultivation in Egypt are from the ninth century: *Arabic Papyri* VI 70 and 204–6, in the latter of which, however, we cannot be sure that the rice mentioned was actually grown in Egypt; and AL-YA'QŪBĪ 187. For later references, see IBN ḤAWQAL I 135, 152; AL-IDRĪSĪ *Description* 175, IBN MAMMĀTĪ 237–9, 248–52; AL-MAQRĪZĪ *Khiṭaṭ* II 14, 18; AL-WAṬWĀṬ ch. 3; AL-WAZZĀN II 499–501; CAHEN "Régime" 14–15; CANARD *passim*; MOSSÉRI *passim*; GOITEIN *A Mediterranean* I 119; and MÜLLER-WODARG (1957) 22ff and (1954) 194. In CASANOVA 155, 275 there is mention of quarters of al-Fusṭāṭ for the rice merchants and the rice millers.

18 AL-IDRĪSĪ *Description* 72. NICCOLI 190 refers to a document of 867–8 which speaks of the export of rice from Sicily.

19 *Calendrier* 76; IBN BAṢṢĀL 142–4; IBN AL-'AWWĀM ed. Banqueri II 27, 55ff, 62–3; AL-'UDHRĪ 17, who speaks of rice in Valencia; LAUTENSACH 60–1. In the fifteenth century rice is not mentioned by AL-QALQASHANDĪ, who discusses crops in detail; nor is it mentioned in SECO DE LUCENA, who has searched in many minor sources, as well as in the major ones, for information on agriculture in Muslim Spain in the fifteenth century. EIXIMENIS 26 shows that rice cultivation in Valencia survived into the Christian period. EANES DE ZURARA 246 spoke of many rice plantations on the island of Gomera in the Canaries in the fifteenth century, and BRUTAILS 18 shows that rice cultivation had spread to Roussillon by the thirteenth century. Dr Miguel Barceló has kindly drawn my attention to ms. fr. 25545 of the Bibliothèque Nationale in Paris, where on fol. 19 rice is mentioned amongst the exports of Majorca around the year 1200.

20 AL-ZUHRĪ 184; POLO 276; IBN BAṬṬŪṬA II 185. That Asiatic rice was brought by the medieval Arabs to the East African coast is stated in PORTÈRES "Vieilles" and "Berceaux"; ANGLADETTE 14; and SCHNELL 140; without, however, any proof being offered. GRANDIDIER AND GRANDIDIER III 1905 make the statement that rice was known in the Comores Islands before the tenth century, which, if true, would suggest an Arab introduction.

21 PORTÈRES *Appellations* 178–9, 207–8, 212, 218. The names in Madagascar are of the *vary* type, suggesting an introduction directly from India.

22 For the cultivation of *O. glaberrima*, a kind of rice indigenous to Africa, see n. 1 above. On the linguistic evidence, see PORTÈRES *Appellations* 176ff.

23 For Arab travellers who mention rice in West Africa, see IBN BAṬṬŪṬA IV 394, 398, 435; AL-IDRĪSĪ *Description* 10, 18; MAUNY *Tableau* 242–3 and "Notes historiques". For the account of one Portuguese explorer, see FERNANDES 15, 39, 47, 57, 59, 75, 81, 95, 99, 115.

4. Hard wheat

1 Unfortunately, there is no specific term in classical Arabic for *Triticum durum*; see CLÉMENT-MULLET *passim*. In Egypt today the terms *qamḥ al-yūsufī* and *qamḥ al-dhakar* (or "male wheat") are sometimes used (see TÄCKHOLM, TÄCKHOLM AND DRAR I 228 and PORTÈRES *Appellations* 40), but no such terms appear in the older texts. The contemporary Syrian term is *qamḥ qasīy*. In North Africa, where all other kinds of wheat had disappeared by the time of the French occupation, *qamḥ* has come to mean hard wheat, and the soft wheats introduced by the French are known as *farina* or *ḥinṭa*. See PORTÈRES *Appellations* 29–30; BOEUF I 25; TRABUT *Répertoire* 261. In the Yemen *burr* denotes hard wheat according to MEYERHOF "Sur un traité" (1943–4) 52 and SCHWEINFURTH *Arabische* 175 (though see also *ibid.* 91, where Forskål reports that *burr* means *T. vulgare* in the Yemen). In the texts, however, the three Arabic terms seem to be interchangeable. IBN AL-BAIṬĀR I 215 states that *ḥinṭa* is *burr*, while in *Tuḥfa* 78 and *Glosario* 318 *ḥinṭa*, *qamḥ* and *burr* are given as synonymous terms for *Triticum* in general (= *ṭridhqa* in Romanic).

2 Cous-cous may also be made from sorghum, barley, millet, rice or soft wheat; see GAST 77, 95; MONTAGNÉ 308; SCHNELL 96, 153, 154; and KOUKI 34. But hard wheat is by far the most common base. For early recipes for cous-cous, see n. 17 below.

3 SMIRES 22–31, 36, 71, 76, 91, 131–2, 152; FERHI 9, 10, 58, 60–72, 77, 78, 81, 84, 92; GAST 93; GOBERT 504ff (who, however, is wrong in suggesting that the *alica* of certain classical texts is hard wheat); KHAYAT AND KEATINGE 136 *et passim*; GUINAUDEAU 61ff.

4 This author has personally seen this practice in the Jordan valley, in Syria and in the Lebanon. Cf. GAST 87–9; FERHI 8, 9; GOBERT 516; and KOUKI 34.

5 In his earlier publications, Vavilov gave a very broad origin to hard wheat: Abyssinia, Eritrea, North Africa, Greece and the coast of Asia Minor. But subsequently he limited the origin to Abyssinia and Eritrea, and suggested that the other regions were secondary centres where new varieties developed. See VAVILOV *Tsentry* 158, "Geographische" 354–5 and *The Origin* 32, 34, 37. See also SCHIEMANN, *Die Entstehung* 119ff; SCHWANITZ 145; HAUDRICOURT AND HÉDIN *L'homme* 112; and ZHUKOVSKIJ 3.

6 For emmer and hard wheat ($2n = 28$), while in soft wheats ($2n = 42$).

7 TÄCKHOLM, TÄCKHOLM AND DRAR I 254–7 and *Karanis*.

8 There is no archeological evidence – at least none that has been examined by modern techniques – of hard wheat at pre-historic or ancient sites in the Near East. See RENFREW 40ff, 202ff and HELBAEK "The paleoethnobotany" 104, "Cereals" *passim*, "Commentary" 350ff and "Plant collecting" 386. HARTMANN 49ff, DIXON "A note" 131ff, BELL 75–6 and A. SCHULZ *Geschichte*, *passim* and "Getreide" 18–20 find no evidence of hard wheat in ancient Egypt, while K. D. WHITE *passim* is unable to identify it in Roman agricultural texts. The suggestion of JASNY 27 *et passim*, repeated in ANDRÉ 321, that certain Greek and Roman texts refer to hard wheat and that hard wheat was "the greatly predominant wheat of classical antiquity", seems altogether without foundation. What is referred to is probably emmer (*Tr. dicoccum*) or poulard (*Tr. turgidum*), both of which have a more ancient history in the Mediterranean. The older archeological finds of cereals must now be re-examined. Only the most careful microscopic and chemical analysis using techniques developed recently by H. Helbaek and others would permit an unambiguous identification of *Tr. durum*. But the outcome of such studies has until now been to show that the common wheat of ancient Egypt was emmer; see HELBAEK "Paleo-ethnobotany" 206–7 and LAUER, TÄCKHOLM AND ÅBERG 127, 156–7. Thus the claim of Peak that hard wheat was grown in Palestine over 3,000 years ago must be dismissed; the other botanists and archeologists who examined the find upon which Peak based his conclusion consider it to have been poulard. The finds from Byzantine Egypt reported in n. 7 above seem more certain, but even these require further analysis. Tentatively, however, it may be accepted that hard wheat reached the lower Nile valley and the Fayyūm by the time of the Roman occupation of Egypt and that it was here that the Arabs first came in contact with this crop. On the other hand, we should not overlook the possibility of an earlier diffusion from Abyssinia to the Arabian peninsula, if indeed Abyssinia is the crop's primary centre.

9 VAVILOV *loc. cit.*; ZHUKOVSKIJ *loc. cit.*; GOUVERNEMENT CHÉRIFIEN *passim*; BOEUF esp. I 19–21; SCHIEMANN *Die Entstehung* 119ff; PORTÈRES *Appellations* 29ff, 40ff; CHEVALIER "Productions" 742–3; OLIVEIRA MARQUES 81, whose sources, unfortunately, do not inspire confidence, but whose conclusions are probably correct; MACK SMITH I 22. As Chevalier and Boeuf point out, the displacement of *Tr. aestivum*, the principal wheat of the Romans in North Africa, was so complete that soft wheats had to be reintroduced by the French. It is interesting to note that ERROUX 25 and CHEVALIER "Productions" 742–3 show that hard wheat is comparatively little grown in the oases of the Sahara. This fact seems to point to its relatively late arrival from the north. In the Levant, too, soft wheat was reintroduced by the French in recent times, after a lengthy period of displacement by hard wheat.

10 "Filāḥa" I 185–6, 190.

11 *Südarabien* 267.

12 *Description* 289.

13 *Geoponika* ed. Beckh (bk III 3); see also A. SCHULZ *Geschichte* 51.

14 HELBAEK "Late Bronze" 90–1.

15 AL-MAQQARĪ *Nafḥ al-ṭīb* I 139 says that "the wheat of Toledo never becomes mothy with the passage of years". See also "Extrait" 643–4, in which the anonymous twelfth-century geographer states that the wheat of Toledo lasts seventy to eighty years and other wheat in Spain lasts up to a hundred years. It is interesting to note that the storability of Spanish wheats was commented upon by a thirteenth-century Chinese author: CHAU JU-KUA 142 stated that the wheats of southern Spain could be stored for tens of years without spoiling.

16 On the making of cous-cous from other grains, see n. 2 above. Most of the examples, however, come from West Africa and are probably late adaptations of older recipes for cous-cous using hard wheat.

17 MAIMONIDES 138, who stated that the semolina could be made of either wheat or barley; "Kitāb al-ṭabīkh" 166–7, which mentions several types of cous-cous, one of which was said to be "known to everyone"; RODINSON "Recherches" 138. These references disprove the commonly held notion that cous-cous is unique to the Maghrib. IDRIS II 588 states that he has been unable to find any references to cous-cous in Zīrid Tunisia (tenth to twelfth centuries). But by Ḥafṣid times (thirteenth to sixteenth centuries) the dish had become popular; see BRUNSCHVIG *La Berbérie* II 271 and n. 4.

18 IBN BAṬṬŪṬA IV 394; GOBERT 513ff; GUAL CAMARENA 422.

19 ALESSIO 263–4.

20 *Ibid.* 265; ARNOLD OF VILANOVA 135, 137; *Libre de sent soví* 182, 183. I am indebted to Professor J. Gulsoy for drawing my attention to these last two works.

21 PELLEGRINI *Gli arabismi* I 207; COROMINAS *Diccionario* I 108; *Diccionario histórico*, *voce* "aletría".

22 AL-FĪRŪZĀBĀDĪ 383, who states that the word designates a foodstuff like thread made from flour; MUḤAMMAD IBN AL-ḤASAN 45; IBN BUṬLĀN *Theatrum* II 30–1 and *Tacuinum* II 73, where the illustrations depict the making of a pasta resembling *fettucini*.

23 SERENI *Note* 364 states that Bar 'Alī describes a pasta made from semolina (?) which resembles a cloth, and might have been similar to lasagna; AL-JAWHARĪ (*voce* ṭ r ā) states that it is a sort of food similar to *hibrīya* or hairs (flakes?). Both of these might have been made from soft wheat, but it seems to this writer that these sources tell of early experimentations to make pasta from hard wheat.

24 "Kitāb al-ṭabīkh" 179, 184.

25 COROMINAS *Diccionario* II 515–17.

26 The legend that Marco Polo introduced the Italians to pasta, which he learned of in China, must be dismissed. According to *Food in Chinese* 169, 200, 217, noodles made of wheat or millet first are mentioned in China during the Sung period and are noted more frequently in Yüan times. The wheat used was almost certainly bread wheat. POLO 152 describes the noodles of China.

5. *Sugar cane*

1 SCHWEINFURTH *Arabische* 108 gives *muddarjand* for the Yemen.

2 HARRISON *et al.* 14.

3 AL-MAS'ŪDĪ ed. Barbier de Meynard VIII 170 wrote of soaking the cane in rosewater before eating it.

4 GOPAL "Sugar-making" 62ff suggests that some form of solid sugar came to be produced in India around the eighth century B.C. and that a white, crystalline sugar was produced by the fifth century B.C. Although these dates may seem early – and on account of the difficulty of dating the texts, doubt is permitted – crystalline sugar appears to have been made in India by the first century, for Dioscorides speaks of Indian sugar as having the consistency of salt. See DIOSCORIDES ed. Wellmann I 167 (bk II 82) and ed. Dubler and Terés II 172 (bk II 80). An Indian document, perhaps of the fourth century, speaks of a grey-white, presumably crystalline, sugar; see DEERR I 449ff and LIPPMANN 50ff. In the year 647, the emperor of China sent a mission to India to learn the secrets of boiling sugar; see LAUFER *Sino-Iranica* 376. Further improvements in the technique of refining sugar, which probably consisted in the use of new clarifying agents such as lime or ashes, seem to have been made in Egypt in the eleventh century, and Egyptian experts brought these skills to China in the Mongol period. See LAUFER *loc. cit.* and POLO 204.

On the techniques of making sugar, see LIPPMANN 50, 98ff, 136–8; MCNAIR *passim*; BERTHIER I 129ff; MARTÍNEZ RUIZ *passim*; and IBN AL-'AWWĀM ed. Banqueri I 393. Some idea of the various types and qualities of medieval sugar may be had from BALDUCCI PEGOLOTTI 362–4, 434–5; GUAL CAMARENA 433–4; ABŪ ḤANĪFA ed. Hamidullah 211–12, 225; AL-KINDĪ 284; LIPPMANN *passim*; MAIMONIDES 141; *Syrian Anatomy*, *passim*; IBN AL-BAIṬĀR II 264, 402 and III 90, 121; IBN WAḤSHĪYA *Medieval* 121; and SCHWARZ "Die Zuckerpressen" 276–7. I am indebted to Professor Gual Camarena for drawing my attention to ms. 4 of the Library of the University of Barcelona, a document of 1455 which on fols. 28v–29v mentions the following kinds of sugar: "sucre cafeti, aquell val mes; sucre Babelony, aquell es bo; sucre de pan de senyor, aquell es bo; sucre de Damas, aquell es avoll; sucre de polç de Alexandra, aquell es avoll; sucre polç de Xipre, aquell es bo; sucre candi, aquell es bo".

5 The Islamic cookbooks abound with recipes using sugar, most of which seem to be of Oriental origin. See, for example, RODINSON "Recherches" 139–41; MUḤAMMAD IBN AL-ḤASAN 208ff; GOBERT 539; and LIPPMANN 112ff. BRESC 79–81 gives some uses of sugar in Norman Sicily. NĀṢIR-I KHUSRAW 158, who visited Cairo in the eleventh century, tells of a banquet offered by the sultan in which the table was decorated with a thousand statuettes of sugar and an orange tree with branches, leaves and fruit also made of sugar. Nor was this a food only for the tables of princes: papyri of the eighth or ninth century suggest that in Egypt sugar was an article of daily household consumption and of trade; while another papyrus, dating from the ninth or tenth century, shows that an Egyptian employer paid his workmen in large quantities of loaf-sugar. See "Texte" 463, 468 and *Arabic Papyri* VI 145ff. Sugar and the many kinds of confection made from it were undoubtedly enormously popular almost everywhere in the Islamic world. However, IBN BAṬṬŪṬA II 365–6 observed that the Uzbek Turks, perhaps better informed about nutrition, considered it degrading to eat sugar or sweets.

6 See, for example, IBN BUṬLĀN ed. Ricci III 92–4; AL-KINDĪ 38, 44, 46, 116, 124, 130, 168, 184, 212; IBN WĀFID *Libre* 62; AL-RĀZĪ *Kitāb* III 161, 236, V 234, 244, VI 12, 69, 108, 251 and VII 60, 80; *Syrian Anatomy* II 233, 254, 256, 262, 264, 265, 268, 269, 270, 276, 352, 415 etc.; and SCHMUCKER 349.

7 IBN AL-'AWWĀM ed. Banqueri I 393.

8 SIMMONDS "Sugarcanes" 104–5; VAVILOV *The Origin* 28, 30; SCHIEMANN *Die Entstehung* 205; CHEVALIER "Recherches"; BRANDES AND SARTORIS 564ff; BOIS III 231ff; CANDOLLE 154ff; ZHUKOVSKIJ 14; HARLAN "Agricultural" 472 n. 34.

9 GOPAL "Sugar-making" 57ff.

10 SCHAFER *The Golden* 152; *Food in Chinese* 57, 147; BRETSCHNEIDER *On the Study* 45–7 and *Botanicon sinicum* I 38, 77.

11 PLINY IV 23 (bk XII 14) states that "Arabia also produces sugar cane, but that grown in India is more esteemed. It is a kind of honey that collects in reeds...It is employed only as a medicine." DIOSCORIDES ed. Wellmann I 167 (bk II 82) and ed. Dubler and Terés II 172 (bk II 80) also stated – although slightly less definitely – that sugar cane was found in Arabia Felix. It is possible that both these authors, who were not well informed about either the plant or Arabia, mistook the place where Roman merchants obtained sugar for the place where the cane was grown. GALEN XII 71 stated only that sugar was brought from Arabia. If the cane was grown in Arabia and sugar manufactured there, it is curious that the "Periplus of the Erythraean Sea", which is a mine of information on first-century Arabia, should speak of sugar-cane cultivation only in India, whence the Abyssinians obtained their sugar. See "Periplus" 65.

12 Nearly all evidence used to support the cultivation of sugar cane in the late Sasanian empire is ambiguous. LIPPMANN 109 points out that sugar cane was not mentioned in the taxation laws of Chosroes I (531–78) and can therefore not have been an important crop. Although the Armenian historian Moses of Khosrene, writing in the second half of the fifth century, stated that "at Elymais, near Gundishapur, precious sugar cane is grown", the text of Moses was probably established in the seventh century and, as it contains many insertions, is not reliable. See LIPPMANN 91. The "sweet cane" referred to in a number of Sasanian chronicles may well be *Sorghum saccharatum* or some other sweet reed. That Sasanian monarchs liked sugar seems clear: *The Pahlavi Text* 18, 23, 25 and al-Tha'ālibī (cited in CHRISTENSEN 471) both say as much, while Theophanes (quoted in FORBES V 104 and DEERR I 68) states that blocks of sugar were captured by Heraclius in his campaigns against Chosroes II in 627. But none of this evidence proves that the sugar was not imported from India. Slightly more compelling evidence comes from the Chinese Sui annals written *c.* 629, which say that Persia produced sugar (see LAUFER *Sino-Iranica* 376–7), and from a passage in AL-BALĀDHURĪ I 427 which suggests that sugar cane was grown in the Sawād area of Iraq at the time of the conquest. It is puzzling, however, that AL-ṬABARĪ 242ff did not list sugar cane as one of the field crops of the Sasanian empire. Nor was it mentioned in the Babylonian Talmud, which contains a great deal of information on the crops of Babylonia in late Sasanian times; see NEWMAN *passim*. The suggestion of LIPPMANN 92ff, taken up by many later writers, that the Nestorian medical school of Gundishapur was responsible for introducing sugar-cane cultivation and sugar manufacture into Persia is, unfortunately, sheer speculation. Only after the Islamic conquest of the Sasanian empire do we get clear evidence of the cane's cultivation: a Chinese source of the second half of the seventh century mentions Persian sugar, and al-Balādhurī noted a tax on land planted with sugar cane imposed by the caliph 'Umar (634–44). See LAUFER *loc. cit.* and LIPPMANN 109. Coming so soon after the conquest of the Sasanian empire, these sources suggest that sugar cane was probably grown in Persia for some decades before the conquest.

13 MOLDENKE 159 suggests that the plant was known in Biblical Palestine, but the sweet cane referred to in the texts may be one of a number of reeds. MOLDENKE AND MOLDENKE 40, 214 seem to doubt that sugar cane was known in pre-Islamic Palestine, as does LÖW *Flora* I 746–65 and IV 148 and *Aramäische* 345. Though many Roman authors mentioned the cane and its product, they clearly have no firsthand knowledge of the plant. Even ISIDORE OF SEVILLE bk I xxii, writing in the late sixth or early seventh century, was no more familiar with the plant than were the ancients; he relied on Galen for his information.

14 See n. 12 above.

15 IBN ḤAWQAL II 250, 251, 254, 288, 307, 308, 313, 314, 318, 319; *Ḥudūd* 108, 124, 130, 134; AL-IṢṬAKHRĪ 120; YĀQŪT I 311, II 49–50, 496–7 and III 5–6, 342; AL-QAZWĪNĪ I 178 and II 102, 134, 136, 233–4; AL-MAS'ŪDĪ ed. Barbier de Meynard VII 405; ABŪ AL-FIDĀ II ii 113, 199; SPULER *Iran* 388; 406; AL-DŪRĪ *Ta'rīkh* 32. IBN KHALDŪN *Muqaddimah* I 362,

citing an "early" source, states that in the time of the caliph Ma'mūn (813–33) the treasury in Baghdad received from the province of al-Ahwāz 30,000 pounds of sugar and from Sijistān 20,000 pounds of sugar-candy. On the possible transmission of sugar cane and sugar manufacture through Hormuz, see SCHWARZ "Die Zuckerpressen".

16 "Filāḥa" I 37, 65–7, II 211, 217, 228, 237, 240, 249, 271, 334, 353, 355 and III 450, 474, 479.

17 Yaḥyā ibn 'Īsa Jazla al-Ḥakīm (d. 1100), who wrote "Risāla fī ṣan'at al-sukkar", ms. 41 in Dār al-Kutub, Cairo.

18 DEERR I 74 misleadingly states that in the seventh century Jacob of Edessa wrote of sugar cane in the Levant. But Jacob made it clear that he was speaking of an Indian plant, and did not mention it amongst the plants grown in his homeland. See HJELT 572.

19 IBN ḤAWQAL I 173; AL-MUQADDASĪ *Aḥsan* 178, 219, 220; AL-DIMASHQĪ 282; NĀṢIR-I KHUSRAW 40, 46; YĀQŪT I 201, III 822 and IV 51, 126; AL-QAZWĪNĪ II 95; AL-MAQRĪZĪ *Khiṭaṭ* I 333; DEERR I 74–6; BENVENISTI 253–6. IBRAHIM *et al.* 63 as well as HAMARNEH report finding over thirty sugar mills on the east bank of the Jordan River during an archeological survey carried out in 1975; these mills all date from Ayyūbid and Mamlūk times.

20 BALDUCCI PEGOLOTTI 85, 99; DEERR I 83–5, who also gives evidence of sugar-cane cultivation in Crete. HEYD II 689 shows that sugar cane was grown in Morea.

21 *Papyrus* 168, 183; *Arabic Papyri* IV 4–10, 81–6 and VI 18–9. Tenth-century references are found in the latter VI 45–7.

22 IBN ḤAWQAL I 135, 137, 140, 162; AL-IDRĪSĪ *Description* 51, 52, 53, 177, 180, 187; YĀQŪT I 767 and III 437; ABŪ AL-FIDĀ II i 140; CAHEN "Regime" 27; AL-MAQRĪZĪ *Khiṭaṭ* I 78, 150, 358–9, 408; MÜLLER-WODARG (1957) 45–8.

23 AL-MAQRĪZĪ *Khiṭaṭ* I 182 and *Description* I 292–4; IBN MAMMĀTĪ 242–52, 266–7 *et passim*; AL-WAṬWĀṬ ch. I iii.

24 AL-MAS'ŪDĪ *Le livre* 35; NĀṢIR-I KHUSRAW 150.

25 BALDUCCI PEGOLOTTI 70; FRESCOBALDI 16; DUFOURCQ 543; DEERR I 93. See also the document reproduced in part in n. 4 above. On the importance of the sugar refining industry in Egypt, see CASANOVA 111–12, 233–4; LABIB *Handelsgeschichte* 319–20, 420–3; GOITEIN *A Mediterranean* I 81, 126 and "Artisans" 864.

26 AL-RĀZĪ "Description" 66, 67, 68, 94 and *Calendrier* 30, 60, 144, 172; IBN ḤAWQAL I 130. Although most authorities state that the references to sugar cane in the *Cordovan Calendar* are the earliest, those from al-Rāzī, who wrote in the first half of the tenth century, are in fact earlier; this author speaks of the plant in the areas of Salobreña, Almuñécar and Elvira.

27 IBN ḤAWQAL I 89; AL-BAKRĪ *Description* 8, 42, 46, 71, 305, 306; AL-IDRĪSĪ *Description* 51, 71, 75; YĀQŪT IV 3–4; AL-'UMARĪ 103, 176; *Extraits* 27, 75–6; BERTHIER I 43ff; VANACKER 677. LIPPMANN 143 claimed that Ibn al-Baiṭār, basing his statement on Abū Ḥanīfa, stated that sugar cane was grown in the area of Tangier. But as is shown in n. 33 below, ABŪ ḤANĪFA ed. Hamidullah spoke of sugar-cane cultivation only in the land of the Zanj, i.e. East Africa. An examination of three manuscripts of Ibn al-Baiṭār in the Bibliothèque Nationale in Paris (no. 2976 fol. 307, no. 2983 fol. 86v and no. 2984 fol. 93v) suggests that Lippmann misread Ṭanja for Zanj; as the writing in two of the manuscripts is not clear, the confusion is understandable. Leclerc, in his translation of IBN AL-BAIṬĀR III 90, has read the manuscript correctly.

28 Ed. Banqueri I 390–3.

29 AL-'UDHRĪ 96; AL-RĀZĪ "Description" 66, 67, 68; YĀQŪT III 316–18; AL-ḤIMYARĪ 27, 30, 136; AL-QAZWĪNĪ II 337; AL-QALQASHANDĪ 20, 21; IBN WĀFID "Tratado" 322; AL-MAQQARĪ *Nafḥ* I 186, 193, who cites Ibn Sa'īd (1213–86). The cultivation of sugar cane is also stated in the sources to have been found at "Shamajla" and "Rayya" in Spain; but I have been unable to locate these, unless "Rayya" is in the region of the Sierra del Rayo lying to the north of Valencia. See also LAUTENSACH 59–60; DEERR I 79ff.

30 *Biblioteca arabo-sicula* 8–10; AMARI *Storia* III ii 808; DEERR I 76–9. Owing to the shortness

of the Arab occupation of Sicily, however, the number of sources which mention the cultivation of sugar cane in Sicily under the Arabs is very limited. But immediately after the Norman occupation, there are other references to the crop. See FALCANDUS *La historia* 186; TRASSELLI *Note* II 126–7, "Produzione" and "Sumário" 58ff; NICCOLI 219–20; and SACCARDO *Cronologia* 340. As Trasselli points out, the fortunes of the sugar industry seem to have fluctuated greatly. At one point, knowledge of sugar refining seems to have died out: Frederick II requested "quod juxta consilium tuum mittimus licteras nostras Riccardo Filangerio, ut inveniat duos homines qui bene sciant facere zuccarum et illos mittat in Panormum pro zuccaro faciendo". See *Historia diplomatica* V 575. The suggestion of TRASSELLI "Sumário" 57–8 and LIPPMANN 144 that sugar cane might have been introduced to Sicily in Byzantine times is speculation. As is pointed out elsewhere in this volume, there is no evidence whatever for a Byzantine role in the introduction of new crops, and such a role seems unlikely.

31 IBN RUSTA 125; 'ARRĀM 417; AL-HAMDĀNĪ *Südarabien* 91, 94, 255, 269; IBN RUSTA 125; IBN JUBAIR II 141; AL-QAZWĪNĪ I 174; MEYERHOF "Sur un traité" (1943–4) 61; GROHMANN *Südarabien* I 256.

32 AL-ZUHRĪ 184; AL-'UMARĪ 10; PANKHURST 213–14.

33 ABŪ ZAID 127; ABŪ ḤANĪFA ed. Hamidullah 211–12; IBN AL-BAIṬĀR III 90; VELHO 31.

34 *Monumenta cartographica* IV 1082. See also AL-'UMARĪ 43 n. 6. Writing in 1506–8, PACHECO PEREIRA 53 and 155 speaks of sugar being sold in the market of a town near Timbuctu and of the cultivation of the cane on São Tomé; the latter may well have been a Portuguese introduction.

6. Old World cotton

1 The term "Old World cotton" is used to distinguish *G. arboreum* L., *G. herbaceum* L. and their ancestors and relatives (which appear to have originated in Asia or Africa) from the possibly more ancient "New World cotton", *G. barbadense* L., *G. hirsutum* L. and their ancestors and relatives (which appear to have originated in some part of the Pacific or in the Americas). Researches of botanists in Russia, America and England during the 1920s showed that these two families are botanically distinct: the Old World species are diploids with thirteen chromosomes ($2n = 26$), while the New World species are amphidiploids with twenty-six chromosomes ($2n = 52$). They can be crossed only with great difficulty. See HARLAND 42ff and ZAITZEV "Un hybride".

2 *G. arboreum* L. and *G. herbaceum* L. are sometimes erroneously referred to as tree-cotton and herbaceous cotton. In fact, both species have perennial forms which develop into bushes or shrubs, and both have "herbaceous", annual forms; the latter were almost certainly late developments.

3 *Kirbās* is given in LÖW *Flora* II 235, while *Ḥudūd* 131 *et passim* gives *karbās*. These forms, deriving directly or indirectly from the Sanskrit *karpasa-i*, are clearly related to the Greek *karpasos* and the Latin *carbasus*. The other names are given in IBN AL-BAIṬĀR III 93, MAIMONIDES 174, AL-MUQADDASĪ *Aḥsan* 70 and ABŪ ḤANĪFA ed. Hamidullah 217, some of whom also mention *ṭūṭ* as an older Arabic name. SCHWEINFURTH *Arabische* 95, 109 gives '*oṭb* and *ajās* as names found in the Yemen in modern times. The existence in early Islamic Arabia of so many names for the cotton plant and its fibre (including *quṭn*), most of which are so clearly different from the Indian names, suggests a considerable antiquity for the fibre, and perhaps for the plant, in the Arabian peninsula.

4 DIETRICH 110 cites Yabuuchi to the effect that cotton yields more fibre per acre than any other textile plant. This fact, combined with its versatility in weaving and the ease of dyeing and washing, makes cotton a highly desirable textile fibre. Although cloths of pure cotton were known in ancient India, in early Islamic times cotton was usually combined with other fibres. See nn. 46–8 below. About the use of cotton in early Islamic paper-making, there is some dispute. CARTER 135 disagrees with the widely held opinion that early Islamic

paper was at least partly made of cotton. IMMAMUDDIN *Some Aspects* 107 cites evidence that cotton was used in paper-making, while LAMM 5 and MÜLLER-WODARG (1957) 39 gives various sources which show that the rag paper of 'Abbāsid and Fāṭimid Egypt was sometimes partially made of cotton. MAZZAOUI "The cotton" 270–1 and LOMBARD 205 also take up the question of the use of cotton in paper-making. HOURANI 106 speaks of ships with cotton sails in the Indian Ocean in early Islamic times. Medical uses of cotton are given in AL-KINDĪ 68; IBN WĀFID *Libre* 34, 68; IBN AL-BAIṬĀR III 93–4; *Syrian Anatomy* II 68, 113, 148, 236–7, 266; and IBN WAḤSHĪYA "Filāḥa" II 213–14.

5 CANDOLLE 402–8.

6 WATT *The Wild*; VAVILOV *The Origin* 28; JOSEPH B. HUTCHINSON *et al. The Evolution* (though, as will be seen in n. 8, the authors appear to have abandoned the view put forward there); ZHUKOVSKIJ 74–81.

7 CHEVALIER "La systématique" and "Le Sahara" 318–19; JOSEPH B. HUTCHINSON "The dissemination"; ROBERTY; MURDOCK 64ff. With regard to Murdock's views, however, see BAKER.

8 HUTCHINSON "New evidence" and *The Application* 11ff. In SANTHANAM AND HUTCHINSON 90 Hutchinson has abandoned the view that *G. herbaceum* var. *africanum* contributed to the development of Old World cotton.

9 Hutchinson's more recent views are found in SANTHANAM AND HUTCHINSON 89ff and in a personal communication to the author. See also an important exploratory work, STEPHENS *Factors*, and two more recent contributions by the same author: "The effects" and "Some problems". In a personal communication to the author Stephens has argued that *G. herbaceum* var. *africanum* is found along old caravan routes, a fact which suggests that it is feral rather than truly wild. One African cotton plant, *G. anomalum* Wawr. and Peyr., is really wild; but although it will produce a weakly fertile hybrid with the Old World cottons, it seems to be only a distant relative of the ancestor or ancestors of these.

10 MARSHALL I 33, 194 and II 585–6; GULATI AND TURNER "A note" and *A Note*, *passim*; CHAUDHURY 25–8. These authors date this material at about 3000 B.C. However, recent revisions in the chronology of Harappan culture, based partly on Carbon-14 datings, suggest that the late-level material from Mohenjo-daro should be dated about 1760 B.C. ±115. See LAL 213–14 and ALLCHIN AND ALLCHIN 337. More recent finds, which may be slightly older, are reported in VISHNU-MITTRE "Paleobotanical" 25. For a find of cotton seeds of comparable age in Nubia, see CHOWDHURY AND BUTH; this find is discussed in n. 25 below.

11 ALLCHIN AND ALLCHIN 264; CLUTTON-BROCK, MITTRE AND GULATI 56–8.

12 These are summarized in GOPAL "Textiles" 60–1.

13 HERODOTUS II 132–5 (bk III 106) and III 178–9 (bk VII 65). The fact that Herodotus describes the trees as "wild" is interesting but, in view of his unreliability on Indian matters, may not be significant. ARRIAN II 352–3 (*Indika* bk VIII 15) also mentions the cotton "tree" but does not say that it grew wild.

14 KAUṬALYA II 168–71.

15 SCHLINGLOFF.

16 *Bṛhatsaṁhitā* (bk XCIV 15) as cited in GOPAL, "Textiles" 61 n. 3. As early as the second century, ARRIAN II 352–3 (*Indika* bk VIII 15) stated that the clothes of the Indians were made of cotton.

17 CTÉSIAS 77.

18 "Periplus" 52, 64–5, 94. On pp. 64–5 it seems to be implied that Egyptian merchants came annually to the Horn of Africa to buy Indian cottons, and on p. 124 the text suggests that Egyptians bought cottons in the Indian port of Barugaza.

19 PHILOSTRATUS I 169 (bk II 20), who uses the word *byssos*; in this context, where it is referred to as an import from India, *byssos* should be taken to mean cotton. As LOMBARD 113–15 has convincingly shown, the term normally refers to "sea wool" obtained from filaments attached to the molluscs *Pinna marina* and *Pinna nobilis*.

20 GOODRICH 409.

21 STEIN *Serindia* II 786, who speaks of cotton cloths found at the Tun-Huang *limes* abandoned in the second century. See also *ibid.* I 435, where cotton fragments are mentioned at Loulan, abandoned in the fourth century; STEIN *Innermost* I 232ff and III 42; and BERGMAN 103–5, 111, 114–17. For Palmyra, see PFISTER *Textiles de Palmyre* I 13, 22, II 16 and III 11, 18 and *Nouveaux textiles* 16, 20–1.

22 GOODRICH 408; BURKILL *Dictionary* I 1103.

23 BRETZL 136ff. The information gleaned on this voyage was used by Theophrastus and Pliny the Elder. See THEOPHRASTUS I 342–5 (bk IV 7) and PLINY IV 29 (bk XII 21–2).

24 For references in Theophrastus and Pliny, see n. 23 above. The information about the Himyaritic graves is given in GROHMANN *Südarabien* VII 260ff and XIII 40ff.

25 POLLUX II 79 (bk VII 75), who says only that "Egyptians" make clothes from mixed linen and cotton fabrics, and describes the "tree" from which cotton is obtained; PLINY IV 152–3 (bk XIII 28) and V 428–9 (bk XIX 2). The text of the Aksumite inscription is given in LITTMANN 33. See also NICHOLSON. Recently, COCKBURN *et al.* 1159 have reported that in a mummy dating 170 B.C. ± 70 was found a ball of cotton wrapped in a linen cloth; some cotton fibres had also been woven into this cloth. The provenance of the mummy is not known, but it is reasonable to assume that it, like most of the other mummies available for autopsy in the west, came from the Aswan region. Though the cotton found here could have been imported, it was probably grown in Nubia; in that case this archeological evidence, if it has been correctly dated, pre-dates the literary evidence. I am indebted to Dr Louise Mackie for drawing my attention to this article. CHOWDHURY AND BUTH report cotton seeds, dating from about 2500 B.C., which are found at a Nubian site. Although the fibres on the seeds were comparable to those on modern specimens of *G. arboreum* and *G. herbaceum*, the authors conclude – for lack of evidence of a Nubian textile industry in such early times – that the seeds, found in animal manure, were used as cattle feed. Whether the plant was wild or domesticated is uncertain.

26 GREISS "Les plus anciens" and *Anatomical* 104–5, 122; GRIFFITH AND CROWFOOT; PFISTER *Les toiles* 10; MASSEY. Miss Elizabeth Crowfoot has kindly sent me two samples (T. 214 and T. 237) of threads from Qaṣr Ibrīm in Egyptian Nubia, dating from the late Meroitic and X-group periods (up to 600); these were identified by the late Dr Veronika Gervers as cotton. The expedition of the Royal Ontario Museum to 'Adda, under the direction of Dr N. Millet, has discovered many fragments of cloth dating from late Meroitic, X-group and early Christian times; some of these, coming from Cemetery III (tombs 26, 645, 778, 807 and 821), were identified by Dr Gervers as cotton.

27 GRIFFITH AND CROWFOOT.

28 This point is discussed in PFISTER "Toiles" 10.

29 Cotton does not seem to have been grown in the Near East in Biblical times. See MOLDENKE 162 and LÖW *Die Flora* II 235–43. However, two identical passages referring to its cultivation appear in later Jewish literature, which may be dated roughly from the third to the fifth centuries: *The Mishnah* 36 (Kil. VII 2) and *Le Talmud de Jérusalem* II 291 (Kil. VII 2). See also GREGORY OF TOURS 499. It has also been shown that cotton was known to the seventh-century writer Jacob of Edessa, but it is not clear from the text whether Jacob had seen the plant growing in the Near East; see HJELT 579. At Palmyra small amounts of cotton or partly cotton cloth have been found, but these are thought to have been imports from India. See PFISTER *Textiles de Palmyre* I 13, 22, II 16 and III 11, 18 and *Nouveaux textiles* 16, 20–1. Similarly, the few pieces of cotton cloth found at the sixth-century site of Zenobia are considered to be Indian; PFISTER *Les textiles de Halabiyeh (Zenobia)* 9, 32. However, in LAMM 8–10 it is suggested that some partly cotton cloths were made in "Syria" in the two centuries before the Arab conquests, as must indeed have been the case if cotton was grown in the region at this time. A passage in the writings of Pausanias in which the author speaks of *byssos* growing in the island of Elis in the Aegean has sometimes been cited as proof of cotton cultivation in ancient Greece. See

PAUSANIUS II 400 (bk V 5). However, this interpretation is almost certainly wrong. The word *byssos*, which also appears on the Rosetta stone, is normally used for "sea wool"; see n. 19 above. Where cotton is intended (as in the texts of Philostratus and Julius Pollux referred to above in nn. 19 and 25) this special meaning is clearly indicated.

30 *Hou Han Shu*, *I Wu Chih* and other works cited in WITTFOGEL AND FÊNG 155–6 n. 74; PELLIOT I 444, 463, 473, 489–91; DIETRICH 111. Evidence of a large cotton industry in Kwangtung is given in SCHAFER *The Vermilion* 180–1.

31 LAUFER *Sino-Iranica* 491–2; DIETRICH 110–11; WITTFOGEL AND FÊNG 157–8 n. 74; GOODRICH 408; PELLIOT I 491; AMANO 482–98. Professor Evelyn Rawski kindly translated the relevant passages of Amano's book for me.

32 CHAU JU-KUA 218; GOODRICH 408.

33 PELLIOT I 456.

34 HARLAND 31; *Mathews' Textile Fibres* 120. It is interesting to note that the present-day distribution of *G. herbaceum* is quite different: on p. 32, Harland gives this as most of India (especially the north-west), Turkey, Persia, Iraq, Turkestan, south-eastern Europe and some areas of Africa.

35 GULATI AND TURNER *A Note* and "A note"; GRIFFITH AND CROWFOOT.

36 ABŪ ḤANĪFA ed. Hamidullah 217.

37 *The Annals* 111, 116; GOOSSENS.

38 See n. 33 above. The fact that cotton was grown in pre-Islamic times in the Jordan valley, a region which is much more northerly than the other areas where cotton was grown in early times, is explained by the exceedingly hot climate of this area, much of which lies below sea level.

39 Yao Ssu-lien (d. 637) *Liang-shu*, cited in CHAU JU-KUA 218. The work of WHYTE on the development of annuals from perennials is of considerable interest; see his "Botanical" and "Cytogenetical". This scholar has postulated that annuals develop from perennials in regions of physiological stress: where rainfall is too little and temperature too low. Such conditions could easily have been encountered as the plant moved from India towards the colder, semi-arid regions of western China. According to Whyte, it was in such regions that the annual varieties of several cereals and grain legumes developed. Thus Whyte's theory, based on botanical evidence, fits well with the literary and archeological evidence presented here.

40 PELLIOT I 491.

41 STEIN *Serindia* I 160.

42 SHA. I am grateful to Dr Hsio-yen Shih for drawing my attention to this report and translating the relevant parts.

43 BERGMAN 56–7, 103–5, 111, 114–17; STEIN *Serindia* I 339, 423, 435. Not all of this material can be easily dated. Bergman suggests *c.* 600–1000 for the piece given on pp. 56–7. The pieces mentioned in STEIN I 435 were found at a site which was abandoned in the fourth century. See also SHIH.

44 SCHAFER *The Golden* 106.

45 E.g. DIETRICH 110. It is difficult to see, however, why the simple techniques of ginning which allowed the industry to be established on a wide scale in India were not adequate for China. For the introduction of new ginning techniques into China, see PELLIOT I 457, 484–5; NEEDHAM IV pt 2 122–4. On the story of the woman who introduced new spinning and weaving techniques, see GOODRICH 408–9; AMANO 495; and PELLIOT 484–5.

46 POLLUX II 79 (bk VII 75).

47 LAMM *passim*; PFISTER "Toiles" 84ff; N. P. BRITTON 29–39; KÜHNEL AND BELLINGER 10, 14, 19. Two early Islamic textile fragments with silk warp and cotton weft are in the collection of the Royal Ontario Museum: Acc. Nos. 963.95.8 (Iraq, late tenth century) and 963.95.3 (Persia, tenth century?). See also GOLOMBERK AND GERVERS. In medieval Europe, too, cotton threads were often used only in the weft. See BORLANDI; GUAL CAMARENA 284–5, 324–6; and WESCHER 2339ff.

48 PFISTER "Toiles" 69ff, 84ff; N. P. BRITTON 74–5; LAMM 144ff; BÜHLER I 11–27; KÜHNEL AND BELLINGER 87–90. See also GOLOMBEK AND GERVERS.

49 PELLIOT I 501–4; AMANO 491–3.

50 Ch'u Hua *Mu mien p'u* [A Treatise on Cotton] as cited by DIETRICH 110. On the basis of the study of many county and prefectural gazetteers, DIETRICH III has concluded that by late Ming and early Ch'ing times between three-fifths and four-fifths of all *hsien* manufactured some cotton cloth.

51 PELLIOT I 425–31 and *passim*; AMANO 482–98.

52 PELLIOT I 501–2; AMANO 491; SCHLINGLOFF 85.

53 AL-IṢṬAKHRĪ 46; IBN ḤAWQAL I 207, 216, 238; AL-ZUHRĪ 252; AL-DŪRĪ *Ta'rīkh* 32; LAMM 218ff; IBN WAḤSHĪYA "Filāḥa II 213–14; LOMBARD 63–4.

54 *Ḥudūd* 102, 105, 132, 143; IBN ḤAWQAL II 296, 330, 354, 358, 369; AL-QAZWĪNĪ II 163; AL-ZUHRĪ 247; LAMM 197ff; LOMBARD 63–4. Cotton is also mentioned in the Būndahishn, a Pahlavi work which was probably not completed until *c.* 881 or perhaps even much later, and is at any rate post-Islamic; see *Pahlavi Texts* xli, xliii, 102.

55 IBN ḤAWQAL II 447, 470, 497; BARTOL'D "Istoriia" 193; AL-ZUHRĪ 243; LAMM 193ff.

56 IBN ḤAWQAL II 293, 354, 369, 371, 422, 436, 437, 447, 463, 469, 470, 497; ABŪ AL-FIDĀ II pt 2 169, 197; *Ḥudūd* 102, 103, 104, 110, 121, 125, 131, 132, 134, 138, 139; AL-YA'QŪBĪ 85; SPULER *Iran* 405; LE STRANGE *Baghdad* 84, 181, 265; SERJEANT "Material" (1942) 80ff and (1946) 129–30, 131ff; LAMM 193ff. KÜHNEL AND BELLINGER list all-cotton cloths made in Iraq or Persia from 866–9 onwards. PELLIOT I 495 cites a Chinese source which mentions the manufacture of cotton goods in Merv by 817.

57 AL-QAZWĪNĪ II 186; AL-BALĀDHURĪ I 113; AL-HAMDĀNĪ *Südarabien* 131; IBN ḤAWQAL II 371–2; IBN AL-'AWWĀM ed. Banqueri II 104; IBN BAṬṬŪṬA II 199; MEYERHOF "Sur un traité" (1943–4) 62; POLO 271; SERJEANT "Material" (1948) 86; LAMM 234ff.

58 AL-MUQADDASĪ *Aḥsan* 176–7, 218–19; YĀQŪT II 21, 308; AL-QAZWĪNĪ I 122, 179; IBN AL-'AWWĀM ed. Banqueri II 195; IBN 'ASĀKIR 117; BENVENISTI 386; LAMM 223–34; ASHTOR "Venetian" 677ff; LOMBARD 67–70.

59 HEYD II 661ff, 684ff; SCHAUBE 161, 162, 197, 214; BALDUCCI PEGOLOTTI *passim*; ASHTOR "Venetian"; MAZZAOUI "The cotton" 266 and *The Cotton, passim.*

60 *Papyrus* 9, 193, 227; *Arabic Papyri* V 86–95; PFISTER "L'introduction" 170; GOITEIN *A Mediterranean* I 105; LAMM 218, 245; IBN ḤAWQAL I 135.

61 "Texte zur Wirtschaftsgeschichte" 463.

62 IBN ḤAWQAL I 135.

63 Cited in LAMM 198.

64 CASANOVA 339.

65 IBN MAMMĀTĪ 240, 241, 244, 248, 250, 252, 265–6; AL-MAQRĪZĪ *Khiṭaṭ* I 182, 337 and II 13, 15, 18, 19; CAHEN "Le régime" 14–15; LAMM 240ff; MÜLLER-WODARG (1957) 38–9; ASHTOR "Venetian" 685ff.

66 SCHAUBE 164; AL-MAQRĪZĪ *Khiṭaṭ* I 136; DUFOURCQ 543; LABIB *Handelsgeschichte* 101, 311–12; ASHTOR "Venetian" 685ff. For evidence of Indian cotton cloths imported into later medieval Egypt, see PFISTER *Les toiles imprimées.*

67 IBN ḤAWQAL I 70, 76, 82; AL-IDRĪSĪ *Description* 109, 122, 130, 156; AL-BAKRĪ *Description* 124; AL-'UMARĪ 111; *Biblioteca arabo-sicula* 134, 137, 148; GOITEIN "La Tunisie" 571; VANACKER 677, map 13; DUFOURCQ 264, 546; *Traités de paix et de commerce* I 221; LOMBARD 71–3.

68 IBN ḤAWQAL I 118 speaks of a part of the market in Palermo set aside for cotton merchants and carders, but it is not clear that in his time cotton was grown locally; ABŪ AL-KHAIR tr. Cherbonneau 26–7; YĀQŪT II 84; AL-ZUHRĪ 176, who mentions that cotton was exported from Sicily; BALDUCCI PEGOLOTTI 111, 367; *Biblioteca arabo-sicula* I 43, 110, 137, 159; AMARI II 444 and III 807; LOMBARD 78–9; SCHAUBE 284. AMARI *loc. cit.* gives evidence of cotton manufacturing in thirteenth-century Sicily.

69 IBN ḤAWQAL I 76, 77; AL-IDRĪSĪ *Description* 70, 81, 84, 85; AL-BAKRĪ *Description* 143, 295; AL-'UMARĪ 80; AL-WAZZĀN I 170, 252; VANACKER 667, map 13.

70 The earliest mention of cotton cultivation in Spain is found in a text of Abū Bakr Aḥmad b. Isḥaq b. Ibrāhīm al-Hamadhānī, written around 903. See ALEMANY BOLUFER "La geografía...en los escritores árabes" 119–27; I am indebted to Dr Miquel Barceló for drawing my attention to this source. Other early references are found in AL-RĀZĪ "Description" 93; *Calendrier* 62; and IBN AL-FAQĪH 53.

71 YĀQŪT I 275, 474; AL-'UDHRĪ 96; AL-ḤIMYARĪ 27; MILLÁS VALLICROSA *Nuevos estudios* 173–82; LAUTENSACH 61–2; DUBLER *Über das Wirtschaftsleben* 49, 60–1, 95; LOMBARD 77–8. AL-ḤIMYARĪ 233 mentions cotton growing at Guadix, while EIXIMENIS 26 and AL-ZUHRĪ 178 mention it at Valencia and in Majorca respectively. I am indebted to Dr Barceló for drawing my attention to the text of al-Zuhrī, which is reproduced in BARCELÓ "Comentaris" 163. See also BARCELÓ "Alguns problemes".

72 ABŪ AL-KHAIR tr. Cherbonneau 26–7; IBN AL-'AWWĀM ed. Banqueri 103ff; IBN BAṢṢĀL 151–3.

73 AL-'UDHRĪ 96; AL-RĀZĪ "Description" 93; AL-ḤIMYARĪ 27; YĀQŪT I 275, who also mentions in I 373 a village in the south of al-Andalus where excellent cotton cloths were made.

74 AL-BAKRĪ *Description* 325–6; AL-IDRĪSĪ *Description* 3; AL-'UMARĪ 66; IBN BAṬṬŪṬA IV 422, 437; MONTEIL; MAUNY "Notes historiques" 698ff and *Tableau* 231–2, 245; CA DA MOSTO 31–2. For cotton in Christian Abyssinia, see AL-QAZWĪNI II 12 and PANKHURST 211ff. It is interesting to note that even as late as the fifteenth and sixteenth centuries many of the Portuguese explorers describing the clothing of the Muslim communities in West Africa contrast this to the nakedness of the pagans. See FERNANDES 13 and PACHECO PEREIRA 69, 73, 125. The accounts of cotton in medieval West Africa do not make clear the kind of plant which was grown. However, one Portuguese voyager in the fifteenth century speaks of tree-cotton growing abundantly in one place on the West African coast and on the island of Gomera in the Canaries. See EANES DE ZURARA 168, 246.

7. *Sour orange, lemon, lime, shaddock*

1 The taxonomy used here follows WEBBER, who has regrouped the various lemons as *C. limon*.

2 Many of the travellers' accounts cited below speak of citrus trees as ornamental plants. IBN KHALDŪN *Muqaddimah* II 295 stated – wrongly – that orange and lime trees had no edible fruits and were therefore largely decorative. He considered their use a sign of decadence. AL-MAQRĪZĪ *Khiṭaṭ* II 38 wrote of the "apple lemon" (*al-laimūn al-tuffāḥī*) as the only citrus fruit which could be eaten without sugar. Various recipes using citrus fruits are given in RODINSON "Recherches" 131, 132, 134, 138, 139, 141, 142, 143, 155–6; MUḤAMMAD IBN AL-ḤASAN 37, 39, 40, 42, 190, 193, 197, 198, 200, 201, 202; and "Kitāb al-ṭabīkh" 245, 252. TANAKA "L'acclimatation" 395 says, without citing a source, that the sour orange was used by medieval Arabs to make a dye. For other information on the uses of citrus trees, see BURKILL *Dictionary* I 561, 566, 569; FONTAINE *passim*; and GILDEMEISTER AND HOFFMANN III 1–107. Medical uses are given in IBN AL-BAIṬĀR III 255–62, 357–8. Just as in the Jewish religion, where the citron is used in the Feast of Tabernacles, so, too, in Christian communities citrus fruits may have had a ceremonial use: AL-MAQRĪZĪ *Khiṭaṭ* II 10, 397 states that on the festival of baptism government employees gave out sugar cane, citrons, sour oranges and lemons.

3 'ABD AL-LAṬĪF tr. Sacy 31. WEBBER 476 states that "it is well known that bad variations occur rather frequently in citrus, and such changed types, unless recognized and eliminated, soon result in the variety becoming a heterogeneous mixture of types".

4 SARTON II i 305; the treatise is by Han Ch'an-chih. For the origin of the grapefruit, see n. 49 below.

5 Ed. Barbier de Meynard II 438–9.

6 TOLKOWSKY 7.

7 ORTA 133v (bk XXXIV).

8 TANAKA *Kankitsu*, "L'acclimatation", "Sur l'origine", "Studies" and "Kankitsu";

WEBBER *passim*; GUILLAUMIN *passim*; CHEVALIER "L'origine géographique"; VAVILOV *The Origin* 25–7; SWINGLE *passim*; ZHUKOVSKIJ 52ff, who suggests that the lime tree may originate in the Malayan archipelago: SCORA 371.

9 TOLKOWSKY 6ff; BURKILL *Dictionary* I 570; SCORA *loc. cit.*

10 TOLKOWSKY 27; THEOPHRASTUS I 311–13 (bk IV iv 2); MOLDENKE AND MOLDENKE 186, 290–1; LÖW *Aramäische* 46 and *Flora* III 284ff; HEHN *Cultivated Plants* 438–43; THOMPSON 313–14.

11 PLINY IV 13 (bk XII 7); TARGIONI-TOZZETTI 193ff.

12 PALLADIUS 132 (bk IV 10); ISIDORE bk XII 8.

13 TOLKOWSKY 51ff.

14 *Ibid.* 100ff.

15 BRETZL 131; LÖW *Flora* III 278ff and IV 149. *The Pahlavi Text* 24 twice gives the word *vātrang* in a late Sasanian text, and it is translated as "lemon". But the correct translation is surely "citron".

16 MEYERHOF "Sur un traité" (1942–3) 62.

17 Ed. Barbier de Meynard II 438–9; see also VIII 336, where the caliph al-Qāhir (932–4) is said to have had a courtyard planted with orange trees brought from India via Oman and Basra.

18 IBN WAḤSHĪYA "Filāḥa" I 70; also II 283; QUSṬŪS 98. It is interesting that there is no mention of the sour orange in the *Geoponika*, which draws on many of the same sources as Qusṭūs.

19 *Ḥudūd* 108, 135; AL-MUQADDASĪ *Aḥsan* 220 and *Description* 7, 181; AL-IṢṬAKHRĪ 120. The poems are given in AL-NUWAIRĪ XI 111ff, who cites *inter alia* poems by Ibn al-Mu'tazz (861–908) and Ibn 'Abbād (938–95).

20 TOLKOWSKY 113ff. However, the only citrus fruit mentioned in the *Cordovan Calendar* of 961 is the citron; see *Calendrier* 36, 76, 172.

21 For the eastern provinces and Iraq, see YĀQŪT I 473 and III 158; AL-QAZWĪNĪ I 177 and II 233–4; ABŪ AL-FIDĀ II 207; *Description of the Province* 47; and MEYERHOF "Sur un traité" (1942–3) 62. For the Levant, see JACQUES DE VITRY 1099, where a detailed description of the fruits is given; IBN JUBAIR III 324; and NĀṢIR-I KHUSRAW 40, 61. For Egypt, see 'ABD AL-LAṬĪF tr. Sacy 31; AL-WAṬWĀṬ ch. 4; ṬAIBŪGHĀ 68; NĀṢIR-I KHUSRAW 150; and AL-MAQRĪZĪ *Khiṭaṭ* I 28 and II 10, 186, 379, 397. The references from the Maghrib are relatively late: AL-'UMARĪ 102, 175; AL-BAKRĪ *Description* 71; AL-WAZZĀN I 263; it should be noted that other references to sour oranges in the translation of AL-BAKRĪ *Description* 15, 104, 228 are mistranslations of *utrujj* (citron). For Spain, see IBN AL-'AWWĀM ed. Banqueri I 320–2; PÉRÈS "Le palmier" 232, 236; DUBLER *Wirtschaftsleben* 60; AL-MAQQARĪ *Nafḥ al-ṭīb* I 145, 193 and IV 200; and GUAL CAMARENA 441–2. For the Yemen, see MEYERHOF "Sur un traité" (1943–4) 61. The evidence for Sicily is not unambiguous. A document of 1002 which states that a prince of Salerno offered "pomi citrini" to some Norman princes has been thought by certain scholars (e.g. FORBES II 49; ALFONSO-SPAGNA 24; CANDOLLE 184) to refer to sour oranges; but it seems equally likely that citrons were meant. See also HEHN *Cultivated Plants* 444–5 and TARGIONI-TOZZETTI 197ff. Immediately after the Norman conquest, however, there is much clear evidence of the cultivation of sour oranges: see FALCANDUS *De rebus* 12–13 and AMARI II 444. TRASSELLI *Note* II 126 and "Promesse" 532 shows the importance of sour oranges in fifteenth-century Sicily; one document mentions a ship laden with 200,000 of the fruits. See also TARGIONI-TOZZETTI 201ff and ALFONSO-SPAGNA 25. All this evidence suggests very strongly that the plant was introduced into Sicily during the Arab occupation.

22 For the sour orange in West Africa, see AL-WAZZĀN II 476 and MAUNY "Notes historiques" 713. For East Africa, see VELHO 30, 31; GALLESIO 240; and PANKHURST 213.

23 The early history of the lemon in India is treated in GLIDDEN; H. M. JOHNSON, who states that there is no literary reference to the lemon in India until the twelfth century; and LAUFER "The lemon", who suggests that the lemon was probably first cultivated between the fourth and ninth centuries. Unfortunately, all these articles need revision.

24 QUSṬŪS 98.

25 AL-IṢṬAKHRĪ 83; IBN ḤAWQAL II 314. It should be noted that references to the lemon in IBN ḤAWQAL 89, 92, 214 and II 314 are mistranslations of *utrujj*

26 See n. 17 above.

27 SARTON II 432–3; IBN AL-BAIṬĀR III 255ff. Excerpts from the poems are given in AL-NUWAIRĪ XI 116.

28 For the lemon in the eastern part of the Islamic world, see YĀQŪT I 385, 395, 672 and II 64; ABŪ AL-FIDĀ II ii 113, 199; AL-QAZWĪNĪ I 177, 266; and *Description of the Province* 39, 47. For the Yemen, see MEYERHOF "Sur un traité" (1943–4) 61, which speaks of *līmūn* and *līmūn ḥāmiḍ* (or *ḥummāḍ*). For the Levant, see JACQUES DE VITRY 1099 and LÖW *Flora* IV 149. For Egypt, see 'ABD AL-LAṬĪF tr. Sacy 31; IBN MAMMĀTĪ 43, 256–7; YĀQŪT IV 152; ṬAIBŪGHĀ 67; NĀṢIR-I KHUSRAW 51, 150, who gives the earliest reference to the lemon in Egypt; and GOITEIN *A Mediterranean* I 121, who has evidence of a considerable trade in lemon juice. For North Africa, see AL-'UMARĪ 102, 175; AL-WAZZĀN I 193, 263; and TORRES BALBÁS "Las ruinas" 290–4. For Spain, see AL-MAQQARĪ *Nafḥ al-ṭīb* IV 200; IBN AL-'AWWĀM ed. Banqueri I 323–4; IBN LUYŪN; AL-ZUHRĪ 204; and "Un libro de cocina" 165. For East Africa, see IBN BAṬṬŪṬA II 191 and AL-'UMARĪ 10; and for West Africa, AL-WAZZĀN II 476 and AL-'UMARĪ 44. There is no evidence of the lemon in Sicily during the Arab occupation. Quite possibly it had reached this part of the Mediterranean only after the Norman conquest of the island, a fact which would help to explain its late diffusion into Italy. See BRESC 71–3; GALLESIO 264ff; ALFONSO-SPAGNA 23; and TARGIONI-TOZZETTI 202ff.

29 IBN WAḤSHĪYA "Filāḥa" I 72. LAUFER "The lemon" 158 says that the synonym given by Ibn Waḥshīya is *hasīya*, but the word in the Cairo manuscript I 72 is clearly *khashīshā*. IBN AL-'AWWĀM ed. Banqueri I 323 gives *hasīya* as name for the lemon in Persian. WEBBER 626, 628 shows that there are limes which are reddish in colour.

30 *The Thousand Nights and a Night* VII 271. Unfortunately, it is difficult, if not impossible, to date this passage. See, however, *Encyclopedia of Islam* 2nd edn *voce* "Alf Laila wa-Laila".

31 AL-QAZWĪNĪ II 83, 160; AL-MUQADDASĪ *Aḥsan* 20; IBN MAMMĀTĪ 238; AL-'UMARĪ 102; MEYERHOF "Sur un traité..." (1943–4) 61.

32 FALCANDUS *La historia* 185, whose editor mistakenly suggests that the author must have meant the lemon, since he speaks of the fruit as bitter; but, as WEBBER 620ff points out, there are both sweet and bitter limes. GUAL CAMARENA 168, 348, who also proposes in his notes the translation "lemon" in spite of the fact that other documents mention both *limons* and *limes*. AL-MAQQARĪ *Nafḥ al-ṭīb* IV 200 also speaks of limes in Seville. See also BRESC 71–3 for *lumie* in Norman Sicily.

33 CHEVALIER "Productions" 772ff and "L'acclimatation" 658; DALZIEL 305–7.

34 For *kubbād*, see below. IBN AL-'AWWĀM ed. Banqueri I 323 states that *zanbū'* and *bustanbūn* have the same meaning, and elsewhere (I 314) he seems to suggest that *zanbū'* is a kind of lime. As the Arabic text given by Banqueri seems corrupt at this point, however, it is impossible to tell what was intended; the French translation is not helpful. *Zanbū'* has been variously translated as "citron", "lemon", "lime", "shaddock", "bergamot", "grapefruit", "poncirus", "a kind of orange" etc. The *Diccionario de la lengua española* of the Real Academia Española (*voce* "azamboa") gives it as a kind of citron with a rough skin. DOZY *Supplément* I 605 also considers it a kind of citron. GHĀLIB II 436 gives bergamot. Of the authors who have recorded the way the word was used in recent centuries, *Tuḥfat* 124 gives its meaning as sour orange in the dialect of Marrakesh; TRABUT *Répertoire* 73 gives it as citron in North African Berber; and DESTAING 66 states that it means lemon in Berber. In the present-day dialects of parts of Tunisia, the word *zimbā'* denotes the grapefruit.

35 ABŪ ḤANĪFA ed. Lewin 40, 69 states clearly that *turunj* is another word (deriving no doubt from the Persian) for *utrujj*, and most Arabic authors use the word in this way. TRABUT *Répertoire* 72–3 records that the word still has this meaning in Berber. However, in Syrian

dialect, Turkish, Sicilian and Catalan, words deriving from *turunj* designate various kinds of oranges, while in Spanish and Portuguese they are used for the grapefruit. See TOLKOWSKY 105; GUAL CAMARENA 441–2; AREZZO 68; and standard dictionaries for Catalan, Turkish, Portuguese and Spanish.

36 BURKILL *Dictionary* I 570; WEBBER 584; AL-MAS'ŪDĪ ed. Barbier de Meynard II 438–9. See also nn. 5, 17 and 26 above. H. M. JOHNSON 50 says that the shaddock was not introduced into India until the seventeenth century. As the Arabs had for centuries been in direct contact with Malaysia, this statement, seemingly at variance with an earlier introduction into the Islamic world, could be correct. However, the word for shaddock in many parts of the Arab world today is *laimūn hindī*, suggesting that the plant reached the Arab world via India.

37 IBN AL-'AWWĀM ed. Banqueri I 315.

38 GAUDEFROY DEMOMBYNES 26; *The Thousand Nights and a Night* II 310 and VIII 272. It should be noted, however, that the meaning of the word *kubbād* is by no means certain. LANE gives *C. limon spongius* Ferrari, while DOZY *Supplément* proposes citron, a kind of lemon, large lemon, large sour orange and poncirus! Several authors, for example TOLKOWSKY 140, have concluded that the *poma Adam* or *poma de Adamo* mentioned in JACQUES DE VITRY 1099 and Burkhardt of Mount Zion was the shaddock. But a careful reading of the texts suggests that this fruit was perhaps not a citrus at all.

39 This information is given by Sacy in a footnote to 'ABD AL-LAṬĪF 117, but I have not been able to find the original text in Ibn Iyās.

40 Cited, for instance, in MAUNY "Notes" 713ff. The text of the statute is given in TARGIONI-TOZZETTI 161, who copied it from Valeriani, *Annali d'agricoltura del Regno Italiano di Filippo Re* XIX 69.

41 AL-BAKRĪ *Description* 104; WEBBER points out that certain "sour" oranges are relatively sweet.

42 Thus, for instance, Schefer, in his edition and translation of NĀṢIR-I KHUSRAW, has consistently translated *turunj* of the Persian text (e.g. on p. 12) as "sweet orange"; see pp. 40, 146, 150, 172.

43 IBN BAṬṬŪṬA III 128.

44 Words of the *portugallo* type may be found in standard dictionaries for Persian, Pashto and nearly all the Mediterranean languages except Spanish and Portuguese. RISSO AND POITEAU 10 give *portugalié* for the dialect of Nice, while SCHWEINFURTH *Arabische* 134 gives *bortuqān hālib* as one of the names in the Yemen. The claim of Grohmann in "Texte" 462–3 that the word *burtuqān* appears in a papyrus of the eighth or ninth century must be an anachronism; as may be seen in pl. LIII, where the papyrus in question is reproduced by Grohmann, the word is at the end of the page and not very legible. For the North African words suggesting a Chinese origin, see SCHWEINFURTH *Arabische* and TRABUT *Répertoire* 73. GALLESIO 295 shows that some of the Indian names are of the "orange-of-China" type, while BURKILL *Dictionary* I 575 states that similar names are found in Malaysia for certain types of sweet orange (though other types of sweet orange seem to have come to Malaysia from India).

45 HEHN *Cultivated* 447; GALLESIO 308 gives evidence that the sweet orange was already common in Sicily by 1525.

46 Thus AL-'UMARĪ 102 and 175 gives only those four for Ifrīqiya and Morocco, while according to GAUDEFROY DEMOMBYNES 26, he lists *utrujj*, *kubbād*, *nāranj* and *līmūn* for Syria. The fourteenth-century Yemeni agricultural treatise mentions *utrujj*, *līmūn ḥāmiḍ*, *nāranj* and *līm ḥālī*; see MEYERHOF "Sur un traité" (1943–4) 65. ṬAIBŪGHĀ 64, 67, 68 gives only *utrujj*, *līmūn* and *nāranj*, which are also the only citrus mentioned by AL-MAQRĪZĪ *Khiṭaṭ* II 397 *et passim* and in AL-NUWAIRĪ XI 111ff. The fourteenth-century lexicographical work of IBN KABAR 56 gives only *turunj*, *nāranj* and *līmūn ḥummāḍ*. For Spain IBN AL-'AWWĀM ed. Banqueri I 314ff gives *utrujj*, *nāranj*, *zanbū'* and *līmūn*, while AL-MAQQARĪ *Nafḥ al-ṭīb* IV 200 lists *nāranj*, *līmūn*, *līm* and *zanbū'*. It is more difficult to

be certain about what kinds of citrus fruits are mentioned in 'ABD AL-LAṬĪF tr. Sacy 31, as he described a number of varieties of "lemons" and a "sweet citron", but he probably was discussing only varieties of the four kinds of citrus mentioned above.

47 JACQUES DE VITRY 1099; MESSEDAGLIA 598, 601; *Libre de sent soví* 63, 77, 87, 91, 96, 97, 108, 109; EIXIMENIS 25; TARGIONI-TOZZETTI 206; GUAL CAMARENA 441. On p. 168 of the last work a document of 1297 (?) is given, in which are mentioned *toronges*, *limos* and *ponssis*; the meaning of the last term, which might be "poncirus", is discussed by GUAL CAMARENA 396.

48 ORTA 133v (bk XXXIV).

49 The appearance of some other varieties of citrus can be approximately dated. The grapefruit developed either out of a mutation of the shaddock or as a cross between the shaddock and a form of orange. It first appeared in the West Indies at the end of the eighteenth century or at the beginning of the nineteenth. See WEBBER 568ff; ROBINSON; and CHAPOT. The clementine, which was first noticed in North Africa in 1902, is probably a cross between the mandarine and the sour orange; see WEBBER 544ff, CHEVALIER "L'origine botanique"; and TRABUT "Les hybrides". The development of other forms of citrus is discussed in WEBBER 642ff.

8. Banana, plantain

1 This is the usual nomenclature, though the plantain is often wrongly referred to as *M. sapientium* L. var. *paradisiaca*. However, as all cultivated varieties of Musaceae are sterile hybrid creations, without wild prototypes, precise botanical names cannot be given; the term *M. cultivars* is perhaps preferable. CHEESMAN (1948) 145ff has argued that the plantain was derived from *M. balbisiana* and its relatives (which are native to Malaysia and Indochina), while the banana is descended from a hybrid of *M. balbisiana* and *M. acuminata* (the latter of which is probably of Malaysian origin). However, SIMMONDS "Bananas" 212 argues that edible fruit first appeared in *M. acuminata* and that *M. balbisiana* contributed to the development of edible varieties only after hybridization with *M. acuminata*. In *Bananas* 300 he postulates that this occurred mainly in India but also in Malaysia and Indochina.

2 Unfortunately, we cannot distinguish the diffusion of the plantain from that of the banana because the Arabic word *mawz* denotes the two plants and their fruits. The word *ṭalḥ*, which appears in the Koran LVI 28 and in AL-AṢMA'Ī 23, 25, 71 is much less commonly encountered and is of uncertain – perhaps changing – meaning. Today it is used mainly to refer to the plantain; but IBN AL-BAIṬĀR II 417, quoting earlier sources, claimed that its ancient meaning was the same as that of *mawz*. On the other hand, ABŪ ḤANĪFA ed. Hamidullah 111–12 and 283–5 stated that *ṭalḥ* was a variety of *mawz* which grew wild in Arabia and, according to some, bore no fruit; and 'ARRĀM 407 and 'ABD AL-LAṬĪF tr. Sacy 34 used both words as if they denoted different plants. It is possible that these writers were not sure of their nomenclature. It is also, we suggest, possible that the older meaning of *ṭalḥ* was neither banana nor plantain, but rather *Ensete*, a plant now widely grown in Abyssinia and other parts of East Africa; it produces no edible fruit, but its rhizomes and inner stalks are eaten. *Ensete* was known in Abyssinia in ancient times and may have been known in ancient Egypt; see SIMMONDS *Bananas passim* and LAURENT-TÄCKHOLM "The plant". The sources do not allow a distinction between the banana and the plantain on the basis of use: the fruits of some bananas are picked green and cooked while, as Cheesman points out, the fruits of some plantains are sweet and eaten raw. An attempt to use the works of early modern botanists, such as Rumphius, Clusius and Orta, in order to determine which of these plants was known in sixteenth-century Spain and West Africa yielded various, inconclusive results. Probably both plants were known throughout the area of diffusion. DALZIEL 467–70, however, maintains that the plantain was introduced into West Africa long before the banana.

3 IBN BAṬṬŪṬA IV 185; RODINSON "Recherches" 138; 'ABD AL-LAṬĪF tr. Sacy 24–5; SIMMONDS *Bananas* 260ff; SCHAFER *The Vermilion* 186–8; MEYERHOF "Sur un traité" (1943–4) 61. Medical uses are given in IBN AL-BAIṬĀR III 343–4, who cites various earlier authors, and SCHMUCKER 489–90.

4 CHEESMAN *passim*; SIMMONDS *Evolution* 69–75, 132ff; VAVILOV *The Origin* 30; CHEVALIER "Observations"; REYNOLDS; ZHUKOVSKIJ 64–5; CHAKRAVOTI; CHANDRARATNA.

5 REYNOLDS 6 mentions references in the Epics and the Pali Buddhist Canon, parts of which were written at least five or six centuries before Christ. The first clearly datable record from ancient India is found in stone representations of the third to first centuries B.C. See TÄCKHOLM, TÄCKHOLM AND DRAR III 599. For Sanskrit taxonomy, see NADKARNI AND NADKARNI I 822.

6 BRETSCHNEIDER *Botanicon* I 38 shows that it is mentioned in the botanical treatise of Ki Han (fl. third to fourth centuries). By late T'ang times the banana was cultivated in many parts of China; see SCHAFER *The Vermilion* 106–8 and *The Golden* 206; and *Food in Chinese* 97.

7 BRETZL 191ff. In THEOPHRASTUS I 314–15 (bk IV 4) there is some confusion between the banana and the fig tree. PLINY IV 17–19 (bk XII 12), in his description of an Indian plant called *pala*, is clearly referring to the banana.

8 ABŪ ḤANĪFA ed. Hamidullah 283–4, writing in the ninth century, stated that the banana originated in Oman, which may indeed have been on the route of its westward migration. IBN WAḤSHĪYA "Filāḥa" I 70ff claims that the banana originated in "Babylon", i.e. Iraq. These assertions at least suggest that the plant had been known for some time in these areas, but not necessarily earlier than the Arab conquest. As suggested above in n. 2, a reference to *ṭalḥ* in the Koran LVI 28 may be evidence that the banana or plantain was known in western Arabia at the time of the Prophet, or it may simply refer to *Ensete*. A pre-Islamic diffusion to the Levant seems improbable since there is no clear ancient Hebrew or Aramaic word for the banana or the plantain: see MOLDENKE AND MOLDENKE 243 and LÖW *Aramäische* 336. LÖW *Flora* II 253–6 and IV 148–9 states that the earliest mention of the banana in Hebrew literature comes from the Gaonen, which was composed between the mid seventh and late thirteenth centuries. Suggestions that the banana was known in ancient Egypt seem unproven; certain wall-paintings which have been thought by one or two scholars to depict the banana may represent *Ensete*, which is native to Abyssinia and may have been known in ancient Egypt. See LAURENT-TÄCKHOLM "The plant". However, a leaf found in an excavation of a Coptic site at Antinoë (which dates from the fifth to seventh centuries) has been claimed to be a banana leaf. See BONNET "Plantes" 7. Even if this identification, which is questionable, is accepted, it does not prove that the banana was grown in pre-Islamic Egypt. It has been suggested that the banana was known in sixth-century Abyssinia, because of a drawing in the Vatican manuscript of Cosmas Indicopleustes which clearly represents the banana tree and is labelled "These are the so-called *moza*, the Indēke fig [or palm?] tree." The assumption that the word "Indēke" is the name of an unidentified place on the Abyssinian coast is based on the fact that the illustration is found opposite the section of the text which discusses Adulis, near Massawa. But the word clearly means "Indian", an interpretation which is supported by the fact that most of the text and all of the references to plants concern India. See COSMAS INDICOPLEUSTIS ed. Winstedt 240 and tr. McCrindle 55 n. 3; TÄCKHOLM, TÄCKHOLM AND DRAR III 558; MAUNY *Notes* 689ff; and WAINWRIGHT.

9 The poem is given in *Diwān al-shi'r* II 274. I am indebted to Professor Pedro Martínez Montávez for drawing my attention to this poem.

10 ABŪ ḤANĪFA ed. Hamidullah 283–5; IBN AL-BAIṬĀR II 343–4; AL-BARQĪ 457–8.

11 QUSṬŪS 26; IBN WAḤSHĪYA "Filāḥa" I and III 493, 494; IBN AL-BAIṬĀR III 343–4; AL-MAS'ŪDĪ ed. Barbier de Meynard VIII 238.

12 AL-MUQADDASĪ *Aḥsan* 80, 187, 205, 220; YĀQŪT II 884 and IV 595; AL-QAZWĪNĪ II 95, 108; 'ABD AL-LAṬĪF tr. Sacy 26.

13 "Papyrus" 19; IBN RUSTA 132; IBN ḤAWQAL I 141; AL-MAS'ŪDĪ ed. Barbier de Meynard II 383.

14 AL-MAQRĪZĪ *Khiṭaṭ* I 48 and 183 and II 11, 19, 186, 325, 384; 'ABD AL-LAṬĪF tr. Sacy 26 31; ṬAIBŪGHĀ 75; AL-WAṬWĀṬ ch. 4; IBN MAMMĀṬĪ 271, 276; NĀṢIR-I KHUSRAW 146, 150; AL-IDRĪSĪ *Description* 57; AL-ZUHRĪ 257, who stated that dates and bananas were the most common fruits of Egypt.

15 AL-BAKRĪ *Description* 41; ABŪ AL-FIDĀ II 198.

16 AL-RĀZĪ "Description" 67; *Calendrier* 144, 172.

17 IBN AL-'AWWĀM ed. Banqueri I 394–6, who cites the eleventh-century agronome Abū al-Khair; AL-ḤIMYARĪ 30, 136; YĀQŪT III 136, 318; AL-QAZWĪNĪ II 337; IBN LUYŪN *passim*; AL-QALQASHANDĪ 21; AL-MAQQARĪ *Nafḥ al-ṭīb* I 186, who cites the thirteenth-century writer Ibn Sa'īd.

18 See n. 8 above and IBN ḤAWQAL I 37.

19 Koran LVI 28; as has been suggested in n. 2 above, however, the word *ṭalḥ* may not refer to the banana at all. References to the cultivation of *mawz* in the Arabian peninsula may be found in ABŪ ḤANĪFA *loc. cit.*; AL-HAMDĀNĪ *Südarabien* 91, 94, 255, 271; 'ARRĀM 414, 420; IBN RUSTA 125, who stated that banana cultivation was very common in the area around San'ā'; AL-ZUHRĪ 271, who claimed that the banana was the principal fruit in the area around Mecca; YĀQŪT III 26, 180, 318, 495 and IV 180, 495; and AL-QAZWĪNĪ II 64. MEYERHOF "Sur un traité" (1943–4) 61 writes of a fourteenth-century agricultural treatise from the Yemen in which a special Yemeni cultivar is mentioned, as well as another from India which had several varieties.

20 See the later part of n. 8 above and WAINWRIGHT.

21 AL-MAS'ŪDĪ ed. Barbier de Meynard III 30.

22 AL-QAZWĪNĪ II 12; AL-'UMARĪ 10.

23 IBN BAṬṬŪṬA II 191 and IV 185.

24 JEFFREYS "Arabs" and KUP 174 argue in favour of an Arab introduction of the banana from East into West Africa, but the evidence – mostly linguistic – is still slight. As will be suggested later in this book, it seems unlikely that the banana was introduced from the north; it could, however, have been diffused across sub-Saharan Africa.

25 The appearance of the banana in Madagascar has been dated variously from remote Bantu or Malay migrations to later Indian migrations. But these hypotheses are purely speculative and an introduction from East Africa in Islamic times seems equally possible. SIMMONDS *Evolution* 143ff suggests that there is "geographic and climatic evidence" which makes a transmission through Arabia and down the east coast of Africa unlikely, but it is difficult to see what this evidence could be. On the contrary, the northern route seems much more probable to this writer.

9. *Coconut palm*

1 AL-NUWAIRĪ XI 129–30 and ABŪ ḤANĪFA ed. Hamidullah 288 and ed. Lewin 36 also give the word *rānij*, while IBN AL-BAIṬĀR I 201 gives *barinj*. AL-MAS'ŪDĪ ed. Barbier de Meynard I 338 mentions *zanj* as another name.

2 ANDERSON 154.

3 ABŪ ḤANĪFA ed. Hamidullah 288–9; AL-NUWAIRĪ *loc. cit.*; ABŪ ZAID AL-ḤASAN 126, 139; IBN BAṬṬŪṬA II 206ff and IV 113, 118, 121, 124, 139; IBN AL-BAIṬĀR III 356–7; MAIMONIDES 53, 126; SCHMUCKER 496; BOIS II 587ff; DAHLGREN 3ff. VELHO 23, writing at the end of the fifteenth century, described boats on the coast of East Africa which had sails of woven palm leaves. GOPAL "Sugar-making" 68–70 states that in India the sap was used to make sugar.

4 The question of the origin of this plant is vexed, the difficulty being that the cultivated coconut has no wild relative in the Old World and yet has clearly been grown there since remote times. There is, on the other hand, a wild coconut palm in Central America, but

its antiquity is uncertain. See BURKILL *Dictionary* I 595; HILL "The original"; CHIOVENDA; SMALL; BARRAU, VAVILOV *The Origin* 28; COOK *passim*; CHILD 4ff; ZHUKOVSKIJ 22; and J. D. SAUER.

5 GOPAL "Sugar-making" 68–70; HILL "The original".

6 Tr. McCrindle 362.

7 SCHAFER *The Vermilion* 174–4; BRETSCHNEIDER *Botanicon* I 38 and *On the Study* 24–5 cite other Chinese references to the coconut from the third or fourth century. According to *Food in Chinese* 97, the coconut palm was grown in South China by T'ang times. By the thirteenth century the tree was apparently grown on the island of Hainan; see CHAU JU-KUA 176 and 183, who (on pp. 48, 60, 77, 89, 96, 155) reports the cultivation of the tree in many parts of the east. ABŪ ḤANĪFA ed. Hamidullah 288 also speaks of the coconut palm as growing in "China", by which he may have meant Indochina.

8 *Pahlavi Texts* 25; CHRISTENSEN 472. On climatic grounds it seems improbable that the plant was ever grown in Persia or Mesopotamia. See also n. 16 below.

9 AL-IDRĪSĪ *India* 25, 27, 33; AL-BĪRŪNĪ I 210; IBN BAṬṬŪṬA IV 120, 228–9; IBN ḤAWQAL II 317; YĀQŪT IV 21, 773; AL-MAS'ŪDĪ ed. Barbier de Meynard I 137–8, 336–9; IBN QUTAIBA 81; *Ḥudūd* 57, 88–90; ABŪ ZAID AL-ḤASAN 126.

10 IBN WAḤSHĪYA "Filāḥa" III 478–9.

11 See n. 3 above. These authors state that the coconut is also mentioned by Ibn Sīnā and al-Rāzī. GOITEIN *Studies* 339 states that coconuts were an important item of trade between Egypt and India.

12 ABŪ ZAID AL-ḤASAN 126.

13 IBN BAṬṬŪṬA II 206ff. GROHMANN *Südarabien* I 229 mentions that the coconut palm still grows in parts of southern Arabia today.

14 AL-MAS'ŪDĪ ed. Pellat II 330; VELHO 23–4; GRAY 24.

15 DALZIEL 497–8 shows that in many West African languages the coconut is referred to as the "whiteman's nut", a term which suggests an introduction in modern times. On the other hand, as is pointed out in MAUNY "Notes" 696, the plant was seen by the Portuguese in West Africa in the sixteenth century; whether the Portuguese had introduced it there, or it was already there when they first arrived, is not known. The various terms for coconut in the Malagasy languages suggest an importation from Malaya or southern India. See BURKILL *Dictionary* I 595.

16 IBN WAḤSHĪYA "Filāḥa" III 478–9.

17 IBN IYĀS IV 747; TÄCKHOLM, TÄCKHOLM AND DRAR II 317.

10. Watermelon

1 Many translators have assumed – wrongly – that the single unmodified word *baṭṭīkh* in the texts necessarily refers to the watermelon. It probably sometimes does; but, as several of the references cited below make clear, it is very often used as a generic term for all melons or for melons belonging to the *Cucumis* family only, while in North Africa it designates the common melon, *Cucumis melo* L. In writing this account I have cited references to the word *baṭṭīkh* used alone only where the context made it absolutely clear that the watermelon was meant. Other references using this name alone have been ignored. For further discussion of taxonomy, see ABŪ ḤANĪFA ed. Lewin 31, 65; MAIMONIDES 29, 52; TRABUT *Répertoire* 72; DUBLER "Temas" *passim*; 'ABD AL-LAṬĪF *Relation* 35; MEYERHOF "Sur un traité" (1943–4) 55; and IBN AL-'AWWĀM ed. Banqueri II 230, 233ff. SCHWEINFURTH *Arabische* 134 gives a number of names used in the Yemen which seem unrelated to other Arabic names; they suggest that the watermelon reached the Yemen in very early times, perhaps directly from India. The terms *jabas* and *baṭṭīkh aḥmar* were noted by the author in the present-day dialects of Syria, the former in the Aleppo region and the latter in Damascus.

2 DALZIEL 54; BURKILL *Dictionary* I 560; IBN ḤAWQAL II 422, who says that melons (probably

watermelons) of Merv were dried and exported all over the world; SCHIEMANN *Die Entstehung* 240–1; AL-RĀZĪ *Kitāb* I 204, 212, VI 145, 156, VII 18 and X 27, 47, 75, 128. That al-Rāzī refers to the watermelon specifically is confirmed by IBN AL-BAITĀR I 240. Other medical uses are given in IBN BUṬLĀN ed. Ricci I 112. GUAL CAMARENA 193 gives evidence of a considerable trade in watermelon seeds in late medieval Europe, while LABIB *Handelsgeschichte* 324 gives references to the export of watermelons from Egypt to Europe in late medieval times.

3 VAVILOV *The Origin* 44; SCHIEMANN *loc. cit.*; CANDOLLE 262–4; CHEVALIER "Le Sahara" 316; SCHWEINFURTH "Sur l'origine"; WHITAKER AND DAVIS 2; DRAR 42, who found the watermelon (possibly an escape?) growing wild near Khartoum.

4 Pictorial and other evidence is presented and discussed in UNGER figs. 30–2; HARTMANN 55; and KEIMER *Die Gartenpflanzen* 18, 24–5, 133. DIXON "Masticatories" 440 and nn. 53–8 goes over the evidence for the watermelon in ancient Egypt: it is likely that much or all of this refers to the colocynth rather than the watermelon. Dr 'Abd al-Gazzar of the Department of Botany of Cairo University kindly examined with me the pre-Islamic archeological material in the Cairo Agricultural Museum which had been identified, probably by Schweinfurth, as watermelon. He found that all material which is clearly pre-Islamic is probably colocynth and all material which is clearly watermelon is of unknown provenance and hence undatable. Thus the leaves from the Twentieth Dynasty, which had been identified as watermelon, are in fact colocynth. Of the seed collection, 4198 (from Tutankhamen's tomb) is not watermelon but some other cucurbit; 4193 (from Thebes) is probably watermelon but without provenance and hence undatable; 1441 (from Dair al-Madīna) is almost certainly colocynth; 4097 (donated by the Egyptian Museum from the Maspero collection) is watermelon but of unrecorded provenance; 4187B is probably watermelon but of uncertain date.

5 MOLDENKE AND MOLDENKE 78–81; LÖW *Flora* I 550–3. The various Aramaic and Hebrew words of the *baṭṭīkh* type given in LÖW *Aramäische* 352 probably all refer to the common melon.

6 TRABUT *Répertoire* 72. The term *dullā' al-hind* appears in the tenth-century *Cordovan Calendar*; see *Calendrier* 130.

7 CHEVALIER *Les productions* 790; DALZIEL 54–5.

8 LAUFER *Sino-Iranica* 438–45, where it is pointed out that a Chinese writer observed the watermelon growing in the lands held by the Kitan in the tenth century; BURKILL *Dictionary* I 560.

9 See n. 1 above.

10 For the various Andalusian variants on this word, see ALVAR LÓPEZ II map 334.

11 IBN AL-'AWWĀM ed. Banqueri II 230, 233ff; 'ABD AL-LAṬĪF *Relation* 35, who says the watermelon is referred to as the Palestinian melon in Egypt; IBN BUṬLĀN ed. Ricci I 112, who speaks of "melones indi id est palestini". ALCOVER AND MOLL VII 332 give the Valencian *melo d'Alger*; they also state that in Urgel and the valley of the Ebro, regions which were Mozarabic until the thirteenth century, the term *melo de moro*, which also suggests an introduction from North Africa, is used. *Glosario* 178–9, a Hispano-Muslim work of the eleventh or twelfth century speaks of the melon of Algiers, the *rīfī* melon (i.e. from the North African Rīf), and the melon of Damascus as if these were all different kinds of melon. Probably the first of these terms was used in medieval Spain to designate the watermelon; the others may have been used for special varieties of watermelons or else for other kinds of melons.

12 AL-RĀZĪ *loc. cit.* in n. 2 above, though it is to be noted that in III 75, 105 this author speaks of the watermelon as a food and not a medicine; ABŪ ḤANĪFA ed. Lewin 31, 65; ORTA 304, who cites many references in Ibn Sīna. The poem, by Abū Ṭālib al-Ma'mūnī (fl. late tenth century), is given in AL-NUWAIRĪ XI 32 and AL-THA'ĀLIBĪ IV 180. Several *ḥadīths* compiled in Kufa in the ninth century mention *khirbiz*, whilst others refer to *baṭṭīkh*; it seems likely that the former concern the watermelon. See AL-BARQĪ 459.

13 I 33.
14 AL-IDRĪSĪ *Description* 25; 'ABD AL-LAṬĪF *Relation* 35; IBN AL-BAIṬĀR I 240; MÜLLER-WODARG (1957) 33, who cites al-Maqrīzī; IBN MAMMĀTĪ 265; AL-GHAZZĪ 37.
15 II 177. An earlier reference to watermelons in Upper Egypt is found in AL-IDRĪSĪ *Description* 25–6, 57.
16 *Calendrier* 130; IBN AL-'AWWĀM ed. Banqueri II 230, 233ff, where the watermelon is the seventh kind of melon mentioned; IBN BAṢṢĀL 169. IBN WĀFID "Tratado" 321 has *badea* in the heading but no reference to the plant in the following text.
17 AL-'UMARĪ 13, 103, 115; MEYERHOF "Sur un traité" (1943–4) 55.

11. Spinach

1 We shall treat here only *Spinacia oleracea* L. and not a large number of other greens which are sometimes – particularly in Africa – referred to as "spinach". These include several members of the *Amaranthus* family which are cultivated very widely in Africa. As many of these are also of Asian origin, they may have been diffused to Africa at about the same time as spinach and over the same routes, but we have no proof. See PORTÈRES "Pousses"; THOMAS 382–3; BUSSON 136ff; and HARRISON *et al.* 160.
2 IBN AL-BAIṬĀR I 60–1; *Tuḥfat* 23; TRABUT *Répertoire* 247.
3 Recipes for preparation of spinach are given in MUḤAMMAD IBN AL-ḤASAN 43, 192, 206 and in "Kitāb al-ṭabīkh" 168. Four other recipes are mentioned in RODINSON "Recherches" 133ff. Medical uses are given in IBN AL-BAIṬĀR *loc. cit.*; SCHMUCKER 67; AL-RĀZĪ *Kitāb al-ḥāwī* V 128 and VI 12; QUSṬŪS 112; and IBN WĀFID *Libre* 89.
4 GIRENKO. Earlier views on the origin of spinach are found in BOIS I 409; GIBAULT 81ff; and CANDOLLE 98ff. VAVILOV *The Origin* gives a "Central Asian" origin. It is interesting to note that IBN AL-BAIṬĀR I 60–1 stated that there was, in his time, a wild spinach similar to the cultivated variety.
5 IBN AL-'AWWĀM ed. Banqueri II 160.
6 Contrary to what is maintained in GUYOT 16 and ABŪ AL-NAṢR 220. IBN WĀFID *Libre* 89 is clearly wrong in stating that it was known to Galen. The hypothesis of BRETSCHNEIDER *Study* 15, 17, according to which it was introduced into China in the second century B.C., is based on a legend which is disproved by LAUFER *Sino-Iranica* 392–3. LÖW *Aramäische* 385–6 gives a medieval Aramaic (i.e. Syriac) word for spinach; in *Flora* he concludes that there was no ancient Hebrew word for the plant.
7 CHRISTENSEN 472 says that Khvadh Arzu mentions a soup made with spinach, flour and vinegar.
8 LAUFER *loc. cit.*, who cites *T'ang hui yao*. BRETSCHNEIDER *Botanicon* I 79 and *Study* 16–17 shows that the plant is mentioned in the Chinese treatise on agriculture by Chung Shu Shu, a work of the seventh or eighth century. See also *Food in Chinese* 155.
9 AL-RĀZĪ *loc. cit.*
10 "Filāḥa" 333. In this reference, which is the only one I have been able to find in Ibn Waḥshīya's work, the writer merely says that a certain plant is a kind of spinach. It would therefore seem that spinach was familiar to his readers. According to later Arab writers, there are other references to spinach in Ibn Waḥshīya's work: IBN AL-BAIṬĀR *loc. cit.* cites *The Nabataean Book of Agriculture* in his discussion of a wild plant which resembles spinach, and a description of Ibn Waḥshīya's recommendations for growing spinach is quoted in AL-NUWAIRĪ XI 77. It may be that in reading this huge work I missed these passages, or they may be absent from the Cairo manuscript. If the plant was well known in Ibn Waḥshīya's time, it is indeed surprising that it should not be discussed in some detail in this work which treats at length a very great number of greens, both wild and cultivated.
11 QUSṬŪS 112.
12 IBN AL-'AWWĀM *loc. cit.*

13 See n. 3 above.

14 IBN AL-'AWWĀM *loc. cit.* and IBN BAṢṢĀL 197–8. The relevant parts of the work of Abū al-Khair (*q.v.* in bibliography) have not been published and may have been lost. The work on spinach by Ibn Ḥajjāj has apparently been lost, though it may have formed part of his *al-Muqni'*, a part of which has recently been discovered and published (see bibliography).

15 IBN AL-BAIṬĀR *loc. cit.*; IBN AL-'AWWĀM *loc. cit.*; AL-NUWAIRĪ *loc. cit.*; AL-QAZWĪNĪ I 272; AL-MAQRĪZĪ *Al-mawā'iẓ* 253; IBN LUYŪN; AL-GHAZZĪ 15, 126; IBN MAMMĀTĪ 240–1; MEYERHOF "Sur un traité" (1943–4) 56.

12. Artichoke

1 The word *kankar*, sometimes thought to designate the artichoke, is a problem. Coming from the Persian *kangar*, which today means cardoon or thistle (see SCHLIMMER 103), the Arabic word seems usually to refer to *Acanthus mollis* L., a plant most often used for its leaves. (See BEDEVIAN 9.) Thus although IBN AL-BAIṬĀR I 432 said that *kankar* is the "*ḥarshuf* of the garden" (and is followed in this by the Moroccan medical glossary *Tuḥfat al-aḥbāb* 95), this same author III 205 states that the plant has leaves longer and wider than lettuce and is the *akanthos* of Dioscorides (ed. Wellmann II 23 (bk III 17), where this term is given as *aqanthūs*). It can therefore hardly have been the artichoke. IBN WAḤSHĪYA *Medieval* 125 may also use the word to denote the acanthus; but in "Filāḥa" I 28 he stated that the plant known in Persian as *kandar* is the wild *kharshuf* of the Arabs and is called *ḥarāshafa* in Nabatean (= Aramaic). ABŪ ḤANĪFA ed. Lewin 112, who does not seem to know the *ḥarshuf* at first hand, but only through Arab sources, said he thought the Persian word *kankar* or *kanqar* was used to designate the cardoon, a plant which was sometimes cultivated but more often found growing wild, and that this plant was known in Arabic by the word *ḥarshuf* or a variant of this word. The Arabic word *kankar* designated the acanthus, a cultivated plant resembling the wild cardoon. SCHWEINFURTH *Arabische* 164 gives *shōk al-ḥamīr* as another Yemeni name. For *qinārīya*, see n. 6 below.

2 A recipe using *kharshuf* is given in "Kitāb al-ṭabīkh" 143, but it is impossible to tell from the text whether the artichoke or the cardoon is meant. Medical uses for *ḥarshuf* are given in IBN AL-BAIṬĀR III 205–6.

3 GIBAULT 13ff; BOIS I 278ff; TARGIONI-TOZZETTI 48–9, 52; CANDOLLE 92–5. ANDRÉ 72 suggests that several Roman authors may have designated the artichoke (or the cardoon) by the word *carduus*. But in fact the descriptions given in PALLADIUS 122 and PLINY V 454 and 518 (bk XIX 19 and 42) say nothing about the plant which suggests that it was not the cardoon; APICIUS 21 (bk III 19) proposes serving the *carduus* with a sauce of hard-boiled eggs, a recipe which seems more suitable for the stems of the cardoon than for the artichoke. THEOPHRASTOS II 31 (bk VI 4) says explicitly that the stem of the *kaktos* is the part eaten and is therefore almost certainly speaking of the cardoon; he does, however, go on to mention another type of "thistle", the *pternix*, which has an edible receptacle but – apparently – inedible bracts. *Geoponika* bk XII 39 also seems to refer to the cardoon. None of the thistle-like plants described in DIOSCORIDES ed. Wellmann II 14–26 (bk III 8–20), mostly belonging to the Compositae family, seems to be the artichoke.

4 TRABUT *Répertoire* 85.

5 In addition to the references cited above, several other Muslim writers speak of the *ḥarshuf*. LOKOTSCH 833 gives a ninth-century Syrian text which uses the word. In the tenth century, Ibn Khālawaih 58 speaks of the *ḥarshaf*, which he says is mentioned by Abū Ḥanīfa; AL-MUQADDASĪ *Aḥsan* 220 says the plant is grown in Palestine. IBN WAḤSHĪYA "Filāḥa" makes many references to the plant: I 75–6, where he speaks of plants with spikes or thorns which are similar to the *ḥarshuf*; II 251, where he speaks of a *ḥarshuf*-like lettuce, probably the acanthus; and II 271–2, 331 and III 471, where he speaks of a "wild *ḥarshuf*" with thorns. It is possible that the *shawk al-darājīn* of IBN BAṢṢĀL 156–7, which Millás

Vallicrosa translates as *cardo espinoso*, is the artichoke, but the description seems to fit the acanthus better.

6 IBN AL-BAIṬĀR I 431 gives the word *qinārīya*, seemingly as the word for artichoke in the "barbarous", i.e. Romanic, language of Spain. This hypothesis seems to be confirmed by the usage in IBN AL-'AWWĀM ed. Banqueri II 302–3, who speaks of the *ḥarshuf* as a plant which grows wild and distinguishes this from the *qinārīya*, presumably the artichoke. The twelfth- or thirteenth-century *Glosario* 320 also probably uses the word to refer to the artichoke: it states that a plant called *ṭūba* (most likely *Onopordon acanthium* L. or Scotch thistle) resembles the *qinārīya*. TRABUT *Répertoire* 85 gives *qinārīya* as one of the North African words for artichoke, and indeed it is the term commonly used today in Tunisia and Algiers (where *kharshuf* is used to designate the cardoon). This linguistic evidence seems to suggest that the artichoke was known in Spain, and perhaps also in North Africa, by the thirteenth century. There is, however, the possibility that it was known much earlier in the Levant, for QUSṬŪS 284 describes the *kanār* as a kind of domestic *ḥarshuf*. It is possible, however, that the word should have been *kankar*, acanthus, but has been incorrectly transcribed.

7 BRESC 73 cites evidence of the artichoke being grown in the gardens of Norman Sicily; the documents distinguish the plant from the cardoon. The earliest evidence of the artichoke in continental Italy seems to be from the fifteenth century: see TARGIONI-TOZZETTI *loc. cit.* and NICCOLI 206. See also PELLEGRINI *Gli arabismi* I 118, 188 and GIBAULT 16ff, who is, however, wrong in imagining that the artichoke was developed in Italy. COROMINAS *Diccionario* I 92 found the first clear reference to the plant in Castilian in a document of 1423, where the word used is *carchofa*. CANDOLLE 92–5 states that the plant did not reach England until the sixteenth century.

13. Colocasia

1 Other Arabic names from the Yemen and North Africa are given in SCHWEINFURTH *Arabische* 104 and TRABUT *Répertoire* 75.

2 'ABD AL-LAṬĪF *Relation* 23; L'ECLUSE lxxv. RODINSON "Recherches" 136 mentions five recipes from a thirteenth-century cookbook.

3 AL-RĀZĪ *Kitāb* V 133; IBN AL-BAIṬĀR III 101; 'ABD AL-LAṬĪF *Relation* 23.

4 HARLAN "Agricultural origins" n. 33 thinks domestication occurred in Burma, while ANDERSON 159 proposes Assam and Burma; GORMAN 56 suggests that cultivation began in Thailand *c.* 9000 B.C.; ZHUKOVSKIJ 12 thinks the origin is Malaysia; and BARRAU 64 points out that colocasia is similar to the *Colocasia esculenta* var. *aquatilis* which grows wild in various regions of Indonesia.

5 Evidence for the use of colocasia in China *c.* 168 B.C. is found in bamboo slips from a tomb in Hunan, while other documents suggest that it was a staple in parts of Han China; see *Food in Chinese* 57, 76. BRETSCHNEIDER *On the Study* says that it is mentioned in a Chinese work of *c.* 100. Evidence from slightly later times is given by LI 254, 256 and SCHAFER *The Vermilion* 182.

6 On the confusion of the ancients, see TÄCKHOLM, TÄCKHOLM AND DRAR II 372ff; CANDOLLE 74–5; BURKILL "The contacts" 84; ANDRÉ 96–7; IBN AL-BAIṬĀR I 41. Unfortunately, the use of the word "colocasia" to refer to other plants has misled many modern authors into the mistaken conclusion that the plant was grown in pre-Islamic times in Egypt, the Levant or Mesopotamia. See, for example, HARTMANN 45; and LÖW *Flora* I 215–18 and *Aramäische* 239–41. TÄCKHOLM, TÄCKHOLM AND DRAR *loc. cit.* survey thoroughly the ancient descriptions of plants called colocasia and arum, and conclude that a passage in Pliny describing a kind of arum might refer to colocasia. But this passage simply states that "it is Egypt especially that produces...the aron. About it and dracontium there has been a sharp controversy, for some have asserted that the two are the same. Glaucius distinguished them by their mode of production, claiming that dracontium is wild aron.

Some have called the root aron, but the stem dracontium, though the latter is a totally different plant. For the aron has a black root, broad and round, and much larger, large enough to fill the hand." See PLINY VII 101–3 (bk XXIV 91). Several points are to be noted. First, it is not clear that Pliny is describing colocasia: there are many other plants which could fit this description equally well, and the statement that the root is black seems to preclude colocasia. Secondly, Glaucius apparently states that there is a wild form of the aron, presumably found either in Egypt or Italy; but colocasia does not grow wild anywhere in Egypt or the Mediterranean basin. Thirdly, there seems no reason to suppose that the aron referred to here is different from aron referred to in PLINY V 483 (bk XIX 30), which, it is said, grows wild in Palastrina and around Reims and which is certainly not colocasia. The *colocaseum* referred to in PALLADIUS 98 is probably *Faba Aegyptica*, which has a bulbous root; see ANDRÉ 96–7. STEPHANUS OF BYZANTIUM I 38, a sixth-century writer, spoke of a plant called *kolosaïon* which grew along a river near Acre, and which was said to have healing powers. But the description of the plant, which was a "grass" with fruit, suggests another identification. In AËTIOS I 91, who probably also wrote in the sixth century, there is a reference to *kolokasion*, which was said to resemble the onion and the turnip, but to have sticky (glutinous?) flesh and to be useful as a detergent and a laxative. Unfortunately, this description is not clear enough to permit identification.

7 "Filāḥa" I 105 and III 540. See also AL-RĀZĪ *Kitāb* V 133, who probably observed it in Mesopotamia, and ABŪ ḤANĪFA ed. Hamidullah 222.

8 RODINSON "Recherches" 136.

9 AL-MAS'ŪDĪ ed. Pellat II 330; AL-MUQADDASĪ *Aḥsan* 220; 'ABD AL-LAṬĪF *Relation* 23; AL-DIMASHQĪ 282.

10 AL-MAS'ŪDĪ *loc. cit.*; 'ABD AL-LAṬĪF *loc. cit.*; AL-MAQRĪZĪ *Khiṭāṭ* I 182; IBN MAMMĀTĪ 267 *et passim*; IBN AL-'AWWĀM ed. Banqueri II 212, where the word *qirqāṣ*, possibly a misreading of the manuscript, is mistranslated by Banqueri. The translation is correctly given in Clément-Mullet's edition (II pt I 416). See also LABIB *Handelsgeschichte* 154, 190. L'ECLUSE lxxv–lxxvi stated that the plant grew in both Egypt and Crete in the sixteenth century.

11 175–6.

12 IBN AL-'AWWĀM ed. Banqueri I 491 and II 212; L'ECLUSE lxxv–lxxvi.

13 YĀQŪT IV mentioned it at Zinguebar in South Arabia, while AL-MAS'ŪDĪ ed. Barbier de Meynard III 30–1 stated that in the land of the Zanj (on the East African coast), the diet had as its base sorghum and a plant called *al-kalārī*, which he said is similar to the colocasia of Syria and Egypt, and which also grew abundantly around the city of Aden. It may be supposed that this plant was in fact colocasia. On its migration to East Africa, see also BURKILL "The rise"; TÄCKHOLM, TÄCKHOLM AND DRAR II 378; and JUMELLE 189.

14 BURKILL "The contacts" 85–7.

15 AL-'UMARĪ 61; IBN BAṬṬŪṬA IV 399.

14. Eggplant

1 Variants of this word found in the sources are *bādinjān*, *bādinjāl* and *barinjān*. ABŪ ḤANĪFA ed. Lewin 21, 66 also gives *ānab*, *waghd* and *ḥadaq*. See also IBN AL-BAIṬĀR I 161.

2 "Filāḥa" II 348ff and *Medieval* 51. Ibn Waḥshīya states that the fruit, seeds, roots and leaves of the plant are edible.

3 "Kibāb al-ṭabīkh" 37, 38, 79, 99, 107, 112, 127, 131, 150–6. Other ways of preparing it are given in MUḤAMMAD IBN AL-ḤASAN 34, 37, 38, 39, 40, 42, 191, 193, 200, 203, 205 and IBN AL-'AWWĀM ed. Banqueri II 250–1. A dish of eggplant with *burān* sauce, served in the time of the caliph al-Mustakfī (mid tenth century), was mentioned by AL-MAS'ŪDĪ ed. Barbier de Meynard VIII 395; it was alleged to whet the dulled appetite. See also RODINSON "Recherches" 133, 135–6, 141, 142, where are mentioned eight other recipes from a thirteenth-century Baghdadi cookbook. In parts of the Middle East today, a saying has

it that a girl should know a hundred ways to prepare eggplant. A fourteenth-century Valencian cookbook gives what must be one of the earliest recipes for eggplant from Christian Europe. See "Libro de cocina" 177.

4 SCHMUCKER 100; AL-RĀZĪ *Kitāb* III 94, 137; IBN WAḤSHĪYA "Filāḥa" II 351.

5 VAVILOV *The Origin* 24, 27; GIBAULT 329ff; BOIS I 355–6; DUBLER "Temas...Sobre la berenjena"; BURKILL "Habits" 37. However, in an earlier discussion Burkill says the eggplant is native to Southeast Asia. See his *Dictionary* II 2044–5.

6 LI 252–60. It is possible, however, that the type of eggplant referred to here is the kind which Vavilov (*loc. cit.*) believed to be native to China. It is described as having a small fruit the size of a marble. By T'ang times (618–907), however, several varieties were known in China; see *Food in Chinese* 93.

7 Certain writers of earlier centuries claimed that the eggplant was mentioned by Theophrastus and Dioscorides, but such an identification seems improbable. See DUNAL 9. It seems impossible to agree with the view of CANDOLLE 287–8 that the plant was known in North Africa in pre-Islamic times; the argument that the Berber word *tar-benjalts* is sufficiently different from the Arabic word to imply an earlier introduction is unconvincing. THOMPSON 331 finds no proof that the plant was known in ancient Assyria. LÖW *Flora* III 377–9 states that the plant is first mentioned in Hebrew sources *c.* A.D. 1000. STERN *Calendrier* 233–4, 366 states that eggplants are depicted in three calendars: the mosaics at Kabr Hiram and Tégée, which date from about the sixth century, and a manuscript of the ninth century in the Vatican Library. The Louvre has kindly supplied me with photographs of the Kabr Hiram mosaics, in which I can find no clear representation of an eggplant. In a later publication, Stern seems to have changed his view and states that the fruits and vegetables represented are gourds and pomegranates (though very clearly one of the vegetables is okra); see STERN "Sur quelques pavements" 26. WEBSTER 128 states that the Vatican manuscript shows melons rather than eggplants. The mosaics at Tégée have not yet been published, and I have been unable to obtain photographs of them.

8 "Filāḥa" II 348ff.

9 ABŪ ḤANĪFA ed. Lewin 66.

10 In particular, the word *ḥadaq* given by ABŪ ḤANĪFA *loc. cit.* seems to be derived from the Sanskrit *vartaku* and *bantaku.*

11 AL-BARQĪ 435 gives five *ḥadiths* concerning the eggplant. IBN WAḤSHĪYA "Filāḥa" II 348–51 is the major treatment, but I have counted ten other references in this work; QUSṬŪS 114–15; IBN AL-BAIṬĀR I 161. Exactly who was the mysterious Ibn Māsawaih is uncertain, but he was probably Māsawaih al-Mardīnī (d. 1015). Although the Arabic text of his work has not been published and has probably been lost, a translation into Latin was published a number of times in the sixteenth and seventeenth centuries with the author's name given as Johannes Mesué. See SARTON I 728–9 (also I 574 for an earlier possibility, an Ibn Māsawaih who died in 857). I have taken the reference to his account on eggplants from IBN AL-BAIṬĀR *loc. cit.*

12 AL-NUWAIRĪ XI 44–5. Another poem is given in AL-MAQQARĪ *Nafḥ al-ṭīb* V 229.

13 NĀṢIR-I KHUSRAW 150; IBN MAMMĀTĪ 204, 239, 240, 247, 250–1, 267–8, 274; AL-MAQRĪZĪ tr. Bouriant I 294.

14 AL-'UMARĪ 103 and 175 observed it in Ifrīqiya (roughly corresponding to modern Tunisia) and in Morocco.

15 *Calendrier* 62, 72, 172, 186; IBN AL-'AWWĀM ed. Banqueri II 245; IBN BAṢṢĀL 173–7.

16 AL-'UMARĪ 13, 44. DALZIEL 433–4 gives a few names in West African languages (e.g. Ti, *a-bela* and Mandinka, *patansi-jato*) which suggest an Arab introduction. CHEVALIER "Les productions" 787 proposed that the cultivation of eggplants in the Saharan oases is very ancient.

17 *Loc. cit.*

18 *Loc. cit.*

19 BURKILL "Habits" 37.
20 MEYERHOF "Sur un traité" (1943–4) 55. Discussions of the eggplant by later Arab writers may be found in IBN MAMMĀTĪ *loc. cit.*; IBN LUYŪN; AL-WAṬWĀṬ ch. 4; AL-MAQRĪZĪ ed. Wiet II 78; AL-GHAZZĪ 29, 37; *Glosario* 167; and IBN JUBAIR II 140.

15. Mango tree

1 ABŪ ḤANĪFA ed. Lewin xxi, 45; IBN BAṬṬŪṬA IV 185. IBN ḤAWQAL II 314 gives *anbāj*. SCHWEINFURTH *Arabische* 87, 168 lists *'amb* as a form which both he and Forskål noted in the Yemen. This is clearly related to the *ambe* of Ceylon, and both must be connected to the Sanskrit *amra*; see CANDOLLE 201. IBN AL-BAIṬĀR I 159 and II 471, who was obviously not familiar with the plant, gives both *'anbā* and *ānbaj* as if they denoted different plants.
2 IBN BAṬṬŪṬA III 125–6 and IV 185; IBN AL-BAIṬĀR I 159; AL-IDRĪSĪ *India* 35. Sources giving medical uses are cited in AL-NAṢR 100–1.
3 MUKHERJEE "The origin", "Origin, distribution" 67 and "The mango"; GANGOLLY *et al.* 3–4; ROBERTSON-PROSCHOWSKY 264; BURKILL "Habits" 16; VAVILOV *The Origin* 26.
4 MUKHERJEE "Origin, distribution" 70; GANGOLLY *et al.* 4–7; AL-IDRĪSĪ *India* 34–5; IBN ḤAWQAL II 314; AL-IṢṬAKHRĪ 83. The last two of these authors mentioned it growing in the province of Sind in the extreme north-west of the Indian sub-continent.
5 LAUFER *Sino-Iranica* 471 states that it was mentioned as a plant growing in Cambodia in the Sui annals, which were written about 629. SCHAFER *The Vermilion* 190–1 points out that in T'ang times (618–907) the mango was still an exotic fruit for the Chinese. Even in Sung times (960–1279) it is mentioned only in medical texts. Today the mango tree grows in central Vietnam, Hainan and on the tip of the Lui-chow peninsula.
6 Ed. Lewin 45.
7 AL-NAṢR 100–1.
8 LAUFER *Sino-Iranica* 552 cites the Chinese *T'ai p'iñ hwan yü ki* ch. 181 p. 13b.
9 IBN BAṬṬŪṬA IV 185.
10 DALZIEL 340 suggests that the mango tree reached Futa Jallon and the upper Niger before the coming of the Europeans. But the various names of the *manku* type in most parts of West Africa suggest a later introduction. MAUNY "Notes" 709 suggests that the mango tree did not reach West Africa till the eighteenth century, while BUSSON puts the introduction in the nineteenth century.
11 BURKILL *Dictionary* II 1403 describes the difficulties of propagating the tree. The introduction of the mango tree into Egypt, the Sudan and Eritrea seems to have occurred within the last two centuries, though SCHWEINFURTH *loc. cit.* mentions that Forskål in 1775 gave the word *'amb* as the name of the plant in Egypt. See *Agriculture in Uganda* 477–8. IBN BAṬṬŪṬA IV 228 saw the tree growing in Sumatra in the fourteenth century, but according to Rumphius it had been introduced to some islands of the Indonesian archipelago only within living memory, that is during the seventeenth century. See BOIS II 144 and RUMPF I 95.

16. The routes

1 On the African centre of plant origins see HARLAN "Agricultural origins" 470–1. The Sabean Lane, linking India to Africa via the Arabian peninsula, has played a crucial role in the diffusion of numerous African crops into Asia and Asian crops into Africa. Amongst the former, MURDOCK 207 lists five which are included in "the seventeen major crops of India": castor, cotton, bulrush millet, sesame and sorghum. To these should perhaps be added the tamarind tree, which now appears to have originated in Madagascar and which was seen in the fourth century B.C. by the Alexandrian expedition to the Persian Gulf and India; see BRETZL 120–32. On the other hand, it is not certain that cotton is of African origin; see the chapter on cotton in this book and A. M. WATSON "The rise"

355ff. About the period over which the Sabean Lane was in operation as a channel for the diffusion of plants and much else, there has been considerable uncertainty. MURDOCK 45, 205ff suggests that the route functioned primarily in the first millennium B.C., while HOURANI 21ff gives evidence of its importance in the third century B.C. KIRK *passim* maintains that the greatest movement over this route took place between 500 B.C. and A.D. 500. However, ALLCHIN AND ALLCHIN 266 state that there is archeological evidence that finger millet and possibly bulrush millet, both of African origin, were cultivated in the southern Deccan in the first half of the second millennium B.C.; see also *Evolutionary Studies* 19–22. Sorghum seems to have reached India from Africa by this time: seeds found in Rajasthan have been dated *c.* 1720 B.C. ±110. See *Evolutionary Studies* 21. Cotton, if it is of African origin, is also relevant here, for it also appears to have been grown in the Indus valley in the first half of the second millennium B.C. and elsewhere in India in the second half of this millennium; see A. M. WATSON "The rise" 356–7. As to the westward movement of plants over this channel, from India to Africa, it seems probable that this did not occur before Islamic times, since the pre-Islamic agriculture of East Africa seems hardly to have been able to receive many of the Indian crops that were to come over this route. Also, as BURKILL "Habits" 33 states, "it has been pointed out by Sir David Prain and me that the African landfall of the Sabaean Lane...was inhospitable to such plants as the greater yam, being far too dry for its thrift. So, too, for other plants whose coming to Africa from the East was delayed until the Yemenite Arabs had so developed their colonies in Zanguebar as to make a home for them. This they did between the 8th and the 11th centuries."

2 The role played by ancient India in the domestication, ennoblement and diffusion of useful plants has not yet been adequately described. See, however, ALLCHIN *passim*; *Evolutionary Studies* 151–60 *et passim*; JOSEPH B. HUTCHINSON "India"; VISHNU-MITTRE "Changing" 583; and GWYNNE.

3 HOURANI 53, 68ff; *Akhbār* xxxviii; BATHURST 92–3. About the exact route followed by sugar cane up the Persian Gulf, there has been a controversy. RITTER maintained that this plant passed through Siraf and thence to al-Ahwāz, where he believed that sugar refining was invented and where indeed the sources tell that sugar was refined (though the cane was not necessarily grown there); see AL-MAS'ŪDĪ ed. Barbier de Meynard VIII 405. However, SCHWARZ "Die Zuckerpressen" maintains that the great circular stones excavated in al-Ahwāz, which were presumed to be used in the crushing of sugar cane, were in fact the bases of pillars! Without giving any evidence, Schwarz suggests Hormuz as the most likely halfway-house for the diffusion of sugar cane from India to Iraq.

4 Ed. Barbier de Meynard II 438–9 and VIII 336.

5 "Filāḥa" I 70.

6 ABŪ ḤANĪFA ed. Hamidullah 283.

7 On pre-Islamic diffusion of crops from the Yemen to Egypt, see SCHWEINFURTH "Sur l'origine". On the settlement of Yemenis in al-Fusṭāṭ, see VADET; on a possible Yemeni presence in the western Sahara, see NORRIS; and on the Yemeni influence in the development of irrigation works and administration in Spain, see GLICK *Irrigation, passim.* On the role of the Yemen as an entrepôt in the spice and drug trade, see MEYERHOF "Sur un traité" (1942–3) 60.

8 On this point, however, see the remarks of Burkill quoted in n. 1 above.

9 ABŪ ZAID 130; FREEMAN-GRENVILLE 21–87; BATHURST 92–3; GRAY 11ff; "The history of Kilwa" 398–9; AL-MAS'ŪDĪ ed. Barbier de Meynard I 206, 231–4, who himself travelled from Oman to East Africa in the company of Sirafi sailors. However, on the question of the Shirazi settlement at Kilwa, see CHITTICK.

10 PORTÈRES *Appellations* 144.

11 One of the three names for eggplant, for instance, in the Malagasy language is *baranjely*, a word which may easily be of Arabic origin. See GRANDIDIER AND GRANDIDIER IV pt 4 62 n. 3.

12 DESCHAMPS 39ff and VÉRIN discuss the dating of the initial and later contacts between Indo-Malaya and Madagascar. See also BURKILL "The rise" 446ff and SOUTHALL.

13 DALZIEL 122, 305–6, 433–4, 541–2, 550.

14 PORTÈRES "Berceaux" 195ff and HAVINDEN 539–40, where it is pointed out that the development of agriculture in the forest regions of West Africa was heavily dependent on imported plants such as colocasia, Asian yams, bananas, plantains, sugar cane and citrus trees. The only indigenous plants of importance to the agriculture of this region are the Guinea yam and the oil palm. MAUNY *Tableau* 228–33 suggests that before agriculture became well established in this region, the gathering of wild fruit, leaves and roots must have been important for subsistence. See also SCHNELL 75ff.

15 MAUNY "La savane".

16 MONTEIL; MAUNY "Notes" 698ff.

17 Indeed, in both East and West Africa the penetration of the new crops may have been largely confined to areas that were predominantly Muslim. On the relatively backward agricultural practices of West Africa, see CHEVALIER AND SACLEUX and AL-BAKRĪ *Description* 300, who relates that at Awdaghast the land on which wheat grew was cultivated by spade and watered by hand. On the land tenure systems of Black Africa, see *African Agrarian.*

18 Byzantium appears to have played no role in the transmission of these or other crops to Europe, except perhaps to eastern Europe, possibly on account of her declining empire, trade and intellectual life. The *Geoponika*, an agricultural manual of the sixth or tenth century, and other Byzantine agricultural writings show little interest in novelty of any kind, confining themselves largely to repeating the advice of the ancients; see TEALL *passim.* Many of these new plants seem to have been unknown to Byzantines, for they appear to have lacked names in medieval Greek. LANGKAVEL *passim* has discovered words for only colocasia, coconut, cotton, rice, sugar, sorghum and eggplant. None of these is mentioned in *Byzantinische Quellen* as crops that were actually grown within the empire.

Contrary to popular legends, there is no evidence of crops being transmitted to continental Europe through the Crusader kingdoms. This failure to diffuse is perhaps explained by the lack of movement between Europe and the Levant of people with any practical experience in growing the new plants, and by the general inability of Crusader agriculture, even in the Levant, to continue growing specialty crops (apart from sugar cane in a narrow band along the coast, where experienced labour from the conquered population was almost certainly used). This point is developed in a larger context in the conclusion to this book. See also MUSSET 315 and RILEY-SMITH 46–7, where it is pointed out that Crusader villages tended to concentrate on subsistence, not cash, crops.

19 Spinach is discussed in CRESCENTIIS bk VI 55, 103; in the Catalan cookery book *Libre de sent soví* 127, 198; and also by the thirteenth-century Catalan physician ARNOLD OF VILANOVA 127, 198, who says it was by his time a common food. See also BEHLING 56; GIBAULT 81ff; BOIS I 409; SACCARDO *Cronologia* 78; TARGIONI-TOZZETTI 77–8; and BRESC 73, 75.

20 CRESCENTIIS bk III 7; NICCOLI 189; HÉMARDINQUER 450–1.

21 TOLKOWSKY 149ff, who seems to be in error in thinking that the sweet-orange tree was known in late medieval Italy; GALLESIO 254ff; GINES ALIÑO 7–8; *Libre de sent soví* 63, 77, 87, 91, 96, 97.

22 ALESSIO 263–5; SERENI "Note" *passim*; GUAL CAMARENA 422.

23 CRESCENTIIS bk III 24 speaks of rice as a medicine only, not as a food and not as a crop. On the introduction of rice into Italy and Spain, see TARGIONI-TOZZETTI 24ff; NICCOLI 190; HEHN *Cultivated Plants* 499–500; GUAL CAMARENA 217–18; and FORBES II 49, where it is argued that the advance of rice through Italy was delayed by the lack of satisfactory irrigation. The Catalan cookery book *Libre de sent sovi* 93–4, 100, 132, 135 gives recipes using rice.

24 On the slow diffusion of the eggplant into late medieval Italy, see SACCARDO *Cronologia* 231; GIBAULT 331ff; BOIS I 355–6; NICCOLI 305. The artichoke does not seem to have made much progress into Italy until the late fifteenth century. See ch. 12 n. 7 above.

25 *Historia diplomatica* v 575. On the probable disappearance of sugar cane from Sicily until the fifteenth century, see TRASSELLI "Lo zucchero"; GAMBI 9ff; and TRASSELLI "Sumário" 58ff.

26 MARTÍNEZ FERRANDO II 19–20.

27 The case of the reconquest of Spain illustrates some of these points. As BISHKO *passim* points out, the newly reconquered areas tended to be used for ranching, no doubt because of their low population density and insecurity. See also KLEIN for further information on the importance of transhumance in reconquered Spain and its disastrous effects on intensive agriculture. The settlers who arrived from France and northern Spain to re-establish sedentary agriculture brought with them the crops and agricultural practices they had known in feudal Europe, where extensive, cereal-dominated agriculture prevailed. See DUBLER *Über das Wirtschaftsleben* 67. Where Muslim cultivators remained on the land, their kind of farming was often placed as a disadvantage: FONTAVELLA GONZÁLES 100 points out that Jaime I reduced the holdings of the conquered population in Gandía to one-quarter of their former size, and distributed the land thus gained to nobles as feudal estates. It may be supposed that many of the Muslim holdings became unviable and were thus sold to the new nobility, and that new patterns of land use appeared. This process must have been hastened by various uprisings of the conquered Muslims which led to their expulsion (e.g. in Valencia *c.* 1248) or their flight, leaving relatively few areas in the hands of Muslim cultivators. See GLICK *Irrigation* 226 and BURNS *Islam* 76. GLICK *op. cit.* 27ff shows that in Valencia after its reconquest by the Christians the irrigation system continued to function on a considerable scale but was used mainly for the production of grains, pulses and vines, i.e. the traditional crops of feudal Europe. With the exception of some rice and sour oranges, the labour-intensive but more productive crops of Islamic times seem to have been largely abandoned, perhaps because a less intensive kind of agriculture was appropriate to a country which was less densely settled. A further turning away from labour-intensive crops at the time of the expulsion of the Moriscos in the seventeenth century is noted by CASEY 34. Although the new patterns of land use in Christian Spain may have been economically rational in view of lower population densities, the impression remains that the Christian conquerors were unable to learn from the conquered population on account of psychological or cultural barriers. GLICK AND PI-SUNYER 143 argue that the thirteenth century in Christian Spain was a time of increasing rigidity and intolerance leading to a virtual obliteration of Muslim culture. In this connection, it is interesting to note that the Castilian translation of the Hispano-Muslim agricultural treatise of Ibn Wāfid does not mention any of the new crops which are studied here, although many of these must surely have been mentioned in the original. The translation concentrates almost entirely on dry faming. See IBN WĀFID "Traducción". It is also significant that *Glosario, passim*, a Hispano-Muslim work of the twelfth or thirteenth century in which 726 plant names are given in the contemporary Romanic or Neo-Latin language of Spain, gives a clear Romanic word for only one of the crops studied in this volume, sorghum. Even in the sixteenth century HERRERA, in his manual on Spanish farming, mentions only one of the new crops, the eggplant. Banana cultivation may have disappeared completely from Christian Spain and had to be reintroduced in the sixteenth century, since the Arabic word *mawz* seems nearly to have disappeared from Iberian languages; see MORAES SILVA *voce* "musa". This word has survived (as *musa*) in only one European dialect, Sicilian; see AREZZO 47 and TRAINA 622. But even in Sicily banana cultivation may have had to be reintroduced in the fifteenth century; see CIFERRI 8. MARTÍNEZ RUIZ 273 discusses the disappearance of sugar-cane cultivation from parts of sixteenth-century Granada.

In Norman Sicily much the same pattern may be observed. Although the early rulers were on the whole tolerant of the Muslim population and many Muslim introductions continued to be grown, at least for a time, the persecution of the Muslims began in the reign of Roger II (1105–30), and during the reign of William II (1166–89) many Muslim cultivators took refuge in the mountains "ob metum Christianorum" while others fled to the Maghrib. Norman, French and Lombard nobles gained control of most of the land, and brought with them peasants from their native regions. Large feudal and ecclesiastical estates often replaced small holdings. The new land use was less intensive, concentrating more heavily on cereals. Though the production of cotton continued, perhaps on a reduced scale, sugar-cane cultivation seems to have disappeared in the thirteenth century and had to be reintroduced. Indigo and henna were also reintroduced by Frederic II, though perhaps not successfully. See PERI I 40ff and II 217ff, 309–22; CICCAGLIONE 329ff; AMARI III ii 805ff; TRASSELLI "Lo zucchero"; CAHEN *Le régime féodal, passim*; S. F. ROMANO 195–6; MACK SMITH I 13ff; and BERCHER *et al. passim.* Some of the same trends seem to appear in southern Italy under the Normans; see GUILLOU 166–7 *et passim.*

17. The agents

1 See ch. 19 below. Sorghum is not mentioned in MUḤAMMAD IBN AL-ḤASAN or in the anonymous "Kitāb al-ṭabīkh", nor is it listed by RODINSON "Recherches" as appearing in the cookery books which he has studied. ASHTOR "The diet" cites a passage from NĀṢIR-I KHUSRAW 35, in which this writer states that at a certain town near Aleppo only wheat was grown, and concludes that sorghum might have been eaten regularly only by ascetics and by others only in times of hardship. To have been available in such times, however, it must have been grown.

2 The importance of the migration of peasants in diffusing crops is perhaps shown by the fact that in the period of classical Islam very few useful plants were diffused from China to the west, in spite of the fact that Muslim merchants had many direct and indirect contacts by land and sea with China; there was even for a time an important community of Arabs living in Canton. This failure to diffuse is all the more surprising when it is remembered that China had a very large range of fruits and vegetables to offer, many of which were not difficult to grow, and in the period of classical Islam much else was diffused from China to the Muslim world. The importance of an experienced peasantry is also shown by examples from Spain and Sicily after the Christian reconquest of those regions. In the first half of the thirteenth century, henna and indigo had to be reintroduced to Sicily by Jews coming from the Maghrib, while at nearly the same time Frederic II had to send to the Levant for "duos homines qui bene sciant facere zuccarum"; see *Historia diplomatica* V 573, 575. It may be assumed that the skills of growing henna and indigo and of refining sugar (and perhaps of growing the cane) had disappeared as Muslims took flight from the land they cultivated and some left the island altogether. Similarly, in the Christian kingdom of Valencia, it seems that the growing of both cotton and sugar cane had disappeared, since Jaime II sent to Sicily for "duos sclavos sarracenos quorum alter sit magistro cotonis et alter de cannamellis", as well as for the seeds of cotton and sugar cane (a fact which shows how little he knew about the latter crop). See the document in MARTÍNEZ FERRANDO II 19–20.

3 Text in BREASTED II sects. 246–87. The reliefs which depict this expedition are reproduced in NAVILLE pls. 69–85. BREASTED II 192–3 gives the inscriptions from Karnak recording the introduction of Syrian plants into Egypt during the reign of Thutmose III (d. 1450 B.C.).

4 *Assyrian Royal* 17.

5 *The Annals* 111, 116; KEIMER *Die Gartenpflanzen* 60; GOOSSENS *passim.*

6 BRETZL *passim.*

7 LAUFER *Sino-Iranica* 190ff; SOOTHILL 10ff.

8 *T'ang hui yao* cited in LAUFER *Sino-Iranica* 393.

9 CHAU JU-KUA 218.

10 LECLERC II 279, 282.

11 AL-MAQRĪZĪ *Khiṭaṭ* II 18; AL-NUWAIRĪ II 18. It is noteworthy, however, that SCHWEINFURTH

"Sur l'origine" says that this melon is found wild in the upper Nile region, while SCHIEMANN *Die Entstehung* 238 states that it is indigenous to the eastern Sudan, Senegambia and Abyssinia. See also HASSIB.

12 AL-MAQRĪZĪ *Khiṭaṭ* II 96; IBN TAGHRĪBIRDĪ II 56–61. See also HITTI 454 and WIET *Cairo* 5.

13 AL-MAQQARĪ *Nafḥ al-ṭīb* II 14–15; AL-KHUSHANĪ 38–41.

14 AL-MAQQARĪ *loc. cit.* Professor Samsó Moya has drawn my attention to the fact that the same legend is given in a work of the grammarian Ibn Hishām (d. 1162).

15 PÉRÈS "Le palmier"; see also GOLVIN "Le palmier".

16 HUICI MIRANDA. I am grateful to Professor Thomas Glick for drawing my attention to this reference. Professor Samsó Moya has pointed out to me that this legend is found in the agricultural treatise of Abū al-Khair (fl. 11th c.?).

17 AL-KHAZRAJĪ II 120; AL-'UMARĪ 12; MEYERHOF "Sur un traité" (1942–3) 58 and (1943–4) 57.

18 *Meyerhof op. cit.* (1942–3) 62.

19 AL-MAS'ŪDĪ ed. Barbier de Meynard VIII 336.

20 TOLKOWSKY 113ff.

21 On the botanical gardens of these kings and the scientists attached to them, see ch. 22.

22 AL-'UDHRĪ 85.

23 AL-KHAZRAJĪ II 108, 120, 287.

24 Text of Ibn Sa'īd in *Monumenta cartographica* VI 1082.

18. *A medium for diffusion*

1 GRÜNEBAUM *Classical* 51, 57–8.

2 *Ibid.* 75 and POLIAK "L'arabisation" 44ff. In many parts of the Islamic world the Arabic language eventually completely displaced the local languages. In Spain, North Africa, Upper Egypt, small parts of the Levant and Persia, however, local languages remained to varying degrees in common use, and *Románico* and Persian were later revived as literary languages. The process of "Arabicization" was gradual. Thus in Syria, for instance, Arabic replaced Greek as the language used in state registers in the year 700/1, and in the Sawād it similarly replaced Persian in the year 694 or shortly thereafter; see AL-BALĀDHURĪ I 301, 465–6 and SPRENGLING *passim.* In the ninth century Arabic replaced Coptic as the language of official documents in Egypt; see BECKER I 113ff, 129–30 and WIET *Cairo* 9. In North Africa, Arabic was used in official documents from the beginning of the eighth century and made headway amongst the people in the ninth century; GOLVIN *Le Magrib* 134–5; *Cambridge History* II 217; and MARÇAIS *La Berbérie* 40–3. On the degree to which Arabic displaced the local languages in Muslim Spain, there is a vast literature and much disagreement; see MENÉNDEZ PIDAL "La invasión".

3 GRÜNEBAUM *Classical* 75 and GRIERSON 244–8. It should be noted that Islamic law – which generally did not apply to Christian and Jewish communities – was in principle not legislated or decreed but rather derived from the Koran, from the reported sayings and doings of the Prophet, from later attempts to extend the principles thought to underlie these, and, in the absence of any applicable principle, from custom (*'urf*) or consensus (*ijmā'*). Except in the last cases, therefore, it was in principle universal for all Muslims. Though its universality was to some extent compromised by the appearance of different legal traditions and by the growth in importance of law-making by decree, the laws governing the Muslim populations of the whole of the classical Islamic world, even after the breakdown of the 'Abbāsid empire, were remarkably similar.

4 GOITEIN *Studies* 303–4 and *A Mediterranean* I 282–95; SOURDEL "Barīd"; GAUDEFROY DEMOMBYNES 258; MACK SMITH I 6; MAKKĪ 87–92; BENVENISTI 269; MEZ 485–517; SOURDEL AND SOURDEL 316. YĀQŪT V 350 mentions a network of smoke or light signals linking Wāsiṭ and Qazwīn.

5 Thus Leclerc has calculated that the thirteenth-century botanist Ibn al-Baiṭār has listed some 200 plants which were unknown to Dioscorides. See IBN AL-BAIṬĀR I xi.

6 On Muslim contacts with India and China, see SOOTHILL *passim*; HOURANI 61ff; *Akhbār* xxxi–xl; and AL-MAS'ŪDĪ ed. Pellat 127ff.

7 To give only one small example of the near universality of Muslim knowledge, the physician al-Rāzī (*c.* 865–*c.* 932) is quoted as saying in his book of remedies that the best kinds of saltwort grew only in Spain and India; AL-BAKRĪ *Jughrāfīya* 126.

8 IBN KHALDŪN *Muqaddimah* I 303.

9 GRÜNEBAUM *Classical* 55; AL-DŪRĪ "Origins" 6. Although the early armies were made up largely of nomads, later armies had large components of Yemeni and others with experience of sedentary agriculture, who could contribute to the agricultural development of the regions where they settled.

10 PELLAT *Le milieu* 9; SYKES II 11, who relies on a variety of secondary works. In Persia new lands were settled variously by groups of Persians, Turks and Arabs; see SPULER *Iran* 247ff and LAMBTON "Iran" 14. According to AL-BALĀDHURĪ I 435–6, Yemeni settlers were in the majority in the region of Kufa. SOURDEL "Baġdād" 263–4 shows that Baghdad was settled not only by the "Nabateans" of the surrounding region, but also by Arabs, Iranians and Irano-Turks, to whom were added slaves from Russia, Nubia and Turkestan; see also *Islam and the Trade* 12.

11 AL-YA'QŪBĪ 173, 174, 176, 177 *et passim*, who has much more information about the diverse peoples who settled in Syria and Palestine; see also POLIAK "L'arabisation" 54 and SHABAN *Islamic* 42.

12 LÉVI-PROVENÇAL *Histoire* I 44ff, 71ff, 81ff and *L'Espagne* 8ff, 21; GUICHARD "Le peuplement"; RIBERA Y TARRAGÓ II 210–47; GLICK *Irrigation* 230; AL-MAQQARĪ tr. Gayangos II 29–9.

13 MACK SMITH I 7.

14 IBN JUBAIR II 120.

15 GOITEIN *Studies* 8.

16 SOURDEL AND SOURDEL 317; SOOTHILL 23–4; HOURANI 61ff; FREEMAN-GRENVILLE 21ff. A citation from the twelfth-century historian Ibn al-Athīr gives an idea of the variety of trade in the port of Aden in the writer's time: goods were apparently found there from India, Zanzibar, Abyssinia, Oman, Kirman and Kish. Cited in HEYD I 379.

17 SCHRIEKE I 15ff; TRIMINGHAM *Islam in East Africa* 1ff and *Islam in West Africa* 24.

18 Ibn Baṣṣāl, for instance, had apparently visited Sicily, Syria, Egypt and Mecca, while Ibn al-Baiṭār, after herborizing in much of the south of Spain, collected plants across the whole of North Africa, in Egypt, Syria and Arabia, and lived for a time in Egypt at the court of the Ayyūbid sultan. See IBN BAṢṢĀL 14, 32; RENAUD 65–6; and IBN AL-BAIṬĀR I vi–ix. MEYERHOF "Esquisse" 3–5 gives a long list of Spanish scientists who went to the east to study and of easterners who came to Spain. See also MAKKĪ 73–5; BOSCH VILÁ *passim*; RIBERA Y TARRAGÓ II 205–10.

19 MAKKĪ 85–6. When Toledo fell to the Christians in 1085, for instance, Ibn Baṣṣāl and Ibn Wāfid, who had been in the employ of the king of Toledo, al-Ma'mūn, fled to the south of Spain where they found new patrons; IBN BAṢṢĀL 14, 32–4. On the flight of refugees from Cordova in 808–9, some of whom founded the city of Fez, thus diffusing their knowledge of agriculture, see LÉVI-PROVENÇAL *Histoire* I 170 and "La fondation". Maimonides fled to Morocco from his native Cordova after that city fell to the Almohads in 1148; he later went to Palestine and finally settled in Egypt.

20 BOSCH VILÁ 19 n. 2; MAKKĪ 69–87; JOMIER 958, where it is pointed out that the mosque of 'Amr ibn al-'Āṣ in al-Fusṭāṭ had lodgings for travellers. The Ṣūfīs provided lodging not only for their fellow believers but also for almost anyone who was sympathetic to their beliefs; see M. G. S. HODGSON II 584 (*voce* "khāniqāh"). For a description of the many ways in which a visitor to Damascus could be subventioned, see IBN JUBAIR III 321, 332–4.

21 Conservative elements, of course, reacted against the taking on of new ways, but with remarkably little effect in the long run. See, for instance, SADAN *passim* and VADET *passim*.

22 On the wealthy classes that were so evident in the cities of classical Islam, and their spending habits, see BULLIET *passim*; AL-MAS'ŪDĪ ed. Barbier de Meynard II 365 and VII

217–18; LÉVI-PROVENÇAL *Histoire* II 118, 142; IBN KHALDŪN *Muqaddimah* I 283, 317, 338ff, 348–52, 458 and II 114, 127; LAMMENS *Le berceau* 165; WIET *Cairo* 25; LAPIDUS *Muslim* 50; GOITEIN *Studies* 224, 228–9; SOURDEL AND SOURDEL 310, 327ff, 442–6, 459, 461; MEZ 147ff; RODINSON "Histoire" 148ff and "Recherches" 98–9, 146; LOMBARD 176–99. GOITEIN *loc. cit.* quotes a passage from al-Shaybānī according to which the Prophet is supposed to have said, "When Allah gives riches to a man, he wants them to be seen on him." A whole genre of Arabic poetry urges that one should enjoy oneself to the full today, for who knows what the morrow may bring?

23 KEIMER *Jardins* 87; WIET *Cairo* 7, 21, 22, 24; AL-MAS'ŪDĪ ed. Barbier de Meynard VIII 336–7; HASSAN 127; NĀṢIR-I KHUSRAW 149, where it is said that in the market of Old Cairo were to be found "rare and precious objects brought from every corner of the world. I saw there objects in [tortoise?] shell, such as boxes, combs, knife handles etc. I also noticed rock crystal of great beauty, which was worked by craftsmen of high taste. This came from the Maghrib, but it was said that they had recently received a finer and more transparent kind from the Red Sea. I saw elephants' tusks from Zanzibar...an ox skin from Abyssinia which looks like a leopard skin and from which slippers are made. From this same country comes a tame bird of great size." On the mania of book collectors in tenth-century Cordova, AL-MAQQARĪ tr. Gayangos I 139–40 quotes this passage from Ibn Sa'īd: "To such an extent did this rage for collection increase that a man in power or holding a situation in the government considered himself obliged to have a library of his own and would spare no trouble or expense in collecting books merely in order that people might say 'such a one has a very fine library'." On the collection of plants, useful and ornamental, see ch. 22.

24 ECHE 13–20.

25 IBN AL-NADĪM tr. Dodge II 586–90, 713; ARNALDEZ *passim*; MIELI *La science* 68ff and *Panorama* 45ff; ECHE 20ff; SARTON I 520ff; STEINSCHNEIDER *Die arabischen, passim*; PINTO.

26 ECHE 21ff; PINTO.

27 AL-MAQRĪZĪ *Description* I 509.

28 WIET *Cairo* 30.

29 ECHE 251. For private libraries in Fatimid Egypt, see MEYERHOF "Über einige".

30 AL-MAQQARĪ tr. Gayangos I xi, 418 and II 168–9; RIBERA Y TARRAGÓ I 191–2; IMAMUDDIN *Some Aspects* 139–42 and *Hispano-Arab* 3ff.

31 AL-MAQQARĪ tr. Gayangos I 139–40; ECHE *passim*; IMAMUDDIN *Some Aspects* 139–42; MEZ 215ff; RIBERA Y TARRAGÓ I 195, 197, 210; IMAMUDDIN *Hispano-Arab* 6–8.

32 HAMILTON 41.

33 MIELI *Panorama* 46; C. G. N. WRIGHT 100ff, who deals with the subsequent assimilation of the Indian system of numerals.

34 MIELI *La science* 69.

35 GHIRSHMAN *Iran* 347. See also RODINSON "Recherches" 148–50 and SPULER *Iran* 289–91. Recent scholarship has tended to dismiss the earlier view that Persian elements were important in the establishment of 'Abbāsid rule and to downplay the importance of Persian traditions. See LASSNER *The Shaping* 3–5.

36 GHIRSHMAN *op. cit.* 348; BRIGGS *passim*; MIELI *Panorama* 5–8; ECHE 43.

37 LECLERC I 278–80, 282; IBN AL-NADĪM tr. Dodge II 862ff. It is interesting to note that IBN AL-BAIṬĀR (*q.v.* I x) in his great book of remedies quotes from about thirty Indian sources. See also MIELI *La science* 69–71.

38 AL-MAS'ŪDĪ ed. Barbier de Meynard I 148–78; AL-BĪRŪNĪ.

39 GRÜNEBAUM "Pluralism" 37–8; SOURDEL AND SOURDEL 259–60.

40 For example, by Ibn Sīnā, who was employed for a time by the Sāmānids in Bukhara, and al-Bīrūnī, who produced most of his work at the court of Maḥmūd of Ghazna.

41 HASSAN 48–9, 127, 288ff; GOITEIN "Changes" 31–2. See also CRESSWELL 301ff; MARÇAIS *L'art* 40–1 and *La Berbérie* 26–8, 48–9, 109, 119, 127, 188ff; RODINSON "Recherches" 101–2; and LAMM *passim.* Among the importations which have been found in the excavations of al-Fusṭāṭ are "Sāmarra" stucco and lustre-ware.

42 GOITEIN "Changes" 18.

43 *Ibid.* 23–4; ASHTOR "Migrations"; PFISTER "L'introduction" 170.

44 GOITEIN *Studies* 329ff.

45 MARÇAIS *L'architecture* 3–5, 60–1, *La Berbérie* 19–130 and "La Berbérie" 277ff; GOLVIN *Le Magrib* 135–7; VONDERHEYDEN 159; GOBERT 539; Solignac *Recherches* 269, who *passim* gives much evidence of the copying of eastern irrigation works. IBN ḤAWQAL I 70 stated that in Tunis were manufactured beautiful polychrome dishes and pottery which were almost as attractive as those imported from Iraq.

46 MAKKĪ *passim*; BOSCH VILÁ *passim*; LÉVI-PROVENÇAL *Histoire* I 106–7, 129ff, 146ff, 186–7, 263ff; BLACHÈRE *passim*; CRESSWELL 226–8; GLICK AND PI-SUNYER *passim*; IMAMUDDIN *Some Aspects* 108, 110, 116; ZEKI *passim*. GUICHARD "Les arabes" and *Structures* shows that one aspect of the *orientalización* of Muslim Spain was a profound change in family structure. On the "Syrianization" of the Spanish landscape, see GLICK *Islamic* 55–6 *et passim*.

47 AL-MAQQARĪ tr. Gayangos II 120–1.

48 See n. 19 above and BOSCH VILÁ 46–7.

49 The outflow from Spain to North Africa was perhaps initiated with the conquest of Morocco by the Umayyads in 973. It was accelerated, however, under the rule of the Berber dynasties, first the Almoravids and then the Almohads, that controlled Muslim Spain and much of North Africa from the mid eleventh to the mid thirteenth century. See MARÇAIS "La Berbérie" *passim*.

19. The pull of demand

1 With the exception of hard wheat, the artichoke and spinach, all of the plants studied in this volume were known in ancient India and all had medical uses. See NADKARNI AND NADKARNI *passim* and WATT *A Dictionary*, *passim*. Indian medicine had a great deal to teach the west, partly because it had access to a different range of medical plants, and partly because it had never known the theory of the humours which was to stultify the growth of western and Middle Eastern pharmacy for more than fifteen centuries. On the other hand, the theory of the humours probably did stimulate the diffusion of plants, for it maintained that every plant had medical virtues. As al-Idrīsī stated, each plant has its power; see MEYERHOF "Die allgemeine Botanik" 226.

2 BRETZL *passim*.

3 IBN AL-NADĪM tr. Dodge II 574–5; MIELI *Panorama* 9; ECHE 43.

4 On the translation of Greek works into Arabic, which has naturally been of much concern to western scholarship, see IBN AL-NADĪM tr. Dodge II 581, 584ff *et passim* and STEINSCHNEIDER *Die arabischen*. Unfortunately, there are no comparable studies of translations from other languages into Arabic, but see SARTON I 520ff; LECLERC I 278ff; MIELI *Panorama* 45ff and *La science* 69ff; IBN AL-NADĪM tr. Dodge II 589–90 *et passim*; and SPRENGLING.

5 LECLERC I 279.

6 "Periplus" 11, 64–5.

7 As is argued in the preceding chapters, the only one of our crops known to have been imported from India into the lands that the Sasanians ruled was rice, and its introduction probably was pre-Sasanian. Other crops which may have been introduced into the Sasanian empire are bananas, sorghum, sugar cane and eggplants; but for none of these is there clear evidence.

8 The Umayyad feast is described in AL-MAS'ŪDĪ ed. Barbier de Meynard V 76; see also VIII 394ff, where is described an elaborate feast offered by the caliph Mustakfī (944–6), after which the talk of the caliph and guests turned to various rare dishes, the ingredients for which included lemons, eggplants, rice and sugar. For the 'Abbāsid feast, see MEZ 432. See also RODINSON "Recherches" 100 and "La Ma'mūniyyat" and SOURDEL AND SOURDEL 392ff.

9 See ch. 18 above. In AL-MAS'ŪDĪ ed. Barbier de Meynard II 364–5 there is described a great celebration in al-Fusṭāṭ offered by the Ikhshīdid ruler Muḥammad ibn Ṭughj. This seems clearly to have been imitating, if not surpassing, similar occasions in Baghdad.

10 Some discussion of the process of acculturation of the Arabs in Persia is given in SPULER *Iran* 249–50. See also SADAN 1374, who skilfully portrays the "pluralism" of Baghdad, where Persian and bedouin traditions existed side by side; in the end, however, he shows how many bedouin traditions in furniture and in other areas were replaced by indigenous customs. GOITEIN *Studies* 252–3 suggests that the middle classes in Egypt assimilated the manners of the upper classes. See also IBN KHALDŪN *Muqaddimah* I 347–8 on the spread of urban luxuries amongst nomadic conquerors, and VADET on the acculturation of the Yemeni in al-Fusṭāṭ. TALBI "Law" 220 describes the luxury in which some great landowners of Ifrīqiya lived.

11 An idea – perhaps only slightly exaggerated – of the extent to which imported foodstuffs were available in the markets of Baghdad is given in the "Tale of the Porter and the Three Ladies of Baghdad". One of the ladies, so the story goes, bought from her fruit merchant apples from Damascus, quinces from Osmanji, peaches from Oman, cucumbers from the Nile valley, Egyptian limes and Sultānī oranges and citrons. See *The Thousand Nights and a Night* I 76.

12 IBN ḤAWQAL I 206–7.

13 "Kitāb al-ṭabīkh"; MUḤAMMAD IBN AL-ḤASAN AL-BAGHDĀDĪ; RODINSON "Recherches"; LA GRANJA.

14 LAMM 50ff, 87ff; PFISTER "L'introduction".

15 PFISTER "L'introduction"; GOITEIN "Artisans" 856–7.

16 AL-IDRĪSĪ 3. It is interesting to note that less than a century earlier, AL-BAKRĪ *Description* 325 stated that the inhabitants of Silla used little loin cloths called *shijjīya*. In the fourteenth century, AL-'UMARĪ 127 stated that West Africans wore clothes of linen and cotton, and that occasionally people could be seen who wore elegant materials imported from Alexandria or Iraq. See also MONTEIL.

20. *Facilitating supply: irrigation*

1 AL-MAQRĪZĪ *Khiṭaṭ* I 182ff; IBN AL-'AWWĀM ed. Banqueri I 391–2. IBN LUYŪN ch. 11 states that sugar cane requires abundant irrigation at planting time and weekly waterings after the shoots come up.

2 ANGLADETTE 25–7 points out that rice can be grown as a non-irrigated crop in regions with adequate rainfall, but it has been shown that the productivity of both land and labour is much higher when rice is heavily irrigated. IBN WAḤSHĪYA "Filāḥa" I 480; IBN LUYŪN ch. 7; IBN AL-'AWWĀM ed. Banqueri II 54–5 (where it is stated that rice could be grown in wet regions without irrigation, but that it was normally an irrigated crop).

3 Cotton is sometimes grown without irrigation, but in the Islamic world it was almost always a heavily irrigated crop; IBN WAḤSHĪYA "Filāḥa" II 213 said it cannot stand dryness; QUSṬŪS AL-RŪMĪ 28–9 said it requires continuous irrigation; and IBN LUYŪN ch. 7 stated that it needs weekly waterings. According to IBN BAṢṢĀL 152–3, there were two systems of growing cotton in the Islamic world: the Spanish system, in which the plant was irrigated every fifteen days after it reached a finger's height, and the Syrian system, in which the land was irrigated once before planting, again when the plant had reached the height of the palm of the hand, and thereafter every fifteen days until the middle of August.

4 WET AND HARLAN 131 and SNOWDEN 204 show that there are now varieties of sorghum which may be grown with as little as 15 to 22 cm of rain or the equivalent in artificial watering, which should come mainly during the period of germination and early growth; however, the crop does best with between 38 and 60 cm of rain or the irrigation equivalent. IBN WAḤSHĪYA "Filāḥa" II 201 states that sorghum should be watered in the same way as rice!

5 See ch. 23.

6 On the decay of ancient irrigation systems in the centuries preceding the Hegira, consult the following: on Arabia, BEEK "The rise" 46; WISSMANN 135ff, 203ff, 308–12 *et passim*; and DOE 59; on Egypt, SCHNEBEL 357–8; FORBES II 32; ROSTOVTZEFF I 480–91; and A. C. JOHNSON *Egypt* 129; on North Africa, KNIGHT *passim*; on Transoxania, TOKAREV 257 and BARTOL'D "Istoriia" *passim*. MAZLOUM 7 states that at the time of the Hegira the canal systems around Aleppo were in ruins. In Spain, the fate of Roman irrigation works during the later centuries of the Empire and during Visigothic rule is not known, but one of the Arab conquerors, Mūsà ibn Nuṣair, is reported to have said that there was not a single canal in the country; see GLICK *Irrigation* 174–206. The decay of Sasanian irrigation is difficult to date without further evidence. It is possible that it began in the early fifth century but was arrested during the reign of Chosroes I, when the countryside seems to have prospered. At any rate, decline became rapid by the last quarter of the sixth century, probably caused by growing insecurity, the rise in power of the military and landed aristocracy, the indirect collection of taxes, frequent changes of monarchs and, finally, invasions. See ALTHEIM AND STIEHL 142ff and R. M. ADAMS *Land* 82.

7 BOAK 22–89; RUSSELL *Late Ancient* 40ff, 71–3, 88ff. Russell suggests that the "plague of Justinian" may have been as devastating as the Black Death of the fourteenth century, which is generally held to have reduced Europe's population by one-third or even one-half.

8 WISSMANN AND HÖFNER 239ff; DOE 59; BOWEN AND ALBRIGHT 75–6; AL-HAMDĀNĪ *Antiquities* 67–9; Koran XXXIV 14, 15; AL-KHAZRAJĪ I 53ff. YĀQŪT IV 382–3, however, seems to write as if the Ma'rib dam was in operation in his time (late twelfth and early thirteenth centuries).

9 PETRIE 37; AL-MAS'ŪDĪ ed. Barbier de Meynard II 374–7.

10 SUSA *Fayaḍānāt* I 205–8 and *Irrigation* 29; R. M. ADAMS *Land* 82; AL-BALĀDHURĪ I 453–5, where the date of the flood is given as 627/8 or 628/9.

11 This device can be powered by animals, and probably was in pre-Islamic times; but no detailed study is available on its history. See, however, GOLVIN "Au souk" *passim*; BRETZL 119–20; DIAS AND GALHANO 126ff; FORBES II 33; BRÄUNLICH 288ff, 472ff; and TARDY.

12 DIAS AND GALHANO 157–61.

13 FORBES II 17, 34–5, 49; PHILON 231; DIAS AND GALHANO 132–44; GOOSSENS 167; R. M. ADAMS *Land* 65; SCHNEBEL 71ff; MÜLLER-WODARG (1954) 188–9, 191.

14 FORBES II 40.

15 The noria is also known in English as the chain of pots, Persian wheel and the water wheel; and in Arabic some of its commoner names are *nā'ūra*, *sāqiya*, *qawādis*, *dūlāb*, *hadīr* and *sāniya*. These terms sometimes denote particular types of noria, but their use varies from country to country and through time. Occasionally they are used for other, quite different, irrigation devices. See the text *infra*.

Evidence is now appearing which suggests that the earliest water wheels or chains of pots were constructed in India; it has even been suggested – improbably – that some scored pots found at Mohenjo-daro had been lashed to a water wheel! See FORBES II 14 and *Concise History* 351, 353–4. Some such device was known in ancient Mesopotamia and in the Sasanian empire; see LAUFER "The noria" and NEWMAN 84. In the west, it seems to have been known as early as the second century B.C. (see L. WHITE 80), and it was described by VITRUVIUS II 304 (bk X 5) in the first century B.C. and by PHILON 209–12, 224 and 225 in the third century A.D.; it is also mentioned by ISIDORE OF SEVILLE bk XX 15. But like a related device, the water mill, which appeared in the west at roughly the same time, the water wheel seems to have been little used in agriculture anywhere in the Roman empire until the fifth or sixth century, when it probably came to be used more widely in Egypt and perhaps elsewhere. See FORBES II 49, SCHNEBEL 74ff, WINLOCK AND CRUM 64ff and JEHUDA 333ff; as MÜLLER-WODARG (1954) 193–4 points out, there was little need for the device in Egypt until irrigated summer crops were introduced. In Nubia, where the lifting of water was perhaps more vital to agriculture, the noria seems to have been widely used from at least the fourth century onwards: see W. Y. ADAMS "An introductory classification of Christian" 251, 261, 262, "An introductory classification of Meroitic" 132, 139, 159, 162–3, "Pottery" 68 and "Progress" 16, where it is shown that noria pots, known as *qawādis*, are common in later Meroitic, X-group and Christian periods. DIAS AND GALHANO 181ff and 231 suggest that water-driven norias and the short-axled animal-powered noria were introduced into the Iberian peninsula by the Arabs, but that other types of animal-powered norias, as well as water-powered norias, existed there in Roman times. Apart from the brief mention of some kind of water wheel in Isidore of Seville, there does not, however, seem to be any hard evidence whatever of the use of any kind of noria in pre-Islamic Iberia.

16 Thus the great pools of Solomon outside Bethlehem were used to provide water to the city of Jerusalem. Smaller reservoirs, too, were mainly for domestic or industrial use. They were used to grow plants only on a small scale. The dams described by REIFENBERG 56–7, BEEK 43 and others are merely water-spreading dams. However, REIFENBERG 60 does describe a pre-Islamic storage dam on the Orontes, and SUSA *Fayaḍānāt* I 203 states that a pre-Islamic dam not far from the later site of Baghdad also stored water. Other storage dams are mentioned in GOBLOT "Kébar". If these really were dams that provided significant amounts of storage, they must have been exceptional. In the main the dams of the great river systems in Egypt and Mesopotamia did not store water. See R. M. ADAMS "Agriculture" 116 and *Land* 13ff; WILLCOCKS AND CRAIG *passim*; GOBLOT "Dans l'ancien" 514–17; and MÜLLER-WODARG (1954) 186. Year-round irrigation appears to have been achieved occasionally in royal gardens, probably through the use of lifting devices; see SINGER I 552–3. On dams in the Hadramawt, see SERJEANT "Some irrigation" 33–57; and for Persia, see GOBLOT "Kébar".

17 GOBLOT "Dans l'ancien" *passim*; FORBES II 12; SINGER I 532–4; GHIRSHMAN *Iran* 182, 203; REIFENBERG 53; KUROS 48ff; HUMLUM "Underjordiske". BEADNELL 167ff attributes the underground canals of the Libyan desert to the Romans, but it seems much more likely that these are Islamic. The operation of the *qanāt* system in present-day Oman is described in detail in WILKINSON *The Organization* and *Water*.

18 R. M. ADAMS *Land* cites sources suggesting that the annual taxes collected in the reign of the caliph 'Umar ibn al-Khaṭṭāb (634–44) averaged only 34 per cent of late Sasanian fiscal revenues. This decline may indicate agricultural decline, and particularly a reduction of the area of land under irrigation; but it may also simply indicate lighter rates of taxation and less efficient collection. It is also very possible that the sources used by Adams were misinformed. See also ch. 24 n. 14.

19 LAPIDUS "Arab settlement" shows that early Arab rulers were interested in increasing revenues through the development of irrigated agriculture, particularly in areas serving new cities. DARKAZALLY 176ff discusses the work of al-Ḥajjāj to promote irrigation. For a number of quotations showing the interest of rulers in the development of agriculture, see the introductory chapter to this book, n. 19. On the repair and extension of irrigation works in the Hijaz, see EL-ALI 252–3. On the attention given to irrigation by 'Abbāsid rulers, see EL-SAMARRAIE 105ff.

20 MAZLOUM 1–6; AL-IDRĪSĪ *Description* 76. Many similar examples may be found, since almost everywhere cities shared their water with the surrounding countryside – an arrangement which often gave rise to conflicts. A famous example is the *ghūṭa* of Damascus, whose irrigation system probably dates from early Islamic times. See KURD 'ALĪ *passim* and TRESSE 471.

21 See n. 17 above; GLICK *Irrigation* 182–4; SOLIGNAC "Travaux" 534, 551–73 and *Recherches* 7, 58; LAUTENSACH 72; OLIVER ASÍN; GOBLOT "Dans l'ancien"; MAZLOUM; HUMLUM "Underjordiske"; VAVILOV AND BUKINICH 547; ABŪ AL-FIDĀ II pt 2 138; and IBN ḤAWQAL II 418–19.

22 On surface canals, see MEZ 451ff and MAGNIN. SPULER *Iran* 386 states that lead pipes were used in Samarkand, while clay tiles were found in the excavations of al-Fusṭāṭ. Stone canals are mentioned in AL-IDRĪSĪ *Description* 103; brick canals in IBN ḤAWQAL I 238 and AL-MUQADDASĪ *Description* 14–15.

23 For dams and weirs, see R. M. ADAMS *Land* figs. 17–22; GLICK *Irrigation* 176–7; BARTOL'D "Istoriia" 135, 140, 160–1, 187; AL-MAQQARĪ *Nafḥ* II 26; MEZ 451ff; MÜLLER-WODARG (1954) 186; GOBLOT "Dans l'ancien" 514ff and "Kébar" 50; SOLIGNAC *Recherches* 275–8; and IBN WAḤSHĪYA "Filāḥa" I 36, where the construction of a small dam is described. For various storage reservoirs, see SOLIGNAC *Recherches* 5ff and 223ff, 255ff, 285ff; ALLAIN; BUGEAT; LAMMENS *Berceau* 26ff; and CRESSWELL 228–30, 291–2.

24 See nn. 11–15 above and (on the Islamic use of the noria) IBN WAḤSHĪYA "Filāḥa" I 26, 35–6 and 72–5, where the noria is described in great detail; AL-MAQQARĪ *Nafḥ* VI 85, where the famous water wheel in the Huerta del Rey of Toledo is described; IBN BAṬṬŪṬA I 141–3, where may be found a description of the great noria of Ḥamāh in Syria, a city which in the fourteenth century was said to have thirty-two of these machines; AL-IDRĪSĪ *Description* 97; AL-GHAZZĪ ch. 2; ABŪ AL-FIDĀ II pt 2 138; AL-WAZZĀN I 234, 243; AL-'UDHRĪ I; BRÄUNLICH 288ff, 472ff; TORRES BALBÁS "Las norias" and "La Albolafia"; CARO BAROJA "Norias" and "Sobre"; NICHOLLS; CAHEN "Le service" 130ff; GIESE "Über die Herkunft" and "Brunnenschöpfräder"; GLICK *Irrigation* 177ff; DIAS AND GALHANO *passim*; BRESC 66–7; COLIN "La noria" and "L'origine"; FORBES II 50; MÜLLER-WODARG (1954) 189–92; LAUTENSACH 70–2; and BARTOL'D "Istoriia" 143. The wheel of the water-powered noria of Ḥamāh on the Orontes has a diameter of 22 m, allowing the water to be raised to nearly that height above the river level. Similarly, in North Africa there may be found animal-powered norias in which the chains are extremely long, making possible the raising of water from very deep wells. Some idea of the efficiency of different types of noria may be had from CAHEN *loc. cit.*

25 SOLIGNAC *Recherches* 5ff, 223ff *et passim*; CRESSWELL 291–2; AL-MUQADDASI *Description* 14–15.

26 DIAS AND GALHANO 182; CARO BAROJA "Sobre" 16–21.

27 DIAS AND GALHANO 188ff, 198; OLIVEIRA MARQUES 193, where it is also suggested that the water-driven noria may not have reached Iberia until Islamic times.

28 The question of storage dams requires much closer investigation; both literary sources and archeological remains need to be studied. However, al-Muqaddasī describes a tenth-century dam on the river Kurr in Fars which seems clearly to be a storage dam; MEZ 451. GOBLOT "Kébar" dates the first known vaulted dam in Iran to *c.* 1300, but new evidence may turn up earlier examples. In any case, the *barrage-poids*, which may also be used for storage, is much earlier.

29 GOBLOT "Dans l'ancien Iran" *passim*; HUMLUM "Underjordiske" *passim*. On the construction of *qanawāt* in the 'Abbāsid east, see KRENKOW and SOLIGNAC "Travaux" 563–4.

30 See n. 24 above; CARO BAROJA "Sobre" 16–21; and GLICK *Irrigation* 177–82. GIESE "Über die Herkunft", "Über portugiesische" 72 and "Brunnenschöpfräder" suggests that the noria was introduced into Sardinia by the Muslims, and that certain kinds of noria were introduced into Portugal in Islamic times. See also n. 15 above.

31 GLICK *Irrigation* 119ff, 240ff.

32 SUSA *Irrigation* 32.

33 See ch. 24 below.

34 In the vast literature of irrigation history may be found assertions which tend to minimize, or even discredit, the contribution of early Islamic times to the development of irrigated agriculture, particularly in Spain, North Africa and the Levant. Thus RIBERA Y TARRAGÓ II 309–13, writing in a long tradition which belittles the Muslim legacy in Spain, argues that the irrigation system of the Huerta of Valencia is pre-Islamic, principally on the grounds that it does not resemble the undoubtedly Muslim system in the region of Marrakesh! In North Africa, GAUCKLER *passim*, following the previous practice of European scholars writing on the region, assigned virtually all the ruined irrigation works of Tunisia to the Romans, an error the enormity of which was finally pointed out in SOLIGNAC *Recherches* and "Travaux", whose careful work is a model to this kind of investigation. In Libya, the *qanawāt* of the desert were attributed by BEADNELL 167ff to the Romans, whereas they are almost certainly Islamic. Again, for the Levant, one reads

in BENVENISTI 263 that "with the Arab conquest a period of decline and decay in irrigated agriculture began". Such assertions need not be taken seriously. To prove for a particular region whether in early Islamic times irrigated agriculture had progressed beyond its classical antecedents requires very careful analysis, and the results may not be unambiguous. The pitfalls are many. Thus, for instance, the opening of new irrigated areas might be counterbalanced by the abandonment of irrigated lands nearby, the shifting of cultivation and settlement being common in desert regions where irrigated lands eventually became overly saline. The impressive evidence presented in the careful work of LAPIDUS "Arab settlement", showing that irrigated agriculture expanded very considerably in a number of areas of Iraq, does not allow us to conclude anything about the expansion or contraction of irrigated farming in the whole of Mesopotamia, since the fate of large areas remains unknown. Archeological work, such as that reported in R. M. ADAMS *Land*, may help to fill in the picture; but this, too, has its limitations. In the first place, it can generally cover only restricted areas, such as the Diyala plains studied by Adams, which are not necessarily typical. Even in such relatively small areas questionable techniques must be used to get an overall picture without undue expenditure of time and money. For a discussion of the shortcomings of Adams's method, see ch. 24 n. 14. For Spain, the problem of assessing the Arab contribution is exacerbated by the small amount of information on Roman irrigation in Iberia and our ignorance of the fate of irrigation in Visigothic times. SCHULTEN *Iberische* I 378–81 gives the available evidence concerning irrigation in Roman and Visigothic Spain, which does not prove the existence of very extensive irrigation works in many areas. A very careful study of the Islamic contribution in the area of Valencia and elsewhere is found in GLICK *Irrigation* 149–242; see also LAUTENSACH 70–8. For Sicily, much work remains to be done; see, however, PIPITONE CANNONE, who argues that the Muslim contribution was very important. It is interesting, and perhaps significant, that in both Spain and Sicily (in the latter of which the Arab occupation was relatively short) the vocabulary of irrigation in post-Islamic times and to this very day is largely of Arabic origin. See AREZZO (Arabic glossary) 23, 34, 38, 46, 59, 63, 73, 74; PELLEGRINI *Gli arabismi* I 55–6 *et passim* and "L'elemento" 712–13; and NEUVONEN 73, 84, 86, 131, 132, 145, 150.

21. Facilitating supply: land tenure

1 On the disparity between legal theory and actual practice, see LØKKEGAARD 5–10, 72–3; POLIAK "Classification" 59, 62; YAḤYĀ IBN ĀDAM 16; QUDĀMA 7–16; ABŪ YŪSUF 11, 14–24; and UDOVITCH 44ff.

2 Koran VII 125 states that the earth belongs to God, and by implication it might be seen as belonging to his Prophet or to his appointed ruler, i.e. the caliph. See 'ABD AL-KADER 10 and LØKKEGAARD 38. The notion that all conquered lands belonged to the State or to the Muslim community seems to have been invented late in the day to rationalize the failure in the Sawād and in certain other areas (e.g. Sicily) to distribute this land as booty; see LØKKEGAARD 39–58; YAḤYĀ IBN ĀDAM 49; and TALBI "Law". But it cannot be thought to have had any practical significance, since such land had originally been treated as private property; see HEYWORTH-DUNNE 14. AL-DĀWŪDĪ II 428 cites the jurist Saḥnūn, who argues that the *status quo* must be accepted regardless of the mode of conquest: that the land was the property of those who were in possession.

3 Specialists in Islamic land tenure will notice that this treatment, by virtue of its generality and its exclusive focus on the question of property rights, does not treat a good number of questions over which much ink has been spilled, both by the classical jurists and by contemporary scholars. These questions include which lands fell into which category (and indeed whether any land fell into several of the categories); which lands paid *kharāj* and which paid *'ushr*; the meaning and extent of *fay'*; etc. For modern treatments of these and related points the reader is referred to LØKKEGAARD *passim*; DENNETT 21ff; LAMBTON

Landlord and Peasant 16ff; AMARI II 16ff; and the introductions by Ben Shemesh to YAḤYĀ IBN ĀDAM, QUDĀMA and ABŪ YŪSUF.

4 EL-ALI 248, 252 points out that private property in agricultural land was common in Medina in the time of the Prophet, who did not try to modify the institution. The confiscation and redistribution of estates in the Hijaz served to widen the sphere of private property. For Iraq and Iran, see LAMBTON *Landlord and Peasant* 21; GIBB 5, 10, 11; POLIAK "L'arabisation" 53; SHABAN *Islamic* 49–50 *et seq.*; ABŪ YŪSUF 23–4; and AL-DĀWŪDĪ II 428. CAHEN "Réflexions" 50 shows that both *kharāj* and *'ushr* lands could be endowed as *waqf* in perpetuity and hence were completely alienable. (*Waqf* is the régime governing land received in mortmain (i.e. inalienable land) by religious and other institutions.) It is now becoming clear that even in Iraq most *ṣawāfī* lands (conquered lands formerly belonging to the Sasanian crown), which were all *fay'* (conquered lands the ultimate ownership of which is seen to reside in the Muslim community or State), quickly became ownerships. Sometimes the former owners returned and had their rights confirmed by the Arabs; in some cases the *dahāqīn* seem to have become the owners; and in still other cases this land seems to have become the property of grantees, of the peasants who farmed it, of the conqueror or of the ruler. Such land could be alienated freely and paid only *kharāj*; no additional rent was paid to the State as landlord. Hence the fiction of ownership by the State or Muslim community had little practical significance. It should be seen simply as a justification of the failure to distribute these lands as booty. According to LØKKEGAARD 57, the rights of non-Muslim holders of *kharāj* land to alienate this property were constrained by a rule of 'Umar II (717–20) which forbad their sale to Muslims. However, such a rule, if it was ever enforced, must have lost its force as conversion to Islam proceeded and as it came to be recognized that these lands would pay *kharāj* regardless of the religion of their holders. See LAMBTON *Landlord and Peasant* 23. In the early period of Islam, a concession of land (known as *iqṭā'*), whether made from the property of the ruler, from State domain or from land belonging to the Muslim community, appears to have been a concession of full rights of ownership – nothing more and nothing less. See CAHEN "L'évolution" 27–8; LAMMENS "Etudes" II 22–3; AL-MAWARDĪ 409ff; and AL-BALĀDHURĪ I 462. DARKAZALLY 161–2 argues that in principle "the ownership of the *iqṭā'* given from the *ṣawāfī* remained with the State", but that the land registers were burned during a revolt of 699–702 and the possessors claimed ownership; in consequence they were obliged by al-Ḥajjāj to pay *kharāj* on these lands instead of merely *'ushr*. IMAMUDDIN "Al-filāḥah" 60, 66 points out that in Spain after the Arab conquest the tenants of the Christian landlords were given property rights over their tenancies. S. F. ROMANO 174 argues that in Sicily the Arab conquerors confiscated and distributed as ownerships the huge imperial lands and church estates, as well as all abandoned or uncultivated lands. For Ifrīqiya see TALBI "Law" 209–10.

5 On the development of a market for land in Iran, see SPULER *Iran* 391–2, and for the Hijaz, see EL-ALI 254. Much more work is needed on this important topic.

6 Communal rights of this kind, which reached their apogee in the open-field system of northern Europe in the Middle Ages, appear to have been dictated there by (*a*) the northern European's insistence on a diet rich in animal products and (*b*) the failure of medieval European agriculture to make use of the full range of available fertilizers, including night soil, the manure of non-field animals and green manure. The large consumption of animal products in northern Europe and the heavy reliance on the manure of field animals implied a very high animal/land ratio and a very low level of cropping. In fact, all the land of the medieval manor was used either wholly or partly for the feeding of animals: the commons and the meadow at all times, the waste and the forest sometimes, and the arable when it grew fodder crops, when it was thrown open to stubble grazing and when it lay fallow. It was therefore not used to the full for growing crops. In those parts of the early Islamic world where sedentary agriculture prevailed, field animals seem to have been much less important both in the diet of the common man and as a source

of fertilizer, and consequently much less land was devoted to their upkeep. Waste and forest were in most areas kept to a minimum; common grazing lands existed in some villages but apparently not in others; and it is not certain that grazing on stubble or even on fallow land was much practised. (In any case, since fallowing was much reduced, the opportunity for grazing fallow land was correspondingly reduced.) The main source of feed seems to have come from fodder crops grown on the arable. In this respect, as in many others, early Islamic agriculture seems to have been closer to the intensive agriculture of China (which has no pasture land in intensively cultivated areas) than to the non-intensive agriculture of Europe. The reduction of the animal/land ratio, and the concomitant increase in the cropping of the land, were in keeping with the high population densities of the early Islamic world, since they led to a considerably greater output of calories (though perhaps not of protein) per land unit. IBN AL-'AWWĀM ed. Banqueri II 7 states that large fields cannot be manured, implying that animals did not pasture on them after harvest or while they lay fallow. GLICK *Irrigation* 22–6 points out that in the irrigated area around Valencia – as doubtless elsewhere – it was forbidden to pasture animals. Pasture lands were established outside the irrigated area. ABŪ YŪSUF 118, 120 speaks of some villages which had common pastures – no doubt outside the irrigated area – and of other villages which had none. The most common fodder crops seem to have been lucerne, clover, trefoil and vetch. See AL-BALĀDHURĪ I 426–8; *Arabic Papyri* VI 19–21, 25–6, 57, 65; and BOLENS *Les méthodes* 129 (where *najīl*, erroneously translated as "pois gris", is given as another fodder crop). In *Description de l' Egypte...Etat moderne* II i 553–4 it is recorded that at the beginning of the nineteenth century field animals in Egypt were fed sorghum, vetch, clover and the stalks of lentils and lupins – all field crops. Of course, in areas controlled by the bedouin or by other nomadic peoples, that is in places where agriculture was not practised, large areas were set aside as grazing reserves, and the rights to both land and water in these areas were held in common by tribes or other groups. But the reduction of the size of such lands by the granting away of portions, and the small area set aside for such lands in the newly conquered territories, suggest that it was a policy to reduce their size in favour of sedentary agriculture. (See LØKKEGAARD 20, 32; GIBB "The fiscal" 5, 11; SHABAN *Islamic* 12–14; 22, 27; POLIAK "L'arabisation" 45; LAMMENS *Le berceau* 56ff; and AL-DŪRĪ "The origins" 5.) Clearly the Islamic laws favouring private ownership of agricultural land derive from the sedentary, rather than the nomadic, traditions of Arabia, as LØKKEGAARD 15, 32 suggests. For the laws and practices concerning village lands held in common, e.g. meadows, bogs, woods, see LØKKEGAARD 36–7.

7 See n. 31 below and FRANTZ 219ff.

8 The large estates appear to have monopolized agriculture in the western part of the Roman empire and in the Sasanian empire. However, in pre-Islamic Byzantium it appears that they had not completely succeeded in displacing peasant operators. For a discussion of some of the literature bearing on this point, see RÉMONDON 300–5. The Egyptian case is discussed in A. C. JOHNSON *Egypt* 69ff, 87ff; DENNETT 69; and HARDY *passim.*

9 The disposition of the lands in the Sawād has occasioned much controversy in the classical literature as well as in contemporary scholarship. See LAMBTON *Landlord and Peasant* 21–3 and SPULER *Iran* 390ff. Whether the ownership actually reverted to tenants where the owners had fled or been killed is not made clear in the sources. But as the intention of this departure from the practice laid down by Muḥammad seems to have been to maintain agricultural production, it may be assumed that tenants often did become *de facto* owners here as elsewhere. On the modest size of the estates in this region, see CAHEN "Fiscalité" 151. For Sicily, see AMARI II 33ff, 41–2; PIPITONE CANNONE "La scuola" 215ff; PERI II 217ff; MACK SMITH I 9; and S. F. ROMANO 174. The decline of the large estates in Egypt is discussed in HARDY 146–8 and DENNETT 69ff. EL-ALI 253 shows that in the seventh and eighth centuries ownerships in the Hijaz were of various sizes.

10 For Spain, see IMAMUDDIN "Al-filāḥa" 60, 66; LÉVI-PROVENÇAL *Histoire* III 198ff and *L'Espagne* 161; AMARI II 38; and VICENS VIVES I 176. For North Africa, see AMARI II 34–8

and TALBI "Law", the latter of whom describes the large estates of Ifrīqiya which competed with medium-sized and smaller estates.

11 See n. 27 below.

12 Many of the geographers and other writers describing cities speak of such areas of market gardens. See, for example, AL-YA'QŪBĪ 38, 79, 202, 229; YĀQŪT IV 787; AL-MAQQARĪ *Nafḥ al-ṭīb* I 155, 164, 183; AL-BAKRĪ *Description* 9, 10, 13, 15, 16, 17, 24, 41, 44, 62, 65, 119; AL-'UMARĪ 157; AL-IDRĪSĪ *Description* 69; IBN ḤAWQAL I 36; NĀṢIR-I KHUSRAW 132, 133 n. 1, 136; DUBLER *Über das Wirtschaftsleben* 89; PELLAT *Le milieu* 16; TORRES BALBÁS "Las ruinas"; CAHEN "Economy" 518–20; GOITEIN *A Mediterranean* I 122; and KURD 'ALI *passim*. For a detailed discussion of the market gardens around Palermo in the thirteenth and fourteenth centuries, when much of the Arab heritage in gardening still remained, see BRESC.

13 The optimum scale of operation must have varied according to kind of crop, soil, watering, labour etc. IBN AL-'AWWĀM ed. Banqueri I 4 states that "a small, compact estate is more advantageous and more productive than a large, fragmented estate".

14 SHABAN *Islamic* 39, 43, 48–50. NEWMAN 161ff, 176 gives examples of the excessive taxation in the late Sasanian empire, where the tax collectors often took more than their due; and DENNETT 66ff, 69, 74 discusses the heavy rates of taxation in late Byzantine Egypt. To be sure, some individuals and some classes of taxpayers were more heavily hit by Islamic than by pre-Islamic taxes. Islamic taxation fell directly on the producer. It abolished the immunities, payments by proxy and collective responsibility which had been so common in the pre-Islamic world.

15 See YAḤYĀ IBN ĀDAM 28, 60–1; QUDĀMA 74–6; IBN 'ABDŪN 10–12; H. I. BELL "Two official" 276; LAMBTON *Landlord and Peasant* xix–xx, xxiii–xxv; GOITEIN *A Mediterranean* II 363; GIBB 40; and DARKAZALLY 188, who cites M. Kurd 'Alī.

16 SHABAN *Islamic* 43; CAHEN "Fiscalité" 145ff. As DENNETT 110ff shows, however, the migration of some peasants to the towns was occasioned by the high poll taxes, and not by the taxes on land or its produce.

17 R. M. ADAMS *Land* 84–5 (who, however, attributes the decline in revenues to private and official corruption, as well as to a possible drop in production).

18 Rural taxes in Egypt were based on the type of crop planted and the flood of the Nile. See DENNETT 65ff, 81, 90ff, 104–5; RABIE *The Financial* 73ff; FRANTZ 123ff; MÜLLER-WODARG (1954) 210–14; and GROHMANN "New discoveries" 169. Calculations made by this writer on the rates of Egyptian taxation given by IBN MAMMĀTĪ 257ff suggest that this rate was also low, usually falling between one-fifth and one-tenth of output.

19 In addition Muslims paid, in theory at least, a tithe for charity, while non-Muslims were subject to a head tax. The main sources for the system of taxation are the legal authorities QUDĀMA IBN JA'FAR, YAḤYĀ IBN ĀDAM, ABŪ YŪSUF and AL-MAWARDĪ, though it should be emphasized that practice did not always conform to the judicial texts. On the other hand, the legal texts do give the impression that their authors were struggling to justify a changing legal reality by reference to the precepts of Islamic law; what the texts prescribed or described may therefore have been close to the reality of their time. For discussions in the secondary literature, the reader is referred to LØKKEGAARD and DENNETT. As LØKKEGAARD 113–14 and CAHEN "Fiscalité" point out, the introduction of the *muqāsama* system must have been very slow, taking a century or more to complete.

20 See, for example, LAMBTON *Landlord and Peasant* 46.

21 AL-BALĀDHURĪ I 429; QUDĀMA 57; YAḤYĀ IBN ĀDAM 77–8, 93–4, 98–100; ABŪ YŪSUF 17, 130, 132; LØKKEGAARD 117.

22 YAḤYĀ IBN ĀDAM 95–6, 99; AL-BALĀDHURĪ I 113, 429. However, cotton seems in fact to have been sometimes taxed; see QUDĀMA 39 and ABŪ YŪSUF 99. The translation of "maize" (for *durra*) in ABŪ YŪSUF 95–6 should be amended to read "sorghum".

23 YAḤYĀ IBN ĀDAM 99. Several sources, however, mention that rice and sugar cane, which were summer crops, were in fact taxed.

24 YAḤYĀ IBN ĀDAM 98; LØKKEGAARD 122–4; AGHNIDES 379.

25 AL-BALĀDHURĪ I 109; YAḤYĀ IBN ĀDAM 77–82; QUDĀMA 37; ABŪ YŪSUF 73, 103–4, 121, 130. Such lands were later taxed at much higher rates; see LØKKEGAARD 122.

26 AL-BALĀDHURĪ I 24–5, 27 shows that the Prophet settled many irrigation disputes, presumably in an attempt to establish a framework that gave security to irrigators. CAPONERA gives a summary of Muslim water law; see also AL-BUKHĀRĪ II 102–11; QUDĀMA 60–3; ABŪ YŪSUF 106, 124–9; YAḤYĀ IBN ĀDAM 67, 71–7; AL-MAWARDĪ 386ff; GLICK *Irrigation, passim*; LAUTENSACH 74ff; SPULER *Iran* 385ff; AGHNIDES 518–21; LØKKEGAARD 20–1, 32; KREMER I 201; and WILKINSON "Islamic" *passim*.

27 On the reclamation of dead land and the enclosure of unused land, see ABŪ YŪSUF 118–23; YAḤYĀ IBN ĀDAM 32, 53, 64–9; QUDĀMA 31–2, 35, 78; AL-BUKHĀRĪ II 97; AL-DĀWŪDĪ 435; AL-MAWARDĪ 379ff and 410ff; AGHNIDES 502–6; 'ABD AL-KADER 6; and LØKKEGAARD 50–78. As R. M. ADAMS "Agriculture" 109 points out, such abandoned lands often were much more productive than long-cultivated lands. On the transfer to the State of ownership of lands not cultivated for two or three years, see YAḤYĀ IBN ĀDAM 68; QUDĀMA 27, 33, 77; ABŪ YŪSUF 76; IBN ḤAWQAL II 296–7; AL-MAQRĪZI *Description* I 274; LAMMENS "Etudes" II 123; AGHNIDES 386; LØKKEGAARD 16–17; TUMA 17; and H. I. BELL "The administration" 285. On the taxation of lands which were not cultivated (but had access to water), see ABŪ YŪSUF 100, 104; AL-BALĀDHURĪ I 426; LØKKEGAARD 116; and AGHNIDES 290, 364.

28 BRUNSCHVIG "'Abd" 33; GOITEIN "Slaves" I; BURNS *Islam* 109; BOLENS *Les méthodes* I. Though slaves were common in the early Islamic world, they seem to have been used mainly in the military, in the household or harem, in the bureaucracy and as personal secretaries. See BRUNSCHVIG "'Abd"; SOURDEL "Ghulām"; LAPIDUS "Evolution" 37–9; and AL-'ABBĀDĪ 9ff. Three exceptions may be noted: NĀṢIR-I KHUSRAW 227 speaks of "30,000" Negro or Abyssinian slaves working in the cultivation of fields and gardens in the area around Bahrain; LAMMENS *Le berceau* gives examples of large-scale use of slaves on some estates in the Hijaz; and TALBI "Law" 214–16 argues that slaves were used on the large estates of ninth-century Ifrīqiya (though not all of his evidence designates these slaves clearly as agricultural workers.) The case of the Zanj in Iraq is also sometimes cited, but the sources state that these African slaves were employed only in the removal of salt encrustations (which were sold) from land that was being reclaimed for agriculture; see POPOVIC. Another apparent exception, cited by PETRUSHEVSKII "Emploi" 4, appears mistaken: *Ḥudūd* 145, which he cites, speaks only of clients (*mawlāyān*), not slaves. The other examples of agricultural slavery cited by PETRUSHEVSKII are of late date. If indeed it is true that slavery and, as we shall argue below, serfdom are virtually absent from the countryside of the early Islamic world, the fact of their disappearance demands an explanation. In the absence of concrete evidence, several factors may be suggested. As LAMBTON *Landlord and Peasant* 17 has argued, "the speed and comparative ease of the Muslim conquest were in all probability in some measure due to the fact that Islām offered the mass of the people release from conditions of intolerable social inferiority". However, we do not learn of any formal freeing of slaves and serfs, except in a text of al-Sarakhsī cited by MORONY. On the other hand, texts do state that on the *ṣawāfī* (or State) lands of the Sawād the former slaves and serfs became free men; see AL-DŪRĪ "The origins" 6 and MORONY. Elsewhere slaves were still technically slaves, even if they were converted to Islam, and according to some authorities even previous owners of booty land became slaves. See QUDĀMA 26.

But the status of serf is not recognized in Islamic law, and it may be that serfs automatically became free men. As GOITEIN *A Mediterranean* I 116–17 points out, the ownership of a village did not give the owner political, judicial or ownership rights over its inhabitants, but only the rights to economic benefits. Slaves may have been manumitted (and thus became clients), especially if they were converted to Islam; according to QUDĀMA 67, the *ṣadaqa* tax could be used to ransom some slaves, especially learned ones, and many others must often have been freed as an act of charity by their masters or by others.

29 FORAND maintains that in the Sawād and possibly elsewhere in the Islamic world the peasants were early tied to the soil. This proposition seems difficult to prove. The attempt to put fugitive peasants back on the land seems to have failed, while texts describing peasants bound to the land do not appear until much later. The binding of peasants to the land in the Roman empire is well known. For similar practices in the Sasanian empire, see MORONY; PIGULEVSKAYA 155–8; LAMBTON *Landlord and Peasant* 13–16 and "Reflections on the role" 286 and WIDENGREN. On the freeing of the peasantry in early Islamic times, see IMAMUDDIN "Al-filāḥah" 60, 61, 66 and AL-DŪRĪ *loc. cit.*

30 GIBB 4–5, 7. In Crusader Palestine, following the Islamic practice, estates had no demesnes and corvées were not known; see BENVENISTI 217 and RILEY-SMITH 45–6. Similarly, in Crusader Valencia, corvée duties were exceedingly light and infrequent; see BURNS "Socio-economic". The use of corvée labour for irrigation is documented in fourteenth-century Egypt and in the twentieth-century Hadramawt; see LAPIDUS *Muslim* 64 and SERJEANT "Some irrigation" 59–60.

31 On the use of sharecropping, see ABŪ YŪSUF 114–17; YAḤYĀ IBN ĀDAM 107; *Arabic Papyri* II 29–72; IMAMUDDIN "Al-filāḥah" 60ff; HEYWORTH DUNNE 41; LÉVI-PROVENÇAL *Histoire* III 266ff; TALBI "Law" 234–5. Of all the forms of exploitation of rural estates, sharecropping is perhaps the one which most favours innovation since both landlord and tenant stand to share in its gains and may well collaborate in its introduction.

32 In the pre-Islamic world wage labour seems to have been unknown in agriculture and was little known in other spheres of production. However, there are many references to it in the Islamic period. IBN ʿABDŪN 125–6 speaks of a place in Seville where agricultural labourers might be hired by the day. See also *Arabic Papyri* II 101–4 and VI 30, 57–9, 73–8, 96; IBN MAMMĀTĪ 277–8; IMAMUDDIN "Al-filāḥah" 62; LAMBTON *Landlord and Peasant* xxviii–xxix; and TALBI "Law" 236. Whether the *akkārūn* mentioned by IBN WAḤSHĪYA "Filāḥa" I 76–7, 100 *et passim* are sharecroppers or wage-earners is not clear, though the fact that they work under a foreman does suggest that they were wage-earners. On the meaning of this term in pre-Islamic Persia see MORONY and ALTHEIM AND STIEHL 170–1.

33 Of course, the institution of slavery was to some extent replaced by clientage, which was another form of tie between men. Clients could be either free or freed men. But as CRONE shows, clientage hardly seems to have restricted the mobility of the peasantry. On the contrary, it seems to have encouraged the movement of peasants to the cities, to the army and to other lands. True, as FORAND 28 has pointed out, fugitive peasants were sometimes returned to the land in the Sawād and possibly elsewhere; documented examples of forcible returns occur in the reigns of ʿAbd al-Malik (685–705) and al-Manṣūr (754–75). Whether such examples show that peasant mobility was seriously curtailed, or simply that it was excessive, is problematic; the latter seems more likely the case. In any event, it is difficult to conclude with FORAND that in the early centuries of Islam the peasantry in the Sawād or in any other region overrun by the Arabs was effectively tied to the soil. Such a conclusion seems to be the result of reading backwards from fifteenth-century and other late texts.

22. *Facilitating supply: gardens*

1 MARÇAIS "Les jardins" *passim*; DICKIE *passim*; SOURDEL AND SOURDEL 292; MEYERHOF "Sur un traité" (1942–3) 58–9; GOITEIN *A Mediterranean* I 122.

2 PÉRÈS *La poésie* 161ff. Garden poems are collected in AL-MAQQARĪ *Nafḥ al-ṭīb* II 21, 25, 72, 74, 75, 80, 181, 182, 186, 189, 190, 193, 194, 197, 199, 208–11; AL-NUWAIRĪ X 251–71; and ABŪ AL-WALĪD *passim*.

3 *La poésie* 161ff.

4 AL-DŪRĪ *Ta'rīkh* 26, 28; PELLAT *Le milieu* 16.

5 YĀQŪT IV 787; AL-DIMASHQĪ 263.

6 IBN ḤAWQAL I 36; NĀṢIR-I KHUSRAW 132, 133 n. 1, 136; WIET *Cairo* 17, 19, 22.

7 AL-BAKRĪ *Description* 9, 10, 13, 15, 16, 17, 24, 41, 44, 62, 65, 110; AL-IDRĪSĪ *Description* 69; AL-'UMARĪ 111–12, 140, 157, 160, 161, 181; AL-WAZZĀN I 99, 106, 204, 285 and II 363; TORRES BALBÁS "Las ruinas" 275ff; MARÇAIS "Les jardins" *passim*.

8 AL-MAQQARĪ *Nafḥ al-ṭīb* I 155, 164, 168ff, 185 and II 14ff; IBN BAṬṬŪṬA IV 368–9; ZEKI 463; DUBLER *Über das Wirtschaftsleben* 89; PÉRÈS *La poésie* 115ff. For gardens in Turkestan, see BARTOL'D "Istoriia" 212, 213, 215; gardens in various other places are described in AL-YA'QŪBĪ 35, 79, 202, 229. The gardens of Norman Sicily, presumably of Islamic origin, are described in BRESC.

9 VIOLLET *passim*.

10 AL-'UMARĪ 111; AL-BAKRĪ *Description* 62; SOLIGNAC *Recherches* 218ff and "Travaux" 528ff; MARÇAIS "Les jardins" 235ff.

11 AL-MAQRĪZĪ *Khiṭaṭ* II 384; WIET *Cairo* 22.

12 AL-'UMARĪ 104, 156, 181ff; AL-QAZWĪNĪ II 73; MARÇAIS "Les jardins" 237.

13 AL-MAQQARĪ *Nafḥ al-ṭīb* II 14ff, 38–41. AL-MUQADDASĪ *Description* 39 described another royal garden in Grenada.

14 AL-'UDHRĪ 85; IBN BAṢṢĀL 14; IBN AL-ABBĀR *Kitāb al-takmila* II 551; DOZY *Recherches* 598; DICKIE *passim*.

15 WILBER 53ff; GOTHEIN 160.

16 BARTOL'D *Turkestan* I 127ff.

17 AL-MAQRĪZĪ *Khiṭaṭ* II 96. Information about royal gardens other than those already mentioned is given in AL-'UMARĪ 112; AL-KHAZRAJĪ II 108, 120, 287; GOTHEIN 146ff; SOURDEL AND SOURDEL 355–6; SOLIGNAC *Recherches* 218ff; VILLIERS-STUART *passim*; and PÉRÈS *La poésie* 115ff.

18 MARÇAIS "Les jardins" 234–5.

19 AL-KHUSHĀNĪ 38–41; AL-MAQQARĪ *Nafḥ al-ṭīb* II 14–15; PÉRÈS "Le palmier". A text of Ibn al-Abbār is given in DOZY *Notices* 34ff.

20 AL-'UDHRĪ 85.

21 MAZAHÉRI 242–3.

22 AL-MAQRĪZĪ *Khiṭaṭ* II 119.

23 *Monumenta cartographica* IV ii 1082; MAUNY *Tableau* 244.

24 AL-KHAZRAJĪ II 108, 120, 287; MEYERHOF "Sur un traité" (1942–3) 58 and (1943–4) 52, 57.

25 MAZAHÉRI 242–3.

26 BOLENS *Les méthodes* 31; MILLÁS VALLICROSA "Un nuevo".

27 ASÍN PALACIOS *Un botánico* 9.

28 LECLERC II 250.

29 IBN AL-ABBĀR *Kitāb al-takmila* II 551; IBN BAṢṢĀL 14ff; IBN WĀFID *El "libre..."* and "La traducción" *passim*; MILLÁS VALLICROSA "Un nuevo"; SHIHĀBĪ *et al.* 901.

30 The earliest botanical gardens in Europe appear to have been those planted by Matthaeus Sylvaticus in Salerno *c.* 1310 and by Gualterius in Venice *c.* 1330. Other European cities and universities did not acquire botanical gardens until the sixteenth and seventeenth centuries: Pisa in 1543, Padua, Parma and Florence in 1545, Bologna in 1568, Leyden in 1577, Leipzig in 1580, Königsberg in 1581, Paris (Le Jardin Royal du Louvre) in 1590, Oxford in 1621 etc. See CHIARUGI; HILL "The history" 195ff; PHILIPPI *passim*; KERNER VON MARILAUN *passim*; KRAUS *Über die Bevölkerung*, *passim*; PAVANI *passim*; and CURSET.

23. An agricultural revolution?

1 Some of the material which follows is presented in greater detail or in a different form in A. M. WATSON "The Arab" and "A medieval".

2 Thus SCHNEBEL 220ff, in discussing the rotations of Hellenistic and Byzantine Egypt, shows no summer cropping at all even along the Nile. See esp. p. 229. See also JEHUDA 36.

3 THEOPHRASTUS II 184–5 (bk VIII 7) mentions only millet and sesame as summer crops. PLINY

220–1, 240–1, 248–51, 266–7 (bk XVIII 10, 18, 22, 31) adds to these lentils, peas, clary (?) and irio (?). Barley, he says, was a winter crop in the Mediterranean, though in parts of Celtic Spain (as in temperate Europe) it could also be sown in summer. In Greece, he adds, all grains, including sesame and millet (which in Italy could be summer crops), were sown as winter crops. This practice probably prevailed in all the hotter parts of the Mediterranean. A spring wheat, known as *trimestre*, is also mentioned in the Roman manuals; but as K. D. WHITE 36–7 points out, this was generally grown only in northern and not Mediterranean Europe. COLUMELLA I 136–9 (bk II ch. 6), however, suggests that farmers in hotter regions might have recourse to a summer crop of *trimestre* when the winter grain crop had failed. ISIDORE OF SEVILLE bk XVII 3 also says *trimestre* could be sown in the spring in times of need. *Trimestre* is probably the summer grain grown in the region of Reims in Roman times; see STERN "Le cycle" 1441–2. Certain Cucurbitaceae, such as cucumbers, gourds and melons, were grown in ancient times as summer garden crops; these could be summer crops, even in hot climates, if some artificial watering was provided. But as is pointed out by STERN *Le calendrier* 366–9, after a thorough examination of all the agricultural calendars of ancient Greece, Rome and Byzantium, as well as all the Latin poems of the months, the field crops of the ancient world were virtually all sown from October to December. *Geoponika*, a Byzantine compendium of the sixth or tenth centuries, is not altogether consistent on the subject of summer crops, probably reflecting the differing practices of the various regions the sources speak of. However, this text seem to imply that wheat and barley were exclusively winter crops, as were pulses, while millet was in some regions a summer crop, as were gourds, cucumbers and hemp. See *Geoponika* 53–4, 66, 75, 76, 365–6 (bk II chs. 14, 25, 38, 40 and bk XII ch. 19). On the lack of summer crops in the Jewish agricultural tradition, see JEHUDA 36, 46, 150–4, where it is shown that virtually no summer crops other than cotton were used in field rotations, though cucumbers, melons, cowpeas, chickpeas, onions, dill and coriander might be grown in the summer, presumably as garden crops.

4 The planting time for most of these crops is shown in the various manuals. It varies slightly with climate. For Spain much of the relevant information is contained in *Le calendrier* 62, 76, 130, 172, 186; IBN AL-'AWWĀM ed. Banqueri II 428ff; and ABŪ AL-KHAIR "Kitāb al-filāḥa" 126–7. In Egypt the flooding of the Nile in late summer changed the timing of the summer season somewhat, as is shown in IBN ḤAWQAL I 135–6 and IBN MAMMĀTĪ 234–70. IBN WAḤSHĪYA "Filāḥa" I 198 states that rice could be a summer or a winter crop in India and Mesopotamia and that sometimes the same plot of land bore two crops of rice in a year, but that in his time it was primarily a summer crop. Other summer crops listed by IBN MAMMĀTĪ *loc. cit.* are swedes, cumin, caraway, *lūbiyā* (= cowpea?), yellow melons, sesame, indigo, radishes and turnips. RABIE "Some technical", drawing on al-Nabulusī, al-Makhzūmī and al-Maqrīzī, adds cucumbers, lettuce and cabbage.

5 Some idea of the early diffusion of these crops may be had from CANDOLLE 136–8, 164, 346; but much more work is needed on the subject.

6 K. D. WHITE 110ff; STEVENS 97; ISIDORE OF SEVILLE bk XVII 2; SCHNEBEL 220ff; JEHUDA 30ff. K. D. WHITE 113, 121–2 shows that "partial legume rotation", i.e. the growing of legumes in alternate years, was known to the Romans; but BOLENS *Les méthodes* 129ff points out that the benefits of legumes were not clearly perceived by the Romans and that such rotations were much more boldly practised in Islamic times. JEHUDA 71 suggests that in the agriculture of the ancients a summer crop would normally be followed by a period of winter fallow (and probably by fallowing in the next summer). NEWMAN 79–81 shows that the standard practice of the Babylonian Jews up to 500 was to crop land only once every two years.

7 SCHNEBEL *loc. cit.* presents the evidence for forty-three cases of land use in different parts of Egypt over a number of years, up to the fourth century. The land was always fallowed in the summer. In alternate winters it was sometimes fallowed, or – more commonly – it was used to grow grass or legumes. As the author points out, this evidence probably

exaggerates the intensity of land use and underestimates the amount of fallowing, since it is taken from leases many of which were for relatively short terms. Land which an owner wished to fallow would normally not be leased until the period of fallow was over, though a lease for a period of years would normally stipulate some fallowing or "conversion" of the land to grass or legumes.

8 JEHUDA 36. CHÉHABI 365 (*voce* "Jachère") gives various Arabic equivalents which, literally translated, mean "resting of the earth"; "changing of the earth" etc. IBN AL-ʿAWWĀM ed. Banqueri II 7–11 uses the term *būr* or *bawr*.

9 IBN AL-ʿAWWĀM ed. Banqueri II 3–4; IBN BAṢṢĀL 369; BOLENS *Les méthodes* 125–7.

10 IBN AL-ʿAWWĀM ed. Banqueri II 3–4; IBN BAṢṢĀL 369.

11 See, for example, NIEBUHR I 289–90, who states that in the Tihāma region of the Yemen the same field would regularly yield three crops per year. BOLENS *Les méthodes* 126 points out that "aucun document ne fournit l'indication du nombre maximum d'années de culture possible, ni la mention de cas d'épuisement total du champ".

12 BOLENS *Les méthodes* 135–7.

13 *Ibid.* 129ff, 137–9.

14 IBN WAḤSHĪYA "Filāḥa" I 170 and II 209, 214, 215.

15 YĀQŪT IV 383; *Ḥudūd* 147. AL-BAKRĪ *Description* 152 noted that in Balīs, in present-day Tunisia, irrigation made it possible to secure two crops of barley from the land.

16 MÜLLER-WODARG (1954) 195; COOPER 99; FRANTZ 86ff, 125. In *Description de l'Egypte...Etat moderne* I 542, 557–83, which describes agricultural conditions in Egypt at the beginning of the nineteenth century, it is stated that in Upper Egypt the land could yield two crops of cotton annually, while in most areas there were three agricultural seasons. IBN MAMMĀTĪ 201ff gives several categories of land which were not cultivated in every season, but it is difficult to know what proportion they were of total land area. HÜTTEROTH AND ABDULFATAH map 5 show the very great importance of summer crops in Levantine agriculture in the late sixteenth century; by this time, however, they must have been much less important than formerly.

17 IBN WAḤSHĪYA "Filāḥa" I 135. Cf. ADRIAN AND GAST 18, 20.

18 POSSOT 147. The same rotation was found in Egypt, according to COOPER 99.

19 IBN WAḤSHĪYA "Filāḥa" I 198, where it is stated that the double cropping of rice was practised in Mesopotamia and India. IBN BAṬṬŪṬA III 133 reported that three crops of rice could be obtained every year from some land in India. RAWSKI 32 cites a document which estimates that in modern China the growing of two crops of rice per year on a piece of land, instead of only one, increases the total yield by 70 to 80 per cent. IBN AL-ʿAWWĀM ed. Banqueri II 61 also speaks of two crops of rice per year.

20 An important advantage of colocasia over the greater yam is that it gives three harvests a year. IBN AL-ʿAWWĀM ed. Banqueri II 160 and IBN BAṢṢĀL 197 state that spinach may be sown throughout the year, while IBN MAMMĀTĪ 267–8 says that several harvests of eggplants may be had per year.

21 NĀṢIR-I KHUSRAW 151.

22 AL-ḤIMYARĪ 30.

23 On multiple cropping in ancient India, as well as intercropping, see *Concise History* 356, 361–2.

24 It is not certain that multiple cropping had reached Arabia Felix or Abyssinia before the rise of Islam, but on account of the climate, rainfall and availability of irrigation it seems likely that it was practised in Arabia Felix. AL-ʿUMARĪ 26 reports that in medieval Abyssinia the land yielded two or even three crops yearly; see also PANKHURST 200, 206–7.

25 IBN WAḤSHĪYA "Filāḥa" I 136–9, 148ff *et passim*; IBN AL-ʿAWWĀM ed. Banqueri I 59–77, 320 and II 230 *et passim*; IBN BAṢṢĀL 55ff; IMAMUDDIN "Al filāḥah" 71–3; BOLENS *Les méthodes* 184ff and "Engrais" *passim*. MÜLLER-WODARG (1954) 216 mentions that *sibākh* was used in Egypt; this term may mean simply manure or it may designate a windborne dusty soil which has gone through a nitrogen cycle. Night soil was of exceptional

importance since it provided a very great supply of excellent fertilizer (that went unused in European agriculture) and thereby reduced, or eliminated, the need to pasture animals on fields and to have large pasture lands and meadows to feed the animal population at times of the year when stubble grazing on the arable was not available. As SLICHER VAN BATH 22 points out, the mixed farming system of Europe (where much better grasslands were available) required that pastures and meadows occupy a land area between 50 and 75 per cent larger than the total areas of arable! Even then, European fields were often underfertilized. The Islamic cultivator clearly had available a much larger range of fertilizers and other materials for the improvement of the soil, and understood their properties better, than his counterpart in earlier times; see K. D. WHITE 125ff; *Geoponika* 60ff (bk II chs. 21ff), where night soil is also mentioned; and JEHUDA 93ff. On the role of animals in early Islamic agriculture, see also ch. 21 n. 6 above; since many animals were kept in stalls rather than grazed, all their manure could be collected.

26 AL-MAQRĪZĪ *Khiṭaṭ* I 182–3 and IBN MAMMĀTĪ 266, for example, state that land to be planted with sugar cane should be ploughed six or seven times, while IBN BAṢṢĀL 151 recommends up to ten ploughings – and manuring – before cotton is planted. See also IBN AL-ʿAWWĀM ed. Banqueri II 28. IBN MAMMĀTĪ 245–6 says that most land to be planted with summer crops should be ploughed two or three times. BRESC 69 states that the market gardens of Norman Sicily, which were probably still in the hands of Muslim cultivators, were ploughed four times before planting. IBN AL-ʿAWWĀM ed. Banqueri II 1ff, 6ff and IBN BAṢṢĀL 62–4 both speak of ploughing as substitute for manuring and sometimes preferable. All three authors, as well as IBN WAḤSHĪYA "Filāḥa" I 135 and 142, stress the importance of occasional ploughings which cut deep into the soil and turn it over (*qalīb*), instead of merely breaking up the surface soil as in normal Mediterranean and Middle Eastern ploughing. It appears that this operation was performed by a heavier type of plough. This may have been similar to the heavy or moldboard plough which was being diffused through the northern parts of medieval Europe. Such a plough would not have been suitable for the regular ploughing of arable land in most of the Mediterranean and the Middle East, but might have been appropriate for these infrequent, deeper ploughings. Another reference to a heavier type of plough is given in RABIE "Some technical" 64.

27 IBN AL-ʿAWWĀM ed. Banqueri II 11–15, where various rotations are given; this author explains that, contrary to ancient practice, wheat should not be grown in successive years on the same land but rather should be combined in rotations with barley and other crops. See also BOLENS *Les méthodes* 129–39, where the importance of legumes, turnips, *trimestre* wheat and catch crops is shown. Amongst the sequences found by Bolens in the manuscript of Abū al-Khair is the following: turnips, flax, broad beans, barley, wheat. How many years such a sequence required is not clear.

28 IBN WAḤSHĪYA "Filāḥa" I 127ff, where different recipes are proposed for earths which are categorized as saline, sweet, bitter, acid, foul, delicate, clayey, heavy, sharp and astringent. See also IBN AL-ʿAWWĀM ed. Banqueri I 69ff and II 5, where the treatment of saline soils is discussed.

29 Many recipes for improving the soil, for example, stressed growing certain crops which benefited the soil's structure or fertility. Sorghum, *trimestre* wheat, legumes, beets, sugar cane (!), rice, various grasses and many other crops were seen to be appropriate to the improvement of specific kinds of soils.

30 See ch. 1 n. 2 above.

31 IBN WAḤSHĪYA "Filāḥa" I 15 states that "there are some places which do not suit certain plants, owing to the blowing of the wind, the different natures of the soil and the kind of water". Much of his manual, and of the other Islamic manuals, is an elaboration of this point. On the types of soils identified by the ancients, see K. D. WHITE 97ff and *Geoponika* 49–52, 63–5 (bk II chs. 9–13, 23). BOLENS *Les méthodes* 66ff summarizes the types mentioned in the Islamic manuals and tries to identify these with the types known to the Romans. On the types of water, see FAHD "Un traité".

32 All the manuals discuss in many places the matching of crops with soil, water and climate; however, the discussion in IBN WAḤSHĪYA "Filāḥa" I 169ff is especially important.

33 IBN WAḤSHĪYA "Filāḥa" I 134–5. AL-BAKRĪ *Jughrāfīya* 80 found it growing on sandy lands in Galicia in Spain. Because of its suitability for marginal areas and its superior yields on good soils, sorghum often displaced millet, which, in some regions, was the principal grain of antiquity.

34 IBN MAMMĀTĪ 204; QUSṬŪS 21. RAWSKI 11 shows that the gazetteers of Ming China recommend rice cultivation as a means of reclaiming land from the sea and improving brackish land. Such lands must have been very common, especially in Lower Iraq and the Nile Delta. The manuals devote considerable space to the cure of saline soils. See IBN WAḤSHĪYA "Filāḥa" I 125–7, 131–2 and IBN AL-'AWWĀM ed. Banqueri I 69ff and II 5. The laws also gave much encouragement to the reclamation of swampland; see ABŪ YŪSUF 122–3 and QUDĀMA IBN JA'FAR 35. On the reclamation of land from the great swamps of Iraq, al-Baṭā'iḥ, see AL-BALĀDHURĪ I 454–6 and LAMMENS "Etudes" II 125ff, 131. For the early Islamic occupation of saline lands in Kuzistan and along the lower Tigris, see R. M. ADAMS "Agriculture" 118, 120. See also AL-IṢṬAKHRĪ 50, who explains that the tides made saline the irrigation water around Basra and yet the area (on account of new crops?) was densely settled and intensively cultivated. For Egyptian reclamation of land, see MÜLLER-WODARG (1954) 216–17.

35 IBN AL-'AWWĀM ed. Banqueri II 104.

36 IBN AL-'AWWĀM ed. Banqueri II 1ff, 7ff; IBN BAṢṢĀL 61–6; BOLENS *Les méthodes* 82.

37 IBN MAMMĀTĪ 221 implied that in areas where year-long irrigation was available summer crops might be grown after winter crops and income would thereby be doubled. He suggested that the construction of a retaining dam on the Alexandrian canal and the consequent provision of perennial irrigation on lands lying below the dam would achieve such an increase in income. IBN ḤAWQAL I 207 recounts how a landowner in Mesopotamia doubled the income of lands by providing more irrigation and shifting from fruit trees to cotton, rice, sesame and wheat.

38 Citrus trees, for instance, could be made to yield at three different times of the year, depending on the timing of irrigation.

39 The participation of rulers and high officials in the grain market did not, however, always help to stabilize prices. For information about their activities in fourteenth-century Egypt and Syria, see LAPIDUS *Muslim Cities* 51–5.

40 The large amounts of labour and the unpleasantness of the work associated with sugar-cane cultivation are well known. In Christian countries, such work has until recently almost always been done by non-European labourers, usually slaves. As is pointed out elsewhere in this volume, slaves do not seem to have been used in early Islamic agriculture. RAWSKI 13, 49 speaks of the great amount of labour required in Chinese rice cultivation and points out that yields can be increased "almost indefinitely" by the application of more labour.

24. *Agriculture in its context*

1 For the Negev, see REIFENBERG 56–7, 97 and EVEN-ARI *et al.* 26–7. In fact, settlement seems to have retreated from the eastern Negev in the sixth century, before the Islamic conquests. The western parts continued to be occupied, though perhaps not so densely, for some time after the Arab conquests. Various Arab raids may account for the decline of the eastern part in late Byzantine times, while the decline of the western part, which like the eastern part had probably been settled mainly to provision the frontier garrisons, may have been due to the disappearance of a political boundary and hence of the military encampments. The decay of Christian monasteries in the area may also account for some of the retreat of settlement. The evidence presented in REIFENBERG *passim* and ASHTOR *A Social* 51 for a decline of settlement in Palestine immediately after the Arab conquests is not satisfactory. In many cases it seems likely that the retreat had already occurred

in later Roman and Byzantine times; in other cases it did not occur until some centuries after the Arab conquest. Much more careful study of these settlements is needed, with particular attention to the dating of materials from the latest levels of occupation. Similarly, it used to be thought that the Arab conquests brought to an end the occupation of the region of the *villes mortes* near Aleppo. See, for instance, TCHALENKO I 431–8. However, it has been shown by SOURDEL-THOMINE *passim* that this area was occupied – and apparently prosperous – in Ayyūbid times, and that settlement ended only with the Mongol conquests! Whether there was any earlier break in occupation is not yet known.

2 In ʿAbbāsid times the frontier of settlement seems to have contracted in the Hijaz, in Transjordania and in eastern Syria. See LAMMENS *Le berceau* 181–2; GRABAR *passim*; SAUVAGET "Remarques"; GRABAR *et al.* I 158.

3 JUYNBOLL 122–4. SHABAN *Islamic* 12–14, 22–7 stresses that one of the great concerns of both Muḥammad and Abū Bakr was the reopening of certain trade routes in the Arabian peninsula. This required controlling nomadic tribes.

4 LAMMENS *Le berceau* 160ff, 175ff, 180–1; POLIAK "L'arabisation" 45–6; SOURDEL AND SOURDEL 271–90; SPULER *Iran* 386; AL-BALĀDHURĪ I 278, 282–3, 298; GRABAR *et al.* I 163. CAHEN "Nomades" gives evidence on the very limited scope of nomadism in the early Islamic world. Nomads were apparently unknown in Muslim Spain; in North Africa they did not appear until the eleventh century; and in Iran and Transoxania they occupied very limited desert regions.

5 See ch. 21 n. 27 above.

6 *Ibid.* and LAMMENS "Etudes" II 123.

7 BARTOL'D "Istoriia" 107–8, 130, 134, 147, 149, 187.

8 SPULER *Iran* 386–7.

9 LAPIDUS "Arab settlement", who shows that the available sources speak mainly of investment by the State in the irrigation of the hinterlands surrounding new cities in Iraq and al-Jazīra. See also GRABAR 14–18 and GRABAR *et al.* I 150–1, 155, 163. R. M. ADAMS "Agriculture" 109–10 shows that in Iraq there is no archeological evidence of any occupation of the lower Karun and Tigris rivers before late Sasanian or early Islamic times. He argues that the settlement of this region in fact took place in early Islamic times. On pp. 118, 120 he gives evidence of the occupation of saline lands in Khuzistan and in the marshy regions of the lower Tigris after the Arab conquest. There can be little doubt that some of the new crops such as sugar cane, which could be grown on salty soil, were a factor promoting settlement in areas of brackish swamplands and salt-encrusted soils. In the opinion of this writer, Adams dates the disappearance of settlement in these areas too early, but the question cannot be resolved without careful archeological work. On the reclamation of marshlands in Iraq, see DARKAZALLY 175ff.

10 LAMMENS *Le berceau* 94ff, 166ff and "Etudes" III 242–3; GRABAR 7ff, 14–18; SAUVAGET "Remarques" *passim*; AL-BALĀDHURĪ I 278, 282–3, 298; GRABAR *et al.* I 150–1, 155, 163. It is true that there are signs of pre-Islamic occupation at some of the sites discussed by Sauvaget and Grabar, but the colonization of these regions in early Islamic times seems to have been much more intensive. SAUVAGET *loc. cit.* argues that many of the "palaces" in the Syrian and Transjordanian desert, once thought to be Roman, Byzantine or Nabatean constructions, were in fact built in Umayyad times. These, he shows, were in their time not isolated "desert palaces", but rather constructions associated with settlements in villages and surrounded by irrigated fields. LAPIDUS "Evolution" 25 gives evidence for the establishment of new frontier settlements along the borders with Byzantium in Syria, Mesopotamia and Armenia, as well as on the Khazar border in Azerbaijan. For eastern Arabia, see WHITCOMB; MASRY 17; R. M. ADAMS, PARR *et al.* 28; and POTTS *et al.* 13ff.

11 VANACKER *passim*. Some idea of the Roman penetration into North Africa may be had from JONES map 5.

12 On the decline of North African agriculture from the eleventh century onwards, see ch. 25.

13 For the Roman penetration into Iberia, see SCHULTEN *Iberische*. Maps 1, 2, 4 and 6 in LAUTENSACH give an indication of the Arab penetration. See also BOLENS *Les méthodes* 8.

14 See R. M. ADAMS *Land* 84ff. On pp. 81–2 Adams states that the Sasanian and early Islamic settlements in the Diyala plains had "roughly comparable population density", while on p. 102 he concludes that the area under cultivation shrank from about 8,000 sq. km in late Sasanian times to about 6,000 sq. km in the mid-ninth century – in spite of considerable reconstruction of irrigation works in late Umayyad and early ʿAbbāsid times. It is of course very possible that the region of the Diyala plains was an exception. But Adams's conclusions are doubtful on a number of grounds. His inferences about the density of settlement in a given period are based almost entirely on very small samples of surface remains of shards. Whether the technique of surface sampling in fact reflects settlement density was not seriously tested; doubt is permitted. The validity of this technique was tested at an Anatolian site by REDMAN AND WATSON, who conclude cautiously that it is "a useful technique for determining where to dig" and that it may produce "testable hypotheses relevant to the total interpretation of the site". Adams's conclusions are also of uncertain value owing to the very great difficulty – if not the impossibility at present – of distinguishing the rural pottery of late Sasanian, Umayyad and early ʿAbbāsid times. He seems to have assigned many shards which could have been early Islamic to the late Sasanian period in order, perhaps, to conform to some preconceived notions about the trends in settlement in the area. Adams does attempt to support his archeological conclusions with literary references which show a decline in taxation revenue for the whole of the Sawād from Sasanian to ʿAbbāsid times; but the figures he cites are not always reliable and do not take account of changes in the rate of taxation (which was almost certainly lower), in the efficiency of collection and remittance, and in the weight, purity and purchasing power of the coins in which the accounts were reckoned. (On the inefficient collection of the *kharāj*, which was diverted into the pockets of the tax collectors, governors and ministers, see TUMA 6–7ff.) In any case, if Adams's conclusions for the Diyala plains are correct, this region could not have been typical. As Adams states on p. 99, "the greatest degree of urbanization prior to modern times [i.e. the rise of Baghdad and Sāmarra] came not as a concomitant of the greatest intensity of land usage but as a sequel to a decline in provincial settlement, irrigation and agricultural production" in the Diyala plains. This pattern could hardly have been general in the Sawād as a whole, and more particularly in the hinterlands of these two great cities; otherwise the populations of these two cities, each of which covered an area at least ten times as great as Ctesiphon, could not have been fed.

15 HOLT 873.

16 AL-MAQQARĪ tr. Gayangos I 84–5, 87. This author also gives a quotation from Ibn Saʿīd, who stated that al-Andalus was so thickly populated that the traveller would find at every step on his road farmsteads, hamlets and villages; in many parts the large cities and populous villages nearly touched one another.

17 TORRES BALBÁS "Las ruinas" 275ff.

18 IBN ḤAWQAL I 80.

19 SOLIGNAC *Recherches* 382; VONDERHEYDEN 241. AL-MUQADDASĪ *Description* 22–3 stated that he knew no region which had more agglomerations of settlement than Ifrīqiya.

20 SUSA *Irrigation* 30; see also AL-IṢṬAKHRĪ 53, where it is stated that between Baghdad and Kufa the land was thickly settled and criss-crossed with irrigation canals.

21 For the Jordan valley, see IBRAHIM *et al.* 63 and HAMARNEH. For eastern Arabia, see R. M. ADAMS, PARR *et al.* 28; POTTS *et al.* 13ff; WHITCOMB *passim*; and MASRY 17.

22 CHEVALIER "Le rôle joué"; PORTÈRES "Berceaux"; HAVINDEN 539–40. The extension of agriculture into forested regions south of the African savanna was dependent on crops such as colocasia, sugar cane, bananas, plantains, citrus trees and the Asian yam.

23 *Papyrus* 152; LAPIDUS "The conversion" 251, who cites Abū Ṣāliḥ; BERCHER *et al.*

24 SUSA *Irrigation* 32.
25 GLICK *Irrigation* 119ff, 240ff.
26 Amongst the new foundations were Baghdad, Basra, Kufa, Wāsiṭ, Sāmarra, al-Fusṭāṭ, Qairawān, al-Mahdīya, Fez and Marrakesh. There seems to be no good account of the rise of new Islamic cities, but see LAPIDUS "Evolution".
27 This argument assumes (*a*) that the per capita consumption of food by urban dwellers and the agricultural labour force did not fall; and (*b*) that the rural dwellers who were not part of the agricultural labour force did not decrease in proportion to the total labour force and that their per capita food consumption did not fall. There seems to be no evidence that these assumptions are unrealistic for the early centuries of Islam.
28 See ch. 19 of this book.
29 Thus RUSSELL *Late Ancient* and "The population" goes to great lengths to cut the population of early Islamic towns and countryside down to what he deems suitable sizes: by assuming that figures for cities must refer to whole provinces; by using very low multipliers for the size of households or the number of inhabitants per hectare; by supposing that the population of metropoles was a constant proportion of the population of the hinterland; by concluding in one case that accounts of tax returns which speak of dinars must have meant dirhems; by assuming that the population of Islamic towns in the Middle Ages was not much different from that of the nineteenth century; etc. Such tactics do much violence to the evidence. On the inadequacy of Russell's method, see DOLS *The Black Death* 196, 198, 202. In the same vein, TORRES BALBÁS "Extensión" has produced very low estimates for the cities of al-Andalus, basing his calculations on the area enclosed by city walls; this approach can produce acceptable results only if reasonable estimates can be made of the density of population within the city walls and if account is taken of the proportion of total population which lived outside the walls. About the proper multiplier to use, i.e. the number of inhabitants per hectare, there can be much dispute. On the one hand, many cities had extremely densely settled areas: IBN ḤAWQAL I 144 tells that the houses in al-Fusṭāṭ (Old Cairo) were five to seven storeys high and might contain as many as 200 people, while in the following century NĀṢIR-I KHUSRAW 146 says that the houses of the city could have up to fourteen storeys. On the other hand, many cities had parks and other open spaces within their walls, and as time went on some cities had abandoned areas. Very conservative estimates, based on the size of the principal mosque, are given for the towns of the eastern Maghrib in LÉZINE 32ff. As the estimates of these three authors all seem excessively low, they are given from here on only when other estimates are available for comparison.
30 ROZMAN 278 states that over the last two millennia, five Chinese cities have had populations of over a million, while many other cities were very large. GERNET 29 estimates that the population of Hangchow from the mid twelfth to the mid thirteenth century was about 500,000, and that at the end of the thirteenth century it was about 900,000. MOTE 39 estimates the population of Soochow in 1229 at 300,000; on pp. 36ff this author argues that urbanization in China occurred along lines that were very different from those of Europe and hence Chinese cities could be much larger. Many of the points he makes seem to apply equally well to Islamic urbanization. However, it should be noted that some cities in the ancient world were also large. Rome, Antioch and Alexandria at their peaks may all have had as many as 500,000 inhabitants. RUSSELL *Late Ancient* 65ff estimates that Rome had about 172,000 inhabitants in the mid fourth century and Alexandria between 121,000 and 215,000 in the late fourth or early fifth century. Russell's figures, as we have pointed out in the preceding note, tend to be much too low, and they pertain to a time when the size of these cities was probably much reduced.
31 Muslim town dwellers were not taxed as such, though merchants and artisans might pay taxes on sales. DENNETT 110–11 and others have described the flight of certain rural populations to the cities in order to escape taxes.
32 *Twentieth-Century Encyclopedia* (in Arabic; *voce* "Baghdād"); LEVI DELLA VIDA 848;

AL-DŪRĪ "Baghdad" 899; HERZFELD 137; LASSNER *The Topography* 282–3 n. 3. RUSSELL *Late Ancient* 89 estimates 300,000; but see R. M. ADAMS *Land* 180 n. 27.

33 HERZFELD 137.

34 CLERGET 126, 238–9; ABU-LUGHOD 37; DOLS *The Black Death* 198–202. These figures do not seem out of keeping with Volney's estimate of 250,000 in the late eighteenth century, nor the estimate of 263,700 made by the Napoleonic expedition at the beginning of the nineteenth century, since by then the population of the city had fallen off considerably as a result of two centuries of plague; see RAYMOND "Les grandes" 209–10 and "Signes". Nor do they seem out of line with information from other sources which speak (perhaps with some exaggeration) of 400,000 soldiers who were billeted in the city in the tenth century, of 100,000 houses in the quarter of al-Qaṭā'i' alone, of 50,000 donkeys to transport wares to and from the markets in the quarter of al-Fusṭāṭ, etc.

35 NĀṢIR-I KHUSRAW 112; on the size and industrial activity of Tinnis, see LOMBARD 161–2.

36 ZIADEH *Life* 97 and *Damascus* 60; DOLS *The Black Death* 195–6, 203–4. RUSSELL *Late Ancient* 101 estimates the population at 15,000 at the time of the Crusades; but see ELISSÉEF III 823–4, who shows that this figure is much too low. It is interesting to note that the fourteenth-century Italian traveller Gucci claims that the city and its suburbs had three times the population of Florence; see *Visit* 143.

37 ZIADEH *Urban* 97. SAUVAGET *Alep* I X, 238 gives estimates for early modern times between 250,000 and 300,000, though the Ottoman census of 1519 counted only 67,344 people. (RUSSELL *Late Ancient* 101 estimates 14,000 at the time of the Crusades!)

38 RUSSELL *Late Ancient* 89, who, however, assigns the overwhelming part of this population to the districts, leaving the city of Hims (on p. 101) only 7,000 inhabitants.

39 MASSIGNON "Explication" 345. PELLAT *Le milieu* 6, however, thinks this estimate too high as it would imply a population of 600,000 for Basra.

40 PELLAT *Le milieu* 5–6 and "Baṣra" 1086; LAPIDUS "Evolution" 26.

41 LAMBTON "Iṣfahān".

42 BULLIET 9–10; see also PETRUSHEVSKII "The socio-economic" 485, who cites enormous (and obviously exaggerated) figures for the massacres at the time of the Mongol conquests: 747,000 at Nishapur, 700,000 or 1,300,000 at Marv and 1,600,000 at Herat.

43 LÉVI-PROVENÇAL *Histoire* III 362–3. The archeologists now excavating parts of the city suggest that the population was as much as a million on account of the very great area covered by the Muslim city, which Lévi-Provençal in his second volume says was about eight times the size of the modern city. A figure of 1,000,000 would accord well with the figures given by various authors, most of them conservative and fairly reliable, cited by AL-MAQQARĪ tr. Gayangos I 214–15: 200,077 houses for the common people and 60,300 for the more important elements; or 113,000 houses for the common people and half that number for the rich; or even 300,000 houses. RUSSELL *Late Ancient* 92 gives Cordova a population of 90,000.

44 FITZGERALD 410.

45 TALBI "Al-Ḳayrawān" 829.

46 Carthage was a settlement of little importance by the sixth century, and its abandonment after the Islamic conquests cannot have released significant numbers of people to settle in other centres. Antioch and Alexandria by no means disappeared; on the contrary, they continued as important cities, though relatively – and perhaps absolutely – they were diminished. IBN JUBAIR I 44, who visited Alexandria in the twelfth century, stated that it had more mosques than any other Islamic city. In the fourteenth century, after the Black Death, the Italian traveller Frescobaldi estimated that the city had a population of 60,000 and that it was twice as large as Damanhur but only half the size of Damietta; see *Visit* 39, 43. The Jewish traveller Meshullam Ben R. Menahem of Volterra stated that at the end of the fifteenth century Alexandria was as big as Florence; see *Jewish Travellers* 159. LABIB "Al-Iskandariyya" estimates its population at 65,000 in the thirteenth century. Antioch also continued to be an important city. According to RUSSELL *Late Ancient* 101,

its population was three times as great as that of Damascus at the time of the Crusades (or about 40,000, as Russell estimates, though as has been pointed out above Russell grossly underestimates the population of Damascus). The abandonment of Ctesiphon was perhaps not of great importance demographically; as R. M. ADAMS *Land* 96, 98 points out, both Baghdad and Sāmarra covered about ten times the area of Ctesiphon. Seleucia was also small in comparison to the great ʿAbbāsid capitals.

47 AL-MAQQARĪ tr. Gayangos I 87, who cites an anonymous author. About the actual size of other cities in Muslim Spain, little concrete information is available. BURNS *Islam* 72ff discusses the seemingly insurmountable difficulties in the way of making a reasonable estimate of Valencia's population after its reconquest. The figures proposed by TORRES BALBÁS "Extensión", as we have pointed out above, all seem manifestly too low.

48 CAHEN "Le service" 142–3. IBN ḤAWQAL I 422 stated that the superintendent of irrigation in Marv had under him more than 10,000 workers and was a more important functionary than the Prefect of Police.

49 On various milling operations in Spain, and on the new types of mills that may have been introduced to Spain in Islamic times, see LAUTENSACH 81. CASANOVA 155 shows that there was a street for rice millers in Cairo.

50 On the heavy investment in sugar refining, see BERTHIER I 129ff; BENVENISTI 253–6; GOITEIN *A Mediterranean* I 81, 126 and "Artisans" 864; LABIB *Handelsgeschichte* 319–20, 421–3; and LAPIDUS *Muslim* 58. Special sections of Cairo and Damascus (and no doubt many other cities) were set aside for sugar refineries; see IBN AL-ʿASĀKIR 268, 269, 280 and CASANOVA 111–12, 233–4. GOITEIN "Changes" 29 states that in Ayyūbid and Mamlūk times "sugar factories simply dominated the landscape of Fusṭāṭ". In the same period there was much cultivation and milling of sugar cane in the Jordan valley, and settlement appears to have been extremely dense; see IBRAHIM *et al.* 63 and HAMARNEH. On the cotton industry, see LOMBARD 66, 151ff.

51 On the development of cotton-using industries, see A. M. WATSON "The rise".

52 The close dependence of a town on its hinterland is made clear in BULLIET 11–12. About the degree of monetization of the rural economy, there has been some dispute. See LØKKEGAARD 103ff; HINDS 23; and ASHTOR "Essai" 65–6. IBN MAMMĀTĪ 257ff shows that in Egypt all taxes were paid in money except those on wheat, barley and faba beans, and that even the landowners' share of the latter crops might be sold. This evidence speaks of a deep penetration of the money economy into the countryside. For the practice in the Fayyūm, see CAHEN "Le régime des impôts" 14–15. See also n. 55 below.

53 HEYD II 611ff, 684ff; SCHAUBE 161, 162, 164, 197, 214; MAZZAOUI "The cotton" 266; LABIB *Handelsgeschichte* 101, 311–12, 320; DUFOURCQ 543; BALDUCCI PEGOLOTTI *passim*.

54 On the class of intermediaries dealing in cotton in Cairo, see LABIB *Handelsgeschichte* 183, 312. CASANOVA 275, 339 shows that special quarters of Cairo were reserved for rice merchants and cotton merchants. Baghdad had a special wharf for cotton merchants and a special market for the trading of cotton; see LE STRANGE *Baghdad* 84, 181, 265.

55 The degree to which early Islamic cities were parasites on the countryside is still problematic. However, nearly all industry, other than usufacture and the processing of some agricultural products, seems to have been located in the cities, and there must therefore have been some flow of urban industrial goods into the countryside. R. M. ADAMS *Land* 100, 101 and CAHEN "Le régime" 14–15 show that in the Diyala plains (*c.* 844) and the Fayyūm (*c.* 1244) by far the greater part of taxes was paid in kind; taxes in cash were levied mainly on specialty crops such as cotton, sugar cane and indigo. Rents, too, were probably normally paid in kind, especially on sharecropping leases, which were the most common form of lease. Thus the payment of taxes and rents would not seem to have deprived the peasantry of all cash income; they might be expected to have some cash left to pay for urban goods and services.

25. Agriculture in retreat

1 For the consequences of the Black Death in the Islamic world, see DOLS *The Black Death* and "The general mortality"; WIET "La grande peste"; and NEUSTADT. DOLS *The Black Death* 218 suggests that the population of Egypt may have declined by about one-quarter or one-third in the first outbreak. He also points out that in Egypt and Syria there was little tendency for population losses to be recovered. The effect of such drastic population losses on agriculture is obvious: lands, especially those which were marginal, would be abandoned or possibly turned over to grazing, and elsewhere cultivation would become less intensive. See DOLS *The Black Death* 154ff.

2 For Egypt, see ASHTOR AND CAHEN and DARRAG; for Tunisia, BRUNSCHVIG *La Berbérie* and SOLIGNAC "Travaux"; for the Ottoman empire, INALCIK 46–7, who estimates that during the sixteenth century Ottoman population increased by 40 per cent in rural areas and 80 per cent in the towns. HÜTTEROTH AND ABDULFATAH 55–7 give clear evidence of a great decline in population in the Levant from the seventeenth to the nineteenth century.

3 JEHUDA 36–7. The problem of salinity of the soil in Mesopotamia is discussed in JACOBSEN AND ADAMS 1252 and R. M. ADAMS *Land* 18, 48, 99. BOLENS *Les méthodes* 134 shows that medieval techniques of maintaining soil fertility and structure were no longer practised in nineteenth-century Algeria.

4 LAMMENS *Le berceau* 169–70, 181; GRABAR; SAUVAGET "Remarques" *passim.*

5 It is perhaps natural that agriculture should have been invented in such regions, since the soil can be tilled with little effort and, if irrigated, can be very productive. In contrast, the great plains of northern Europe, which had more potential, needed to be cleared and once cleared were more difficult to plough effectively because of the heavy clay soils.

6 SPULER *Iran* 464; LØKKEGAARD 94–100; AL-DŪRĪ "The origins" 13–14; AMEDROZ 824; CAHEN "L'évolution" 29.

7 ABŪ YŪSUF 105ff; QUDĀMA 74–6.

8 LØKKEGAARD 67–70; AL-DŪRĪ "The origins" 5, 9, 14, 17; CAHEN "L'évolution" 31–4; LAMBTON *Landlord* 25–6. MORONY points out that the *taljiʿa*, or a form of it, was known in seventh-century Iraq, where some *dahāqīn* saved their lands by placing them under the protection of powerful Muslims.

9 CAHEN "Réflexions" *passim*; MORONY 14; LØKKEGAARD 53; HEYWORTH-DUNNE 19; LAMBTON *Landlord* 27–8.

10 HÜTTEROTH AND ABDULFATAH map 4 show that the revenues of *waqf* land were often sent to distant beneficiaries whose sources of income were often widely scattered.

11 *Ibid.* map 4.

12 HEFFENING; EL-SAMARRAIE 43–4; CAHEN *loc. cit.*; LAMBTON *loc. cit.*; GOITEIN "Changes" 29–30.

13 Although the agricultural history of the Islamic world under its new conquerors is largely unwritten, some works are useful. For the effects of the Banū Hilāl invasion, which TALBI "Law" 222ff points out was preceded by a series of devastating famines beginning in 1004, see also AL-IDRĪSĪ *Description* 40, 41 *et passim*; IBN KHALDŪN *Histoire* I 46 *et passim*; MARÇAIS *La Berbérie* 193–228; PONCET; PLANHOL 134–62; and IDRIS 206ff. The consequences of the Saljūq conquests are touched upon in R. M. ADAMS *Land* 87–8; PLANHOL 220ff; CAHEN *La Syrie* 472ff and "L'évolution" 38ff; LAMBTON *Landlord* 53ff; and BOSWORTH "Barbarian" 9ff. For the Mongols, see PETRUSHEVSKII *Zemledelle*, "The socio-economic" 484ff and "L'état"; ALI-ZADE; R. M. ADAMS *Land* 106ff; BARTOL'D *Turkestan* and *Histoire* 141ff; SOURDEL-THOMINE 200; LAMBTON "Aspects", "Reflections on the role" 298ff and *Landlord* 77ff; and PLANHOL 210ff. The general decline of agriculture in Khuzistan and Iraq is discussed in R. M. ADAMS "Agriculture" 120ff and *Land* 84ff; SUSA *Fayaḍānāt* II *passim*; AL-DŪRĪ *Taʾrīkh* 13ff; and CAHEN "Notes croisades" 308–9. As we have argued elsewhere, and as other works seem to confirm, Adams seems to have placed too early a date on the beginning of ʿAbbāsid agricultural decline. See also IBN ḤAWQAL I 205ff. On the general spread of nomadism, see CAHEN "Nomades" 97ff and PLANHOL *passim.*

AYALON 92, 94, 95, 99, 100 shows that nomadic tribes were settled in many parts of Syria in Mamlūk times, presumably with adverse effects on agriculture. DEERR I 72 points out that the plantations of sugar cane in Persia appear to have been lost after the Mongol conquests; sugar cane was replanted there only in the sixteenth century.

14 CAHEN "Iḳṭāʿ" 1088 and "L'évolution" 28–30; LØKKEGAARD 62, 189–90; QUDĀMA 36; LAMBTON *Landlord* 26–7.

15 See CAHEN "Iḳṭāʿ" and "L'évolution"; LAMBTON "Reflections...iqṭāʿ" and *Landlord* 28–30, 53ff; AL-DŪRĪ "The origins" 12ff and *Ta'rīkh* 5ff; RABIE "The size" and *The Financial*; LØKKEGAARD 14ff; and CHALMETA GENDRÓN *passim*. It should be noted that the meaning of the term *iqṭāʿ* changed over time. As was stated in ch. 21, the term during the early centuries of Islam meant simply the concession of the rights of ownership. See CAHEN "L'évolution" 26ff; MORONY *passim*; LAPIDUS "Arab"; AL-DŪRĪ "The origins" 3ff; YAḤYĀ 62–3; and QUDĀMA 34–6.

16 RABIE *The Financial*, following a text of al-Maqrīzī, states that all of the land of Egypt was held in *iqṭāʿ* by the time of Saladin, but CAHEN "Iḳṭāʿ" 1090 suggests that the State kept direct control of more than half of the land in Egypt. On the increasing pervasiveness of the *iqṭāʿ*, see CAHEN "L'évolution" *passim*.

17 The Egyptian case is described in CAHEN "L'évolution" 37–8, 45ff and "Iḳṭāʿ" 1089–90; RABIE "The size" and *The Financial*; COOPER; and ASHTOR AND CAHEN. It seems that in Egypt the holders of *iqṭāʿāt* could not exceed the levels of taxation prescribed by the central government, and much of what was collected had to be turned over to the government. These differences may well account for the periodic prosperity of Egyptian agriculture from the eleventh century onwards, when the agriculture of most other regions was in full decline.

18 CAHEN "L'évolution" *passim*; FORAND 34, who, in the view of this writer, dates much too early the appearance of *adscriptio glebae*.

19 It should be noted that the deterioration of Levantine agriculture pre-dates the arrival of the Crusaders, some decline having taken place under Saljūq rule. See n. 9 above.

20 In the coastal strip of the Holy Land, in Cyprus and perhaps for a brief time in the Jordan valley, intensive agriculture on the Islamic model persisted under the Christian conquerors. See CAHEN "Notes...croisades" 287, 293; DEERR I 84–6; BRAUDEL I 122–5; BALDUCCI PEGOLOTTI 77ff; HEYD *passim*; SCHAUBE *passim*; and RICHARD 340–2, 346–7. Indeed, the growing market in Europe for exotic products, particularly cotton and sugar, may actually have stimulated the spread of certain new crops in these regions and fostered a more intensive land use. These exceptions may be instructive. Although nothing is known about the landholding arrangements which permitted the survival and perhaps spread of such crops, it seems almost certain that in all these regions the care of these crops was left in the hands of Muslim workers or converts to Christianity, who alone had the necessary skills. Most of them seem to have become serfs or slaves, and Muslim slaves were added from time to time to the labour force. An incident which occurred in the early fifteenth century is very revealing. Between the years 1400 and 1415, about 1,500 slaves were captured by Cypriots from the sultan of Egypt; the king of Cyprus refused to return these on the grounds that they were essential for the cultivation of sugar cane. Christian peasants, in Cyprus as elsewhere, were seemingly unable or unwilling to perform this laborious work, which free peasants performed in the Muslim world; sugar cane, it seems, was cultivated in the Christian world only where slaves or Muslim serfs were available. See PRAWER "Etude" (1953) 165; RICHARD 351–2; *Documents chypriotes* 137.

21 PRAWER *Histoire* I 507 and "Etude" (1952) 31ff; PERI I 40–1; CICCAGLIONE 332, 340, 343–4; BURNS *Islam* 37ff, 334; GLICK AND PI-SUNYER 151; GLICK *Irrigation* 231ff, who points out that in the kingdom of Valencia the Muslims who remained were mainly in mountainous regions where grazing and non-intensive agriculture were practised. In Sicily, too, the Muslims gradually became concentrated largely in mountainous regions.

22 On the lack of demesne, see CAHEN "Notes...croisades" 297; RILEY-SMITH 45–6; PRAWER *Histoire* I 466, 519 and "Etude" (1952) 40 and (1953) 165, in the latter of which it is

pointed out that a kind of *réserve* could be found around Tyre on which specialty crops, but no cereals, were grown. Since demesnes were generally absent, labour services tended to be light, if they existed at all. None the less, the status of the conquered peasants continually worsened as they were reduced to a kind of serfdom and made liable to heavier payments. See PRAWER *Histoire* I 506ff; CAHEN "Notes...croisades" 298ff; CICCAGLIONI 328–9, 344; IBN JUBAIR I 33 and II 353 and CHALANDON II 500.

23 On the formation of large manors, which sometimes incorporated smaller ownerships, see PRAWER *Histoire* I 506ff; CAHEN "Notes...croisades" 290ff; CICCAGLIONE 329; GUILLOU 166–7; FONTAVELLA GONZÁLEZ 100; ROMANO 195–6; DOUGLAS 178; CHALANDON II 493ff, 510ff and BURNS *Islam* 105, who points out that in the irrigated area around the city of Valencia the units remained relatively small. In other *huertas* on the Spanish coastland, where the irrigation communities were to a large extent self-governing, relatively small ownerships may also have been able to resist with some success the more general trend towards the feudalization of the land and its cultivators, and the domination of the large estates.

24 On biennial cropping in the Holy Land, see CAHEN "Notes...croisades" 287, 297 and PRAWER "Etude" (1952) 43ff. GLICK *Irrigation* 29–30 points out that even on irrigated land in the Valencian Huerta it is doubtful that multiple cropping was practised by the Christians.

25 Of course, cereals and pulses had also been the principal crops even in the Golden Age of Islamic farming. The change is one of degree, not of absolutes. GLICK *Irrigation* 27 shows that even on irrigated land around Valencia the Christians grew almost exclusively cereals and pulses, the exceptions being some sour oranges and rice. See also CAHEN "Notes...croisades" 293, where it is mentioned that the Crusaders also cultivated vines extensively and some rice; RILEY-SMITH 46–7, who argues that Crusader villages produced mainly subsistence crops; PRAWER "Etude" (1952) 42–3, who points out that even on the coastal plain around Tyre cereals were the principal crops; and DUBLER *Über* 67. CASEY 34, 36ff, in discussing the general decline of the Huerta de Valencia after the expulsion of the Moriscos, points out that the Christians reoriented the agriculture of the region away from sugar cane and rice towards mulberry trees and vines, which required less labour. On the appearance of large-scale grazing in frontier lands, see BISHKO; and on the appearance of what seems to be waste land or abandoned land, see CAHEN "Notes...croisades" 294; PRAWER "Etude" (1952) 31ff; and PERI II 218–19. RICHARD 337–8 argues that, in spite of the export of considerable quantities of sugar and cotton from Cyprus, cultivated land there was used principally for the growing of grains and pulses; he suggests that the role of this island as a "colonial economy" has been exaggerated.

26 As ASHTOR "Levantine" and DEERR I 193–4 point out, the decline of sugar-cane cultivation and of the sugar industry in Egypt and the Levant dates from the beginning of the fifteenth century. This was probably due to the increase of sugar production in Sicily, Cyprus and Spain during the fifteenth century. See TRASSELLI "Produzione" and "Sumário"; GAMBI 12ff; DEERR I 84–6; and FONTAVELLA GONZÁLEZ 127–8. By the end of the fifteenth century, however, sugar cultivation had largely moved to the islands of the eastern Atlantic. See *Documentos sobre* III 116; EANES DE ZURARA 48, 57; FERNANDES 115, 141; MAUNY "Notes" 695ff; MAGALHÃES GODINHO 337, 342; BRAUDEL I 141–2; OLIVEIRA MARQUES 250; and MASEFIELD 276ff. It should be noted that the Portuguese had also introduced sour oranges, lemons and rice to these islands and probably to parts of the coast of West Africa; but it is not clear whether these introductions had any significant effect on the Mediterranean. See PACHECO PEREIRA 157; FERNANDES 127, 129, 135, 155; CHEVALIER "L'acclimatation" 660, 667–72; and OLIVEIRA MARQUES 255.

27 WEE I 306; ASHTOR "Levantine"; DEERR I 86; MASEFIELD 287–9.

28 TÄCKHOLM, TÄCKHOLM AND DRAR I 500–4 show that in the fifteenth century sugar was being imported into Egypt from Madeira, while by the seventeenth century Egypt was receiving her sugar from India. See also GAMBI 13–17 and DEERR I *passim*.

29 The longer-stapled cottons of the New World, *Gossypium barbadense* L. and *Gossypium hirsutum* L., tended to replace the Old World cottons, while *Musa nana* and Tahitian sugar cane tended to replace the types of bananas and sugar cane that had been diffused through the medieval Islamic world. On sugar cane, see BLUME and the notes to the map on sugar cane in BERTIN, HÉMARDINQUER *et al.*

30 See GAMBI 13–17, 30; MASEFIELD 288ff; TRASSELLI "Produzione" and "Sumário"; MARTÍNEZ RUIZ 273; VUILLET *passim*; CRINO "Importanza"; MARÇAIS *La Berbérie* 178; ALPINO II 38; LAUTENSACH 160; BLUME 20; and CASEY 34, 36ff. HÜTTEROTH AND ABDULFATAH 83–5 and map 5 show no evidence of sugar-cane cultivation in the Levant in the late sixteenth century; some rice was still grown around Lake Tiberias and on the shores of the Jordan and Yarmuk rivers, and cotton was common in many localities. In *Description de l'Egypte... Etat moderne* II i 521 and 547 it is stated that at the beginning of the nineteenth century rice was cultivated in Egypt only in the northern part of the Delta, while sugar cane was grown only in the province of Girgeh. One exception to the general pattern seems to be rice, the cultivation of which spread through parts of northern Italy and southern France in the late fifteenth and sixteenth centuries; see TARGIONI-TOZZETTI 24–6; NICCOLI 190; and GEORLETTE.

31 SCHWEINFURTH "Was Afrika"; MASEFIELD *passim*.

Works cited

Anonymous works and collections are listed in alphabetical order by title.

Primary sources

'Abd al-Laṭīf al-Baghdādī (1162–1231). *The Eastern Key. Kitāb al-ifāda wa'l-i 'tibār*, ed. and tr. K. H. Zand, J. A. Videau and I. E. Videau. London, 1965.

Relation de l'Egypte par Abd-allatif, médecin arabe de Bagdad, tr. S. de Sacy. Paris, 1810.

Abū al-Fidā (1273–1331). *Géographie d'Aboulféda*, ed. and tr. M. Reinaud. 3 vols. Paris, 1840–83.

Abū Ḥamid al-Gharnāṭī (1080–1169/70). *Abū Ḥamid el Granadino y su relación de viaje por tierras eurasiáticas*, ed. and tr. C. E. Dubler. Madrid, 1953.

Abū Ḥanīfa al-Dīnawarī (d. 895). *The Book of Plants of Abū Ḥanīfa ad-Dīnawarī. Parts of the Alphabetical Section*, ed. B. Lewin. Uppsala Universitets Årsskrift x. Uppsala, 1953.

Le dictionnaire botanique d'Abū Ḥanīfa ad-Dīnawarī, ed. M. Hamidullah. Cairo, 1973.

Abū al-Khair (fl. 11th c.?). "Kitāb al-filāḥa". Ms. 4764 fols. 61–180, Bibliothèque Nationale, Paris.

Kitāb al-filāḥa ou le Livre de la Culture, part. tr. A. Cherbonneau. Bibliothèque arabe–française v. Algiers, 1946.

Abū al-Walīd (= al-Ḥimyarī, 1308–69). *Al-badī' fī waçf ar-rabī'*, ed. H. Pérès. Rabat, 1940.

Abū Yūsuf (731?–798). *Taxation in Islam II: Abū Yūsuf's Kitāb al-Kharāj*, ed. and tr. A. Ben Shemesh. Leyden/London, 1969.

Abū Zaid al-Ḥasan al-Sīrāfī (wrote *c.* 916). "Informations sur la Chine et l'Inde", in *Voyage du marchand arabe Sulaymān en Inde et en Chine*, tr. G. Ferrand. Paris, 1922. 77–140.

Aëtios of Amida (fl. 6th c.?). *Libri medicinales I–VIII*, ed. A. Olivieri. 2 vols. Leipzig, 1935–50.

[Anon. (wrote 851)] *Akhbār al-ṣīn wal-hind. Relation de la Chine et de l'Inde*, ed. and tr. J. Sauvaget. Paris, 1948.

Alpino, Prosper (1553–1617). *De plantis Aegypti liber*. 2 vols. Leyden, 1735.

Annals of Sennacherib, The, ed. D. D. Luckenbill. Chicago, 1924.

pseudo-Apicius (compiled 4th or 5th c.). *De re coquinaria*, ed. M. E. Milham. Leipzig, 1969.

[Coll.] *Arabic Papyri in the Egyptian Library*, ed. A. Grohmann. 6 vols. Cairo, 1934–62.

Arnold of Vilanova (d. 1313?). *Obres catalanes II. Escrits mèdics.* Barcelona, 1947.

'Arrām ibn al-Aṣbagh (wrote *c.* 845). "Kitāb asmā' jibāl al-Tihāma wa makāniha", in *Nawādir al-makhṭūṭāt*. Cairo, 1954. V 388–421.
Arrian (96 – *c.* 180). *History of Alexander and Indica*, ed. and tr. E. I. Robson. 2 vols. London/Cambridge, Mass., 1946–7.
al-Aṣma'ī (d. 828?). *Kitāb al-nabāt*, ed. A. Y. al-Ghanim. Cairo, 1972.
[Coll.] *Assyrian Royal Inscriptions*, pt 2, ed. A. K. Grayson. Wiesbaden, 1976.
Babylonian Talmud, The (compiled 3rd–5th c.), ed. and tr. I. Epstein. 34 vols. London, 1935–48.
al-Badrī, Tāqī al-Dīn (fl. 15th c.). *Nuzhat al-anām fī maḥāsin al-Sha'm*. Baghdad, 1922.
al-Bakrī (d. 1094). *Description de l'Afrique septentrionale*, ed. and tr. MacGuckin de Slane. Algiers, 1913.
Jughrāfīyat al-Andalus wa Ūrūbā, ed. 'Abd al-Raḥmān 'Alī al-Ḥajjī. Beirut, 1968.
al-Balādhurī (d. 892). *The Origins of the Islamic State*, tr. P. K. Hitti and F. C. Murgotten. 2 vols. New York, 1916–24.
Balducci Pegolotti, F. (fl. 1310–47). *La pratica della mercatura*, ed. A. Evans. Cambridge, Mass., 1936.
al-Barqī, Abū Ja'far Aḥmad ibn Khālid (d. 887). *Kitāb al-mahāṣin*. Al-Najaf, 1974.
[Coll.] *Biblioteca arabo-sicula*, ed. M. Amari. Leipzig, 1857.
al-Bīrūnī (973–1050?). *Alberuni's India*, tr. E. Sachau. 2 vols. London, 1910.
al-Bukhārī, Muḥammad ibn Ismā'īl (810–70). *Les traditions islamiques*, tr. O. Houdas and W. Marçais. 4 vols. Paris, 1903–14.
[Coll.] *Byzantinische Quellen zur Länder- und Völkerkunde*, ed. K. Dietrich. 2 vols. Leipzig, 1912.
Ca da Mosto, A. (d. 1483). *The Voyages of Cadamosto*, tr. G. R. Crone. Hakluyt Society Works, 2nd ser., LXXX (1937).
[Anon. (wrote 961)] *Le calendrier de Cordoue*, ed. and tr. C. Pellat. Leyden, 1961.
Celsus, Aulus Cornelius (fl. 1st c.). *De medicina*, ed. and tr. W. G. Spencer. 3 vols. London, 1948–53.
Chau Ju-Kua (wrote 1225). *His Work on the Chinese and Arab Trade in the Twelfth and Thirteenth Centuries, entitled "Chu-fan-chï"*, ed. and tr. F. Hirth and W. W. Rockhill. Amsterdam, 1966.
[Coll.] *Colección diplomática de Jaime I, el Conquistador*, ed. A. Huici. Valencia, 1919.
Columella (fl. 1st c.). *De re rustica*, ed. and tr. H. B. Ash. 3 vols. London/Cambridge, Mass., 1941–55.
Cosmas Idicopleustis (fl. 6th c.). *The Christian Topography of Cosmas, an Egyptian Monk*, tr. J. W. McCrindle. London, 1897.
The Christian Topography of Cosmas Indicopleustis, ed. E. O. Winstedt. Cambridge, 1909.
Crescentiis, Petrus de (1230–1321). *Liber ruralium commodorum*. Florence, 1478.
Ctésias (fl. 5th c. B.C.). *La Perse, l'Inde. Les sommaires de Photius*, ed. and tr. R. Henry. Brussels, 1947.
al-Dāwūdī, Abū Isḥāq Ja'far ibn Naṣr (d. 1011). "Le régime foncier en Sicile au Moyen Age (IXe et Xe siècles)", ed. and tr. H. H. Abdul Wahhab and F. Dachraoui. In *Études d'orientalisme dédiées à la mémoire de Lévi-Provençal*. 2 vols. Paris, 1962. II 399–444.
Description de l'Égypte: ou recueil des observations et des recherches qui ont été faites en Egypte pendant l'expédition de l'armée française. 22 vols. Paris, 1809–29.
[Coll.] *Description du Maghreb et de l'Europe au IIIe–IXe siècle*, ed. M. Hadj-Sadok. Bibliothèque arabe–française VI. Algiers, 1949.
[Anon. (wrote 1340)] *Description of the Province of Fars in Persia at the Beginning of the Fourteenth Century A.D.*, tr. G. Le Strange. Asiatic Society Monographs XIV. London, 1912.

al-Dimashqī (d. 1327). *Manuel de la cosmographie arabe*, tr. A. F. Mehren. Amsterdam, 1964.
Diodorus of Sicily (fl. 1st c. B.C.). *Diodorus of Sicily*, ed. and tr. C. H. Oldfather and F. R. Walton. 10 vols. London, 1933–47.
Diokletians Preisedikt (issued 301), ed. S. Lauffer. Berlin, 1971.
Dioscorides, Pedanios (fl. 1st c.). *De materia medica libri quinque*, ed. M. Wellmann. 3 vols. Berlin, 1906–14.
La "Materia Médica" de Dioscórides. Transmisión medieval y renacentista, ed. C. E. Dubler and E. Terés. 6 vols. Barcelona, 1953–9.
[Coll.] *Diplomi greci ed arabi de Sicilia*, I, ed. and tr. S. Cusa. Palermo, 1868.
[Coll.] *Diwān al-shi'r al-'arabī*, ed. A. A. Sa'īd. 2 vols. Beirut, 1963–4.
[Coll.] *Documentos sôbre a expansão portuguesa*, ed. V. Magalhães Godinho. 3 vols. Lisbon, 1943–56.
[Coll.] *Documents chypriotes des Archives du Vatican*, ed. J. Richard. Bibliothèque archéologique et historique de l'Institut Français de Beyrouth LXXIII. Paris, 1962.
Dodoens, R. (1517–85). *A New Herball or Historie of Plants*, tr. H. Lyte. London, 1595.
Eanes de Zurara, G. (d. 1474?). *Chronique de Guinée*. Dakar, 1960.
Eiximenis, Francesc (*c.* 1349 – *c.* 1410). *Regiment de la cosa pública*, ed. D. De Molins de Rei. Barcelona, 1927.
[Anon. (wrote 4th c.?)] *Expositio totius mundi et gentium*, ed. and tr. J. Rougé. Paris, 1966.
[Anon. (fl. 12th c.)] "Extrait de la description d'Espagne tiré de l'ouvrage du géographe anonyme d'Almeria", ed. and tr. R. Basset. In *Homenaje a Francisco Codera*. Zaragoza, 1904. 619–47.
[Coll.] *Extraits inédits relatifs au Maghreb*, tr. E. Fagnan. Algiers, 1924.
Falcandus, Hugo (fl. late 12th c.). *De rebus gestis in Siciliae Regno*. Paris, 1550.
La historia o Liber de Regno Sicilie e la epistola ad Petrum Panormitane ecclesie thesaurium, ed. G. B. Siragusa. Fonti per la storia d'Italia XXII. Rome, 1897.
Fernandes, V. (wrote 1506–7). *Descripçam de Cepta por sua costa de Mauritania e Ethiopia*, ed. and tr. T. Monod, A. Teixeira da Mota and R. Mauny. Bissau, 1951.
al-Fīrūzābādī (1329 – *c.* 1414). *Mukhtār al-qāmūs*. Cairo, 1963.
Frescobaldi, Leonardo (wrote 1384). *Viaggio in Terrasanta*, ed. E. Emanuelli. Novara, 1961.
Galen (*c.* 130 – *c.* 200). *Claudii Galeni opera omnia*, ed. C. G. Kühn. 20 vols. Leipzig, 1821–33.
[Coll.] *Geoponika sive Cassiani Bassi scholastici de re rustica eclogae* (6th c.? or 10th c.?), ed. H. Beckh. Leipzig, 1895.
al-Ghāfiqī (d. *c.* 1160). *Kitāb jāmi' al-mufradāt* (as abridged by Barhebraeus), ed. and tr. M. Meyerhof and G. P. Sohby. Cairo, 1932.
al-Ghazzī (wrote 1529). "Jāmi' fawā'id al-malāḥa fī'l-filāḥa". Agric. Ms. 134, Dār al-Kutub, Cairo.
[Anon. (fl. 11th or 12th c.)] *Glosario de voces romances registrados por un botánico anónimo hispano-musulmán (siglos XI–XII)*, ed. M. Asín Palacios. Madrid/Granada, 1943.
Gregory of Tours (*c.* 540–94). "Liber in gloria martyrum", in *Monumenta Germaniae historica. Scriptorum rerum Merovingicarum*. Hanover, 1885. I/I 487–561.
[Coll.] *Habices de las mezquitas de la ciudad de Granada y sus alquerías* (late 15th c.), ed. C. Villanueva Rico. Madrid, 1961.
Hājji Khalīfa (= Kātib Čelebī) (1608–58). *Lexicon bibliographicum et encyclopaedicum*, ed. G. Flügel. 7 vols. London, 1835–58.
al-Hamdānī (893?–945?). *The Antiquities of South Arabia*, tr. N. A. Faris. Princeton, 1938.

Südarabien nach al Hamdānī's "Beschreibung der arabischen Halbinsel", tr. L. Forrer. Leipzig, 1942.
Herodotus (fl. 5th c. B.C.). *Herodotus*, ed. and tr. A. D. Godley. 4 vols. London/New York, 1921–4.
Herrera, Gabriel Alonso de (wrote *c.* 1513). *Obra de agricultura*, ed. and tr. T. Glick, Valencia, 1979.
al-Ḥimyarī (ms. of 1461; author's dates unknown). *La péninsule ibérique au moyen-âge d'après le "Kitāb al-mi'tār fī ḥabar al-aktār"*, ed. and tr. E. Lévi-Provençal. Leyden, 1938.
[Coll.] *Historia diplomatica Friderici Secundi*, ed. J. A. Huillard-Bréholles. 6 vols. in 11. Paris, 1852–61.
[Anon.] "History of Kilwa, The", ed. S. A. Strong. *Journal of the Royal Asiatic Society* (1895) 385–430.
[Anon. (wrote 982)] *Ḥudūd al-'ālam*, tr. V. Minorsky. London, 1937.
Ibn al-Abbār (1199–1260). "Apéndice a la edición Codera de la 'Tecmila' de Aben al-Abbar", ed. M. Alcarón and C. A. González Palencia. In *Miscelánea de estudios y textos árabes*. Madrid, 1915.
Kitāb al-takmila li-kitāb al-ṣila, ed. F. Codera. 2 vols. Bibliotheca Arabico-Hispana V–VI. Madrid, 1866–7.
Ibn 'Abd al-Ḥakam, Abū al-Qāsim 'Abd al-Raḥmān (*c.* 798/9–871). *The History of the Conquest of Egypt, North Africa and Spain, Known as the Futūḥ Miṣr*, ed. C. C. Torrey. New Haven, 1922.
Ibn 'Abdūn (fl. 11th–12th c.). *Séville musulmane au début du XIIe siècle. Le traité d'Ibn 'Abdūn sur la vie urbaine et les corps des métiers*, tr. E. Lévi-Provençal. Paris, 1947.
Ibn 'Asākir, 'Alī ben Ḥasan (1105–76). *La description de Damas d'Ibn 'Asākir*, tr. N. Elisséeff. Damascus, 1959.
Ibn al-'Awwām (fl. 12th c.). *Kitāb al-filāḥa*, ed. and tr. J. A. Banqueri. 2 vols. Madrid, 1802.
Le livre de l'agriculture d'Ibn al-Awam, tr. J.-J. Clément-Mullet. 2 vols. in 3 pts. Paris, 1864–7.
Ibn al-Baiṭār (1197?–1248). *Traité des simples*, tr. L. Leclerc. 3 vols. Notices et extraits des manuscrits de la Bibliothèque Nationale XXIII, XXV, XXVI. Paris, 1877–83.
Ibn Baṣṣāl (?) (d. 1105). *Kitāb al-filāḥa*, ed. and tr. J. M. Millás Vallicrosa and M. Aziman. Tetuan, 1955.
Ibn Baṭṭūṭa (b. 1304). *Voyages d'Ibn Batoutah*, ed. and tr. C. Defrémery and B. R. Sanguinetti. 4 vols. Paris, 1853–8.
Ibn Buṭlān (= Abul Kasem de Baldac, d. 1066; text revised till 14th c.). *Tacuinum sanitatis*, ed. and tr. F. Unterkircher, H. Saxer and C. H. Talbot. 3 vols. Graz, 1967.
Theatrum sanitatis di Ububuchucasym de Baldach, ed. F. M. Ricci. 3 vols. Parma, 1970–1.
Ibn al-Faqīh (wrote *c.* 903). "Description du Maghreb et de l'Europe au IIIe–IXe siècle", ed. and tr. M. Hadj-Sadok. Bibliothèque arabe–française VI. Algiers, 1949. 30–61.
Ibn Ḥajjāj (wrote 1073/4). "Un capítulo de la obra agronómica de Ibn Ḥajjāj", ed. J. Millás Vallicrosa and L. Martínez Martín. *Tamuda* VI (1958) 45–69.
Ibn Ḥammād (d. 1231). *Histoire des rois 'obaidites*, ed. M. Vonderheyden. Algiers, 1927.
Ibn Ḥawqal (wrote *c.* 988). *Configuration de la terre*, tr. J. H. Kramers and G. Wiet. 2 vols. Paris, 1964.
Ibn Iyās (1448–1524). *Badā'i' al-zuhūr fī waqā'i' al-duhūr*, ed. M. Mustafa. 5 vols. Cairo, 1960.

Ibn Jubair (1145–1217). *Voyages*, tr. M. Gaudefroy Demombynes. 4 vols. Paris, 1949–65.
Ibn Kabar, Shams al-Riāsa Abū al-Barakāt (d. 1324). "Les livres III et IV (animaux et végétaux) de la *Scala Magna* de Schams-ar-Riāsah", ed. V. Loret. *Annales du Service des Antiquités de l'Egypte* I (1899) 48–63, 215–29.
Ibn Khālawaih (d. 980/1). *Kitāb al-shajar*, ed. S. Nagelberg. Kirchhain, 1909.
Ibn Khaldūn (1332–82). *Histoire des Berbères*, tr. MacGuckin de Slane. 4 vols. Paris, 1925–56.
The Muqaddimah, tr. F. Rosenthal. 3 vols. New York, 1958.
Ibn Khallikān (1211–82). *Ibn Khallikān's Biographical Dictionary*, tr. MacGuckin de Slane. 4 vols. Paris/London, 1843–71.
Ibn Khurdādhbih (820?–911?). "Le livre des routes et des provinces", ed. and tr. C. Barbier de Meynard. *Journal asiatique* 6th ser. V (1865) 5–127, 227–96, 446–532.
Ibn Luyūn (1282–1349). *Kitāb ibdā' al-malāḥa wa inhā' al-rajāḥa fī uṣūl ṣinā'at al-filāḥa.* Ms. 1352, Bibliothèque Générale, Rabat.
Ibn Mammātī (d. 1209). *Kitāb qawānīn al-dawāwīn*, ed. A. S. 'Aṭīya. Cairo, 1943.
Ibn al-Nadīm (d. 995). *Al-fihrist*, ed. G. Flügel. 2 vols. Leipzig, 1871–2.
The Fihrist of al-Nadīm, tr. B. Dodge. 2 vols. New York, 1970.
Ibn Qutaiba (828–89). *The 'Uyūn al-Akhbār of Ibn Qutayba*, tr. L. Kopf. Paris/Leyden, 1949.
Ibn Rusta (wrote after 903). *Les atours précieux*, tr. G. Wiet. Cairo, 1955.
Ibn Sarābiyūn (fl. 902–45). "Description of Mesopotamia and Baghdad...", ed. and tr. G. Le Strange. *Journal of the Royal Asiatic Society* 1895, 1–76, 255–315.
Ibn Taghrībirdī (*c.* 1411–70). *Al-nujūm al-zāhira*, ed. T. G. J. Juynboll. 2 vols. Leyden, 1851.
Ibn Wāfid (1007/8–1074). *El "Libre de les medicines particulars". Versión catalana del texto árabe*, ed. L. Faraudo de Saint Germain. Barcelona, 1943.
"La traducción castellana del 'Tratado de agricultura' de Ibn Wāfid", ed. J. M. Millás Vallicrosa. *Al-Ándalus* VIII (1943) 281–332.
Ibn Waḥshīya (wrote ? 903/4). "Al-filāḥa al-nabaṭīya". Agr. Ms. 490, Dār al-Kutub, Cairo.[1]
Medieval Arabic Toxicology. The Book of Poisons of Ibn Waḥshīya and its Relation to Early Indian and Greek Texts, ed. and tr. Martin Levey. Transactions of the American Philosophical Society, new ser., LVI pt 7. Philadelphia, 1966.
al-Idrīsī (fl. 12th c.). *Description de l'Afrique et de l'Espagne*, ed. and tr. R. Dozy and M. J. de Goeje. Leyden, 1866.
India and the Neighbouring Territories, tr. S. Maqbul Ahmad. Aligarh, 1954.
Isidore of Seville (*c.* 560–636). *Etymologiarum sive originum Libri XX*, ed. M. W. Lindsay. 2 vols. Oxford, 1911.
al-Iṣṭakhrī (fl. 10th c.). *Das Buch der Länder*, tr. A. D. Mordtmann. Hamburg, 1845.
Jacob of Edessa (633–708). *Etudes sur l'Hexaméron de Jacques d'Edesse*, ed. and tr. A. Hjelt. Helsingford, 1892. [Texts in appendices]
Jacques de Vitry (d. 1240). "Historia Hierosolimitana". In *Gesta Dei per Francos sive*

[1] The dating of this work has been, and will be, the subject of much controversy; see the article on the author in the second edition of the *Encyclopedia of Islam*. However, a careful reading of the entire text has persuaded this writer that a substantial part of the work was composed at the beginning of the tenth century. Only this dating makes it possible to explain extensive parts of the text: the references to Baghdad, Basra, Wāsiṭ and Kufa, all of which were to all intents and purposes founded in the Islamic period; the discussions of Islam and of the Arab conquest of Persia; and the frequent mention of new crops, unknown to the region of "Babylonia" in Sasanian times. These sections are not, as has been suggested, a light overlayer in a text the greater part of which is more ancient. They are, on the contrary, deeply embedded in the text and a fundamental part of it. Even the discussions of superstitions which were once thought to be much more ancient can sometimes be shown to belong to the time of Ibn Waḥshīya.

orientalium expeditionum et Regni Francorum Hierosolimitani, ed. J. Bongars. 2 vols. Hanover, 1611. I 1047–145.

al-Jawharī (d. *c.* 1010). *Tāj al-lugha wa ṣiḥāḥ al-'arabīya.* 2 vols. Bulaq, 1865.

[Coll.] *Jewish Travellers*, ed. and tr. E. N. Adler. London, 1930.

Kauṭalya (fl. late 4th c. B.C.?). *The Kauṭilīya Arthaśāstra*, ed. and tr. R. P. Kangle. 3 vols. Bombay, 1960–5.

al-Khazrajī, 'Alī ibn Ḥasan (d. 1409). *The Pearl Strings. A History of the Resúliyy Dynasty of Yemen*, ed. and tr. M. 'Asal and J. W. Redhouse. 5 vols. Leyden/London, 1906–18.

al-Khushanī (fl. 10th c.). *Historia de los jueces de Córdoba por Aljoxaní*, ed. and tr. J. Ribera. Madrid, 1914.

al-Kindī, Abū 'Umar Muḥammad ibn Yūsuf (897–961). *Governors and Judges of Egypt*, ed. R. Guest. Leyden/London, 1912.

al-Kindī, Ya'qūb ibn Isḥāq (d. *c.* 873). *The Medical Formulary or "Aqrabādhīn" of al-Kindī*, ed. and tr. M. Levey. Madison, 1966.

[Anon. (fl. 13th c.)] "Kitāb al-ṭabīkh fī al-Maghrib wal-Andalus", ed. A. Huici Miranda. In *Revista del Instituto de Estudios Islámicos en Madrid* IX–X (1961–2) Arabic section, 12–256. [*Vide* also *Traducción española de un manuscrito anónimo del siglo XIII sobre la cocina hispano-magribī*, tr. A. Huici Miranda. Madrid, 1966]

L'Ecluse, Charles de (= Clusius, 1526–1609). *Rariorum plantarum historia.* Antwerp, 1601.

[Anon. (wrote early 14th c.?)] *Libre de sent soví* (*receptari de cuina*), ed. R. Grewe. Barcelona, 1979.

[Anon. (wrote 14th c.)] "Libro de cocina del siglo XIV, Un", ed. J. Osset Merle. *Boletín de la Sociedad Castellonense de Cultura* XVI (1935) 156–77.

Maimonides, M. (1135–1204). *Sharḥ asmā' al-'aqqār*, ed. and tr. M. Meyerhof. Mémoires présentés à l'Institut d'Egypte XLI. Cairo, 1940.

"Manu" (compiled 1st c. B.C. onwards). *The Laws of Manu*, tr. M. Müller. Sacred Books of the East XXV. Oxford, 1886.

al-Maqqarī, Aḥmad Ibn Muḥammad (*c.* 1591/2–1632). *Nafḥ al-ṭīb*, ed. Muḥammad M. 'Abd al-Ḥamīd. 10 vols. Cairo, 1949.

The History of the Mohammedan Dynasties in Spain, tr. P. de Gayangos. 2 vols. London, 1840–3.

al-Maqrīzī (1364–1442). *Description topographique et historique de l'Égypte* I–II, tr. U. Bouriant. Paris, 1895–1900. III–IV, tr. P. Casanova. Cairo, 1906–20.

Al-khiṭaṭ al-Maqrīzīya. 3 vols. in 9. Al-Shaiyāḥ (Lebanon), 1959.

Al-mawā'iẓ wali'tibār fī dhikr al-khiṭaṭ wal-āthār, ed. G. Wiet. 5 vols. Cairo, 1911–27.

al-Mas'ūdī (d. 956?). *Le livre de l'avertissement*, tr. B. Carra de Vaux. Paris, 1896.

Les prairies d'or, ed. and tr. C. Barbier de Meynard and P. de Courteille. 9 vols. Paris, 1861–77.

Les prairies d'or, tr. Barbier de Meynard and P. de Courteille, rev. C. Pellat (in progress). Paris, 1962– .

al-Mawardī (972–1058). *Les statuts gouvernementaux*, tr. E. Fagnan. Algiers, 1915.

Mishnah, The (compiled up to early 3rd c.), tr. H. Danby. London, 1933.

[Coll.] *Monumenta cartographica Africae et Aegypti*, ed. Prince Yusuf Kamal. 4 vols. Cairo, 1926–51.

Muḥammad ibn al-Ḥasan ibn Muḥammad ibn al-Karīm al-Kātib al-Baghdādī (wrote 1226). "A Baghdad cookery book", tr. A. J. Arberry, *Islamic Culture* XIII (1939) 21–47, 189–214.

al-Muqaddasī (wrote *c.* 985–90). *Aḥsan at-taqāsīm fī ma'rifat al-aqālīm*, tr. A. Miquel. Damascus, 1963.

Description de l'Occident musulman, ed. and tr. C. Pellat. Algiers, 1950.

Nāṣir-i Khusraw (1003–61?). *Sefer nameh*, ed. and tr. C. Schefer. Paris, 1861.

Niebuhr, M. (1733–1815). *Travels in Arabia and Other Countries in the East*, tr. R. Heron. 2 vols. Edinburgh, 1792.
al-Nuwairī (1279–1332). *Nihāyat al-arab fī funūn al-adab*. 18 vols. Cairo, 1923–65.
Orta, García da (fl. 16th c.). *Colloquies on the Simples and Drugs of India*, ed. and tr. Conde de Ficalho and Sir Clements Markham. London, 1913.
Coloquios dos simples, e drogas he cousas mediçinais da India, e assi dalguas frutas... Goa, 1563.
Pacheco Pereira, D. (wrote *c.* 1506–8). *Esmeraldo de situ orbis*, ed. R. Mauny. Bissau, 1956.
[Anon. (wrote 6th or 7th c.)] *Pahlavi Text "King Husrau and his Boy, The,"* tr. J. M. Unvala. Paris, 1922. [The appendix to this volume contains the Arabic version of the story given by al-Tha'ālibī]
[Coll.] *Pahlavi Texts*, tr. E. W. West. Sacred Books of the East v. Oxford, 1890.
Palladius (fl. between 3rd c. and 6th c.). *Opus agriculturae*, ed. J. C. Schmidt. Leipzig, 1898.
[Coll.] "Papyrus arabes du Louvre", ed. J. David-Weill. *Journal of the Economic and Social History of the Orient* VIII (1965) 277–311; XIV (1971) 1–19.
[Coll.] *Papyrus Erzherzog Rainer. Führer durch die Ausstellung*, ed. J. Karabaček. Vienna, 1894.
Pausanias (d. *c.* 470–65 B.C.?). *Description of Greece*, ed. and tr. W. H. Jones. 4 vols. London, 1918.
[Anon. (fl. 1st c.)] "Periplus Maris Erythraei", in *The Commerce and Navigation of the Erythraean Sea*, tr. J. W. McCrindle. Calcutta/Bombay/London, 1879.
Philon of Byzantium (fl. late 3rd c.). "Le livre des appareils pneumatiques et des machines hydrauliques par Philon de Byzance", ed. and tr. Carra de Vaux. *Notices et extraits des manuscrits de la Bibliothèque Nationale* XXXVIII (1903) 27–235.
Philostratus (170 – *c.* 245). *The Life of Apollonius of Tyana*, ed. and tr. J. S. Phillimore. 2 vols. London/New York, 1912.
Piloti, Emmanuel (wrote 1420). *Traité d'Emmanuel Piloti sur le passage en Terre Sainte*, ed. H. Dopp. Paris/Louvain, 1958.
Pliny the Elder (23–79). *Historia naturalis*, ed. and tr. H. Rockham. 10 vols. London/Cambridge, Mass. 1942–62.
Pollux, Julius (fl. later 2nd c. B.C.). *Onomasticon*, ed. W. Dindorf. 5 vols. in 4. Leipzig, 1824.
Polo, Marco (1254–1324). *The Travels of Marco Polo*, tr. R. E. Latham. Harmondsworth, 1958.
Possot, D. (wrote 1532). *Le voyage de la Terre Sainte*, ed. C. Schefer. Recueil de Voyages XI. Paris, 1890.
al-Qalqashandī (d. 1418). *Un tratado árabe del siglo XV sobre España. Extraído del "Subh al-A'shā"*, tr. L. Seco de Lucena Parades. Granada, 1942.
al-Qazwīnī (*c.* 1203–83). *Kitāb 'ajā'ib al-makhlūqāt wa gharā'ib al-mawjūdāt*, ed. F. Wüstenfeld. 2 vols. Göttingen, 1847–8.
Qudāma Ibn Ja'far (fl. 10th c.). *Taxation in Islam II: Qudāma b. Ja'far's "Kitāb al-Kharāj"*, ed. and tr. A. Ben Shemesh. London/Leyden, 1965.
Qusṭūs al-Rūmī (?) (transl.? 10th c.). *Al-filāḥa al-rūmīya*. Cairo, 1876.[2]

[1]The introduction to this work claims that it is by Qusṭūs the Greek, who may be Cassianus Bassus (fl. 6th c.), and that it was translated into Arabic by Sarjīs ibn Hilyā. It is quite possible that both these statements are wrong; medieval Arab writers, such as Ibn al-'Awwām, appear confused on the authorship of the book and on its translator. A careful comparison of this work with the Byzantine *Geoponika* of the tenth century does, however, reveal one important point very clearly: at the time of the translation of this work into Arabic, or shortly before, some new material was incorporated which is not found in any of the classical or Byzantine sources on which it and the *Geoponika* draw. In particular, a few new crops, not known in earlier times, are mentioned.

al-Rāzī, Aḥmad ibn Muḥammad (888?–955?). "La 'Description de l'Espagne' d'Aḥmad al-Rāzī", tr. E. Lévi-Provençal. *Al-Ándalus* XVIII (1953) 51–108.
al-Rāzī, Abū Bakr Muḥammad ibn Zakarīyā (= Rhazes, *c.* 865 – *c.* 932). *Kitāb al-ḥāwī fīl ṭibb.* 17 vols. Hyderabad/Deccan, 1955–64.
[Coll.] *Régestes des délibérations du Sénat de Venise concernant la Romanie*, ed. F. Thiriet. 3 vols. Paris, 1958–61.
Rufinus (fl. 13th c.). *The Herbal of Rufinus*, ed. L. Thorndike. Chicago, 1946.
al-Ruhāwī, Ayyūb (= Job of Edessa, d. *c.* 835). *Encyclopedia of Philosophical and Natural Sciences as Taught in Baghdad about A.D. 817; or Book of Treasures*, ed. and tr. A. Mingana. Cambridge, 1935.
Rumpf, G. E. (= Rumphius, 1627?–1702). *Herbarium amboinensis*... 7 vols. Amsterdam, 1741–55.
al-Ṣābī (970–1056). *Rusūm dār al-khilāfa*, ed. M. 'Awād. Baghdad, 1964.
Stephanus of Byzantium (= Grammaticus, fl. 6th c.). *Stephanus Byzantinus cum annotationibus*, ed. W. Dindorf. 4 vols. Leipzig, 1825.
Strabo (b. *c.* 63 B.C.). *The Geography of Strabo*, ed. and tr. H. L. Jones. 8 vols. London/New York, 1917–32.
al-Suyūṭī (1445–1505). *Ḥusn al-muḥāḍara fī ta'rīkh Miṣr wal-Qāhira.* 2 vols. Cairo, 1967–8.
[Anon. (date uncertain)] *Syrian Anatomy, Pathology and Therapeutics, or "The Book of Medicines"*, ed. and tr. E. A. W. Budge. 2 vols. Oxford, 1913.
al-Ṭabarī (839–923). *Geschichte der Perser und Araber zur Zeit der Sasaniden*, tr. T. Nöldeke. Leyden, 1879.
Ṭaibūghā al-Shariklamishi (d. 1394?). "Al-filāḥa al-muntakhaba". Agric. Ms. 22, Dār al-Kutub, Cairo.
Talmud de Jérusalem, Le (compiled 3rd–8th c.), tr. M. Schwab. 11 vols. Paris, 1878–90.
"Texte zur Wirtschaftsgeschichte Ägyptens in arabischer Zeit", ed. A. Grohmann. *Archív Orientální* VII (1935) 437–72.
al-Tha'ālibī, 'Abd al-Malik b. Muḥammad (d. 1038). *Yatīmat al-dahr.* 4 vols. Damascus, 1885.
Theophrastus (370 B.C.–*c.* 285 B.C.). *Enquiry into Plants*, ed. and tr. Sir A. Hort. 2 vols. London/New York, 1916.
[Anon. (written down 8th–16th c.)] *Thousand Nights and a Night, The*, tr. R. Burton. 10 vols. Benares, 1885–6.
[Coll.] *Traités de paix et de commerce et documents divers concernant les relations des Chrétiens avec les Arabes au moyen âge*, ed. L. de Mas Latrie. 2 vols. Paris, 1866.
[Coll.] *Trois traités hispaniques de ḥisba* (*texte arabe*), ed. E. Lévi-Provençal. Cairo, 1955.
[Anon. (fl. 17th or 18th c.?)] *Tuḥfat al-aḥbāb. Glossaire de la matière médicale marocaine*, ed. and tr. H. P. J. Renaud and G. Colin. Paris, 1934.
al-'Udhrī (1002/3–1085/6). *Nuṣūṣ 'an al-Andalus*, ed. 'Abd al-'Azīz al-Ahwānī. Madrid, 1965.
al-'Umarī, Ibn Faḍl Allāh (1301–49). *Masālik al-abṣār fī mamālik al-amṣār*, tr. L. J. M. Gaudefroy Demombynes. Paris, 1928.
Velho, Alvara (wrote 1497–9). *Roteiro da primeira viagem de Vasco da Gama (1497–1499)*, ed. A. Fontoura da Costa. Lisbon, 1960.
[Coll.] *Visit to the Holy Places of Egypt, Sinai, Palestine and Syria in 1384 by Frescobaldi, Gucci & Sigoli, A*, tr. T. Bellorni and B. Bagatti. Jerusalem, 1948.
Vitruvius (fl. 1st c. B.C.). *Vitruvius on Architecture*, ed. and tr. F. Granger, 2 vols. London/New York, 1931–4.
Walahfrid Strabo (807?–849). *Hortulus Wilahfrid Strabo*, tr. R. Payne. Pittsburgh, 1966.
al-Waṭwāṭ (1235–1318). "Mabāhij al-fikar wa manāhij al-'ibar". Natural Sciences and Chemistry Ms. No. 324, Dār al-Kutub, Cairo.

al-Wazzān, al-Ḥasan ben Muḥammad (= Leo Africanus, fl. early 16th c.). *Description de l'Afrique*, ed. and tr. A. Epaulard. 2 vols. Paris, 1856.
Yaḥyā Ibn Ādam (b. 757). *Taxation in Islam I: Yaḥyā Ibn Ādam's "Kitāb al-Kharāj"*, ed. and tr. A. Ben Shemesh. Leyden, 1958.
al-Ya'qūbī (wrote 889). *Les pays*, tr. G. Wiet. Cairo, 1937.
Yāqūt, Ibn 'Abd Allāh al-Ḥamāwī (1179–1229). *Jacut's Geographisches Wörterbuch*, ed. F. Wüstenfeld. 6 vols. Leipzig, 1866–70.
al-Zuhrī, 'Abd Allāh Muḥammad b. Abī Bakr (fl. 12th c.). *Kitāb al-jughrāfīya*, ed. M. Hadj-Sadok. Damascus, 1968.

Secondary works

al-'Abbādī, A. M. *Los esclavos en España*. Madrid, 1953.
'Abd al-Kader, A. "Land, property and land tenure in Islam", *Islamic Quarterly* v (1959) 4–11.
'Abd el Jalil, J. "L'Islam et la technique", *Studia missionalia* xi (1961) 7–27.
Abū al-Naṣr, A. *Ta'rīkh al-nabāt*. Beirut, 1963.
Abu-Lughod, J. L. *Cairo*. Princeton, 1971.
Adams, R. M. "Agriculture and urban life in early southwestern Iran", *Science* cxxxvi (1962) 109–22.
Land Behind Baghdad. A History of Settlement on the Diyala Plains. Chicago/London, 1965.
Adams, R. M. and H. Nissen. *The Uruk Countryside*. Chicago/London, 1972.
Adams, R. M., P. J. Parr, M. Ibrahim and A. S. al-Mughamnum. "Saudi Arabian archeological reconnaissance 1976", *Atlal. Journal of Saudi Arabian Archeology* i (1977) 21–40.
Adams, W. Y. "An introductory classification of Christian Nubian pottery", *Kush. Journal of the Sudan Antiquities Service* x (1962) 245–88.
"An introductory classification of Meroitic pottery", *Kush. Journal of the Sudan Antiquities Service* xii (1964) 126–94.
"Pottery kiln excavations", *Kush. Journal of the Sudan Antiquities Service* x (1962) 62–75.
Adams, W. Y. "Progress report on Nubian pottery: i. The native wares", *Kush. Journal of the Sudan Antiquities Service* xv (1967–8) 1–50.
Adrian, J. and M. Gast. *Mils et Sorgho en Ahaggar*. Paris, 1965.
African Agrarian Systems, ed. D. Biebuyck. London, 1963.
Aghnides, N. P. *Mohammedan Theories of Finance*. New York, 1916.
Agricoltura e mondo rurale in Occidente nell'alto medioevo. Settimane di studio del Centro Italiano di Studi sull'Alto Medioevo xiii. Spoleto, 1965.
Agriculture in Uganda, ed. J. D. Tothill. London, 1940.
Alcover, A. and F. Moll. *Diccionari Català–Valencià–Balear*. 10 vols. Palma de Mallorca, 1930–62.
Alemany Bolufer, J. "La geografía de la península Ibérica en los escritores árabes", *Revista del Centro de Estudios Históricos de Granada y su Reino* ix (1919) 109–72; x (1920) 1–29.
"La geografía de la península Ibérica en los pueblos cristianos desde San Isidoro hasta el siglo xvi", *Revista del Centro de Estudios Históricos de Granada y su Reino* xii (1922) 1–64.
"La geografía de la península Ibérica en los textos de los escritores griegos y latinos", *Revista de archivos, bibliotecas y museos* xxi (1909) 463–78; xxii (1910) 1–34; xxiii (1910) 45–80; xxiv (1911) 96–104.
Alessio, G. "Storia linguistica di un antico cibo rituale: i maccheroni", *Atti della Accademia Pontaniana* new ser. viii (1958–9) 261–80.
Alfonso-Spagna, F. *Precetti sulla coltivazione degli agrumi in Sicilia*. Palermo, 1869.

Ali, S. A. El-. "Muslim estates in Hidjaz in the first century A.H.", *Journal of the Economic and Social History of the Orient* II (1959) 247–61.
Ali-Zade, A. "The agrarian system in Azerbaijan in the XIII–XIV centuries". In *Akten des vier-und-zwanzigsten Internationalen Orientisten-Kongresses München*. Wiesbaden, 1959. 339–42.
Allain, C. "Les citernes et les margelles de Sisi Bou-Othman", *Hespéris* XXXVIII (1951) 423–40.
Allchin, B. and R. Allchin. *The Birth of Indian Civilization*. Baltimore, 1968.
Allchin, F. R. "Early cultivated plants in India and Pakistan", in *The Domestication and Exploitation of Plants and Animals*, ed. P. J. Ucko and G. W. Dimbleby. London, 1969. 323–9.
Alpino, P. *De plantis Aegypti liber*. 2 vols. Leyden, 1735.
Altheim, F. and R. Stiehl. *Ein Asiatischer Staat. Feudalismus unter den Sasaniden und ihren Nachbarn*. Wiesbaden, 1954.
Alvar López, M. *Atlas lingüístico y etnográfico de Andalucía*. 6 vols. Granada, 1961–73.
Amades, J. *Vocabulari dels pastors*. Barcelona, 1932.
Amano, Motonosuke. *Chūgoku nōgyō-shi kenkyū*. Tokyo, 1962.
Amari, M. *Storia dei Musulmani di Sicilia*. 3 vols. Florence, 1854–72.
Amedroz, H. F. "Abbasid administration in its decay, from the Tajarib al-Umam", *Journal of the Royal Asiatic Society* 1913, 823–42.
Anderson, E. *Plants, Man and Life*. London, 1954.
André, J. *Lexique des termes de botanique en Latin*. Paris, 1956.
Angladette, A. *Le Riz*. Techniques agricoles et productions tropicales V–VII. Paris, 1966.
Aquilar, F. *Plants de la lengua catalana*. Vich, 1861.
Arezzo, F. G. *Sicilia. Miscellanea di studi storici, giuridici ed economici sulla Sicilia; glossario di voci siciliane derivate dal greco, latino, arabo, spagnuolo, francese, tedesco etc.* Palermo, 1950.
Arnaldez, R. "Science et philosophie dans la civilisation de Baġdād sous les premiers 'Abbasides", *Arabica* IX (1962) 357–73.
Ashtor, E. "The diet of salaried classes in the medieval Near East", *Journal of Asian History* IV (1970) 1–24.
Ashtor, E. "Essai sur les prix et les salaires dans l'Empire Califien", *Rivista degli studi orientali* XXXVI (1961) 19–69.
"Levantine sugar industry in the late Middle Ages – a case of technological decline", in *The Islamic Middle East, 700–1900*, ed. A. L. Udovitch. Princeton, 1981. 91–132.
"Migrations de l'Irak vers les pays méditerranéens", *Annales: économies, sociétés, civilisations* XXVII (1972) 185–214.
A Social and Economic History of the Near East in the Middle Ages. London, 1976.
"The Venetian cotton trade in Syria in the later Middle Ages", *Studi medievali* 3rd ser. XVII (1976) 675–715.
Ashtor, E. and C. Cahen. "Débat sur l'évolution économico-sociale de l'Egypte à la fin du Moyen Age, à propos d'un livre récent", *Journal of the Economic and Social History of the Orient* XII (1969) 102–11.
Asín Palacios, M. "Avempace botánico", *Al-Ándalus* V (1940) 255–99.
Un botánico arábigoándaluz desconocido. Madrid, 1942.
Contribución a la toponimía árabe de España. Madrid/Granada, 1944.
Ayalon, D. "The Wafdīya in the Mamlūk kingdom", *Islamic Culture* XXV (1951) 89–105.
Bahġat, A. *Les manufactures d'étoffe en Egypte au Moyen Age*. Cairo, 1904.
Bailey, H. W. "Medicinal plant names in Uigur Turkish", in *Mélanges Köprülü*. Istanbul, 1953. 51–6.

Baker, H. G. "Comments on the thesis that there was a major centre of plant domestication near the headwaters of the river Niger", *Journal of African History* III (1962) 229–33.
Barceló, M. "Alguns problemes d'història agrària mallorquina suggerits pel text d'al-Zuhrī", *Recerques* VIII (1978).
"Comentaris a un text sobre Mallorca del geògraf al-Zuhri (s. VI/XII)", *Mayurqa* XIV (1975) 155–64.
Barrau, J. "Histoire et préhistoire des horticoles de l'Océanie tropicale", *Journal de la Société des Océanistes* XXI (1965) 55–78.
Bartlett, H. H. "Sumatran plants collected in Asahan and Karoland, with notes on their vernacular names", *Papers of the Michigan Academy of Science, Arts and Letters* VI (1926) 1–66.
Bartol'd, V. V. *Histoire des Turcs d'Asie Centrale*, tr. M. Donskis. Paris, 1945.
"Istoriia orosheniia Turkestana". In *Sochineniia.* 8 vols. Moscow, 1963–73. III 97–233.
Turkestan v épokhu mongol'skago nashestviia. 2 vols. St Petersburg, 1898–1900.
Bathurst, R. D. "Maritime trade and Imamate government: two principal themes in the history of Oman to 1728". In *The Arabian Peninsula: Society and Politics*, ed. D. Hopwood. London, 1972.
Beadnell, H. J. *An Egyptian Oasis.* London, 1909.
Becker, C. H. *Beiträge zur Geschichte Ägyptens unter dem Islam.* 2 vols. Strassburg, 1902–3.
Beckett, P. "Qanāts-Persia", *Journal of the Iran Society* I (1952) 125–33.
Bedevian, A. K. *Illustrated Polyglottic Dictionary of Plant Names.* Cairo, 1936.
Beek, G. van. "The Rise and fall of Arabia Felix", *Scientific American* CCXXI (Dec. 1969) 36–46.
Behling, L. *Die Pflanzenwelt der mittelalterlichen Malerei.* Cologne/Graz, 1967.
Bell, G. D. H. "The comparative phylogeny of the temperate cereals". In *Essays on Crop Plant Evolution*, ed. Sir J. Hutchinson. Cambridge, 1965. 70–102.
Bell, H. I. "The administration of Egypt under the Umayyad khalifs", *Byzantinische Zeitschrift* XVIII (1928) 278–86.
"Two official letters of the Arab period", *Journal of Egyptian Archaeology* XII (1926) 276–9.
Benvenisti, M. *The Crusaders in the Holy Land.* Jerusalem, 1970.
Bercher, H., A. Courteaux and J. Mouton. "Monreale, des terres et des hommes, leur exploitation". Unpublished thèse de maîtrise en histoire. Université de Paris VIII–Vincennes, 1973.
Bergman, F. *Archaeological Researches in Sinkiang.* Reports from the Scientific Expedition to the North-Western Provinces of China under the Leadership of Sven Hedin VII. Stockholm, 1939.
Berque, J. "Les Hilaliens repentis ou l'Algérie rurale au XVe siècle d'après un manuscrit jurisprudentiel", *Annales: économies, sociétés, civilisations* XXV (1970) 1325–53.
Berrall, J. S. *Illustrated History of Gardens.* New York, 1966.
Berthier, P. *Les anciennes sucreries du Maroc et leurs réseaux hydrauliques.* 2 vols. Rabat, 1966.
Bertin, J., J.-J. Hémardinquer, M. Keul and W. Randles. *Atlas des cultures vivrières.* Paris/The Hague, 1971.
Bey, A. I. *Dictionnaire des noms des plantes.* Cairo, 1930.
Bezuneh, T. and A. Feleke. "The production and utilization of the genus *Ensete* in Ethiopia", *Economic Botany* XX (1966) 65–70.
Bishko, C. J. "The Castilian as plainsman: the medieval ranching frontier in La Mancha and Extramadura". In *The New World Looks at its History*, ed. A. R. Lewis. Austin, 1958. 47–69.

Blachère, R. "Un pionnier de la culture arabe en Espagne au xe siècle. Saīd de Baghdad" *Hespéris*, xvi (1933) 99–121.

Blasquez, J. M. *Estructura económica y social de Hispania durante la Anarquía militar y el Bajo Imperio*. Madrid, 1964.

Blume, H. "Zuckerrohranbau in Andalusien verglichen mit dem Rohranbau in Louisiana", *Die Erde* LXXXVIII (1957) 10–38.

Boak, A. E. R. *Manpower Shortage and the Fall of the Roman Empire in the West*. Ann Arbor, 1955.

Boeuf, F. *Le Blé en Tunisie*. 2 vols. Tunis, 1932–5.

Bois, D. *Les plantes alimentaires chez tous les peuples et à travers les âges*. 4 vols. Paris, 1927–37.

Boissier, E. *Flora orientalis, sive enumeratio plantarum in oriente a Graecia et Aegypto ad Indiae fines hucusque observatarum*. 5 vols. Basle, 1867–88.

Bolens, L. "De l'idéologie aristotélicienne à l'empirisme médiéval: les sols dans l'agronomie hispano-arabe", *Annales: économies, sociétés, civilisations* XXX (1975) 1062–83.

"L'eau et l'irrigation d'après les traités d'agronomie andalous au moyen-âge (xie–xiie siècles)", *Options méditerranéennes* Dec. 1972, 64–77.

"Engrais et protection de la fertilité dans l'agronomie hispano-arabe, xie–xiie siècles", *Etudes rurales* XLVI (1972) 34–60.

Les méthodes culturales au Moyen-Age d'après les traités d'agronomie andalous: traditions et techniques. Geneva, 1974.

Bonnet, E. *Etudes sur deux manuscrits médico-botaniques exécutés en Italie aux XIVe et XVe siècles*. Paris, 1898.

"Plantes antiques des nécropoles d'Antinoé", *Journal de botanique* XIX (1905) 5–12.

Bonsor, G. *The Archeological Expedition Along the Guadalquivir*. New York, 1931.

Borasio, L. *Il Vercellese*. Vercelli, 1929.

Borlandi, F. "'Futaniers' et futaines dans l'Italie du moyen âge". In *Hommage à Lucien Febvre*. 2 vols. Paris, 1953. II 133–40.

Boronat y Barrachina, P. *Los moriscos españoles y su expulsión: estudio histórico–crítico*. 2 vols. Valencia, 1901.

Bosch Vilá, J. *El oriente árabe en el desarrollo de la Marca Superior*. Madrid, 1954.

Boswell, V. "Our vegetable travellers", *National Geographic Magazine* XCVI (1949) 145–217.

Bosworth, C. E. "Barbarian incursions: the coming of the Turks into the Islamic world". In *Islamic Civilisation, 950–1150*, ed. D. H. Richards. Oxford, 1973. 1–16.

Bouvier, R. *Les migrations végétales*. Paris, 1946.

Bouza Brey, F. *Noticias históricas sobre la introducción del cultivo del Maíz en Galicia*. Madrid, 1953.

Bowen, R. L. and F. P. Albright. *Archaeological Discoveries in Southern Arabia*. Baltimore, 1958.

Brandes, E. W. and G. B. Sartoris. "Sugarcane: its origin and improvement". In *U.S. Department of Agriculture Yearbook, 1936*. Washington, 1936. 561–623.

Braudel, F. *La Méditerranée et le monde méditerranéen à l'époque de Philippe II*. 2 vols. Paris, 1966.

Bräunlich, E. H. "The well in ancient Arabia", *Islamica* I (1925) 41–76, 288–343, 454–528.

Breasted, J. H. *Ancient Records of Egypt*. 5 vols. Chicago, 1906–7.

Bresc, H. "Les jardins de Palerme (1290–1460)", *Mélanges de l'Ecole Française de Rome* LXXXIV (1972) 55–127.

Bretschneider, E. *Botanicon sinicum*. Pt I in *Journal of the North-China Branch of the Royal Asiatic Society* new ser. XVI (1881) 18–230; pts II–III published as a monograph, Shanghai, 1892–5.

On the Study and Value of Chinese Botanical Works, with Notes on the History of Plants and Geographical Botany from Chinese Sources. Foochow, 1871.

Bretzl, H. *Botanische Forschungen des Alexanderzuges*. Leipzig, 1903.

Briggs, G. W. "Brief outline of Indo-Iranian contacts". In *Oriental Studies in Honour of Cursetji Erachji Pavry*, ed. J. D. C. Pavry. London, 1953. 55–60.

Britton, N. L. "Botanical gardens. Origin and development", *Bulletin of the New York Botanical Gardens* I (1897) 62–77.

Britton, N. P. *A Study of Some Early Islamic Textiles in the Museum of Fine Arts, Boston*. Boston, 1938.

Broun, A. F. and R. E. Massey. *Flora of the Sudan*. London, 1929.

Brunhes, J. *L'irrigation. Ses conditions géographiques, ses modes et son organisation dans la péninsule ibérique et dans l'Afrique du Nord*. Paris, 1902.

Brunschvig, R. "'Abd", *Encyclopedia of Islam* 2nd edn, II 24–40.

La Berbérie Orientale sous les Ḥafṣides. 2 vols. Paris, 1940–7.

Brutails, J.-A. *Etude sur la condition des populations rurales de Roussillon au Moyen Age*. Paris, 1891.

Bugeat, L. "Notes sur les citernes", *Ibla* XX (1957) 155–7.

Bühler, A. *Ikat, Batik, Plangi. Reservemusterungen auf Garn und Stoff aus Vorderasien, Zentralasien, Südosteuropa und Nordafrika*. 3 vols. Basel, 1972.

Bulliet, R. W. *The Patricians of Nishapur. A Study in Medieval Islamic Social History*. Cambridge, Mass., 1972.

Bunard, V. "Les anciens herbiers et les jardins botaniques", *Cosmos* new ser. XXI (1891) 118–22, 201–4.

Buret, M.-T. "Le vocabulaire arabe du jardinage à Sefrou", *Hespéris* XX (1935) 73–9.

Burkill, I. "The contacts of the Portuguese with African food plants which gave words such as 'yam' to European languages", *Proceedings of the Linnean Society of London* CL (1937–8) 84–95.

"The cultivated races of sorghum", *Kew Bulletin* 1937, 112–19.

A Dictionary of the Economic Products of the Malay Peninsula. 2 vols. London, 1935.

"Habits of man and the origins of the cultivated plants of the world", *Proceedings of the Linnean Society of London* CLXIV (1951–2) 12–41.

"The rise and decline of the greater yam in the service of man", *Advancement of Science* VII (1950–1) 443–8.

Burnouf, E. *Dictionnaire classique sanscrit–français*. Paris, 1866.

Burns, R. I. *The Crusader Kingdom of Valencia*. 2 vols. Cambridge, Mass., 1967.

"Irrigation taxes in early Mudejar Valencia: the problem of the *Alfarda*", *Speculum* XLIV (1969) 560–7.

Islam under the Crusaders. Princeton, 1973.

"Socio-economic structure and continuity: medieval Spanish Islam in the tax records of Crusader Valencia". In *The Islamic Middle East, 700–1900*, ed. A. Udovitch. Princeton, 1981. 251–82.

Busson, F. *Plantes alimentaires de l'Ouest africain*. Marseilles, 1965.

Butler, A. J. *The Arab Conquest of Egypt and the Last Thirty Years of the Roman Dominion*. Oxford, 1902.

Cadevall y Diars, J. *Flora de Catalunya*. 5 vols. Barcelona, 1925–33.

Cahen, C. "Douanes et commerce dans les ports méditerranéens de l'Egypte médiéval d'après le Minhādj d'al-Makhzūmī", *Journal of the Economic and Social History of the Orient* VII (1964) 217–34.

"Economy, society, institutions". In *The Cambridge History of Islam*. Cambridge, 1970. II 510–38.

"L'évolution de l'iqṭā' du IXe au XIIIe siècle", *Annales: économies, sociétés, civilisations* VIII (1953) 25–52.

"La féodalité et les institutions politiques de l'Orient latin". In *XII Convegno "Volta"*. Rome, 1957. 167–91.

"Fiscalité, propriété, antagonismes sociaux en Haute-Mésopotamie au temps des premiers 'Abbāsides", *Arabica* I (1954) 136–52.

"Īghār", *Encyclopedia of Islam* 2nd edn, III 1051.

"Iḳṭā'" *Encyclopedia of Islam* 2nd edn, III 1088–91.

"Nomades et sédentaires dans le monde musulman du milieu du Moyen Age". In *Islamic Civilisation, 950–1150*, ed. D. H. Richards. Oxford, 1973.

"Notes pour une histoire de l'agriculture dans les pays musulmans médiévaux", *Journal of the Economic and Social History of the Orient* XIV (1971) 63–8.

"Notes sur l'histoire des croisades et de l'Orient Latin II: le régime rural syrien au temps de la domination franque", *Bulletin de la Faculté des Lettres de Strasbourg* XXIX (1950–1) 286–310.

"Réflexions sur le *waqf* ancien", *Studia islamica* XIV (1961) 37–56.

"Le régime des impôts dans le Fayyūm ayyūbide", *Arabica* III (1956) 8–30.

Le régime féodal de l'Italie normande Paris, 1940.

"Le service de l'irrigation en Iraq au début du XIe siècle", *Bulletin d'études orientales* XIII (1949–51) 117–43.

La Syrie du Nord à l'époque des croisades. Paris, 1940.

Cambridge History of Islam, The, ed. P. M. Holt, A. K. S. Lambton and B. Lewis. 2 vols. Cambridge, 1970.

Campbell, D. *Arabian Medicine and its Influence on the Middle Ages*. London, 1926.

Canard, M. "Le Riz dans le Proche Orient aux premiers siècles de l'Islam", *Arabica* VI (1959) 113–31.

Candolle, A. de. *Origin of Cultivated Plants*. London/New York, 1967.

Capmany y de Montpalau, A. de. *Memorias históricas*. 4 vols. Barcelona, 1961.

Caponera, D. A. *Water Laws in Moslem Countries*. Rome, 1954.

Carnoy, A. *Dictionnaire étymologique des noms grecs des plantes*. Louvain, 1959.

Caro Baroja, J. *Los moriscos del Reino de Granada*. Madrid, 1957.

"Norias, azudes, aceñas", *Revista de dialectología y tradiciones populares* X (1954) 29–160.

Los pueblos de España. Ensayo de etnología. Barcelona, 1946.

"Sobre la historia de la noria de tiro", *Revista de dialectología y tradiciones populares* XI (1955) 15–79.

Carter, T. F. *The Invention of Printing in China and its Spread Westwards*. 2nd edn. New York, 1955.

Casanova, P. *Essai de reconstitution de la ville d'Al Fousṭâṭ ou Miṣr*. Mémoires de l'Institut Français d'Archéologie Orientale XXXV. 1919.

Casey, J. "Moriscos and the depopulation of Valencia", *Past and Present* L (1971) 19–40.

Ceccaldi, M. *Dictionnaire corse–français*. Paris, 1968.

Cessi, R. "Alvise Cornaro e la bonificà veneziana del secolo XVI", *Accademia dei Lincei, classe dei scienze morale* 6th ser. XIII (1936) 301–23.

Chabaud, B. *Les jardins de la Côte d'Azur. Histoire et description*. Toulon, 1910.

Chakravoti, A. K. "Origin of Cultivated bananas of South East Asia", *Indian Journal of Genetics and Plant Breeding* XI (1951) 34–46.

Chalandon, F. *Histoire de la domination normande en Italie et Sicile*. 2 vols. Paris, 1907.

Chalmeta Gendrón, P. "Feudalismo en al-Andalus?" *Orientalia hispanica* I (1974) 168–94.

Champion, J. *Le Bananier*. Paris, 1963.

Champion, J., *et al*. "Le Bananier aux îles Canaries", *Fruits* XVII (1962) 105–11.

Chandraratna, M. F. "The origin of the cultivated races of banana", *Indian Journal of Genetics and Plant Breeding* XI (1951) 29–33.

Chang, K.-C. *The Archaeology of Ancient China*. New Haven/London, 1977.
"The beginnings of agriculture in the Far East", *Antiquity* XLIV (1970) 175–85.
Early Chinese Civilization. Anthropological Perspectives. Cambridge, Mass., 1976.
Chang, T.-T. "The origin and early cultures of the cereal grains and food legumes". Paper presented at the Conference on the Origins of Chinese Civilization, Berkeley, 1978.
"The origin, evolution, cultivation, dissemination, and diversification of Asian and African rices", *Euphytica* XXV (1976) 425–41.
"The rice cultures". In *The Early History of Agriculture*, ed. Sir J. Hutchinson, J. G. G. Clark, E. M. Jope and R. Riley. Oxford, 1977. 143–57.
Chapot, H. "Pamplemousses, pomelos ou grape-fruits et tangelos", *Revue internationale de botanique appliquée et d'agriculture tropicale* XXX (1950) 62–75.
Chatterjee, C. "Notes on the origin and distribution of wild and cultivated rices", *Indian Journal of Genetics and Plant Breeding* XI (1951) 18–22.
Chattopadhyaya, B. D. "Irrigation in early medieval Rajasthan", *Journal of the Economic and Social History of the Orient* XVI (1973) 298–316.
Chaudhury, N. C. *Mohenjo-daro and the Civilization of Ancient India with References to Agriculture*. Calcutta, n.d.
Chauvin, V. C. *Bibliographie des oeuvres arabes ou relatives aux Arabes publiées dans l'Europe chrétienne de 1810 à 1885*. 12 vols. Liége, 1892–1922.
Cheesman, E. E. "Classification of the bananas", *Kew Bulletin* 1947, 97–117; 1948, 11–28, 145–57, 323–8; 1949, 23–8, 133–7, 265–72, 445–52; 1950, 27–31, 151 5.
Chéhabi, M. *Dictionnaire français–arabe des termes agricoles*. Cairo, 1957.
Cherbonneau, A. "Notices et extraits du *Kitab al-flaha* d'Abou-Abd-Allah-Mohammed-ben-el-Husseïn" [in fact Abū al-Khair], *Annales de la colonisation algérienne* V (1854) 339–51.
Chevalier, A. "L'acclimatation des Citrus en Afrique tropicale", *Revue de botanique appliquée et d'agriculture tropicale* XV (1935) 658–75.
"Ce que l'Amérique a donné à l'Ancien Monde", *Revue de botanique appliquée et d'agriculture tropicale* XVI (1936) 348–64, 417–41.
Le Coton. 2nd edn. Paris, 1949.
"La culture non irriguée du Coton par les indigènes", *Revue de botanique appliquée et d'agriculture coloniale* III (1923) 261–5.
Les fruits exotiques. Paris, 1953.
"Mandariniers et orangers", *Revue internationale de botanique appliquée et d'agriculture tropicale* XXVII (1947) 495–8.
"Observations sur quelques Bananiers sauvages et cultivés", *Revue de botanique appliquée et d'agriculture tropicale* XIV (1934) 506–21.
"L'origine botanique d'un Agrume hybride: le Clémentinier", *Revue de botanique appliquée et d'agriculture tropicale* XIX (1939) 428–30.
"L'origine géographique des *Aurantiocées* (Agrumes) cultivées et les étapes de leur amélioration spécialement en Indochine", *Revue de botanique appliquée et d'agriculture tropicale* XXIII (1943) 15–25.
"L'origine, la culture et l'usage des cinq Hibiscus de la section Abelmoschus", *Revue de botanique appliquée et d'agriculture tropicale* XX (1940) 319–28, 402–19.
"L'outillage agricole des primitifs et son amélioration", *Revue de botanique appliquée et d'agriculture tropicale* IV (1924) 569–80.
"Les productions végétales du Sahara", *Revue de botanique appliquée et d'agriculture tropicale* XII (1932) 668–924.
"Recherches biologiques sur la Canne à sucre et sur les genres apparentés", *Revue internationale de botanique appliquée et d'agriculture tropicale* XXIX (1949) 109–17.
"Le rôle de l'Homme dans la diffusion des plantes tropicales: échanges d'espèces

entre l'Afrique tropicale et l'Amérique du Sud", *Revue de botanique appliquée et d'agriculture tropicale* XI (1931) 633–50.

"Le rôle joué par les migrations humaines dans la répartition actuelle de quelques végétaux". In *Congrès de l'Association Française pour l'Avancement des Sciences*. Liège, 1924. 990–6.

"Le Sahara, centre d'origine des plantes cultivées". In *La vie dans la région désertique nord tropicale de l'ancien monde*. Mémoires de la Société de Biogéographie VI. Paris, 1938. 307–22.

"Sur la première introduction de quelques plantes cultivées en Normandie, d'après le Journal de Sir Gilles de Gouberville (1549–1562)", *Comptes rendus de l'Académie des Sciences* CCXVIII (1944) 297–300.

"Sur un Citrus d'apparence spontanée vivant dans la forêt dense de l'Ouest africain", *Revue internationale de botanique appliquée et d'agriculture tropicale* XXIX (1949) 355–66.

"La systématique des Cotonniers cultivés ou ayant été cultivés anciennement en Afrique tropicale", *Revue internationale de botanique appliquée et d'agriculture tropicale* XXVIII (1948) 228–41.

Végétaux utiles de l'Afrique tropicale française. Paris, 1905.

Chevalier, A. and L. Joléaud. "Les origines et l'évolution de l'agriculture méditerranéenne", *Revue de botanique appliquée et d'agriculture tropicale* XIX (1939) 613–62.

Chevalier, A. and R. P. Sacleux. "Les techniques de l'agriculture indigène en Afrique noire", *Revue internationale de botanique appliquée et d'agriculture tropicale* XX (1940) 263–71.

Chiarugi, A. "Le date di fondazione dei primi orti botanici del mondo", *Nuovo giornale botanico italiano* new ser. LX (1953) 785–839.

Child, R. *Coconuts*. London, 1964.

Chiovenda, E. "La culla del Cocco", *Webbia* V (1923) 359–449.

Chittick, N. "The 'Shirazi' colonization of East Africa", *Journal of African History* IV (1963) 179–90.

Chowdhury, K. A. and G. M. Buth. "Cotton seeds from the Neolithic in Egyptian Nubia and the origin of Old World cottons", *Biological Journal of the Linnean Society* III (1971) 303–12.

Christensen, A. *L'Iran sous les Sassanides*. 2nd edn. Copenhagen, 1944.

Ciccaglione, F. "La vita economica siciliana nel periodo normanno–svevo", *Archivio storico per la Sicilia orientale* X (1913) 321–45.

Ciferri, R. *L'industria del banano in Sicilia*. Rome, 1936.

Citrus Industry, The, I: History, Botany and Breeding, ed. H. J. Webber and L. D. Batchelor. Berkeley/Los Angeles, 1946.

Clarici, P. B. *Istoria e coltura delle piante*. Venice, 1726.

Clark, J. D. "The spread of food production in sub-Saharan Africa", *Journal of African History* III (1962) 211–28.

Clément-Mullet, J. J. "Sur les noms des céréales chez les anciens et en particulier chez les Arabes", *Journal asiatique* 6th ser. V (1865) 185–226.

Clerget, M. *Le Caire*. Cairo, 1934.

Clifford, D. *A History of Garden Design*. London, 1962.

Clutton-Brock, J., V. Mittre and A. N. Gulati. *Technical Reports on Archeological Remains*. Poona, 1961.

Cockburn, A., R. A. Barraco, T. A. Reyman and W. H. Peck. "Autopsy of an Egyptian mummy", *Science* CLXXXVII (1975) 1155–60.

Coit, J. E. "Carob or St. John's Bread", *Economic Botany* V (1951) 82–96.

Colin, G. S. "La noria marocaine et les machines hydrauliques dans le monde arabe", *Hespéris* XIV (1932) 22–60.

"L'origine des norias de Fès", *Hespéris* XVI (1933) 156–7.

Colmeiro, M. *Diccionario de los diversos nombres vulgares de muchas plantas.* Madrid, 1871.
Examen histórico–critico de los trabajos concernientes a la flora hispano–lusitana. Madrid, 1885.
Enumeración y revisión de las plantas de la península hispano–lusitana. 5 vols. Madrid, 1896.
Concise History of Science in India, A, ed. D. M. Bose, S. N. Sen and B. V. Subbarayappa. New Delhi, 1971.
Cook, O. F. *The Origins and Distribution of the Cocoa Palm.* Washington, 1901.
Cooper, R. "Land classification terminology and the assessment of the *kharāj* tax in medieval Egypt", *Journal of the Economic and Social History of the Orient* XVII (1974) 91–102.
Corominas, J. *Diccionario crítico–etimológico de la lengua castellana.* 4 vols. Berne, 1954–7.
"Mots catalans d'origen arabic", *Bulletí de dialectología catalana* XXIV (1936) 1–81.
Cortés, F. and L. Granell. "Vocabulari valencià del conreu, molinatge i comerç de l'arròs", *Revista valenciana de filología* II (1952) 67–97.
Cortesi, F. "Piante officinaci e della medicina popolare delle colonie italiane d'Africa e regioni limitrofi", *Rassegna economica coloniale* XXIV (1936) 71–126.
Cotte, J. and C. Cotte. *Etude sur les Blés d'antiquité.* Paris, 1912.
Cox, E. H. M. *Plant Hunting in China.* London, 1945.
Coyaud, Y. *Le Riz.* Saigon, 1950.
Cresswell, K. A. C. *Early Muslim Architecture.* Harmondsworth, 1958.
Crino, S. "Come si coltovava la canna da zucchero in Sicilia", *Agricoltura coloniale* XVII (1923) 81–9.
"Importanza della cotonicoltura siciliana per la soluzione del problema cotoniero nazionale", *Bollettino della Reale Società Geografica d'Italia* XII (1923) 432–512.
Crisp, F. *Mediaeval Gardens.* 2 vols. London, 1924.
Crone, P. "Umayyad clientage". Typescript of a paper presented at the conference on the economic history of the Middle East, Princeton, 1974.
Crowfoot, J. W. *The Island of Meroë.* 19th Memoir of the Archeological Survey of Egypt. London, 1911.
Curset, G. "Sur les jardins botaniques parisiens au XVIe siècle", *Journal d'agriculture tropicale et de botanique appliquée* XIII (1966) 385–404.
Dahlgren, B. E. *The Coco Palm.* Chicago, 1922.
Dalziel, J. M. *The Useful Plants of West Tropical Africa.* London, 1948.
Danechi, M. H. *Vocabulaires agricoles en langue persane.* Paris, 1963.
Dantin Cereceda, J. *Catálogo metódico de las plantas cultivadas en España y las principales especies arbóreas.* Madrid, 1920.
Daressy, G. "Le Riz dans l'Egypte antique", *Bulletin de l'Institut d'Egypte* IV (1921–2) 35–7.
Darkazally, B. "Al-Ḥajjāj ibn Yūsuf al-Thaqafī: the consolidation of Umayyad authority in Iraq (75–95 A.H./694–714 A.D.)". Unpublished Ph.D. thesis, University of Toronto, 1977.
Darlington, C. D. and J. Ammal. *Chromosome Atlas of Flowering Plants.* London, 1945.
Darrag, A. *L'Egypte sous le règne de Barsbay.* Damascus, 1961.
Daumas, M. *Histoire générale des techniques.* Paris, 1962.
Deerr, N. *The History of Sugar.* 2 vols. London, 1949–50.
Dennett, D. C. *Conversion and the Poll Tax in Early Islam.* Cambridge, Mass., 1950.
Deschamps, H. *Histoire de Madagascar.* Paris, 1965.
Destaing, E. *Vocabulaire français–berbère.* Paris, 1938.
Devie, M. *Dictionnaire étymologique des mots d'origine orientale.* Paris, 1876.
Dias, J. *Os arados portugueses e as suas prováveis origens.* Coimbra, 1948.

Dias, J. and F. Galhano. *Aparelhos de elevar a água de rega.* Oporto, 1953.
Diccionario histórico de la lengua española, ed. R. Lapesa Melgar *et al.* In progress. Madrid, 1972– .
Dickie, J. "Notas sobre la jardinería árabe en la España musulmana", *Miscelánea de estudios árabes y hebráicos* XIV–XV (1965–6) 75–86.
Dietrich, C. "Cotton culture and manufacture in early Ch'ing China". In *Economic Organization in Chinese Society,* ed. W. E. Wilmott. Stanford, 1972.
Diop, C. A. *L'Afrique noire pré-coloniale.* Paris, 1960.
Dixon, D. M. "Masticatories in ancient Egypt", *Journal of Human Evolution* I (1972) 433–49.
"A note on cereals in ancient Egypt". In *The Domestication and Exploitation of Plants and Animals,* ed. P. J. Ucko and G. W. Dimbleby. London, 1969. 131–42.
Djaït, H. "Les Yamanites à Kūfa au 1er siècle de l'Hégire", *Journal of the Economic and Social History of the Orient* XIX (1976) 148–81.
Doe, B. *Southern Arabia.* London, 1971.
Doggett, H. "The Development of cultivated sorghum". In *Essays on Crop Plant Evolution* ed. Sir J. Hutchinson. Cambridge, 1965. 50–69.
Dols, M. *The Black Death in the Middle East.* Princeton, 1977.
"The general mortality of the Black Death in the Mamlūk empire". In *The Islamic Middle East, 700–1900,* ed. A. Udovitch. Princeton, 1981. 397–428.
Doñate Sebastia, J.-M. "Existencia de un maíz europeo anterior al descubrimiento del Nuevo Mundo", *Boletín de la Sociedad Castellonense de Cultura* XXXVII (1961) 6–12.
Douglas, D. C. *The Norman Achievement, 1050–1100.* London, 1969.
Dozy, R. P. A. *Notices sur quelques manuscrits arabes.* Leyden, 1847–51.
Dozy, R. P. A. *Recherches sur l'histoire politique et littéraire de l'Espagne pendant le Moyen Age* I. Leyden, 1849.
Supplément aux dictionnaires arabes. 2 vols. Leyden, 1927.
Dozy, R. P. A. and W. H. Engelman. *Glossaire des mots espagnols et portugais dérivés de l'arabe.* Leyden, 1869.
Drar, M. *A Botanic Expedition to the Sudan,* ed. V. Täckholm. Cairo, 1970.
Dubler, C. E. *Estudio sobra la transmisión medieval y renacentista de la "Materia medica" de Dioscorides.* Barcelona, 1953.
"Temas geográfico-lingüísticos I. Sobre la berengena", *Al-Ándalus* VII (1942) 367–89.
"Temas geográfico-lingüísticos II. Badea–Sandía" *Al-Ándalus* VIII (1943) 383–413.
Über das Wirtschaftsleben auf der Iberischen Halbinsel vom XI. zum XIII. Jahrhundert. Romanica Helvetica XXII. Geneva, 1943.
Dudgeon, G. C. *Egyptian Agricultural Products. Gossypium Spp.* Cairo, 1917.
Dufourcq, C.-E. *L'Espagne catalane et le Maghrib aux XIIIe et XIVe siècles.* Paris, 1966.
Dunal, M. F. *Histoire naturelle, médicale et économique des Solanum.* Paris/Strasbourg/Montpellier, 1813.
Dunlop, D. M. *Arab Science in the West.* Karachi, 1966.
Durán Cañameras, F. *El notariado en Lérida y sus comarcas.* Lerida, 1955.
al-Dūrī, A. A. "Baghdād", *Encyclopedia of Islam* 2nd edn, I 894–908.
"The origins of iqṭā' in Islam", *Al-Abḥāth* XXII (1969) 3–22.
Ta'rīkh al-'Irāq al-iqtiṣādī. Baghdad, 1948.
Ebeid, R. Y. *Bibliography of Medieval Arabic and Jewish Medicine and Allied Sciences.* London, 1971.
Eche, Y. *Les bibliothèques arabes publiques et semi-publiques en Mésopotamie, en Syrie et en Egypte au moyen âge.* Damascus, 1967.
Elisséeff, N. *Nur ad-Dīn.* 3 vols. Damascus, 1967.

Erroux, J. *Les Blés des oasis sahariennes*. Algiers, n.d.
Even-Ari, M., L. Shanan and N. Tadmor. *The Negev. The Challenge of a Desert*. Cambridge, Mass., 1971.
Evolutionary Studies in World Crops, ed. Sir J. Hutchinson. London/New York, 1974.
Fahd, T. "L'histoire de l'agriculture en Irak: *Al-filāḥa an-nabaṭiyya*". In *Handbuch der Orientalistik*, ed. B. Spuler. VI 276–377.
"Un traité des eaux dans *Al-filāḥa an-nabaṭiyya* (hydrogéologie, hydraulique agricole, hydrologie)". In *Atti del convengo internazionale sul tema. La Persia nel medioevo*. Quaderni dell'Accademia Nazionale dei Lincei CLX, 1971. 279–326.
Ferhi, Y. *Grandes recettes de la cuisine algérienne*. Algiers, 1970.
Ferrer y Parpal, J. *Diccionario menorquin castellano*. 2 vols. Mahon, 1883.
Fischer, H. *Mittelalterliche Pflanzenkunde*. Munich, 1929.
Fischer-Benzon, R. von. *Altdeutsches Gartenflora*. Kiel/Leipzig, 1894.
Fitzgerald, W. *Africa*. London, 1967.
Floridia, S. "Storia degli agrumi in Sicilia", *Archivio storico per la Sicilia orientale* 2nd ser. VIII (1932) 1–20.
Foaden, G. P. and F. Fletcher. *Textbook of Egyptian Agriculture*. 2 vols. Cairo, 1908–10.
Fogg, W. H. "The domestication of *Setaria italica* (L.) Beauv.: a study of the process and origin of cereal agriculture in China". Paper presented at the Conference on the Origins of Chinese Civilization, Berkeley, 1978.
Fontaine, M. "Produits secondaires retirés des Limes acides, des Citrons et des Bergamotes", *Revue de botanique appliquée* VI (1926) 601–24.
Fontavella González, V. *La huerta de Gandía*. Zaragoza, 1952.
Food in Chinese Culture, ed. K.-C. Chang. New Haven/London, 1977.
Forand, P. G. "The status of the land and the inhabitants of the Sawād during the first two centuries of Islām", *Journal of the Economic and Social History of the Orient* XIV (1971) 25–37.
Forbes, R. J. *Studies in Ancient Technology*. 9 vols. Leyden, 1955–64.
Foureau, F. *Essai de catalogue des noms arabes et berbères des plantes, arbustes et arbres*. Paris, 1896.
Frantz, G. M. "Savings and investment in medieval Egypt". Unpublished Ph.D. thesis, University of Michigan, 1978.
Freeman-Grenville, H. S. P. *The Medieval History of the Coast of Tanganyika*. London, 1962.
Freytag, G. W. *Lexicon Arabico–Latinum*. 4 vols. Halle a. d. S., 1830–7.
Fuchs, L. *De historia stirpium* (*Historia plantarum*). Lyon, 1549.
Gadea M. *Trigos españoles*. Madrid, 1954.
Gallesio, G. *Traité du Citrus*. Paris, 1811.
Gambi, L. *Geografia delle piante da zucchero in Italia*. Università di Napoli, Memorie di geografia economica XII. Naples, 1955.
Gangolly, S. R., R. Singh, S. L. Katyal *et al. The Mango*. New Delhi, 1957.
Garber, E. D. *Cytotaxonomic Studies in the Genus "Sorghum"*. University of California Publications in Botany XXIII vi. Berkeley/Los Angeles, 1950.
Garcia de Diego, V. *Diccionario etimológico español y hispánico*. Madrid, 1954.
García Gómez, E. "Sobre agricultura arabigoandaluza", *Al-Ándalus* X (1945) 137–46.
García-Badell y Abadía, G. *Introducción a la historia de la agricultura española*. Madrid, 1963.
Gast, M. *Alimentation des populations de l'Ahaggar. Etude ethnographique*. Paris, 1968.
Gauckler, P. *Enquête sur les installations hydrauliques romaines en Tunisie*. 2 vols. Paris/Tunis, 1901–2.
Gaudefroy Demombynes, L. J. M. *La Syrie à l'époque des Mamelouks*. Paris, 1923.
Georlette, R. "La culture du riz en Camargue", *Annales de Gembloux* LXII (1956) 65–75.

Gernet, J. *Daily Life in China on the Eve of the Mongol Invasion, 1250–1276*. New York, 1962.
Gerth van Wijk, H. L. *A Dictionary of Plant Names*. 2 vols. The Hague, 1911.
Ghālib, Adwār (Edouard). *Al-mawsū'a fī 'ulūm al-ṭabī'a*. 3 vols. Beirut, 1965–6.
Ghirshman, R. *Iran*. Harmondsworth, 1954.
Parthes et Sassanides. Paris, 1962.
Gibault, G. *Histoire des légumes*. Paris, 1912.
Gibb, H. A. R. "The fiscal rescript of 'Umar II", *Arabica* II (1955) 1–40.
Gidon, F. "Notes sur l'archéologie de l'alimentation", *Bulletin de la Société d'Antiquaires de Normandie* XLIV (1937) 290–309.
Giese, W. "Brunnenschöpfräder der Mancha", *Zeitschrift für Romanische Philologie* LIV (1934) 517–22.
"Über die Herkunft der sardischen Brunnenschöpfräder". In *Miscelânea de estudos a memoria de Cláudio Basto*. Oporto, 1948. 378–88.
"Über portugiesische Brunnen", *Wörter und Sachen* XI (1928) 65–73.
Gildemeister, E. and F. Hoffmann. *The Volatile Oils*, tr. E. Kremers. 2nd edn. 3 vols. London, 1913–22.
Gines Aliño, B. *Tratado completo del naranjo*. Valencia, 1892.
Giralt y Raventós, E. *Los estudios de historia agraria en España desde 1940 a 1961. Orientaciones bibliográficas*. Barcelona, 1962.
Girenko, M. M. "O klassifiktsii spinata", *Trudy po prikladnoi botanike, genetike i selektsii* XL (1968) 28–36.
Glick, T. *Irrigation and Society in Medieval Valencia*. Cambridge, Mass., 1970.
Islamic and Christian Spain in the Early Middle Ages. Princeton, 1979.
Glick, T. and O. Pi-Sunyer. "Acculturation as an explanatory concept in Spanish history", *Comparative Studies in Society and History* XI (1969) 136–54.
Glidden, H. W. "The lemon in Asia and Europe", *Journal of the American Oriental Society* LVII (1937) 381–96.
Gobert, E. G. "Les références historiques des nourritures tunisiennes", *Cahiers de Tunisie* III (1955) 501–42.
Goblot, H. "Dans l'ancien Iran, les techniques de l'eau et la grande historie", *Annales: économies, sociétés, civilisations* XVIII (1963) 499–520.
"Kébar en Iran, sans doute le plus ancien des barrages-voûtes (1300 environ)", *Science, progrès, découverte* MMMXXXLVIII (1965) 50–6.
Godefroy, F. *Dictionnaire de l'ancienne langue française et de tous ses dialectes*. Paris, 1898.
Goitein, S. D. "Artisans en Mediterranée orientale au haut moyen âge", *Annales: économies, sociétés, civilisations* XIX (1964) 847–68.
"Changes in the Middle East (950–1150) as illustrated by the documents of the Cairo Geniza". In *Islamic Civilisation, 950–1150*, ed. D. H. Richards. Oxford, 1973. 17–32.
A Mediterranean Society. 2 vols. to date. Berkeley, 1967– .
"Slaves and slave girls in the Cairo Geniza records", *Arabica* IX (1962) 1–20.
Studies in Islamic History and Institutions. Leyden, 1966.
"La Tunisie du XIe siècle à la lumière des documents de la *Geniza* du Caire". In *Etudes d'orientalisme dédiées à la mémoire de Lévi-Provençal*. 2 vols. Paris, 1962. II 559–79.
Golombek, L. and V. Gervers. "Tiraz fabrics in the Royal Ontario Museum". In *Studies in Textile History in Memory of Harold Burnham*, ed. V. Gervers. Toronto, 1977. 82–125.
Golvin, L. "Au souk des artisans du tamis (Sfax)", *Ibla* VIII (1945) 15–41.
Le Magrib central à l'époque des Zirides. Paris, 1957.
"Le palmier dans le décor musulman d'Occident", *Hespéris Tamuda* II (1961) 145–60.

Gonzáles Palencia, C. A. *El Arzobispo don Raimundo de Toledo*. Madrid, 1942.
Los mozárabes de Toledo en los siglos XII y XIII. 4 vols. Madrid, 1926–30.
"Notas sobre el régimen de riejos en la región de Veruela en los siglos XII y XIII", *Al-Ândalus* x (1945) 79–88.
Goodrich, L. C. "Cotton in China", *Isis* xxxiv (1942–3) 408–10.
Goossens, G. "Le Coton en Assyrie", *Annuaire de l'Institut de Philosophie et d'Histoire Orientales et Slaves* xii (1952) 167–76.
Gopal, L. *The Economic Life of Northern India c. A.D. 700–1200*. Delhi/Patna, 1965.
"Sugar-making in ancient India", *Journal of the Economic and Social History of the Orient* vii (1964) 57–72.
"Textiles in ancient India", *Journal of the Economic and Social History of the Orient* iv (1961) 53–69.
Gorman, C. F. "*A priori* models and Thai prehistory: a reconsideration of the beginnings of agriculture in southeastern Asia". In *Origins of Agriculture*, ed. C. A. Reed. The Hague/Paris, 1977. 385–412.
"Modèles a priori et préhistoire de la Thailande", *Etudes rurales* liii (1974) 41–71.
Gothein, M.-L. *A History of Garden Art*. New York, 1966.
Gottschalk, A. *Histoire de l'alimentation et de la gastronomie de la préhistoire jusqu'à nos jours*. 2 vols. Paris, 1948.
Gouvernement chérifien. *Etudes préliminaires sur les Blés durs marocains*. Paris, 1922.
Grabar, O. "Umayyad 'palace' and the 'Abbasid 'revolution'", *Studia Islamica* xviii (1963) 5–18.
Grabar, O., R. Holod, J. Knustad, W. Trousdale *et al. City in the Desert. Qasr al-Hayr East*. 2 vols. Cambridge, Mass., 1978.
Grandidier, A. and G. Grandidier. *Histoire physique, naturelle et politique de Madagascar*. 39 vols. Paris, 1885–1958.
Gray, Sir John. *History of Zanzibar from the Middle Ages to 1856*. London, 1962.
Gregorio, G. de and C. F. Seybold. "Glossario delle voci siciliane di origine araba", *Studi glottologici italiani* iii (1903) 225–51.
Greiss, A. M. *Anatomical Identification of Some Ancient Egyptian Plant Materials*. Mémoires de l'Institut d'Egypte lv. Cario, 1957.
"Les plus anciens spécimens de tissus et de fibres de coton découverts en Egypte", *Chronique d'Egypte* xxvii (1952) 321–3.
Grierson, P. "The monetary reforms of 'Abd al-Malik", *Journal of the Economic and Social History of the Orient* iii (1960) 241–64.
Griffith, F. L. and G. M. Crowfoot. "On the early use of cotton in the Nile valley", *Journal of Egyptian Archaeology* xx (1934) 5–12.
Grimal, P. *Les jardins romains à la fin de la République et aux deux premiers siècles de l'Empire*. Paris, 1943.
Grist, D. H. *Rice*. London, 1959.
Grohmann, A. "New discoveries in Arabic papyri. An Arabic tax-account book (Inv. No. 1400). Found in Umm El Bureigāt (Tebfynis) in 1916", *Bulletin de l'Institut d'Egypte* xxxii (1949–50) 159–70.
Südarabien als Wirtschaftsgebiet. 2 vols. Schriften der Philosophischen Fakultät der Deutschen Universität in Prag vii and xiii. Prague, 1930–3.
Gromort, G. *Jardins d'Espagne*. Paris, 1926.
Grünebaum, G. von. *Classical Islam. A History, 600–1258*. London, 1970.
"Pluralism in the Islamic world", *Islamic Studies* i no. 2 (1962) 37–59.
Gual Camarena, M. *Vocabulario del comercio medieval*. Tarragona, 1968.
Guichard, P. "Les Arabes ont bien envahi l'Espagne", *Annales: économies, sociétés, civilisations* xxix (1974) 1483–513.
"Le peuplement de la région de Valence aux deux premiers siècles de la domination musulmane", *Mélanges de la Casa de Velasquez* v (1969) 103–58.

Structures sociales "orientales" et "occidentales" dans l'Espagne musulmane. Paris/The Hague, 1977.
Guillaumin, A. "Classification, origine et phylogénie des Hespérides", *Revue de botanique appliquée et d'agriculture tropicale* XII (1932) 543–7.
Guillou, A. "Italie méridionale byzantine ou Byzantins en Italie méridionale?" *Byzantion* XLIV (1974) 152–90.
Guinaudeau, Z. *Fès vu par sa cuisine.* Rabat, n.d.
Gulati, A. N. and A. J. Turner. *A Note on the Early History of Cotton.* Indian Central Cotton Committee Technological Laboratory, Bulletin XVII. Bombay, 1928.
"A Note on the early history of cotton", *Journal of the Textile Institute* XX (1929) Transactions 1–9.
Guyot, L. *Histoire des plantes cultivées.* Paris, 1963.
Gwynne, M. D. "The origin and spread of some domestic food plants of Eastern Africa". In *East Africa and the Orient. Cultural Syntheses in Pre-colonial Times,* ed. H. N. Chittick and R. I. Rotberg. New York/London, 1975. 248–71.
Hagerty, M. J. "Comments on writings concerning Chinese sorghums", *Harvard Journal of Asiatic Studies* V (1940) 234–61.
Hamarneh, S. "Zirā'at qaṣab al-sukkar wa ṣinā'atuhu 'inda al-'Arab al-Muslimīn, *Annual of the Department of Antiquities* [of Jordan] XXII (1977–8) 12–19.
Hamidullah, M. "L'Afrique découvre l'Amérique avant Christophe Colombe", *Présence africaine* XVII–XVIII (1958) 178–83.
Hamilton, R. W. *Khirbat al Mafjar. An Arabian Mansion in the Jordan Valley.* Oxford, 1959.
Hardy, E. R. *The Large Estates of Byzantine Egypt.* New York, 1931.
Harlan, J. R. "Agricultural origins: centers and noncenters", *Science* CLXXIV (1971) 468–74.
Crops and Man. Madison, 1975.
"The origins of cereal agriculture in the Old World". In *Origins of Agriculture,* ed. C. A. Reed. The Hague/Paris, 1977. 327–83.
"Plant and animal distribution in relation to domestication". In *The Early History of Agriculture,* ed. J. B. Hutchinson, J. G. G. Clark, E. M. Jope and R. Riley. Oxford, 1977, 13–25.
Harlan, J. R. and J. M. J. De Wet. "A simplified classification of cultivated sorghum", *Crop Science* XII (1972) 172–6.
Harlan, J. R. and A. Stemler. "The races of sorghum in Africa". In *Origins of African Plant Domestication,* ed. J. R. Harlan, J. M. J. De Wet and A. Stemler. The Hague/Paris, 1976. 465–78.
Harland, S. C. *The Genetics of Cotton.* London, 1939.
Harrison, S. G., G. B. Masefield and M. Wallis. *The Oxford Book of Food Plants.* Oxford, 1969.
Hartmann, F. *L'agriculture dans l'ancienne Egypte.* Paris, 1923.
Hassan, Z. M. *Les Tulunides.* Paris, 1933.
Hassib, M. *Cucurbitaceae in Egypt.* Cairo, 1938.
Haudricourt, A.-G. and J. Brunhes Delamare. *L'homme et la charrue à travers le monde.* Paris, 1956.
Haudricourt, A.-G. and L. Hédin. *L'homme et les plantes cultivées.* Paris, 1943.
"Recherches sur l'histoire des plantes cultivées", *Revue internationale de botanique appliquée et d'agriculture tropicale* XXXIII (1953) 537–45.
Havinden, M. A. "The history of crop cultivation in West Africa: a bibliographical guide", *Economic History Review* 2nd ser. XXIII (1970) 532–55.
Hedrick, U. P. *Sturtevant's Notes on Edible Plants.* Report of the New York Agricultural Experiment Station, 1919, II. Albany, 1919.
Heers, J. *Gênes au XVe siècle.* Paris, 1961.
Heffening, W. "Waḳf", *Encyclopedia of Islam,* 1st edn, V 1096–103.

Hegener, H. *Die Terminologie der Hanfkultur im katalanischen Sprachgebiet*. Hamburg, 1938.
Hehn, V. *Cultivated Plants and Domestic Animals in their Migration from Asia to Europe*, ed. J. S. Stallybrass. London, 1891.
Kulturpflanzen und Hausthiere in ihrem Übergang aus Asien nach Griechenland und Italien sowie in das übrige Europa. Berlin, 1887.
Helbaek, H. "Cereals and seed grasses in Phase A". In R. J. Braidwood and L. J. Braidwood, *Excavations in the Plain of Antioch* I. Chicago, 1960.
"Commentary on the phylogenesis of *Triticum* and *Hordeum*", *Economic Botany* XX (1966) 350–60.
"Domestication of food plants in the Old World", *Science* XXX (1959) 365–72.
"First impressions of the Çatal Hüyük plant husbandry", *Anatolian Studies* XIV (1964) 151–3.
"The Fyrkat grain: a geographical and chronological study of rye", in A. Olsen, E. Roesdahl and H. W. Schmidt, *Fyrkat. En jysk vikingeborg*. Copenhagen, 1975.
"Late Bronze Age and Byzantine crops at Beycesultan in Anatolia", *Anatolian Studies* XI (1961) 77–97.
"Die Paläoethnobotanik des Nahen Ostens und Europas". In *Opuscula ethnologica memoriae Ludovici Biró sacra*. Budapest, 1959.
"Paleo-ethnobotany". In *Science in Archeology*, ed. D. Brothwell and E. Higgs. 2nd edn. London, 1969.
"The paleoethnobotany of the Near East and Europe". In R. J. Braidwood and B. Howe, *Prehistoric Investigations in Iraqi Kurdistan*. Oriental Institute of the University of Chicago, Studies in Ancient Oriental Civilization XXXI (1960) 99–118.
"Plant collecting, dry farming, and irrigation agriculture in prehistoric Deh Luran". In *Prehistory and the Ecology of the Deh Luran Plain*, ed. F. Hole, K. V. Flannery and J. A. Neeley. Ann Arbor, 1969. 383–426.
Hémardinquer, J.-J. "L'introduction du Maïs et la culture des Sorghos dans l'ancienne France", *Bulletin philologique et historique* (1963) 429–59.
Henslow, G. *Medieval Works of the Fourteenth Century, Together with a List of Plants Recorded in Contemporary Writings with their Identification*. London, 1899.
Herzfeld, E. *Geschichte der Stadt Samarra*. Die Ausgrabungen von Samarra VI. Hamburg, 1948.
Heske, F. "Historiche Bedeutung der Bodenbenützung und des Bodenmissbrauches im Islamischen Orient", *Proceedings of the Twenty-second Congress of Orientalists* VI. Leyden, 1957. 263–69.
Heyd, W. *Histoire du commerce du Levant au Moyen-Age*. 2 vols. Leipzig, 1885–6.
Heyworth-Dunne, G. *Land Tenure in Islam, 630 A.D. – 1951 A.D.* Cairo, 1952.
Hill, A. W. "The history and function of botanical gardens", *Annals of the Missouri Botanical Garden* II (1915) 185–240.
"The original home and mode of dispersal of the coconut", *Nature, Lond.* CXXIV (1929) 133–4, 151–3.
Hinds, M. "Some economic issues in third/ninth century Iraq". Paper presented at the Princeton conference on the economic history of the Near East, 1974.
Hitti, P. K. *History of the Arabs*. 6th edn. London, 1956.
Hjelt, A. "Pflanzennamen aus dem Hexaëmeron Jacob's von Edessa". In *Orientalische Studien Theodor Nöldeke*, ed. C. Bezold. 2 vols. Giessen, 1906. I 571–9.
Ho, Ping-ti. *The Cradle of the East*. Hong Kong/Chicago, 1975.
"The indigenous origins of Chinese agriculture". In *Origins of Agriculture* ed. C. A. Reed. The Hague/Paris, 1977. 411–84.
Hodgson, M. G. S. *Venture of Islam. Conscience and History in World Civilization*. 3 vols. Chicago, 1974.
Hodgson, R. G. *La culture fruitière en Tunisie*. Tunis, 1931.
Hollingsworth, T. H. *Historical Demography*. London, 1969.

Holt, P. M. "Al-Fayyūm", *Encyclopedia of Islam* 2nd edn, II 872–3.
Hooker, J. D. *A Flora of British India*. London, 1875–97.
Hoops, J. *Waldbäume und Kulturpflanzen im germanischen Altertum*. Strassburg, 1905.
Hourani, G. *Arab Seafaring in the Indian Ocean in Ancient and Early Medieval Times*. Beirut, 1963.
Huici Miranda, A. "Al-Ghazāl" *Encyclopedia of Islam* 2nd edn., II 1038.
Humlum, J. *La géographie de l'Afghanistan*. Copenhagen, 1959.
"Underjordiske vandingskanaler: kareze, qanat, foggara", *Kulturgeografi* XVI (1965) 81–132.
Hutchinson, John and J. M. Dalziel. *Flora of West Tropical Africa*. 2 vols. London, 1927–31.
Hutchinson, Joseph B. *The Application of Genetics to Cotton Improvement*. Cambridge, 1959.
"Crop plant evolution in the Indian subcontinent". In *Evolutionary Studies in World Crops*, ed. J. B. Hutchinson. Cambridge, 1974. 151–60.
"The dissemination of cotton in Africa", *Empire Cotton Growing Review* XXVI (1949) 256–70.
"India: local and introduced crops". In *The Early History of Agriculture*, ed. J. B. Hutchinson, J. G. G. Clark, E. M. Jope and R. Riley. Oxford, 1977. 129–41.
"New evidence on the origin of the Old World cottons", *Heredity* VIII (1954) 225–41.
Hutchinson, Joseph B., R. Silow and S. G. Stephens. *The Evolution of Gossypium*. Oxford, 1947.
Hütteroth, W.-D. and K. Abdulfatah. *Historical Geography of Palestine, Transjordan and Southern Syria in the Late 16th Century*. Erlanger Geographische Arbeiten, Sonderband v. Erlangen, 1977.
Ibañez, E. *Diccionario rifeño –Español*. Madrid, 1949.
Ibrahim, M., J. A. Sauer and K. Yassine. "The East Jordan Valley Survey, 1975", *Bulletin of the American Schools of Oriental Research* CCXXII (1976) 41–66.
Idris, H. R. *La Berbérie Orientale sous les Zirides. Xe–XIIe siècle*. 2 vols. Paris, 1962.
Imamuddin, S. M. "Al-filāḥah (farming) in Muslim Spain", *Islamic Studies* I iv (1962) 51–89.
Hispano-Arab Libraries. Karachi, 1961.
Some Aspects of the Socio-Economic and Cultural History of Muslim Spain, 711–1492 A.D. Leyden, 1965.
Inalcik, H. *The Ottoman Empire*. London, 1973.
Irvine, F. R. "Vocabularies of plant names in Nigerian languages with botanical equivalents". Typescript in the library of Kew Gardens.
'Īsà, Aḥmad. *Ta'rīkh al-nabāt 'ind al-'arab*. Cairo, 1944.
[Coll.] *Islam and the Trade of Asia*, ed. D. S. Richards. Oxford, 1970.
Jacobsen, T. and R. M. Adams. "Salt and silt in ancient Mesopotamian agriculture", *Science* CXXVIII (1958) 1251–8.
Jasny, N. *The Wheats of Classical Antiquity*. Johns Hopkins University Studies in Historical and Political Science ser. LXII no. 3. Baltimore, 1944.
Jeffreys, M. D. W. "Arabs introduce African exotic plants", *Islamic Review* XLIV (1956) 31–3.
"The history of maize in Africa", *Southern African Journal of Science* L (1954) 197–200.
"Pre-Columbian maize in Africa", *Nature, Lond.* CLXXII (1953) 965–6.
Jehuda, Feliks. *Ha-Ḥakla'ut be-Erets-Yisrael bi-tekufat ha-Mishna veha-Talmud*. Jerusalem, 1963.
Johnson, A. C. *Egypt and the Roman Empire*. Ann Arbor, 1951.
Roman Egypt in the Reign of Diocletian. An Economic Survey of Rome II. Paterson, 1959.

Johnson, A. C. and L. C. West. *Byzantine Egypt*. Princeton, 1949.
Johnson, Helen M. "The lemon in India", *Journal of the American Oriental Society* LVI (1936) 47–50.
Jomier, J. "Al-Fusṭāṭ", *Encyclopedia of Islam* 2nd edn, II 957–9.
Jones, A. H. M. *The Later Roman Empire*. 3 vols. plus maps. Oxford, 1964.
Joret, C. *Les plantes dans l'antiquité et au moyen âge*. 2 vols. Paris, 1897–1904.
Jumelle, H. "Les Aracées de Madagascar", *Annales du Musée Colonial de Marseille* 3rd ser. VII (1919) 179–89.
Juynboll, G. H. A. "The qurrā' in early Islamic history", *Journal of the Economic and Social History of the Orient* XVI (1973) 113–29.
Kammerer, A. *L'histoire antique d'Abyssinie*. Paris, 1926.
Karanis. The Temples, Coin Hoards, Botanical and Zoological Reports. Seasons 1924–31, ed. A. E. R. Boak. University of Michigan Studies, Humanistic Series XXX (1930).
Kāshif, Sayyida Ismā'īl. *Aḥmad bin Ṭūlūn*. Cairo, 1965.
Miṣr fī 'aṣr al-wulāh. Cairo, n.d.
Keimer, L. *Die Gartenpflanzen im alten Ägypten*. Hamburg/Berlin, 1924.
Jardins zoologiques d'Egypte. Cairo, 1954.
Kerner von Marilaun, A. *Die botanische Gärten, ihre Aufgabe in der Vergangenheit, Gegenwart und Zukunft*. Innsbruck, 1874.
Khayat, M. K. and M. C. Keatinge. *Food from the Arab World*. Beirut, 1969.
Kirk, W. "The N. E. monsoon and some aspects of African history", *Journal of African History* III (1962) 263–7.
Klein, J. *The Mesta*. Cambridge, Mass., 1920.
Kluge, F. *Etymologisches Wörterbuch der deutschen Sprache*. Berlin, 1934.
Knight, M. M. "Water and the course of empire in North Africa", *Quarterly Journal of Economics* XLIII (1928–9) 44–93.
Koenig, P. "Über die ägyptische Banane", *Die Ernährung der Pflanze* XXV (1929) 445–8.
Kouki, M. *Cuisine et pâtisserie tunisiennes*. Tunis, 1977.
Kraus, G. *Geschichte der Pflanzeneinführung in die europaïschen botanischen Gärten*. Leipzig, 1894.
Über die Bevölkerung Europas mit fremden Pflanzen. Leipzig, 1891.
Kremer, A. von. *Culturgeschichte des Orients unter den Chalifen*. 2 vols. Vienna, 1875–7.
Krenkow, F. "The construction of subterranean water supplies during the Abbaside Caliphate", *Glasgow University Oriental Society Transactions* XIII (1947–9) 23–32.
Kühnel, E. and L. Bellinger. *Washington D.C. Textile Museum. Catalogue of Dated Tiraz Fabrics*. Washington, 1952.
Kup, A. P. *A History of Sierra Leone, 1400–1787*. Cambridge, 1961.
Kurd 'Alī, M. *Ghūṭa Dimashq*. Damascus, 1953.
Kuros, G.-R. *Irans Kampf um Wasser*. Berlin, 1943.
Labarge, M. W. *A Baronial Household of the Thirteenth Century*. London, 1965.
Labib, S. Y. *Handelsgeschichte Ägyptens im Spätmittelalter*. Wiesbaden, 1965.
"Al-Iskandariyya", *Encyclopedia of Islam* 2nd edn, IV 132–7.
la Blanchère, D. *L'aménagement de l'eau et l'installation dans l'Afrique ancienne*. Paris, 1895.
Lacarra, J. M. *La reconquista española y la repoblación del país*. Zaragoza, 1951.
Lacvivier, R. de. *Quelques noms des plantes et synonymes français–catalans*. Perpignan, 1920.
La Granja, F. *La cocina arábigo–andaluza según un manuscrito inédito*. Madrid, 1960.
Lal. B. B. "A picture emerges: an assessment of the Carbon-14 datings of the protohistoric cultures of the Indo-Pakistan sub-continent", *Ancient India* XVIII–XIX (1962–3) 208–21.
Lambton, A. K. S. "Aspects of Saljūk–Ghuzz settlement in Persia". In *Islamic*

Civilization, 950–1150, ed. D. H. Richards. Oxford, 1973.
"Iran", *Encyclopedia of Islam* 2nd edn, IV 1–33.
"Iṣfahān", *Encyclopedia of Islam* 2nd edn, IV 100.
Landlord and Peasant in Persia. London, 1953.
"Reflections on the iqṭā'". In *Arabic and Islamic Studies in Honour of Hamilton A. R. Gibb*, ed. G. Makdisi. Cambridge, Mass., 1965.
"Reflections on the role of agriculture in medieval Persia". In *The Islamic Middle East, 700–1900*, ed. A. Udovitch. Princeton, 1981. 283–312.
Lamm, C. J. *Cotton In Medieval Textiles of the Near East*. Paris, 1937.
Lammens, H. *Le berceau de l'Islam*. Rome, 1914.
"Etudes sur le règne du Calife Omaiyade Mo'awia Ier", *Mélanges de la Faculté Orientale de l'Université Saint-Joseph de Beyrouth* I (1906) 1–108; II (1907) 1–172; III (1908) 145–312.
Lane, E. W. *An Arabic–English Lexicon*. 8 vols. London, 1863–93.
Lange, E. *Botanische Beiträge zur mitteleuropäischen Siedlungsgeschichte*. Berlin, 1971.
Langkavel, B. *Botanik der späteren Griechen vom 3. bis zum 13. Jahrhunderte*. Berlin, 1866.
Laoust, E. "Le nom de la charrue et de ses accessoires chez les Berbères", *Archives berbères* III (1918) 4–30.
"Au sujet de la charrue berbère", *Hespéris* X (1930) 37–47.
Lapidus, I. "Arab settlement and economic development of Iraq and Iran in the age of the Umayyad and early Abbasid caliphs". In *The Islamic Middle East, 700–1900*, ed. A. Udovitch. Princeton, 1981. 177–208.
"The conversion of Egypt to Islam", *Israel Oriental Studies* II (1972) 248–62.
"The evolution of Muslim urban society", *Comparative Studies in Society and History* XV (1973) 21–50.
Muslim Cities in the Later Middle Ages. Cambridge, Mass., 1967.
Lasinio, F. *Delle voce italiane di origine orientale*. Florence, 1866.
Lassner, J. *The Shaping of 'Abbāsid Rule*. Princeton, 1980.
The Topography of Baghdad in the Early Middle Ages. Detroit, 1970.
Latynin, B. A. "Voprosy istorii irrigatsii drevnei Fergany", *Institut Ethnografii. Kratkie soobshcheniia* XXVI (1957) 12–15.
Lauer, J. P., V. L. Täckholm and E. Åberg. "Les plantes découvertes dans les souterrains de l'enceinte du roi Zoser à Saqqarah (IIIe dynastie)", *Bulletin de l'Institut d'Egypte* XXXII (1949–50) 121–57.
Laufer, B. "The lemon in China and elsewhere", *Journal of the American Oriental Society* LIV (1934) 143–60.
"The noria or Persian wheel". In *Oriental Studies in Honor of Cursetji Erachji Pavry*, ed. J. D. C. Pavry. London, 1933. 238–50.
Sino-Iranica. Chinese Contributions to the History of Civilization in Ancient Iran. Chicago, 1919.
Laurent-Täckholm, V. *Faraos blomster*. Stockholm, 1951.
"The plant of Nagada", *Annales du Service des Antiquités de l'Egypte* LI (1951) 299–312.
Lautensach, H. *Maurische Züge im geographischen Bild der Iberischen Halbinsel*. Bonn, 1960.
Lázaro e Ibiza, B. *Compendio de la flora española*. 3 vols. Madrid, 1920.
Leclerc, N. L. *Histoire de la médecine arabe*. 2 vols. Paris, 1876.
Leeuwen, A. van. "L'eau en Tunisie: essai de bibliographie", *Ibla* XX (1957) 173–7.
Le Strange, G. *Baghdad During the Abbasid Caliphate*. Oxford, 1924.
"Description of Persia and Mesopotamia in the year 1340 A.D. from the Nuzhat-al-Ḳulūb of Ḥamd-Allah Mustawfī", *Journal of the Royal Asiatic Society* (1902) 49–74.

Levi della Vida, G. "Baghdad", *Enciclopedia italiana* v (1930) 848.
Levillain, L. *Examen critique des chartes mérovingiennes et carolingiennes de l'Abbaye de Corbie*. Paris, 1902.
Lévi-Provençal, E. *L'Espagne musulmane au Xe siècle. Institutions et vie sociale*. Paris, 1932.
"La fondation de Fès", *Annales de l'Institut d'Etudes Orientales d'Alger* IV (1938) 25–53.
Histoire de l'Espagne musulmane. 3 vols. Paris/Leyden, 1950–3.
Lézine, A. *Deux villes d'Ifriqiya*. Paris, 1971.
Li, Hui-lin. "The vegetables of ancient China", *Economic Botany* XXIII (1969) 253–60.
Lippmann, E. von. *Geschichte des Zuckers*. Leipzig, 1890.
Littmann, E. *Deutsche Aksum-Expedition* IV. Berlin, 1913.
Lloyd, J. V. *Origin and History of All the Pharmacopeial Vegetable Drugs, Chemicals and Preparations, I: Vegetable Drugs*. Cincinnati, 1929.
Løkkegaard, F. *Islamic Taxation in the Classic Period with Special Reference to Circumstances in Iraq*. Copenhagen, 1950.
Lokotsch, K. *Etymologisches Wörterbuch der europäischen (germanischen, romanischen und slavischen) Wörter orientalischen Ursprungs*. Heidelberg, 1927.
Lombard, M. *Les textiles dans le monde musulman du VIIe au XIIe siècle*. Paris/The Hague/New York, 1978.
Lopez de Meneses, A. *Los consulados catalanes de Alejandría y Damasco en el Reinado de Pedro el Ceremonioso*. Zaragoza, 1956.
Lourie, E. "Free Moslems in the Balearics under Christian rule in the thirteenth century", *Speculum* XLV (1970) 624–49.
Löw, I. *Aramäische Pflanzennamen*. Leipzig, 1881.
Die Flora der Juden. 4 vols. in 6. Vienna/Leipzig, 1926–34.
Mack Smith, D. *A History of Sicily*. 2 vols. New York, 1969.
McNair, J. B. *Sugar and Sugar-Making*. Chicago, 1927.
Madan, C. L., B. M. Kapur and R. K. Gupta. "Saffron", *Economic Botany* XX (1966) 377–85.
Magalhães Godinho, V. "A economia das Canárias nos séculos XIV e XV", *Revista de história* (São Paulo) X (1952) 311–48.
Magnin, J. "L'eau de Zaghouan", *Ibla* XX (1947) 89–93.
Makkī, Maḥmūd 'Alī. "Ensayo sobre las aportaciones orientales en la España Musulmana", *Revista del Instituto de Estudios Islámicos en Madrid* IX–X (1961–2) 65–231.
Marçais, G. *L'architecture musulmane d'Occident*. Paris, 1954.
L'art musulman. Paris, 1962.
"La Berbérie du VIIe au XVIe siècle". In *Deuxième congrès national des sciences historiques*. Algiers, 1932. 277–87.
La Berbérie musulmane et l'Orient au Moyen Age. Paris, 1946.
"Les jardins de l'Islam". In *Mélanges d'histoire et d'archéologie de l'Occident musulman*. 2 vols. Algiers, 1957. I 233–44.
Maria d'Aleppo, P. G. Calvaruso and G. M. Calvaruso. *Le fonti arabiche nel dialetto siciliano*. Rome, 1910.
Marshall, Sir John. *Mohenjo-daro and the Indus Civilization*. 3 vols. London, 1931.
Martínez Ferrando, J. E. *Jaime II de Aragón*. 2 vols. Barcelona, 1948.
Martínez Ruiz, J. "Notas sobre el refinado del azúcar de caña entre los moriscos granadinos: estudio léxico", *Revista de dialectología y tradiciones populares* XX (1964) 271–88.
Martínez Santa-Olalla, J. "Cereales y plantas de la cultura ibero-sahariana en Almizarague (Almería)", *Cuadernos de historia primitiva* I (1946) 35–45.

Masefield, G. B. "Crops and livestock". In *Cambridge Economic History of Europe* IV. Cambridge, 1967. 276–301.
Masry, A. H. "The historic legacy of Saudi Arabia", *Atlal. The Journal of Saudi Arabian Archeology* I (1977) 9–19.
Massey, R. E. "A note on the early history of cotton", *Sudan Notes and Records* VI (1923) 231.
Massignon, L. "Explication du plan de Kufa". In *Mélanges Maspéro*. 3 vols. in 7. Cairo, 1934–40. III 334–60.
Le Maroc dans les premières années du XVIe siècle: tableau géographique d'après Léon l'Africain. Algiers, 1906.
Materialy po istorii zemledeliia S.S.S.R., ed. P. A. Zhukovskii. 2 vols. Moscow, 1956.
Mathews' Textile Fibres. Their Physical, Microscopic and Chemical Properties. 6th edn, ed. H. R. Mauersberger. New York/London, 1954.
Mauny, R. "Notes historiques autour des principales plantes cultivées d'Afrique occidentale", *Bulletin de l'Institut Français d'Afrique Noire* XV (1953) 684–730.
"L'ouest africain chez les géographes arabes au Moyen Age". In *Première conférence internationale des africanistes de l'Ouest. Comptes rendus* II. Dakar, 1951. 503–8.
"La savane nilo-tchadienne, voie de pénétration des influences égyptiennes et orientales?" In *Conferencia internacional de Africanistas occidentales* II. Madrid, 1954. 83–115.
Tableau géographique de l'ouest africain au moyen âge. Dakar, 1961.
Maurizio, A. *Histoire de l'alimentation végétale*. Paris, 1932.
Mazahéri, A. A. *La vie quotidienne des Musulmans au Moyen Age*. Paris, 1951.
Mazloum, S. *L'ancienne canalisation d'eau d'Alep*. Documents d'études orientales V. Damascus, 1936.
Mazzaoui, M. *The Cotton Industry of Medieval Italy*. Cambridge, 1981.
"The cotton industry of northern Italy in the late Middle Ages: 1150–1450", *Journal of Economic History* XXXII (1972) 262–86.
Mekinassi, A. *Léxico de las palabras españolas de origen árabe*. Tetuan, 1973.
Menéndez Pidal, R. "La invasión musulmana y las lenguas ibéricas". In *Etudes d'orientalisme dédiées à la mémoire de Lévi-Provençal*. 2 vols. Paris, 1962. I 191–6.
Orígenes del español. 3rd edn. Madrid, 1950.
Messedaglia, L. "Le piante alimentari del *Tacuinum sanitatis*, manoscritto miniato della Biblioteca Nazionale di Parigi", *Atti del Reale Istituto Veneto di Scienze, Lettere ed Arti* XCVI (1936–7) 571–681.
Meyer, E. H. F. *Geschichte der Botanik*. 4 vols. Königsberg, 1854–7.
Meyerhof, M. "Die allgemeine Botanik und Pharmacologie des Edrisi", *Archiv für Geschichte der Mathematik, der Naturwissenschaft und der Technik* XII (1930) 225–36.
"Esquisse d'histoire de la pharmacologie et botanique chez les Musulmans d'Espagne", *Al-Ándalus* III (1935) 1–41.
"Essai sur les noms portugais de drogues dérivés de l'arabe", *Petrus Nonius* II (1938) 1–8, 95–6.
"Sur un traité d'agriculture composé par un sultan yéménite du XIVe siècle", *Bulletin de l'Institut d'Egypte* XXV (1942–3) 54–63; XXVI (1943–4) 51–65.
"Über die Pharmacologie und Botanik des arabischen Geographen, Edrisi", *Archiv für Geschichte der Mathematik, der Naturwissenschaft und der Technik* XII (1929) 45–53.
"Über einige Privatbibliotheken im Fatimidischen Ägypten", *Rivista degli studi orientali* XII (1929–30) 286–90.
Mez, A. *The Renaissance of Islam*. Patna, 1937.

Mieli, A. *Panorama general de historia de la ciencia, II: El mundo islámico.* 2nd edn. Buenos Aires, 1952.
La science arabe et son rôle dans l'évolution scientifique mondiale. Leyden, 1966.
Millás Vallicrosa, J. M. *La ciencia geopónica entre los autores hispanoárabes.* Madrid, 1954.
"Los cinco últimos capítulos de la obra agronómica de Ibn Baṣṣāl", *Tamuda* I (1953) 47–58.
Estudios sobre historia de la ciencia española. Barcelona, 1949.
Nuevas aportaciones para el estudio de la transmisión de la ciencia a Europa a través de España. Barcelona, 1943.
"Un nuevo manuscrito de la obra agronómica de al Tignari", *Tamuda* I (1953) 85–6.
Nuevos estudios sobre historia de la ciencia española. Barcelona, 1960.
Las traducciones orientales en los manuscritos de la Biblioteca Catedral de Toledo. Madrid, 1942.
Miquel, A. *La géographie humaine du monde musulman jusqu'au milieu du 11e siècle.* Paris/The Hague, 1967.
Moldenke, H. "The economic plants of the Bible", *Economic Botany* VIII (1954) 152–63.
Moldenke, H. and A. L. Moldenke. *The Plants of the Bible.* Waltham, Mass., 1952.
Monneret de Villard, U. *La scultura ad Ahnās. Note sull'origine dell'arte copta.* Milan, 1923.
Montagné, P. *Nouveau Larousse gastronomique*, rev. R. J. Courtine. Paris, 1960.
Monteil, V. "Le Coton chez les Noirs", *Bulletin du Comité d'Etudes Historiques et Scientifiques de l'A.O.F.* IX (1926) 585–684.
Monteil, V. and C. Sauvage. *Contribution à l'étude de la flore du Sahara occidental.* 2 vols. Paris, 1949–53.
Moraes Silva, A. de. *Grande dicionário da língua portuguesa.* 12 vols. Lisbon, 1949–59.
Moreland, W. H. *India at the Death of Akbar.* London, 1920.
Morony, M. "Landholding in seventh century Iraq: a comparison of late-Sasanian and early Islamic patterns". In *The Islamic Middle East, 700–900*, ed. A. L. Udovitch. Princeton, 1980.
Moscati, Sabatino. *The World of the Phoenicians*, tr. A. Hamilton. London, 1968.
Mossèri, V. M. "Sur l'origine du Riz et l'histoire de sa culture en Egypte", *Bulletin de l'Institut d'Egypte* IV (1922) 25–34.
Mote, F. W. "A millennium of Chinese urban history: form, time and space concepts in Soochow", *Rice University Studies* IV pt 4 (1973) 35–65.
Mukherjee, S. K. "The mango", *Economic Botany* VII (1953) 130–62.
"Origin, distribution and phylogenetic affinities of the species of *Mangifera* Linn.", *Journal of the Linnean Society of London. Botany* LV (1953) 65–83.
"The origin of mango", *Indian Journal of Genetics and Plant Breeding* XI (1951) 49–56.
Müller-Wodarg, D. "Die Landwirtschaft Ägyptens in der frühen 'Abbāsidenzeit, 750–969 n. Chr. (132–358 d.H.)", *Der Islam* XXXI (1954) 174–227; XXXII (1957) 14–78, 141–67; XXXIII (1958) 310–21.
Muñoz Perez, J. and J. Benito Arranz. *Guía bibliográfica para una geografía agraria de España.* Madrid, 1961.
Murdock, G. P. *Africa: Its Peoples and their Culture History.* New York, 1959.
Musset, R. "Le rôle du monde méditerranéen dans l'expansion des plantes de grande culture intertropicales". In *Deuxième Congrès National des Sciences Historiques.* Algiers, 1932. 313–16.
Nadkarni, K. M. and A. K. Nadkarni. *Indian Materia Medica.* 3rd edn. 2 vols. Bombay/Panvel, 1955.
Nallino, C. A. "Tracce di opere greche giunte agli Arabi per trafila Pehlevica". In

A Volume of Oriental Studies Presented to Edward G. Browne, ed. T. W. Arnold and R. A. Nicholson. Cambridge, 1922. 345–63.

al-Naṣr, A. A. *Ta'rīkh al-nabāt*. Beirut, 1962.

Naville, E. *The Temple of Deir el Bahari*, pt III. London, 1898.

Needham, J. *Science and Civilisation in China*. 5 vols. in 9 to date. Cambridge, 1954– .

Neustadt, D. "The plague and its effects upon the Mamluk army", *Journal of the Royal Asiatic Society* 1946, 67–73.

Neuvonen, E. K. *Los arabismos del español en el siglo XIII*. Studia orientalia X, pt I. Helsinki, 1942.

Newman, J. *Agricultural Life of the Jews of Babylonia Between the Years 200 C.E. and 500 C.E.* London, 1932.

Niccoli, V. *Saggio storico e bibliografico dell'agricoltura italiana dalle origini al 1900*. Turin, 1902.

Nicholls, W. "The saqia in Dongola province", *Sudan Notes and Records* I (1918) 21–4.

Nicholson, G. E. "The production, history, uses and relationships of cotton (*Gossypium* spp.) in Ethiopia", *Economic Botany* XIV (1960) 3–36.

Noiret, H. *Documents inédits pour servir à l'histoire de la domination vénitienne en Crète*. Bibliothèque des Ecoles Françaises d'Athènes et de Rome LXI. Paris, 1892.

Norris, H. T. "Yemenis in the western Sahara", *Journal of African History* III (1962) 317–22.

d'Oliveira Feijão, R. *Elucidário fitológico* II Lisbon, 1961.

Oliveira Marques, A. H. de. *Introdução à história da agricultura em Portugal*. Lisbon, 1968.

Oliver Asín, J. *Historia del nombre "Madrid"*. Madrid, 1959.

Orientalische Studien Theodor Nödelke, ed. C. Bezold. 2 vols. Giessen, 1906.

Pales, L. *L'alimentation en A.O.F.* Dakar, 1954.

Pankhurst, R. *An Introduction to the Economic History of Ethiopia*. London, 1961.

Pavani, E. "Intorno ai giardini botanici", *Bolletino della Società Adriatica di Scienzi Naturali in Trieste* IX (1886) 51–93.

Pellat, C. "Baṣra" *Encyclopedia of Islam* 2nd edn, I 1085–7.

Le milieu baṣrien et la formation de Ǧāḥiẓ. Paris, 1953.

Pellegrini, G.-B. *Gli arabismi nelle lingue neolatine con speciale riguardo all'Italia*. 2 vols. Brescia, 1972.

"L'elemento arabo nelle lingue neolatine". In *L'Occidente e l'Islam nell'alto Medioevo*. Settimane di studio del Centro Italiano di Studi sull'alto Medioevo XII (1965) ii 697–790.

Pelliot, P. *Notes on Marco Polo*. 2 vols. Paris, 1959–63.

Pereira Coutinho, A. X. *A flora de Portugal*. Paris, 1913.

Pérès, H. "Le palmier en Espagne musulmane". In *Mélanges Gaudefroy-Demombynes*. Cairo, 1935–45. 224–39.

La poésie andalouse en arabe classique au XIe siècle. Paris, 1953.

Peri, I. *Città e campagna in Sicilia*. 2 vols. Palermo, 1953–6.

Petrie, W. M. F. *Ehnasya*. London, 1905.

Petrushevskii, I. P. "L'état de l'agriculture en Iran aux XIIIe–XIVe siècles", *Utchenié zap* CXCV (1956) 69–113.

"Emploi du labeur d'esclaves en Iran et dans les pays limitrophes dans le bas Moyen Age". In *XXV Congrès des Orientalistes. Conférences présentées par la délégation de l'URSS*. Moscow, 1960.

"The socio-economic condition of Iran under the Il-Khans". In *Cambridge History of Iran* V. Cambridge, 1968. 483–537.

Zemledelle i agrarnye otnosheniia v Irane XIII–XIV vekov. Leningrad, 1960.

Pfister, R. "L'introduction du Coton en Egypte musulmane", *Revue des arts asiatiques* XI (1937) 167–72.

Nouveaux textiles de Palmyre. Paris, 1937.
"Le rôle de l'Iran dans les textiles d'Antinoé", *Ars Islamica* XIII–XIV (1948) 46–74.
Les textiles de Halabiyeh (Zenobia). Paris, 1951.
Textiles de Palmyre. 3 vols. Paris, 1934–40.
"Toiles à inscriptions abbasides et fatimides", *Bulletin d'études orientales* XI (1945–6) 47–90.
Les toiles imprimées de Fostat et de l'Hindoustan. Paris, 1938.
Philippi, F. *Los jardines botánicos*. Santiago de Chile, 1878.
Piddington, H. *An English Index to the Plants of India*. Calcutta, 1832.
Piédallu, A. *Le Sorgho. Son histoire, ses applications*. Paris, 1923.
Pignauvin, G. *L'hydraulique en Tunisie d'après les Romains*. Tunis, 1932.
Pigulevskaya, N. *Les villes de l'état iranien aux époques parthe et sassanide*. Paris, 1963.
Pines, S. "What was original in Arab science?" In *Scientific Change*, ed. A. C. Crombie. London, 1963. 181–205.
Pinto, O. "Le biblioteche degli Arabi nell'età degli Abbasidi", *La bibliofilia* XXX (1928) 1939–65.
Pipitone Cannone, A. "Governo delle acque e case rurale nella Sicilia musulmana", *Problemi Mediterranei* XVI (1939) 273–82.
"La scuola degli Arabi: l'agricoltura in Sicilia sotto i musulmani e nel periodo normanno-suevo", *Problemi Mediterranei* XVI (1939) 204–17.
Planhol, X. de. *Fondements géographiques de l'histoire de l'Islam*. Paris, 1968.
Poliak, A. N. "L'arabisation de l'Orient sémitique", *Revue des études islamiques* XII (1938) 35–63.
"Classification of lands in Islamic Law and its technical terms", *American Journal of Semitic Languages and Literatures* LVII (1940) 50–62.
Poncet, J. "Le mythe de la 'catastrophe' hilalienne", *Annales: économies, sociétés, civilisations* XXII (1967) 1099–120. See also the discussion in *ibid*. XIII (1968) 390–6, 660–2.
Pons Boigues, F. *Ensayo bio-bibliográfico sobre los historiadores y geografos arábigo-españoles*. Madrid, 1898.
Popenoe, P. "The distribution of the date-palm", *Geographic Review* XVI (1926) 117–21.
Popovic, A. "Les facteurs économiques et la révolte des Zanǧ". Paper presented at the Princeton conference on the economic and social history of the Middle East, 1974.
Porru, V. *Nou dizionariu universali Sardu–Italianu*. Casteddu, 1832.
Portères, R. *Les appellations des céréales en Afrique*. Paris, 1959. (Also published as a series of articles in *Journal d'agriculture tropicale et de botanique appliquée* V–VI 1958–9.)
"Berceaux agricoles primaires sur le continent africain", *Journal of African History* III (1962) 195–210.
"Genres botaniques privilégiés dans les néolithiques céréaliers et origine présumée indienne de l'agriculture céréalière de l'Afrique Tropicale", *Journal de l'agriculture tropicale et de botanique appliquée* XIII (1966) 607–11.
"Géographie alimentaire, berceaux agricoles et migrations des plantes cultivées en Afrique intertropicale", *Comptes-rendus sommaires des séances de la Société Biogéographique* 1951, 16–21.
"Pousses et feuilles alimentaires employées par les peuplades de la zone montagneuse forestière de l'Ouest africain (des Monts de Loma au Massif des Dans)". In *Première Conférence Internationale des Africanistes de l'Ouest*. Dakar, 1951. II 71–81.
"Vieilles cultures de l'Afrique intertropicale", *L'agronomie tropicale* V (1950) 489–507.
Post, G. E. and J. E. Dinsmore. *Flora of Syria, Palestine and Sinai*. 2 vols. Beirut, 1932–3.

Potts, D., A. S. Mughanum, J. Frye and D. Sanders. "Comprehensive archeological survey programme: preliminary report on the second phase of the Eastern Province Survey 1397/1977", *Atlal. The Journal of Saudi Arabian Archeology* II (1978) 7–27.

Prawer, J. "Etude de quelques problèmes agraires et sociaux d'une seigneurie croisée au XIIIe siècle", *Byzantion* XXII (1952) 5–61; XXIII (1953) 143–70.

Histoire du Royaume Latin de Jérusalem. 2 vols. Paris, 1969–70.

Preston, H. G. *Rural Conditions in the Kingdom of Jerusalem*. Philadelphia, 1903.

Rabie, H. *The Financial System of Egypt A.H. 564–741/A.D. 1169–1341*. London, 1972.

"The size and value of the *Iqṭā'* in Egypt, 564–741 A.H./1169–1341 A.D.". In *Studies in the Economic History of the Middle East*, ed. M. A. Cook. London, 1970. 129–38.

"Some technical aspects of agriculture in medieval Egypt". In *The Islamic Middle East, 700–1900*, ed. A. Udovitch. Princeton, 1981. 59–90.

Rawski, E. S. *Agricultural Change and the Peasant Economy of South China*. Cambridge, Mass., 1972.

Raymond, A. "Les grandes épidémies de peste au Caire aux XVIIe et XVIIIe siècles", *Bulletin d'études orientales* XXV (1972) 203–10.

"Signes urbains et étude de la population des grandes villes arabes à l'époque ottomane", *Bulletin d'études orientales* XXVII (1974) 183–93.

Reconquista española y la repoblación del país, La. Zaragoza, 1951.

Redman, C. L. and P. J. Watson. "Systematic, intensive surface collection", *American Antiquity* XXXV (1970) 279–91.

Reifenberg, A. *The Struggle Between the Desert and the Sown. Rise and Fall of Agriculture in the Levant*. Jerusalem, 1955.

Rémondon, R. *La crise de l'Empire Romain*. Paris, 1964.

Renaud, H. P. J. "La contribution des Arabes à la connaissance des espèces végétales: les botanistes musulmans", *Bulletin de la Société des Sciences Naturelles du Maroc* XV (1935) 58–71.

Renfrew, J. M. *Paleoethnobotany*. London, 1973.

Reynolds, P. K. *The Earliest Evidence of Banana Culture*. American Oriental Society, Supplements XII. Baltimore, 1951.

Ribera y Tarragó, *Disertaciones y opúsculos*. 2 vols. Madrid, 1928.

Richard, J. "Une économie coloniale? Chypre et ses ressources agricoles au Moyen-Age" *Internationale Zeitschrift für Byzantinistik* V (1977) 331–52.

Richter, G. *Das Geschichtsbild der arabischen Historiker des Mittelalters*. Tübingen, 1933.

Riley-Smith, J. *The Feudal Nobility and the Kingdom of Jerusalem, 1174–1277*. London, 1973.

Rilki, M. *Das Pflanzenkleid der Mittelmeerländer*. 3 vols. Bern, 1943–48.

Risso, A. and A. Poiteau. *Histoire naturelle des Orangers*. Paris, 1818.

Ritter, C. *Über die geographische Verbreitung des Zuckerrohrs*. Berlin, 1840.

Robertson-Proschowsky, A. "Etudes récentes sur la culture du Manguier", *Revue de botanique appliquée et agriculture coloniale* IV (1924) 263–72.

Roberty, G. "Hypothèses sur l'origine et les migrations des Cotonniers cultivés et notes sur les Cotonniers sauvages", *Candollea* VII (1938) 297–360.

Robinson, T. R. "Grapefruit and pummelo", *Economic Botany* VI (1952) 228–45.

Rodinson, M. "Histoire économique et histoire des classes sociales dans le monde musulman". In *Studies in the Economic History of the Middle East*, ed. M. A. Cook. London, 1970.

"La Ma'mūniyyat en Orient et en Occident". In *Etudes d'orientalisme dédiées à la mémoire de Lévi-Provençal*. 2 vols. Paris, 1962. II 733–47.

"Recherches sur les documents arabes relatifs à la cuisine", *Revue des études islamiques* XVII (1949) 95–165.
Rokseth, P. *Terminologie de la culture des céréales à Majorque*. Barcelona, 1923.
Rolland, E. *Flore populaire ou histoire naturelle des plantes dans leurs rapports avec la linguistique et le folklore*. 11 vols. Paris, 1967.
Romano, R. "Les prix au Moyen Age: Proche-Orient et Occident chrétien", *Annales: économies, sociétés, civilisations* XVIII (1963) 699–703.
Romano, S. F. *Breve storia della Sicilia*. Torino, 1964.
Rosenthal, F. *The Herb. Hashish versus Medieval Muslim Society*. Leyden, 1971.
A History of Muslim Historiography. Leiden, 1952.
Rostovtzeff, M. *The Social and Economic History of the Roman Empire*. 2 vols. Oxford, 1957.
Roxburgh, W. *Flora Indica; or Description of Indian Plants*. 2 vols. Serampore, 1820–4.
Rozman, G. *Urban Networks in Ch'ing China and Tokugawa Japan*. Princeton, 1973.
Russell, J. C. *Late Ancient and Medieval Population*. Transactions of the American Philosophical Society, new ser. XLVIII iii. Philadelphia, 1958.
Medieval Cities and their Regions. Newton Abbot, 1972.
"The population of medieval Egypt", *Journal of the American Research Center in Egypt* V (1966) 69–82.
Saccardo, P. A. *La botanica in Italia*. 2 vols. Venice, 1895–1901.
Cronologia della flora italiana. Padua, 1909.
Sadan, J. "Meubles et acculturation: Bédouins et sédentaires dans la civilisation califienne", *Annales: économies, sociétés, civilisations* XXV (1970) 1354–75.
Salin, E. *La civilisation mérovingienne*. 4 vols. Paris, 1949–59.
El-Samarraie, H. A. *Agriculture in Iraq During the Third Century, A.H.* Beirut, 1972.
Sankalia, H. D., *et al. From History to Pre-History at Nevasa*. Poona, 1961.
Santhanam, V. and Joseph B. Hutchinson. "Cotton", in *Evolutionary Studies in World Crops*, ed. Sir J. Hutchinson. Cambridge, 1974. 89–100.
Sarton, G. *Introduction to the History of Science*. 3 vols. in 5. Washington, 1927–48.
Sauer, C. O. *Agricultural Origins and Dispersals*. New York, 1952.
Sauer, J. D. "A reevaluation of the coconut as an indicator of human dispersal". In *Man Across the Sea*, ed. C. L. Riley *et al.* Austin/London, 1971. 309–19.
Sauvaget, J. *Alep*. 2 vols. Paris, 1941.
"Remarques sur les monuments omeyyades", *Journal asiatique* CCXXXI (1939) 1–59.
Sbath, P. "L'ouvrage géoponique d'Anatolius de Bérytos (IVe siècle)", *Bulletin de l'Institut d'Egypte* XIII (1930–1) 47–54.
Schafer, E. H. *The Golden Peaches of Samarkand. A Study of T'ang Exotics*. Berkeley/Los Angeles, 1963.
The Vermilion Bird. T'ang Images of the South. Berkeley/Los Angeles, 1967.
Schaube, A. *Handelsgeschichte der romanischen Völker des Mittelmeergebiets bis zum Ende der Kreuzzüge*. Munich/Berlin, 1906.
Schiemann, E. "Einkorn im alten Aegypten?" *Der Züchter* XXIV (1954) 139–99.
Die Entstehung der Kulturpflanzen. Berlin, 1932.
"Gedanken zur Genzentrentheorie Vavilovs", *Die Naturwissenschaften* XXVII (1939) 377–83, 394–401.
"Die Geschichte der Kulturpflanzen im Wandel der biologischen Methoden", *Saetryk af Botanisk Tiasskrift* LI (1954) 308–29.
"Neue Untersuchungen an Secale africanum Stapf", *Botanische Jahrbücher* LXXV (1950) 196–205.
Schlimmer, J. L. *Terminologie médico-pharmaceutique et anthropologique française–persane*. Teheran, 1874.
Schlingloff, D. "Cotton-manufacture in ancient India", *Journal of the Economic and Social History of the Orient* XVII (1974) 81–90.

Schmidt, G. A. *Die landwirtschaftlichen Nutzpflanzen Afrikas*. Berlin, 1942.
Schmucker, W. *Die pflanzliche und mineralische Materia Medica im "Firdaus al-Ḥikma" des Ṭabarī*. Bonner Orientalische Studien, new ser. XVIII. Bonn, 1969.
Schnebel, M. *Die Landwirtschaft im hellenistischen Ägypten*. Munich, 1925.
Schnell, R. *Plantes alimentaires et vie agricole de l'Afrique Noire*. Paris, 1957.
Schrieke, B. *Indonesian Sociological Studies*. 2 vols. The Hague, 1966.
Schulten, A. *Estrabon. Geografía de Iberia*. Fontes Hispanicae Antiquae VI. Barcelona, 1952.
Iberische Landeskunde. Geographie des antiken Spanien. 2 vols. Strasbourg/Kehl, 1955–7.
Schulz, A. *Die Geschichte der kultivierten Getreide*. Halle a. d. S., 1913.
"Die Getreide der alten Aegypter", *Abhandlungen der Naturforschenden Gesellschaft zu Halle a. d. S.* New Ser. V (1916) 5–39.
Schulz, H. *Vorlesungen über Wirkung und Anwendung der deutschen Arzneipflanzen*. Ulm/Donau, 1955.
Schwanitz, F. *The Origin of Cultivated Plants*. Cambridge, Mass., 1966.
Schwarz, P. *Iran im Mittelalter nach den arabischen Geographen*. 5 vols. Leipzig, 1896–1925.
"Die Zuckerpressen von Ahwāz", *Der Islam* VI (1916) 269–79.
Schweinfurth, G. "Aegyptens auswärtige Beziehungen hinsichtlich der Culturgewächse", *Verhandlungen der Berliner Anthropologishen Gesellschaft*, meeting of 18 July 1891. 649–69.
Arabische Pflanzennamen aus Aegypten, Algerien und Jemen. Berlin, 1912.
Sur certains rapports entre l'Arabie Heureuse et l'ancienne Egypte. Geneva, 1970.
"Sur l'origine africaine des plantes cultivées en Egypte", *Bulletin de l'Institut Egyptien* XII (1872–3) 200–6.
"Was Afrika an Kulturpflanzen Amerika zu verdanken hat und was es ihm gab". In *Festschrift Eduard Seler*. Stuttgart, 1922. 503–42.
Schweitzer, C. "Muslim waterworks", *Islamic Culture* XIII (1939) 79–82.
Scora, R. W. "On the history and origin of citrus", *Bulletin of the Torrey Botanical Club* CII (1975) 309–75.
Seco de Lucena, L. "La civilización hispanomusulmana del siglo XV", typescript, in press.
Segré, A. "Note sulla storia dei cereali nell'antichità", *Aegyptus* XXX (1950) 161–97.
Semple, E. C. *The Geography of the Mediterranean Region. Its Relation to Ancient History*. New York, 1931.
Sereni, E. "Note di storia dell'alimentazione nel mezzogiorno: i Napoletani da 'Mangiafoglia' a 'Mangiamaccheroni'", *Chronache meridionali* V (1958) 272–95, 353–77, 398–422.
Storia del paesaggio agrario italiano. Bari, 1961.
Serjeant, R. B. "Material for a history of Islamic textiles up to the Mongol conquest", *Ars Islamica* IX (1942) 54–92; X (1943) 73–104; XI–XII (1946) 98–145; XIII–XIV (1948) 75–117; XV–XVI (1951) 29–85.
"Some irrigation systems in Ḥaḍramawt", *Bulletin of the School of Oriental and Africa Studies* XXVII (1964) 33–76.
Sha, Bi-ti. "Cong kaogufajueziliao kan Xinjiang qudai de mianhua zhongzhi he fangzhi", *Wenwu* 1973, 48–51.
Shaban, M. A. *The 'Abbāsid Revolution*. Cambridge, 1970.
Islamic History A.D. 600–750 (A.H. 132). A New Interpretation. Cambridge, 1971.
Shih, H.-Y. "Textile finds in the People's Republic of China". In *Studies in Textile History*, ed. V. Gervers. Toronto, 1977.
Shihābī, M. "Al-filāḥa al-andalusīya", *Revue de l'Académie Arabe de Damas* XI (1931) 193–200.

"Kutub al-filāḥa al-'arabīya", *Revue de l'Académie Arabe de Damas* XXXV (1960) 529–40.
"Vocabulaire des principaux termes de sociologie végétale 'phyto-sociologique'", *Revue de l'Académie Arabe de Damas* XXXIII (1958) 21–35.
Shihābī, M., G. S. Colin, A. K. S. Lambton, H. Inalcik and I. Habib. "Filāḥa", *Encyclopedia of Islam* 2nd edn, II 899–910.
Silvestre de Sacy, A. "Sur la nature et les révolutions du droit de propriété territoriale en Egypte depuis la conquête de ce pays par les Musulmans jusqu'à l'expédition des Français", *Mémoires de l'Institut Royal de France* I (1815); V (1821); VII (1824).
Simmonds, N. W. *Bananas*. London, 1959.
"Bananas". In *Evolution of Crop Plants*, ed. N. W. Simmonds. London/New York, 1979. 211–15.
The Evolution of the Bananas. London, 1962.
"Sugarcanes". In *Evolution of Crop Plants*, ed. N. W. Simmonds. London/New York, 1979. 104–8.
Simonet, F. J. *Glosario de voces ibéricos y latinas usadas entre los Mozárabes*. Madrid, 1888.
Simoons, F. J. "Some questions on the economic prehistory of Ethiopia", *Journal of African History* VI (1965) 1–12.
Singer, C. J., E. J. Holmyard, A. R. Hall *et al. A History of Technology*. 5 vols. New York/London 1954–8.
Slicher van Bath, B. *The Agrarian History of Western Europe, A.D. 500–1800*. London, 1963.
Small, J. K. "The coconut-palm – *Cocos nucifera*", *Journal of the New York Botanical Gardens* XXX (1929) 153–61.
Smires, L. B. *La cuisine marocaine*. Paris, 1970.
Smith, A. "Qanats", *Journal of the Iran Society* I (1951) 86–90.
Smith, C. E. "Plant fibers and civilization – cotton, a case in point", *Economic Botany* XIX (1965) 71–82.
Snowden, J. D. *The Cultivated Races of Sorghum*. London, 1936.
Solignac, M. *Recherches sur les installations hydrauliques de Kairouan et des steppes tunisiennes du VIIe au XIe siècle (J.C.)*. Algiers, 1953.
"Travaux hydrauliques hafsides de Tunis". In *Deuxième congrès de la Fédération des Sociétés Savantes de l'Afrique du Nord*. Algiers, 1936. 519–80.
Soothill, W. E. *China and the West*. London/Oxford, 1925.
Sourdel, D. "Baġdād, capitale du nouvel empire 'Abbāside", *Arabica* IX (1962) 251–65.
"Barīd", *Encyclopedia of Islam* 2nd edn, I 1045–7.
"Ghulām", *Encyclopedia of Islam* 2nd edn, II 1079–81.
Sourdel, D. and J. Sourdel. *La civilisation de l'Islam classique*. Paris, 1968.
Sourdel-Thomine, J. "Le peuplement de la région des 'villes mortes' (Syrie du Nord) à l'époque ayyūbide", *Arabica* I (1954) 187–200.
Sousa, A. de. *Antiqua Lusitania. De geographia, de populo, de moribus, de re rustica*. Rio de Janeiro, 1958.
Southall, A. "The problem of Malagasy origins". In *East Africa and the Orient. Cultural Syntheses in Pre-colonial Times*, ed. H. N. Chittick and R. I. Rotberg. New York/London, 1975. 192–215.
Sprengling, M. "From Persian to Arabic", *American Journal of Semitic Languages and Literatures* LVI (1939) 175–224, 325–36; LVII (1940) 302–5.
Spuler, B. *Iran in früh-Islamischer Zeit*. Wiesbaden, 1952.
Die Mongolen in Iran. Berlin, 1955.
Steiger, A. *Contribución a la fonética del hispano–árabe y de los arabismos en el ibero–románico y el siciliano*. Madrid, 1932.

Stein, A. *Innermost Asia*. 4 vols. Oxford, 1928.
Serindia. 5 vols. Oxford, 1921.

Steinschneider, M. *Die arabischen Übersetzungen aus dem Griechischen*. Berlin, 1889–96.
Die hebraïschen Übersetzungen des Mittelalters und die Juden als Dolmetscher. Berlin, 1893.

Stemler, A. B. L., J. R. Harlan and J. M. J. De Wet. "Evolutionary history of cultivated sorghums (*Sorghum bicolor* [Linn.] Moench) of Ethiopia", *Bulletin of the Torrey Botanical Club* CII (1975) 325–33.

Stephens, S. G. "The effects of domestication on certain seed and fiber properties of perennial forms of cotton, *Gossypium hirsutum* L.", *American Naturalist* XCIX (1965) 355–72.
Factors Affecting Seed Dispersal in "Gossypium" and their Possible Evolutionary Significance. North Carolina Agricultural Experiment Station Technical Bulletin CXXXI. Raleigh, 1958.
"Some problems of interpreting transoceanic dispersal of New World cottons". In *Man Across the Sea*, ed. C. L. Riley *et al.* Austin/London, 1971. 401–15.

Stern, H. *Le calendrier de 354. Etude sur son texte et ses illustrations*. Paris, 1953.
"Le cycle des mois de la Porte de Mars à Reims". In *Hommages à Albert Grenier*, ed. M. Renard. 3 vols. Brussels, 1962. III 1441–6.
"Sur quelques pavements paléo-chrétiens du Liban", *Cahiers archéologiques* XV (1965) 21–37.

Stevens, C. E. "Agriculture and rural life in the later Roman Empire". In *Cambridge Economic History of Europe* I. Cambridge, 1966. 92–124.

Streck, M. "Ḳanāt", *Encyclopédie de l'Islam* 1st edn, II 751–3.

Surūr, M. J. *Miṣr fī 'aṣr al-dawla al-Fāṭimīya*. Cairo, 1960.

Susa, A. *Fayaḍānāt Baghdād fī al-ta'rīkh*. 3 vols. Baghdad, 1963–5.
Irrigation in Iraq. Its History and Development. Baghdad, 1945.
Rayy Sāmarrā. 2 vols. Baghdad, 1948.

Swingle, W. T. "The botany of citrus and its wild relatives of the orange subfamily". In *The Citrus Industry, I: History, Botany and Breeding*, ed. H. J. Webber and L. D. Batchelor. Berkeley/Los Angeles, 1943. 129–474.

Sykes, P. M. *A History of Persia*. 2 vols. London, 1915.

Täckholm, V., G. Täckholm and M. Drar. *Flora of Egypt*. 7 vols. to date. Cairo, 1941– .

Talbi, M. "Al-Ḳayrawān", *Encyclopedia of Islam* 2nd edn, IV 824–32.
"Law and economy in Ifrīqiya (Tunisia) in the third Islamic century: agriculture and the role of slaves in the country's economy". In *The Islamic Middle East, 700–1900*, ed. A. Udovitch. Princeton, 1981. 209–49.

Tanaka, T. "L'acclimatation des Citrus hors de leur pays d'origine", *Revue de botanique appliquée et d'agriculture tropicale* XIII (1933) 389–98, 480–94.
"The best oranges of the Far East", *Journal of Heredity* XX (1929) 37–45.
Kankitsu no kenkyu. Tokyo, 1933.
"Kankitsu-zoku kigeu ron", *Studia citrologica* II (1928) 19–32.
"Studies in the origin of citrus flora of various localities", *Proceedings of the Japanese Association for the Advancement of Science* X (1935) 570–6.
"Sur l'origine et la délimitation de l'espèce chez les Citrus", *Revue de botanique appliquée* IX (1929) 723–4.

Tardy, P. "Quelques réflexions sur les puits et leur usage en Tunisie", *Ibla* XX (1957) 159–66.

Targioni-Tozzetti, A. *Cenni storici sulla introduzione di varie piante nell'agricoltura ed orticoltura toscana*. Florence, 1853.

Tchalenko, G. *Villages antiques de la Syrie du Nord*. 3 vols. Paris, 1953–8.

Teall, J. L. "Byzantine agricultural tradition", *Dumbarton Oaks Papers* XXV (1971) 33–59.

Teixeira da Mota, A. and A. Carreira. "*Milho zaburro* and *milho maçaroca* in Guinea and in the Islands of Cabo Verde", *Africa* XXXVI (1966) 73–84.
Thomas, J. M. C. "Notes d'ethnobotanique africaine: plantes utilisées dans la région de Lobaye", *Journal d'agriculture tropicale et de botanique appliquée* VI (1959) 353–90.
Thompson, R. C. *A Dictionary of Assyrian Botany*. London, 1949.
Tokarev, S. A. "The study of the early history of agriculture in the territory of the U.S.S.R. in 1945–1955". In *Men and Cultures: Selected Papers of the Fifth International Congress of Anthropological and Ethnological Sciences*, ed. A. F. C. Wallace. Philadelphia, 1960.
Tolkowsky, S. *Hesperides: A History of the Culture and Use of Citrus Fruits*. Westminster, 1937.
Tolstov, S. P. and B. B. Andrianov. "Novye materialy po istorii razvitiia irrigatsii v Khorezme", *Institut Etnografii. Kratkie soobshcheniia* XXVI (1957) 5–11.
Torres Balbás, L. "La Albolafia de Córdoba y la gran noria toledana", *Al-Ándalus* VII (1942) 461–9.
"Almería islámica", *Al-Ándalus* XXII (1957) 411–53.
"Extensión y demografía de las ciudades hispanomusulmanas", *Studia Islamica* III (1955) 35–59.
"Las norias fluviales en España", *Al-Ándalus* V (1940) 195–208.
"Las ruinas de Belyūnes o Bullones", *Tamuda* V (1957) 275–96.
Trabut, L. "Les hybrides de *Citrus nobilis*: la Clémentine", *Revue de botanique appliquée* VI (1926) 484–9.
Répertoire des noms indigènes des plantes spontanées, cultivées et utilisées dans le Nord de l'Afrique. Algiers, 1935.
Traina, A. *Nuovo vocabulario siciliano–italiano*. Palermo, 1868.
Trasselli, C. *Note per la storia dei banchi in Sicilia nel XV secolo*. 2 vols. Palermo, 1959–68.
"Produzione e commercio dello zucchero in Sicilia dal XIII al XIX secolo", *Economia e storia* II (1955) 325–42.
"Promesse e lettere di cambio nel '400 siciliano". In *Studi in onore di Amintore Fanfani*. Milan, 1962. III 523–43.
"Sumário duma história do açúcar siciliano", *Do tempo e da história* II (1968) 50–78.
"Lo zucchero siciliano dai Normanni ai Martini". Unpublished typescript available from the author.
Tresse, R. "L'irrigation dans la Ghouta de Damas", *Revue des études islamiques* III (1929) 463–559.
Trimingham, J. S. *Islam in East Africa*. Oxford, 1964.
Islam in West Africa. Oxford, 1959.
Trotter, A. *Flora economica della Libia*. Rome, 1915.
Tuma, E. H. "Early Arab economic policies (1st/7th – 4th/10th centuries)", *Islamic Studies* IV (1965) 1–23.
Udovitch, A. L. *Partnership and Profit in Medieval Islam*. Princeton, 1970.
Unger, A. *Die Pflanzen des alten Aegypten*. Vienna, 1859.
Uphof, J. C. T. *Dictionary of Economic Plants*. Würzburg, 1959.
Vadet, J.-C. "L'acculturation des sud-arabiques de Fusṭāṭ au lendemain de la conquête arabe", *Bulletin d'études orientales* XII (1969) 7–14.
Vanacker, C. "Géographie économique de l'Afrique du Nord selon les auteurs arabes, du XIe siècle au milieu du XIIe siècle", *Annales: économies, sociétés, civilisations* XXVIII (1973) 659–80.
Vavilov, N. "Geographische Genzentren unserer Kulturpflanzen". In *Verhandlungen des V internationalen Kongresses für Vererbungswissenschaft, Berlin 1927* (Supplement vol. I of *Zeitschrift für induktive Abstammungs- und Vererbungslehre*). Leipzig, 1928. 342–69.

The Origin, Immunity and Breeding of Cultivated Plants. Chronica Botanica XII. Waltham, 1951.

Tsentry proiskhozhdeniia kul'turnykh rastenii. Leningrad, 1926.

Vavilov, N. I. and D. K. Bukinich. *Agricultural Afghanistan*. Leningrad, 1929.

Verhulst, A. E. "L'agriculture médiévale et ses problèmes", *Studi medievali* I (1960) 619–704.

Vérin, P. "Austronesian contribution to the culture of Madagascar: some archeological problems". In *East Africa and the Orient. Cultural Syntheses in Pre-colonial Times*, ed. H. N. Chittick and R. I. Rotberg. New York/London, 1975. 164–91.

Vicens Vives, J. *Historia social y económica de España y América*. 5 vols. Barcelona, 1957–9.

Villiers-Stuart, C. M. *Gardens of the Great Mughals*. London, 1913.

Spanish Gardens. Their History, Type and Features. London, 1929.

Viollet, H. "Description du palais de al-Moutasim à Samara", *Mémoires de l'Académie des Inscriptions et Belles-Lettres* XII ii (1913) 567–94.

de Visiani, R. *Dell'origine ed anzianità dell'orto botanico di Padova*. Padua, 1839.

Vishnu-Mittre. "Changing economy in ancient India". In *The Early History of Agriculture*, ed. Joseph B. Hutchinson, J. G. G. Clark, E. M. Jope and R. Riley. Oxford, 1977. 569–80.

"Paleobotanical evidence in India". In *Evolutionary Studies in World Crops*, ed. Sir J. Hutchinson. Cambridge, 1974. 3–30.

"Protohistoric records of agriculture in ancient India", *Transactions of the Bose Research Institute* XXXI (1968) 86–106.

Vitali, G. and E. Bartolozzi. *Strumenti agricoli indigeni dell'Africa Orientale Italiana*. Florence, 1939.

Vladimirtsov, B. I. *Le régime social des Mongols. Le féodalisme nomade*. Paris, 1948.

Vonderheyden, M. *La Berbérie orientale sous la dynastie des Benoû'l-Arlab 800–909*. Paris, 1927.

Vuillet, J. "Les jardins royaux de Provence et le jardin botanique et d'acclimatation de la Marine de Toulon", *Revue internationale de botanique appliquée et d'agriculture tropicale* XX (1940) 694–721.

Wagner, M. L. "Zu einigen arabischen Wörtern des Sizilianischen und Süditalienischen", *Zeitschrift für Romanische Philologie* LII (1932) 641–70.

Wainwright, F. A. "The coming of the banana to Uganda", *Uganda Journal* XVI (1952) 145–7.

Watson, A. M. "The Arab agricultural revolution and its diffusion", *Journal of Economic History* XXXIV (1974) 8–35.

"A medieval green revolution". In *The Islamic Middle East, 700–1900*, ed. A. Udovitch. Princeton, 1981. 29–58.

"The rise and spread of Old World cotton". In *Studies in Textile History in Memory of Harold Burnham*, ed. V. Gervers. Toronto, 1977. 355–68.

Watson, J. F. *Index to the Native and Scientific Names of Indian and Other Economic Plants and Products*. London, 1868.

Watson, W. "Early cereal cultivation in China". In *The Domestication and Exploitation of Plants and Cereals*, ed. P. J. Ucko and G. W. Dimbleby. London, 1969. 397–402.

Watt, Sir George. *The Commercial Products of India*. London, 1908.

A Dictionary of the Economic Products of India. 6 vols. Calcutta, 1889–93.

The Wild and Cultivated Cotton Plants of the World. London, 1907.

Webber, H. J. "The cultivated varieties of citrus". In *The Citrus Industry, I: History, Botany and Breeding*, ed. H. J. Webber and L. D. Batchelor. Berkeley/Los Angeles, 1943. 475–668.

Webster, J. C. *The Labours of the Months in Antique and Medieval Art.* Evanston/Chicago, 1938.

Wee, H. van der. *The Growth of the Antwerp Market and the European Economy.* 3 vols. The Hague, 1963.

Wescher, H. "Cotton and cotton trade in the Middle Ages", *CIBA Review* LXIV (1948) 2322–60.

Wet, J. M. J. De and J. R. Harlan. "The origin and domestication of *Sorghum bicolor*", *Economic Botany* XXV (1971) 128–35.

Wet, J. M. J. De and J. P. Huckaby. "The origin of *Sorghum bicolor*. II. Distribution and domestication", *Evolution* XXXI (1967) 787–802.

Whitaker, T. W. and G. N. Davis. *Cucurbits.* London, 1962.

Whitcomb, D. S. "The archeology of al-Ḥasā' oasis in the Islamic period", *Atlal. The Journal of Saudi Arabian Archeology* II (1978) 95–106.

White, K. D. *Roman Farming.* London, 1970.

White, L. *Medieval Technology and Social Change.* Oxford, 1962.

Whyte, R. O. "The botanical Neolithic revolution", *Human Ecology* V (1977) 209–22.

"Cytogenetical response to physiological stress", *Indian Journal of Genetics and Plant Breeding* XXXIV A (1974) 1125–9.

"An environmental interpretation of the origin of Asian cereals", *Indian Journal of Genetics and Plant Breeding* XXXIV A (1974) 1–11.

Widengren, G. "Recherches sur le féodalisme iranien", *Orientalia suecana* V (1956) 79–182.

Wiener, L. *Africa and the Discovery of America.* 3 vols. Philadelphia, 1920–22.

Wiet, G. *Cairo. City of Art and Commerce.* Norman, Okla., 1964.

"La grande peste noire en Syrie et en Egypte". In *Etudes d'orientalisme dédiées à la mémoire de Lévi-Provençal.* 2 vols. Paris, 1962. I 367–84.

Wilber, D. N. *Persian Gardens and Garden Pavilions.* Tokyo, 1962.

Wilkinson, J. C. "Islamic water law with special reference to oasis settlement", *Journal of Arid Environment* I (1978) 87–96.

The Organization of the Falaj Irrigation System in Oman. School of Geography (University of Oxford) Research Papers X. Oxford, 1974.

Water and Tribal Settlement in South-East Arabia. A Study of the Aflāj of Oman. Oxford, 1977.

Willcocks, W. and J. I. Craig. *Egyptian Irrigation.* 2 vols. London/New York, 1913.

Williamson, J. *The Useful Plants of Nyasaland.* Zomba, 1955.

Winlock, H. E. and W. E. Crum. *The Monastery of Epiphanus at Thebes* I. New York, 1926.

Wissmann, H. von. *Zur Geschichte und Landeskunde von Alt-Südarabien.* Vienna, 1964.

Wissmann, H. von and M. Höfner. *Beiträge zur historischen Geographie des vorislamischen Südarabien.* Akademie der Wissenschaften und der Literatur, Abhandlungen der Geistes- und Sozialwissenschaftlichen Klasse, Jahrgang 1952 IV. Wiesbaden, 1952.

Wittfogel, K. and Fêng Chia-Shêng. *History of Chinese Society. Liao (907–1125).* Transactions of the American Philosophical Society, new ser. XXXVI. Philadelphia, 1949.

Wright, C. G. N. *The Writing of Arabic Numerals.* London, 1952.

Wright, R. *The Story of Gardening.* New York, 1963.

Wrigley, C. "Speculation on the economic prehistory of Africa", *Journal of African History* I (1960) 189–203.

Yin, Huan-Chang and Chung-i Li. "Kiang-su Hsin-yi hsien San-li-tun ku weu-hua i-chih – ti erh tz'u fa-chüeh chien chieh", *Kaogu* (1960) VII 20–2.

Zaitzev, G. S. "A hybrid between Asiatic and American cotton plants", *Agricultural Journal of India* XXI (1926) 460–70.

"Un hybride entre les Cotonniers asiatiques et américains: *Gossypium herbaceum* L. et *G. hirsutum* L.", *Revue de botanique appliquée* V (1925) 628–9.

Zangheri, R. "Gli studi di storia dell'agricoltura nell'ultimo ventennio", *Studi storici* VIII (1967) 669–95.

Zeki, A. "Mémoire sur les relations entre l'Egypte et l'Espagne pendant l'occupation musulmane". In *Homenaje a Francisco Codera*. Zaragoza, 1904. 455–81.

Zhukovskij, P. M. *Cultivated Plants and their Wild Relatives*, tr. P. S. Hudson. Farnham Royal, 1962.

Ziadeh, N. *Damascus under the Mamluks*. Norman, Okla., 1964.

Life in Syria under the Early Mamlūks. Westport, Conn., 1970.

Index

'Abbāsids, 91, 94, 96, 129; *see also names of individual caliphs*
'Abd Allāh ibn Ṭāhir, governor of Egypt, 89
'Abd al-Laṭīf al-Baghdādī, 1, 42, 67
'Abd al-Raḥmān I, of Spain, 89, 118
'Abd al-Raḥmān II, of Spain, 89
Abū Ḥanīfa al-Dīnawarī, botanist, 35, 54, 59, 70, 72, 80, 94
Abū al-Khair, agronome, 14, 41, 62, 68, 70
Abū Zaid al-Sirāfī, traveller, 14, 56
Abyssinia, 14, 78, 80, 92, 125, 171 n. 2
  banana in, 54
  cotton in, 34, 35
  eggplant in, 71
  hard wheat in, 20, 21
  plough in, 82
  rice in, 17
  sugar cane in, 29–30
  watermelon in, 61
Afḍal, al-, Fāṭimid vizier, 118
Africa, East, 77, 80–1, 82, 93, 100; *see also* Abyssinia
  banana in, 54
  coconut palm in, 56
  colocasia in, 68
  cotton in, 41
  mango tree in, 72–3
  rice in, 15, 17–18
  sorghum in, 14
  sour orange in, 46
  sugar cane in, 29
Africa, West, 81–2, 95, 97, 131
  banana in, 54
  coconut palm in, 6–7
  colocasia in, 68–9
  cotton in, 41, 102
  eggplant in, 71
  mango tree in, 72
  rice in, 18–19
  sorghum in, 14
  sour orange in, 46
Aghlabid dynasty, 97, 118
Aleppo (Ḥalab), 13, 107, 191 n. 6
Alexander, botanical observations of his expeditions in India and the Persian Gulf, 11, 15, 34, 51, 89, 99
alfalfa, 89
annual varieties, development of, 4, 37–8, 154–5 n. 7, 165 n. 39
Anṣārī, al-, 1
Arabia Felix, 15, 29–30, 77, 78, 80–1, 89, 90, 119, 124, 125, 202 n. 11
  banana in, 54
  coconut palm in, 56
  colocasia in, 28
  cotton in, 31, 40
  eggplant in, 70, 71
  hard wheat in, 21
  irrigation works of, 104, 191 n. 6
  lime in, 48
  rice in, 90
  sorghum in, 13
  sour orange in, 46
  sugar cane in, 25, 29–30
  watermelon in, 61, 174 n. 1
Arabian Gulf, *see* Persian Gulf
Aristobolus, 15
artichoke, 5, 64–5
Aṣma'ī, al-, philologist, 94
aubergine, *see* eggplant
'Azīz, al-, Fāṭimid caliph, 95

Babylonia, *see* Mesopotamia and Babylonia
Baghdād, 1, 40, 89, 90, 94, 95, 96, 97, 130, 131, 133
Bakrī, al-, geographer, 14, 21, 49, 54
Balkh, 17
  lemon in, 46
  sour orange in, 45
  sugar cane in, 26
banana, plantain, 51–4, 57, 77, 80, 81, 82, 103, 118, 145, 184 n. 27
Banū Hilāl, 6, 143
Baṣra, al-, 1, 45, 48, 80, 90, 92, 117, 130, 131, 133

bedouin, *see* nomads
beer
from banana and plantain, 49
from sorghum, 9
Berber language and peoples, 11, 49, 58, 64, 68, 92, 169 nn. 34–5, 180 n. 7, 189 n. 49
Bīrūnī, al-, scholar, 96, 188 n. 40
Black Death, *see* plague
Boccaccio, Giovanni, 22
bread
from hard wheat, 20
from rice, 15, 151 n. 4
from sorghum, 9
Byzantium, 82; *see also* Egypt, Byzantine
taxation in, 14–15, 196 n. 8

Cairo, al-Fusṭāṭ, 190 n. 9, 192 n. 22
bananas exported to, 54
cotton in, 40
exotic goods in, 3
gardens of, 118
population of, 133, 207 n. 29
rice merchants in, 5
sugar cane near, 28
Calendar of Cordova, 14, 54, 60, 71
Candolle, Alphonse de, 4, 31
Caspian Sea, 17
sugar cane in, 26
Chad, 9, 19
China, 89, 96, 185 n. 2, 207 n. 30
banana in, 51
citrus in, 43, 44
coconut palm in, 55
colocasia in, 66
cotton in, 34–5, 37, 39
eggplant in, 70, 71
mango in, 72
rice in, 15, 103
spinach in, 62
sorghum in, 11
sugar cane in, 25
watermelon in, 59
citron, 42, 43, 44, 48
citrus, 1, 42–50, 72, 77, 80, 81, 82–3, 89–90, 101, 102, 184 n. 27; *see also* citron
coconut palm and coconuts, 55–7, 77, 80, 81, 127, 135
collectors in early Islamic world, 89, 94–6, 117, 145
colocasia, 57, 66–9, 77, 81, 82, 103, 123, 124, 127
colocynth, 58
commendation, 142
cookery of Islamic world, 9, 15, 20, 22–3, 24, 31, 42, 51, 58, 64, 66, 70, 72, 101, 102
Cordova, 45, 90, 95, 97, 118, 134, 187 n. 19
Cordovan Calendar, see *Calendar of Cordova*
Cosmas Indicopleustis, 53, 55, 56
cotton, New World, 41, 145, 162 n. 1
cotton, Old World, 31–41, 77, 81, 82–3, 89, 100, 101, 102, 103, 115, 123, 124, 127, 135, 145, 150 n. 10, 185 n. 27
cous-cous, 20, 22
cowpea, 77
Crusaders and Crusader kingdoms, 28, 82, 83, 143, 144
Ctésias, 32
cultivars, development of new, 1, 126, 150 nn. 11–12, 154 n. 11
Cyprus, 82, 144
cotton in, 40, 124
sugar cane in, 124

Damascus (Dimashq), 28, 97, 118, 133, 149 n. 2, 192 n. 20
date palm, 89, 118
dead lands, reclamation of, 112, 116, 127, 130
Dioscorides, Pedanios, 11, 26, 99, 186 n. 5
Diyala plains, 130, 194 n. 34

Ecluse, Charles de l', 68
eggplant, 15, 57, 70–1, 77, 81, 102, 123, 124, 127
Egypt, ancient, possible crop introductions into
citrus, 46–8
sorghum, 11
watermelon, 58, 175 n. 4
Egypt, Byzantine, 20, 124, 172 n. 8, 191 nn. 6 and 15, 196 n. 8
Egypt, Islamic, 80, 124, 125, 131, 139; *see also* Egypt, Upper
banana in, 54
citrus in, 48, 80
coconut palm in, 57
colocasia in, 66, 67
cotton in, 40, 102
eggplant in, 70
irrigation in, 104
rice in, 17
sugar cane in, 28
taxation in, 143, 197 n. 18
Egypt, Upper, 80
cotton in, 34
sorghum in, 13, 14
sugar cane in, 28
Eiximenis, Francesc, 50
emmer, 20
Ensete, 51, 72, 171 n. 2, 172 n. 8
estates, size of, 113–14, 128
Ethiopia, *see* Abyssinia

fallowing, 123, 124, 125, 126
Fāṭimid dynasty, 97, 118
Fayyūm, al-, 17, 131
cotton in, 40
hard wheat in, 157 n. 8
sugar cane in, 28
Fergana, 72

fertilizing, 125, 128
Fez (Fās), 118, 134
Fīrūzābādī, al-, lexicographer, 22
fodder, animal, 9, 195–6 n. 6
Frederick II of Sicily, 83
Fusṭāṭ, al-, *see* Cairo

gardens, botanical, commercial and ornamental, 6, 87, 89, 90, 114, 117–19
  poems about, 6, 117
Geoponika (Byzantine), 21
Granada (Gharnāṭa), Vega of
  banana in, 54
  irrigation of, 125
  sugar cane in, 29
grape vine, 89
grapefruit, 42
Gregory of Tours, 34
Guadalquivir river and valley, 131
  sugar cane in, 29
Guadix (Wādī Āsh), 40, 119

Ḥaḍramawt, *see* Arabia Felix
Ḥafṣid dynasty, 118
Ḥakam II, al-, Caliph of Spain, 95
Ḥākim, al-, Fāṭimid Caliph of Egypt, 95
Hamdānī, al-, geographer, 21
Hārūn al-Rashīd, 72, 96, 100
Hatshepsut, queen, 88
henna, 123
Herodotus, 11, 32
Ḥimṣ, 133
Ḥimyarī, al-, geographer, 125
Ḥudūd al-ʿālam, 12

Iaxartes river, 130
Ibn al-ʿAwwām, agronome, 14, 29, 41, 48, 71, 103, 124, 127
Ibn Baṣṣāl, agronome, 41, 62, 71, 119, 187 nn. 18–19
Ibn Baṭṭūṭa, traveller, 17, 49, 56, 69, 72
Ibn Buṭlān, physician, 18, 22, 23, 43, 60, 63
Ibn Ḥawqal, geographer, 12, 17, 26, 40, 46, 101
Ibn Iyās, historian, 48, 133
Ibn Jāmiʿ, his treatise on the lemon, 46
Ibn Jubair, traveller, 92
Ibn Khaldūn, historian, 5, 6, 92
Ibn Luyūn, poet, 103
Ibn Māsawaih, physician, 54, 70
Ibn al-Rūmī, poet, 54
Ibn Rusta, scholar, 1, 54
Ibn Saʿīd, geographer and historian, 30
Ibn Sīna (= Avicenna), scholar, 59, 70, 188 n. 40
Ibn Ṭūlūn, Aḥmad, ruler of Egypt, 96
Ibn Wāfid, agronome, 62, 119, 184 n. 27, 187 n. 19
Ibn Waḥshīya, agronome, xiii, 1, 13, 21, 26, 40, 45, 47, 54, 57, 59, 62, 66, 68, 70, 71, 80, 103, 125, 219 n. 1
Idrīsī, al-, geographer, 28, 102, 107, 189 n. 11
Idrīsid dynasty, 97
Ifrīqiya, 108, 118, 131, 139, 198 n. 28
  banana in, 54
  citrus in, 49
  cotton in, 40
  sorghum in, 12
  sugar cane in, 28
  watermelon in, 61
īghār (taxation immunity), 143
Īl Khans, 119
India, in pre-Islamic times, 6, 89, 95, 96, 100, 125
  citrus in, 44
  coconut palm in, 2
  cotton in, 32–3, 34
  eggplant in, 70
  mango tree in, 72
  receives, domesticates, improves and diffuses plants, 77–8, 89
  rice in, 15
  sorghum in, 9, 11, 14
  spinach in, 62
  sugar cane in, 24–5
Indian numerals, 95
indigo, 100, 123, 135, 145, 184–5 n. 27, 185 n. 1
industries linked to new crops, 134–5
iqṭāʿ, 143–4, 195 n. 4
Iran, Islamic, 130
  citrus in, 45, 89–90
  cotton in, 40
  eggplant in, 70
  rice in, 17
  sorghum in, 12
  sugar cane in, 26
Iraq, Islamic, 17, 80, 111, 130, 131, 195 n. 4, 206 n. 14
  banana in, 54
  citrus in, 45, 46–8, 80, 90
  coconuts and coconut palm in, 55, 57
  colocasia in, 66
  cotton in, 40
  land tenure and taxation in, 113, 115
  mango tree in, 72
  rice in, 17, 124
  sorghum in, 13
irrigation, 103–11, 126, 127, 128, 130
  European, 83
  laws, 80, 116
  remains of works, 5
  taxation of irrigated lands, 115–16
  technology, 80, 84
Iṣfahān, 133
Isho Bar ʿAlī, 22
Isidore of Seville, 44
Iṣṭakhrī, al-, geographer, 12, 46

Italy; *see also* Sicily
  artichoke in, 178 n. 7
  citrus in, 49, 82–3
  colocasia in, 68
  hard wheat in, 22–3
  rice in, 83
  sorghum in, 12, 81

Jacob of Edessa, 15
Jacques de Vitry, 50
Jāḥiẓ, al-, writer, 1
Jaime II, of Aragon, 83
Java
  cotton in, 35, 89
  sorghum in, 11
Jawharī, al-, lexicographer, 22
Jazīra, al-, *see* Iraq, Islamic
Jordan valley, 80, 83, 131
  banana in, 54
  cotton in, 34
  rice in, 15, 78
  sugar cane in, 28

Kanem
  eggplant in, 71
  sugar cane in, 30, 90, 119
Khālid ibn Yazīd ibn Mu'āwiya, caliph, 94
Khurāsān, cotton in, 40
Kilwa, 81
Kirmān, city and province, 12
  sugar cane in, 26
Kūfa, 70, 133
kumquat, 44

land tenure, 112–16
lemon, *see* citrus
Levant and Palestine, 80, 83, 129; *see also* Jordan valley
  banana in, 54
  citrus in, 45, 48, 50, 80
  colocasia in, 66, 67
  cotton in, 40
  rice in, 17
  sugar cane in, 28
libraries, 94, 95
lime, *see* citrus

macaroni, *see* pasta
Madagascar, possible Islamic introductions into, 81
  of banana, 54
  of coconut palm, 57
  of colocasia, 68
  of sorghum, 14, 81
Maghrib, al-, *see* Ifrīqiya; Morocco
Mahdī, al-, 'Abbāsid caliph, 96, 100, 115
Maimonides, 22
maize, 146
Majorca
  cotton in, 40
  rice in, 17
Malaya, 81
  centre of plant origin, 77
  citrus in, 44, 45, 46, 48
  coconut palm in, 55, 57
  colocasia in, 66
  cotton in, 35
  watermelon in, 59
Mālik al-Ashraf, al-, Rasūlid sultan, 90
Ma'mūn, al-, 'Abbāsid caliph, 45
mandarine, 44, 48
mango, 54, 57, 72–3, 77, 80, 81, 103
Manṣūr, al-, 'Abbāsid caliph, 115
Manṣūr, al-, chamberlain, 45, 90
manuals of farming, Arabic, 60, 93, 119, 124, 125, 126, 127, 149 n. 5; *see also* *names of authors*
Maqqarī, al-, historian, 21, 95, 134
Maqrīzī, al-, historian, 54, 142
Ma'rib dam, 104, 124
Marrakesh (Marrākush), 118
  sugar cane near, 28
Marv (Marw), 133
Mas'ūdī, al-, geographer and historian, 14, 28, 42, 45, 46, 48, 54, 56, 80, 81, 96
mawqūf, 142
Mecca (Makka), 92
medical uses of plants, 1, 9, 15, 24, 31, 42, 44, 51, 55–6, 58, 59, 60, 62, 64, 66, 70, 72, 99, 135, 155–6 n. 13
melon, 58, 89, 174 n. 1, 175 n. 11; *see also* watermelon
  'Abdallāwī, 89
Mesopotamia and Babylonia, pre-Islamic, 11–12, 15, 26, 38, 80; *see also* Sasanian empire
migration of peasants, 5–6, 80, 87, 90, 92, 116, 150 nn. 16–17, 199 n. 33; *see also* Yemeni emigrants
millets, 9, 11, 77, 123, 151 n. 2, 152 nn. 15 and 17, 153 n. 36, 181–2 n. 1, 200–1 n. 3
Mishna, 34
Mogadishu (Maqadishū), 17
  banana in, 54
  mango in, 72
Mohenjo-daro, 11, 32, 35, 191 n. 15
Morocco, 95, 107, 130, 131
  colocasia in, 67–8
  cotton in, 40
  rice in, 17
  sorghum in, 12
  sugar cane in, 28–9
  watermelon in, 61
Mu'āwiya I, Umayyad caliph, 94
Muḥammad the Prophet, 91, 115, 129, 188 n. 22, 196 n. 9, 198 n. 26
Muqaddasī, al-, geographer, 17, 54
muqāsama taxation, 115
muqāṭa'a, 116
Mustakfī, al-, 'Abbāsid caliph, 179 n. 3, 189 n. 8

Mu'taṣim, al-, 'Abbāsid caliph, 150–1 n. 18
Mu'taṣim ibn Ṣumādiḥ, al-, King of Almería, 90, 118

Nāṣir-i Khusraw, traveller, 28, 125, 133
Negev, 129
Niebuhr, M., traveller, 14, 151 n. 3
Nimrud dam, 104
Nineveh, 11
Nīshāpūr, 133
Niṣibīn, 17, 117
nomads, 6, 129–30, 141, 143, 196 n. 6
noodles, *see* pasta
Normans in Sicily, 143, 161–2 n. 30, 168 n. 21, 169 nn. 28 and 32, 184 n. 27, 200 n. 8
Nubia, 34, 35, 78, 191 n. 15

Oman ('Umān), 80
  banana in, 54
  coconuts in, 56
  lemon in, 46
  mango in, 72
  sailors and merchants from, 56, 78, 81
  sour orange in, 45, 90
  sugar cane in, 30
orange, sour, *see* citrus
orange, sweet, 42, 43, 44, 48, 49, 146
Orta, García da, 43, 50
Ottoman empire, 139, 142
ownership of land, 112–14
Oxus river, 130

Pahlavi language, *see* Persian language
paleo-ethnobotany, 4
Palermo (Balarm), 29, 92
Palestine, *see* Levant and Palestine; Jordan valley
Palladius, agronome, 44
paper, 31
pasta, 20, 22–3
peasantry, freedom of, 115, 116, 128, 142, 144; *see also* migration of peasants
Pemba, 14, 81
Persia, Islamic, *see* Iran
Persia, pre-Islamic, *see* Sasanian empire
Persian Gulf, 78, 80, 89; *see also* Alexander
  cotton in, 32, 34
  sorghum in, 12
  sugar cane in, 26
Persian language, 12, 59, 70, 78, 151 n. 2, 153 n. 26, 154 n. 12, 168 n. 15, 169 n. 35, 177 n. 1, 186 n. 2
plague
  6th and 7th centuries, 191 n. 7
  14th and 15th centuries, 139, 210 n. 1
plantain, *see* banana
Pliny the Elder, 12, 26, 34, 44
plough, ploughing, 82, 125, 128
Pollux, Julius, 34, 39
Polo, Marco, 17, 40
pomegranate, 89, 118
population
  growth in rural areas, 129–32
  growth in urban areas, 132–4
  levels in Europe, 83
Portuguese, possible plant introductions by, 19, 49, 145, 162 n. 34, 174 n. 15
Portuguese explorers find crops growing in Africa, 81
  bananas, 54
  cotton, 167 n. 74
  rice, 19

Qāhir, al-, 'Abbāsid caliph, 80, 90
Qairawān, 108, 118, 134
Qalāwūn, Mamlūk sultan, 119
Qazwīnī, al-, geographer and historian, 54, 60
Qusṭūs al-Rūmī, agronome, 45, 46, 54, 59, 62, 70, 221 n. 2

rawḍīya poems, 117
Rāzi, al-, geographer, 21
Rāzī, al- (= Rhazes), physician, 59, 62, 70
rice, African (*Oryza glaberrima*), 18, 82, 154 n. 1
rice, Asiatic, 14, 15–19, 77, 81, 82, 83, 99, 100, 101, 102, 103, 119, 123, 124, 127, 145, 184 n. 27
  milling of, 134–5
  trade in, 135, 156 nn. 17–18
Roman empire, 199 n. 29
  sugar in, 26
  taxation in, 114–15, 191 n. 15
rotation of crops, 123, 124, 125, 126
Ruṣāfa, al-, palace, 89
Rustamid dynasty, 97

Sabean lane, 29, 57, 59, 77, 78
Samarkand (Samarqand), 71
Sāmarra, 96, 101, 118, 133
San'ā', 1, 124
Sanskrit language and texts, 12, 46, 51, 55, 70, 77, 78, 94, 95, 96, 152 n. 8, 153 n. 26, 154 n. 2, 162 n. 3, 172 n. 5, 181 n. 1
Sasanian empire, 78, 99, 100, 191 n. 15, 197 n. 14, 199 n. 29; *see also* Mesopotamia and Babylon
  possible introductions into of crops studied in this volume, 11, 15, 26, 44, 55, 62, 78, 114–15
Sawād, al-, *see* Iraq
science, Islamic, 145–6
Sennacherib, king, 11, 38, 89
Seville (Ishbīliya), 29, 118, 119
shaddock, *see* citrus
Shafrān, al-, botanist, 119
Sicily, 17, 80, 82, 83, 92, 113, 131, 144, 185 n. 1, 194 n. 34, 196 n. 9, 197 n. 12; *see also* Normans in Sicily; Palermo

Sicily (*cont.*)
artichoke in, 178 n. 7
banana in, 184 n. 27
citrus in, 46, 49
cotton in, 40, 127, 185 n. 27
rice in, 17
sugar cane in, 28, 29, 83, 185 n. 27
Siddhanta, 95
Sijilmāsa, 21
Sind, al-, 17, 78, 95, 96
coconut palm in, 55
lime in, 48
sour orange in, 45
sugar cane in, 26
Sinkiang, cotton in, 38, 39
Sirāf, 78
sailors and merchants from, 81
slaves, used in agriculture, 116
Socotra (Suquṭra), 40
sorghum, 9–14, 17, 77, 81, 82, 87, 115, 123, 124, 126, 130
Sous (al-Sūs), *see* Morocco
spaghetti, *see* pasta
Spain, 80, 83, 89–90, 91, 97–8, 108, 117, 118–19, 130, 134, 144, 184 n. 27, 194 n. 34, 195 n. 4
artichoke in, 64
banana in, 54, 184 n. 27
citrus in, 45, 50, 82–3, 90
colocasia in, 68
cotton in, 40, 73, 127, 185 n. 1
eggplant in, 70–1
hard wheat in, 21
land tenure in, 113
rice in, 17
sorghum in, 14
spinach in, 62
sugar cane in, 28–9, 184 n. 27
spinach, 62–3, 82, 125
Strabo, geographer, 15
Sudan, 9
sugar, sugar cane, 24–30, 42, 77, 81, 82, 83, 90, 99, 100, 101, 102, 103, 118, 123, 145, 185 n. 27
refining industry, 83, 135
trade in, 127, 128
summer crops, 103, 104, 115, 123, 124

Tabrīz, 119
taifa kingdoms of Spain, 97, 118, 119
talji'a, 142
Talmud
Babylonian, 11
Palestinian, 34
tangerine, 42
taxation
of land and crops, 114–16, 143, 144, 192 n. 18, 206 n. 14
of urban dwellers, 133
tax farming, 141–2
Tha'ālibī, al-, writer and anthologist, 40
Thebes, 11
Theophrastus, 99
Thousand Nights and a Night, 48, 190 n. 11
Tiberias, lake, 28
cotton around, 34
Tiglath-pileser I, king, 88
Tignarī, al-, agronome, 119
Tinnis (Tinnīs), 133
Tlemcen (Tilimsān), 118
tobacco, 146
Toledo (Ṭulaiṭula), 97, 118, 119, 158 n. 15
hard wheat in, 21
Huerta del Rey, 118, 119, 193 n. 24
tomato, 146
translation of scientific texts into Arabic, 94, 100
Tūnis, 118

'Udhrī, al-, geographer, 90, 118
Uganda, 9, 54
'Umar I, Umayyad caliph, 26, 192 n. 18
'Umarī, al-, geographer, 21, 48, 54, 61, 67, 69
Umayyad dynasty of Spain, 21, 48, 54, 61, 67, 69
Umayyad dynasty of Syria, 91, 94, 129

Valencia (Balansiya) and its Huerta, 17, 40, 50, 110, 118, 131, 184 n. 27, 185 n. 1, 194 n. 34, 199 n. 30, 209 n. 47, 212 nn. 23–5
Vedic texts, 59, 77, 78
voyages of discovery, European, 145, 146; *see also* Portuguese

Wadebuli, sailors from Dabhol, 81
waqf, 142
watermelon, 57, 58–61, 77, 123, 127
wheat, hard, 5, 20–3, 83, 102, 127, 130

Yaḥya ibn Khālid, vizier, 100
Yāqūt, geographer, 13
Yemen (Yaman), *see* Arabia Felix
Yemeni emigrants, 80, 88, 92, 97, 150 n. 16, 182 n. 1, 190 n. 10
Yemeni sailors and merchants, 81

Zabīd, 119
Zanzibar, 80, 81
banana in, 54
coconut palm in, 57
sugar cane in, 30
Ziryāb, musician, 97
Zuhrī, al-, geographer, 17

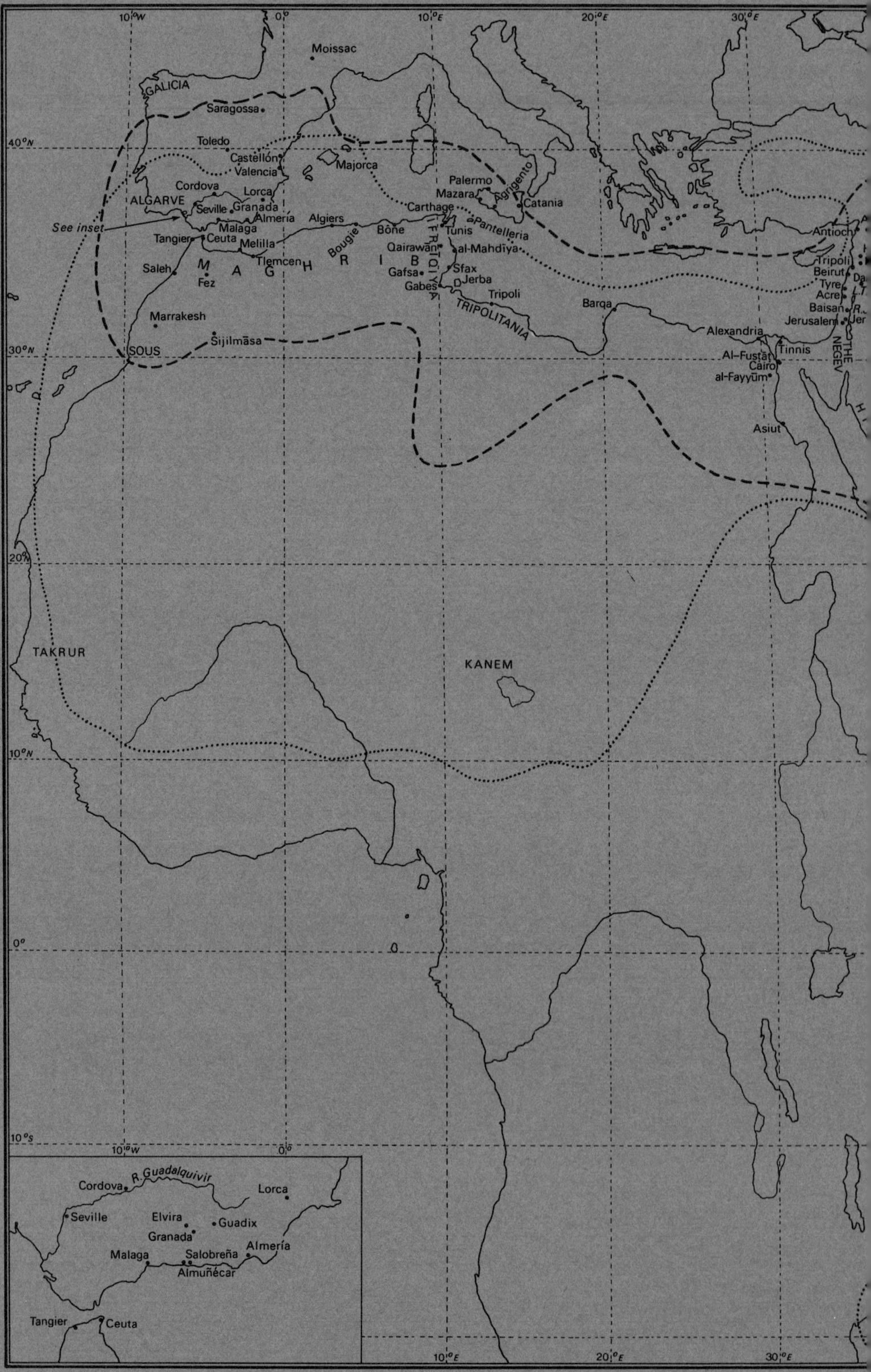

10°W
0°
10°E
20°E
30°E
40°N
30°N
20°N
10°N
0°
10°S
Moissac
GALICIA
Saragossa
Toledo
Castellón
Valencia
Majorca
Cordova
Lorca
ALGARVE
Seville
Granada
Almería
Malaga
See inset
Tangier
Ceuta
Melilla
Algiers
Bougie
Bône
Tlemcen
Saleh
Fez
MAGHRIB
Marrakesh
Sijilmāsa
SOUS
Palermo
Mazara
Agrigento
Catania
Carthage
Pantelleria
Tunis
Qairawān
al-Mahdīya
IFRĪQIYA
Sfax
Gafsa
Gabes
Jerba
Tripoli
TRIPOLITANIA
Barqa
Alexandria
Tinnis
Al-Fusṭāṭ
Cairo
al-Fayyūm
Asiut
Antioch
Tripoli
Beirut
Tyre
Acre
Baisan
Jerusalem
THE NEGEV
TAKRUR
KANEM
Cordova
R. Guadalquivir
Lorca
Seville
Elvira
Guadix
Granada
Almería
Malaga
Salobreña
Almuñécar
Tangier
Ceuta